Dearest Dawn Marie —

Welcome to another year —
and 366 (one extra for Leap Year!)
more stories of encouragement,
faith, hope and love to
accompany you on your
journey through 2020.

May you know His abundant
blessings through any trials
that will make your faith stronger.
His love for you is perfect,
and you are so very precious
to Him!

I love you, my dear sister,
and thank God for placing us
in our wonderful family.

May 2020 be a wonderful
year for you — full of love
and laughter, joy, wisdom
and contentment.

Much love always —
Jeri

DAILY GUIDEPOSTS

2020

Guideposts

New York

Daily Guideposts 2020

Published by Guideposts Books & Inspirational Media
110 William Street
New York, New York 10038
Guideposts.org

Acknowledgments

Every attempt has been made to credit the sources of copyrighted material used in this book. If any such acknowledgment has been inadvertently omitted or miscredited, receipt of such information would be appreciated.

Scripture quotations marked (AMP) are taken from the *Amplified Bible*. Copyright © 2015 by The Lockman Foundation, La Habra, CA 90631. All rights reserved.

Scripture quotations marked (CEB) are taken from the *Common English Bible*. Copyright © 2011 by Common English Bible.

Scripture quotations marked (CEV) are taken from *Holy Bible: Contemporary English Version*. Copyright © 1995 American Bible Society.

Scripture quotations marked (CSB) are taken from *The Christian Standard Bible*. Copyright © 2017 by Holman Bible Publishers. Used by permission.

Scripture quotations marked (ESV) are taken from the *Holy Bible, English Standard Version*. Copyright © 2001 by Crossway Bibles, a division of Good News Publishers. Used by permission. All rights reserved.

Scripture quotations marked (GNT) are taken from the *Holy Bible, Good News Translation*. Copyright © 1992 by American Bible Society.

Scripture quotations marked (GW) are taken from *GOD'S WORD Translation*. Copyright © 1995 by God's Word to the Nations. Used by permission of Baker Publishing Group.

Scripture quotations marked (HCSB) are taken from the *Holman Christian Standard Bible*. Copyright © 1999, 2000, 2002, 2003, 2009 by Holman Bible Publishers, Nashville, Tennessee. All rights reserved.

Scripture quotations marked (JPS) are taken from *Tanakh: A New Translation of the Holy Scriptures according to the Traditional Hebrew Text*. Copyright © 1985 by the Jewish Publication Society. All rights reserved.

Scripture quotations marked (ICB) are taken from *The Holy Bible, International Children's Bible*®. Copyright © 1986, 1988, 1999, 2015 by Tommy Nelson™, a division of Thomas Nelson. Used by permission.

Scripture quotations marked (ISV) are taken from the *Holy Bible, International Standard Version*. Copyright © 1995–2014 by ISV Foundation. All rights reserved internationally. Used by permission of Davidson Press, LLC.

Scripture quotations marked (KJV) are taken from the *King James Version of the Bible*.

Scripture quotations marked (MSG) are taken from *The Message*. Copyright © 1993, 1994, 1995, 1996, 2000, 2001, 2002 by Eugene H. Peterson.

Scripture quotations marked (NASB) are taken from the *New American Standard Bible*. Copyright © 1960, 1962, 1963, 1968, 1971, 1972, 1973, 1975, 1977, 1995 by the Lockman Foundation. Used by permission.

Scripture quotations marked (NCV) are taken from *The Holy Bible, New Century Version*. Copyright © 2005 by Thomas Nelson, Inc.

Scripture quotations marked (NET) are taken from the *NET Bible*®. Copyright ©1996–2006 by Biblical Studies Press, L.L.C. http://netbible.com All rights reserved.

Scripture quotations marked (NIV) are taken from the *Holy Bible, New International Version*. Copyright © 1973, 1978, 1984, 2011 by Biblica, Inc. Used by permission of Zondervan. All rights reserved worldwide. www.zondervan.com

Scripture quotations marked (NKJV) are taken from *The Holy Bible, New King James Version*. Copyright © 1982 by Thomas Nelson, Inc.

Scripture quotations marked (NLT) are from the *Holy Bible, New Living Translation*. Copyright © 1996, 2004, 2007 by Tyndale House Foundation. Used by permission of Tyndale House Publishers Inc., Carol Stream, Illinois 60188. All rights reserved.

Scripture quotations marked (NRSV) are taken from the *New Revised Standard Version Bible*. Copyright © 1989 by the Division of Christian Education of the National Council of the Churches of Christ in the United States of America. Used by permission. All rights reserved.

Scripture quotations marked (RSV) are taken from the *Revised Standard Version of the Bible*. Copyright © 1946, 1952, 1971 by Division of Christian Education of the National Council of Churches of Christ in the United States of America. Used by permission.

Scripture quotations marked (TLB) are taken from *The Living Bible*. Copyright © 1971 by Tyndale House Publishers, Wheaton, Illinois 60187. All rights reserved.

Cover and interior design by Müllerhaus
Cover photo by Shutterstock
Monthly page opener photos by Shutterstock
Indexed by Frances Lennie
Typeset by Aptara

Printed and bound in the United States of America
10 9 8 7 6 5 4 3 2 1

Hello, Friends,

This year Guideposts celebrates our 75th anniversary! While we remain grounded in our dynamic history, we are most excited to continue to spread the message that anything is possible with hope, faith, and prayer.

Welcome to *Daily Guideposts 2020*. Whether you're a longtime reader of this devotional or are discovering it for the first time, we welcome you with love and the expectation of great things to come.

The theme for this year is "He Performs Wonders" based on Job 5:9: "He performs wonders that cannot be fathomed, miracles that cannot be counted." (NIV)

In 2019 we debuted the alternate title *Walking in Grace*, for those readers who prefer that name, and we are using it again in 2020. Whichever name they appear under, these devotions are sure to uplift and inspire you throughout the year.

What a marvelous reminder of God's majesty, power, and faithfulness! Despite life's ups and downs, it's important to remember that every day God is still making miracles and causing wonderful things to happen.

As we leap into 2020 and a new decade, our contributors continue to share what's in their hearts—from daily lessons and blessings to disappointments followed by moments of grace. Shawnelle Eliasen recalls an ocean-side encounter with her son that prompts her to leave her cares in God's hands. Scott Walker muses about the meaning of retirement, but realizes that there's always work to be done in God's kingdom. Jacqueline Wheelock reminds us of the importance of taking time out to pause and praise, and Julie Garmon learns about hope and God's miraculous timing when her daughter finally gets pregnant after years of infertility.

We're delighted to share several new series this year. Elizabeth Sherrill leads with a marvelous series titled "Firsts," which was inspired by the loss of John, her beloved husband of seven decades. As a new chapter unfolded and she faced the challenges of the first days of widowhood, she thought about other first times in her life and wondered, "What if I could maintain the thrill of discovery, the heightened awareness that comes with first-times?"

Kim Taylor Henry takes us on a "Journey to the Holy Land" and shares the sights, sounds, and revelations of walking where Jesus walked. Debbie Macomber invites us along on her adventures in "Packing Light." In "Praying in Public," Marci Alborghetti writes about the wonders and miracles she encountered when she stepped out in faith, and out of her comfort zone, and met prayer needs of friends, family, neighbors, and yes, even strangers. In "The Friendship of Women," Roberta Messner prompts us to reflect on the blessed connections in our lives, and Sabra Ciancanelli's "Sundays of Advent" series warms our hearts and joyfully prepares us for Christmas.

We're happy to welcome new writers Tia McCollors, Kenneth Sampson, Jolynda Strandberg, and Gayle T. Williams. And we say fare-well, thank you, and blessings to our friends Natalie Perkins, Melody Swang, and Marion Bond West.

This year, as we move forward in faith, we'll face joys and sorrows, celebrations and stormy days, but if we look and listen, we'll also experience His wonders and miracles. Get ready to meet God each day and as you do, think about Job 5:9. Allow His wonder and miracles to light your path this year, and remain encouraged for all that is to come. Never forget: God still "performs wonders that cannot be fathomed, miracles that cannot be counted."

Faithfully yours,
The Editors of Guideposts

P.S. We love hearing from you! Let us know what *Daily Guideposts* means to you by e-mailing DailyGPEditors@guideposts.org or by writing to Guideposts Books & Inspirational Media, 39 Old Ridgebury Road #27, Danbury, CT 06810. You can also keep up with your *Daily Guideposts* friends on Facebook.com/dailyguideposts.

Going Digital? Especially for You!

Get one-year instant access to the digital edition of *Daily Guideposts* delivered straight to your e-mail. You'll be able to enjoy its daily inspi-ration and Scripture anytime, anywhere, on your computer, phone, or tablet. Visit DailyGuideposts.org/DG2020 and enter this code: wonder.

JANUARY

*Always be prepared to give an answer
to everyone who asks you to give the
reason for the hope that you have.*

—1 Peter 3:15 (NIV)

New Year's Day, Wednesday, January 1

FIRSTS: Day One

"Behold, I make all things new." —Revelation 21:5 (RSV)

January first! The first day of a brand-new year, the first day of a brand-new decade. It's started me thinking about all the first-days in my life. The big ones. Joyful—the birth of our first child. Challenging—my first days of widowhood. I'm thinking about the small firsts too. My first pair of high heels. My first airplane trip. What if I could maintain the thrill of discovery, the heightened awareness, that comes with first-times?

My father did—with oranges. "I saw my first orange when I was fifteen," he'd tell us. "Never tasted one until I was nearly thirty." Whereas, my childhood oranges were commonplace, I'd find him in the kitchen, cradling an orange in his hand, sniffing it, stroking the rough skin, a kind of wonderment in his eyes.

Our friend Tomu, in Uganda, never got over the marvel of reading. "Look!" he would say. "Little black marks. They talk to me!" The first one in his family to go to school, he remembered when the little black marks were only that.

Has the very abundance of my life, I wondered, *made me less grateful?*

When my husband, John, and I lived for a few months in Normandy, we got to know an elderly priest who, as clergy numbers fell in France, served five separate parishes: Four had daily communion, all had two services on Sunday. How, we asked him once, could he keep repeating the same words over and over with seeming freshness? "But they're never the same!" he said, though we'd heard him intone the identical phrases day after day. "Each time I say them they feel brand new!"

> *Lord, Who makes all things new, help me to recapture*
> *in this new year the wonder of the very first time.*
> —Elizabeth Sherrill

Digging Deeper: Psalm 65:11; Isaiah 43:18–19

JOURNEY TO THE HOLY LAND: Freed from Fear

There is a time for everything, and a season for every activity under the heavens.... —Ecclesiastes 3:1 (NIV)

I've never been much of a bucket-list person. If ever something was on mine, it was to visit Jerusalem and the Holy Land. But for years, fear of danger had kept me away. Then a tour invitation popped up on social media and something inside me said, "Go!" We booked the trip.

I've read the Bible through many times, but never paid much attention to where those divine events took place. Locations were simply names attached to vague, conjured images of quaint dusty villages, a manger scene, or camel-hued earth. Then, amazingly, I was there, standing, walking, gazing on holy ground. I saw Nazareth, Jerusalem, Cana, the Sea of Galilee, the Mount of Olives, Gethsemane, the Jordan River, the Valley of Armageddon, and Mount Zion. I visited the places where Jesus multiplied the loaves and fishes, where Elijah challenged Baal worshippers to a fire contest, and where Jesus was baptized. My head spun. Locations were no longer words to be skimmed over. The Bible was coming to life in a new way.

To say that I was overwhelmed is an understatement. There was more than I could absorb, most of it quite different from what I'd expected. But what surprised me most was the absence of fear. From the moment I booked the reservations, through nine days of assimilating all I saw, not once was I afraid. God filled me with peace as he showed me his beloved land.

Thank You, Lord, for taking away my fear and telling me it was time to experience your sacred land.
—Kim Taylor Henry

Digging Deeper: Isaiah 41:10, 54:14

I remember the days of old; I meditate on all you have done;
I reflect on the work of your hands. —Psalm 143:5 (CSB)

My mom pulled a giant purple tub into the dining room. She lifted the lid, where I saw dozens of old photo albums.

"It might be in here," she said.

I was searching for one photo in particular—me as a four-year-old, sitting on Grandpa's lap in his big leather chair. The search started after a recent dream I'd had about him, which made me remember that this photo of us existed. But a couple of hours passed and no luck.

"Sorry, sweetheart," my mom said. It was getting late, so she went upstairs to get ready for bed. An hour later, I heard her footsteps coming down the stairs, back into the dining room where I had settled in to read for the night. There, in her hand, was the photo.

Except it wasn't exactly how I remembered it. Instead of just sitting on his lap, the photo showed my arms wrapped around him in that chair. The image revealed just how much I loved Grandpa.

All of a sudden, looking at that photo, I could smell his house in western Kansas. I could smell the leather chair. I could smell him. I hadn't been in that house for twenty-five years, but my senses were in that room again.

I felt Jesus come in close, telling me that this is what it's like for Father God to redeem something we thought was forever gone. Jesus's breath carried the smells I knew as a girl. Something deep in my spirit felt God exhale over me, reminding me that He's always been there for me, even at that age when I didn't know Him. And that He remembers this moment, and all other moments, better than I ever could.

Tender Father, I'm overwhelmed by Your unwavering affection
for me and how You've been with me since my heart first beat.
—Desiree Cole

Digging Deeper: 1 Chronicles 16:15; Psalm 78:35

You also must help us by prayer, so that many will give thanks
on our behalf for the blessing granted us in answer to many prayers.
—2 Corinthians 1:11 (RSV)

This year, 2020, *Guideposts* celebrates its seventy-fifth anniversary. The first story in the first issue of the magazine was by Eddie Rickenbacker, a hero of both World War I and World War II. In his article "I Believe in Prayer," Rickenbacker told of how prayer had sustained him in various near disasters, including being lost at sea in the South Pacific for twenty-four days.

Inspired by his words, readers sent in their own stories and shared their own needs for prayer. Soon the small staff of this fledging magazine was gathering every Monday morning at 9:45 to pray for the readers' needs.

Today the prayer requests come in a variety of ways, through social media (I love it when there are photos, by e-mail, by snail mail (sometimes the handwriting itself says a lot). We get thousands of requests, more than a million a year, and they're shared through cyberspace where countless others can add their prayers.

And at 9:45 AM in a downtown office where magazines and books are created to go out to millions of readers, a group of us gather around a conference room table, read prayer requests aloud, and bow our heads. We believe in prayer. Always have.

God, how glad I am that I can offer my prayers to keep all in Your care.
—Rick Hamlin

Digging Deeper: Psalm 122:6; Philippians 1:19; James 5:14–16

Sunday, January 5

Remember the message that...you believed and trusted.
—1 Corinthians 15:1 (CEV)

Ialways read with a pencil and highlighter, meticulously identifying gems from a text and adding notes. But I've wondered if the time spent doing this is worthwhile because I rarely review what I've learned.

Early in my faith, I read every book I could find by Dr. Norman Vincent Peale. His books brought clear understanding of Jesus's teachings and the insights to apply them. A couple of years ago, craving to read something again by Dr. Peale, I ordered his devotional book, *Positive Living Day by Day*. Wow! It's a collection of many of Dr. Peale's biblical teachings that drew me to seek a deeper faith. The powerful impact of revisiting messages I had long trusted inspired me to add the book to my daily reading, along with the Bible and *Daily Guideposts*.

I'm finding great value in returning to past reading treasures. Last year, I focused on identifying faith practices that most changed my life—such as trusting God rather than depending on my understanding and being intentional about keeping a time for prayer each day. Some days I see progress from the previous year's notes. Other days I find gaps, such as the note I found today from two years ago today: "Drop the negative mind chatter when things don't go my way." Time to prioritize this one.

This year, instead of selecting a Bible version I haven't read, I'll reread one, and pay special attention to my past notes and highlights. In my current edition of *Daily Guideposts*, I'm noting God's daily miracles.

The few extra minutes of daily reflection is bringing new understanding to my faith, a deeper awareness of God's guiding presence, and ongoing opportunities for growth.

Lord, inspire us to revisit Your messages that our lives depend on,
that we will seek an ever-closer relationship with You.
—John Dilworth

Digging Deeper: Deuteronomy 6:5–9; Luke 24:8; Revelation 3:13

On coming to the house, they saw the child with his mother Mary, and they bowed down and worshiped him. Then they opened their treasures and presented him with gifts of gold, frankincense and myrrh.
—Matthew 2:11 (NIV)

A few days after Christmas, my wife, daughter, son-in-law, and I traveled to Madrid, Spain, for one week. Walking through the city streets, I noticed that the stores were swamped with shoppers and large crowds of people were gathered in a celebratory spirit everywhere I looked. This struck me as curious; the holiday festivities were in full swing in Madrid, but back home in the States, things tend to quiet down after Christmas and New Year's Day. I asked my daughter why the celebratory mood. She replied, "The people are getting ready for Three Kings Day, or as they say in Spanish *Dia de los Reyes Magos* on January 6."

This holiday is also known as The Feast of the Epiphany, one of the oldest Christian feasts, which commemorates the time when three kings, also known as the Three Wise Men, visited the infant Jesus in Bethlehem. Just as when the Wise Men delivered gifts to baby Jesus, in Spain children receive their Christmas gifts in celebration of this day. My father told me stories about celebrating this holiday as a child growing up in Puerto Rico. Each year, he would fill a small box with grass for the camels to eat—camels that the three kings were said to have ridden.

I enjoyed my visit to Madrid immensely. It reminded me of the time I cofounded a Hispanic congregation on Three Kings Day in Boston. Every year, we celebrated this day with music, food, worship, and gifts for the children. These were joyous celebrations much like what our family discovered on the streets of Spain.

Thank You, Lord, for special times to remember and to focus on You.
—Pablo Diaz

Digging Deeper: Isaiah 60:6; Matthew 2:1–2

Tuesday, January 7

"Do not be afraid, nor be dismayed, for the Lord your God is with you wherever you go." —Joshua 1:9 (NKJV)

In an e-mail to one of my brainy friends, I mentioned that Macedonia might join NASA, which could cause tensions in the region. He e-mailed back with a laughing emoji and wrote, "Are you saying that now those pesky Macedonians are causing trouble in outer space?"

Of course, he knew I meant NATO and so did I, but little slipups that amused me in my fifties can really unnerve me in my sixties. And I am convinced that I have more to worry about than most people my age.

Alzheimer's has taken a toll in my family. My mother and both of her sisters died of it, as did their father. Now some of my older cousins on that side of the family are showing symptoms. So for me every little slip of the tongue, every dumb auto-corrected typo, every forgotten name spells doom.

Later another friend, Todd, asked me, "If there were a test that could tell you if you're going to get Alzheimer's, would you take it?"

I thought for a moment and then said, "Probably not, if there wasn't anything I could do about it."

Todd smiled. "Isn't that pretty much true of the future in general? We have very little idea what will happen to us. There's not much we can do about it except live one day at a time and trust that God will guide us."

It was a lesson I should have been able to glean for myself. Trust is one of the tenets of my faith. Yet I often allow fear and anxiety to cloud my thinking and undermine my outlook. I don't always trust that a loving God has laid a path before me. I shook Todd's hand, grateful for the reminder to trust God.

Lord, I must not be fearful of the future, despite its great unknowns, for You are always there.
—Edward Grinnan

Digging Deeper: Psalm 139:7–10; Isaiah 41:10, 46:4

May the favor of the Lord our God rest on us; establish the work of our hands for us.... —Psalm 90:17 (NIV)

At lunchtime, I usually throw together a sandwich. I eat it in my home office, in front of my computer with a view of swaying oak branches outside the window. But my workload is light this week. This noon I changed my venue. With plate and cup, I settled into a living room chair. Nagging questions quickly surfaced: *Should I be pushing to generate new projects? or stepping back to catch my breath?* In the respite, my eyes rested on a tableau of framed prints that defines the interior wall across the room.

I started collecting the pieces decades ago for my first apartment when I clipped a tinted photo from a perfume ad. Then at a yard sale, I found an Andrew Wyeth—an inviting empty chair beside a window. My mom gave me her heirloom copy of Millet's *The Gleaners*, still in its vintage frame. I later added prints bought at museum shops: a Vermeer *Girl with the Red Hat*, a Sargent mother and daughter, a Morisot, and more, twelve in all.

It had been too long since I'd spent time with the personalized gallery. This noon's vantage point reminded me that in this apartment I'd grouped the scenes by universal themes. Those on the right depict labor: subjects ironing laundry, peeling onions, harvesting fields. Those on the left strike a meditative pose: serene portraits, dreamy lovers, inspired musicians.

A few moments with the art settled my spirit. In the array I saw the interplaying modes of life, even of a particular day. *It's not all demanding work. It's not all rest or reflection. Why not make room for both?*

I plan to eat tomorrow's sandwich away from my desk, maybe outside under the oak. The sandwich will nourish my body. A new vista might nourish and replenish my soul.

Lord, help me to find a good balance between work and rest.
—Evelyn Bence

Digging Deeper: Ecclesiastes 3:1–11; Isaiah 30:15–18

Thursday, January 9

Our Lord Jesus Christ himself and God our Father loved us and through grace gave us eternal comfort and a good hope. —2 Thessalonians 2:16 (CEB)

On January 9, 1961, my friend Carol and I were drinking chocolate malts in our dorm room at Oklahoma State University when my uncle called. "Your dad died an hour ago," he said. "Get your clothes together. I'll drive you home."

That night remains indelibly etched in my mind. On the anniversary of his death last year, it was sorrow on top of sorrow: two of my grandchildren were still grieving their father's unexpected death and struggling to face life without him.

My private pity party was in full swing when my friend Pat called. Pat, a homebound widow, is the most positive, Jesus-loving, and encouraging woman I've ever known. "I got some greeting cards in the mail," she said. "A devotion you wrote years ago was on the back of one. It was about the blizzard that hit right after you and Don [my husband] moved to Copeland. I loved it!"

That memory was clear too. We were snowed in—nothing but snow as far as I could see. I didn't know a single person and I'd never felt so hopeless and alone. Then the telephone rang. "I'm Audrey, your neighbor," a cheery voice said. "You can't see my house but I'm only a couple of miles east. If you need anything, just telephone. I'll find a way to reach you."

Audrey's call years ago and Pat's call when I was sad were powerful reminders that Jesus is always present. He was there when my dad lost his battle with cancer. He is with my heartbroken grandchildren and with our family as we help them deal with their grief. All we have to do is speak His name.

Lord of comfort and hope, thank You for being as near to
Your sorrowing children as a whispered prayer or anguished sigh.
All we have to do is speak Your name.
—Penney Schwab

Digging Deeper: Psalm 18:6; Matthew 5:4; John 14:18–19

I will draw upon the spirit that is on you and put it upon them…
—Numbers 11:17 (JPS)

I've been practicing spiritual direction for a number of years now, trying to serve as a conduit for the awareness of God's blessings. The people who come to me seek to be more sensitive to the divine in their lives. In the past year, I've been privileged to work with a woman who had been doing this for more than twenty years with a different advisor. When her previous advisor retired, she received a referral to me, and we started working together.

She was a caring and passionate person, and after a few months, it became clear that she was also a woman with deep spiritual gifts. However, she was uncertain of her ability to apply these gifts to her own problems. So my hope for her became a prayer that she would come to recognize what seemed so apparent to me—that she only needed to relax and trust. I asked God to help me help her understand how deeply she had integrated God into her life—a rich gift whose solidity I could only acknowledge, and whose strength I had no wish to weaken.

Several months after I began praying for her to have confidence in herself, she said she felt called to try to move away from formal direction for a while. She was hesitant to speak with me about it, I think, because she didn't want to hurt my feelings. I reassured her that I not only understood, but I was happy for her and proud of her. She had made the often difficult decision to stop consistently depending on someone else to show her the path on which she was already walking.

And I told her that if at any point she felt she needed a companion to walk with her for a while, I would be happy to share her journey once again.

Thank You, Lord, for the moments when You allow me to do Your work.
—Rhoda Blecker

Digging Deeper: Exodus 31:3; Numbers 11:25

A good person leaves an inheritance for their children's children...
—Proverbs 13:22 (NIV)

Iinherited my ironing board from my mother-in-law Sybil. It's your standard metal one with a cushion and a floral cover, complete with a nails-on-the-chalkboard, high-pitched squeak that makes the cats run out of the room every time I open it.

Throwing the ironing board into the back of my husband's truck when we were cleaning out his mom's house after she died was really an afterthought. No one else wanted it and I didn't have one. I'd just been using the table covered with a thick blanket, but rather than put it in the dumpster, we brought it home.

Now every time I iron a shirt for a special occasion—a performance of our son Solomon's band, a wedding, or a funeral—I look at the two stained spots where Sybil let the iron sit a little too long and its silhouette is burned in a perfect shadow. I wonder, *What happened?*

As I iron out the wrinkles, I think about how much grace Sybil brought into our lives. The strength of faith she had when she faced the grief of losing her husband and then her oldest son. How she always looked so put together, hair in place, lipstick on. Even on the last day of her life, her granddaughter made sure her nails were done and her lips were colored because she knew Sybil would have wanted them that way.

The ironing board helps me feel her love and the universal love of being a mom, of supporting those we care about by ironing out what we can and doing everything in our power to help them get ready to be their best.

Heavenly Father, thank You for the beautiful people You bring into our lives, and the lessons they teach us. Thank You for reassuring us that those in heaven are still with us, especially on our special days.
—Sabra Ciancanelli

Digging Deeper: Psalm 63:4; 1 Peter 1:3–4

"If you remain in me and I in you, you will bear much fruit; apart from me you can do nothing." —John 15:5 (NIV)

Eight of us were sitting around a table at a church leadership meeting. Our pastor, who'd come to our church a year earlier, joined us.

"How long have you all been teaching?" he asked.

Wanting to impress, I responded first. "My husband and I taught high school Sunday school for almost twenty years, then married couples for two years."

He nodded, then asked the woman beside me. "How about you?"

"I've lost track of the years," she said, "but I'll never forget the day I walked into Sunday school and said, "My life is falling apart, I have nothing to give."

Her honesty sliced straight through my puffed-up pride.

Our pastor said, "I bet it was your best lesson ever."

"You're right. That was the day we stopped pretending we were fine and admitted we couldn't make it without God."

It felt as if the Father, Son, and Holy Spirit had pulled up a chair and joined our conversation.

"Reminds me of a youth camp I led a few years ago," the pastor said. "I'd prepared pages of notes, but I couldn't get the youngsters' attention. Everything went south. Harder I tried, the worse it got."

"What'd you do?" I asked.

"The only thing I could do. I lay on my face in prayer."

"In front of the youth group?" I said.

"Yep. In the middle of the room."

I imagined a pastor stretched out on the floor, begging God for help.

"What did the kids do?" I asked, barely breathing.

"They joined me on the floor. Facedown. Praying. Then God showed up and we had a revival."

Lord, there's no other way to survive aside from total dependence on You.
                    —Julie Garmon

Digging Deeper: Jeremiah 10:23; Philippians 4:13

Monday, January 13

These days should be remembered and observed in every generation by every family, and in every province and in every city....—Esther 9:28 (NIV)

It was purging time. I stuffed worn quilts, old pots, and broken toys into large garbage bags. I glanced over at the high folding chair near the window, the one my mother begged me to get rid of with each visit. "One of these days the boys are going to kill themselves on that thing," she'd say.

I opened the chair in the middle of the living room. It's where I sat, five years old, as Mami clipped my long hair into a short pixie style. It was where she cut everyone's hair. This chair was also our ladder, where Papi would stand to replace lightbulbs, where I would stand reaching over the plastic Christmas tree to place the star.

My mother had hemmed countless pants as I stood on it, clenched with fear she would poke me with pins. It was my favorite chair at the table, because it was so high, and I was so short.

Through the years it served the same purposes for my children—lightbulbs, Christmas trees, haircuts, a favorite chair at the table for my little boys. I did my best to keep it intact but nothing I did could mend the damage of so many years. As much as I hated to admit it, it was time to let go.

I took several pictures from different angles, wiping away tears as I did. It's a chair. I know. But it's also a piece of my history, intimately connected to the ones I love. I was thankful to my beloved chair for serving us so well, but even more so for my family, their love, and the beautiful memories that gave a simple chair so much meaning.

Lord, Thank You for the gifts of memories and for people who give each memory such life.
—Karen Valentin

Digging Deeper: Psalm 133:1; Philippians 1:3–5

"Do not fear, for I am with you.... Surely I will uphold you with My righteous right hand."—Isaiah 41:10 (NASB)

Tonight as I sat at my desk and stared at my computer screen, my golden retriever, Buddy, walked up and placed his large, handsome muzzle on my forearm. Nuzzling closer, he demanded my attention.

Gazing into his deep and loving brown eyes, I realized that Buddy represents our third generation of golden retrievers. When we moved from Texas to Georgia nine years ago, our Chevrolet Suburban was a Noah's Ark that carried not only my wife, Beth, and me, but also Buddy, his aging parents, Beau and Muffy, and his brother and littermate, Bear. Today, Buddy is the only one still living. Nine years is a long time in the life of a dog.

Slowly I stopped writing in order to bend down and hold Buddy's front paw in my two hands. A dog must trust you to give you his paw to hold. And Buddy trusts me with his life—for food, shelter, medical care, and the love that Beth and I commit to him.

Tonight Buddy has reminded me that I must place my aging paw into God's big hand too. I need to be reassured that God's love for me is unquestionable, enduring, and forever. If I can love my dog with all my heart, how much more does God love you and me!

Father, thank You for animals that depend upon us for goodness and teach us to trust You as Our Heavenly Father. Amen.
—Scott Walker

Digging Deeper: Psalms 4:8, 91:2; Isaiah 46:4

Wednesday, January 15

Whatever you do, work at it wholeheartedly as though you were doing it for the Lord and not merely for people. —Colossians 3:23 (ISV)

"So, you are an author."

"Yes." I say slowly, while I eye the retired gentlemen sitting next to me, a stranger at an event I was attending with my husband.

"My daughter thinks I should write a book," he tells me.

I nod, knowingly. The words might vary, but the desire to get a life on paper remains constant in the hundreds of conversations I've had since my memoir was published and people discover that I'm an author.

"Don't do it." I steady the plate of appetizers on my lap.

He stares at me in surprise. "What do you mean, 'Don't do it'?"

"Write one story. Maybe how you met your wife. Then write another story—a day you got in trouble as a child. Then another story."

He smiles. Nods. "I could do that."

"Writing an entire book is too daunting. Most people give up."

"I understand."

"Your children and grandchildren will treasure whatever you write—even if it isn't an entire book."

His faded blue eyes track mine. "I like that. When I built my first airplane, many people wondered at the enormity of the task."

It's my turn for surprise. "You built an airplane?"

"Yes."

"Where?"

"In my garage."

"How did you do it?"

He laughs. "The same way you wrote your book. Piece by piece."

Sometimes I try to accomplish too much, Jesus, and I become
overwhelmed. Give me strength to do the next right thing today.
—Lynne Hartke

Digging Deeper: Proverbs 3:6; Colossians 3:17

Wishing to justify himself, he said to Jesus, "And who is my neighbor?"
—Luke 10:29 (NASB)

*B*roke *and broken down.*

The words kept running through my mind. Three weeks of ministry concert dates and a couple of thousand miles under our wheels, my family and I were finally pointed toward home when our old motorhome decided enough was enough. Now we were stuck in a junkyard garage on the edge of a windswept plain in the middle of nowhere. I wasn't sure I could even afford the tow, let alone labor and parts.

God and I thumb-wrestled, and my bitterness edged out. *Lord, why now? Why here?*

Desperate to hurry things along, I looked down at the elderly mechanic. "Hey, man, is there anything I can do to help?"

He blinked at me through thick glasses. "Actually, yeah, can you grab a half-inch wrench out of the tool box and hold that bolt right there?"

A few minutes later, I was covered in grease to my elbows.

An hour after that, I realized that the man on the other side of the engine wasn't just an oil-smeared face. His name was Bob. He'd lost the wife of his youth to cancer. Recently he'd come out of retirement to make the extra cash he needed to raise his two grandsons.

Why here? Why now? Simple—because God loved Bob.

As we talked on through the hours, I realized that I loved Bob too. My bitterness had tumbled off over the grass with the prairie wind.

Later, I held my breath as the shop owner totaled the bill.

Then he smiled. "You know what? I'm only gonna charge you for parts. The rest is on me. Bob really needed someone to talk to."

I left humbled. Bob and I'd worn the grease, but the Great Mechanic had done the work.

Lord, help me to see past myself, so that I might see You.
—Buck Storm

Digging Deeper: Isaiah 1:17; John 13:34

Friday, January 17

I am not ashamed of the gospel, because it is the power of God that brings salvation to everyone who believes: first to the Jew, then to the Gentile. —Romans 1:16 (NIV)

As though youth ministry isn't spontaneous enough, this past year we allowed our students to choose the verse that would guide their study, their activity, and eventually their mission work. None of the adults was quite sure what the students would come up with or how it would all work out. For a planner like me, this caused some anxiety, and I was somewhat hesitant about it.

After two weeks, the majority of the students chose Romans 1:16. All the adults gasped at the profoundness of this selection. You see, our youth group was a military youth group overseas. Our students had experienced an intense amount of transition laced with the reality of having parents placed in harm's way regularly. In addition to this transient lifestyle, living overseas brings the sober reality of security concerns, which become a part of daily life in efforts to keep US personnel safe. The chosen Scripture was emblazoned on T-shirts worn as an act of faith. It was bold, and it was faith affirming. Our young people were more committed than we had ever thought!

Because of this prayerful and bold choice of Scripture, this past year our youth group inspired an entire community. Students, leaders, and parents prayed this Scripture as we planned and facilitated our programs and events, knowing the Lord would guide our actions. All of these faith-filled experiences taught me that not only do I need to make room for the Lord's spontaneity, but I also need to embrace the uncertainty of military life. Great things happen when the Word directs our paths and changes our hearts!

Lord, help me to remember that You are always faithful and always true. Help me to be open to Your will in both expected and unexpected ways.
—Jolynda Strandberg

Digging Deeper: Isaiah 6:8; 1 Corinthians 12:27

A wise son maketh a glad father.... —Proverbs 10:1 (KJV)

Would you like a refill on your Coke?" the waitress asks, approaching our table in the restaurant where Harrison, my son and I are enjoying a boys' night out.

"Uh," Harrison says, glancing at me, "Uh, sure."

"Harrison," I say, "Don't you think—?" and then, I catch myself.

I have to laugh, as I look at him, sitting there, hesitating somewhere between boy and man.

I've always tried to help him balance his choices between what's good for him and what's not. Cokes were always an occasional treat, not a habit.

Harrison is on his way to college in Washington, DC. We've spent hours imagining his future adventures. He is such a fine young man of whom I am exceedingly proud.

Yet here I am, on the cusp of squelching his order of a second Coke.

I kick back in the booth and grin at Harrison.

On the inside, though, I'm letting go. Not letting him go, mind you, but letting go of that notion that somehow I can control his future.

In many ways, Harrison is already who he'll always be. That pleases me. It doesn't mean he's a carbon copy of anyone, especially me. When I was his age, I loved football. Harrison's passion is drama. I liked big, noisy parties. Harrison finds pleasure in small friend-gatherings, listening to music and discussing subjects that would've been beyond me at his age.

My grin widens. "What, Dad?" he asks, refilled glass before him.

I don't have words to describe how good God has been to me through the ups and downs of raising Harrison, so I grin some more and cherish the moment.

I'm already looking ahead, imagining Harrison on a distant Saturday, wandering through DC, giant-size Coke in hand, perfectly content.

Father God, we raised him together. I hope
You are as proud of him as I am.
—Brock Kidd

Digging Deeper: Psalm 127:3; Proverbs 22:6

Sunday, January 19

Therefore, if anyone is in Christ, he is a new creation; old things have passed away; behold, all things have become new. —2 Corinthians 5:17 (NKJV)

It was Sunday morning and I was eager for a day of worship, Bible teaching, and connection with my church community. My church's coffee-bar ministry is a delight for this coffee-enthusiast, and each Sunday morning I grab a sweet and bold cup of dark roast.

This Sunday was no different, as I held the warm, comforting treat in my hands. As I turned to leave the coffee line, an earring fell off. I attempted to snatch the runaway earring but I tilted too abruptly, spilling coffee on the lobby floor.

What is wrong with me today? I thought, adding up this third accident that morning. Earlier my youngest daughter had spilled orange juice on the kitchen floor. Soon after, I'd spilled gooey hair gel on my family room hardwood floors.

After flagging a church volunteer to help with the spill, I walked into the sanctuary with my head and spirits low. Why was I so clumsy when other women around me seemed so poised and graceful?

When my pastor took to the podium, he opened his sermon with a personal anecdote fit for a television sitcom. He told the story of going to a fast-food restaurant that had led to a back-and-forth trip from the restaurant to the ATM and back again. Each trip he'd forgotten something—his wallet, retrieving his money from the ATM, taking his food from the employee at the restaurant window. At the end of his story, the entire church roared with laughter, and I along with them.

Through the pastor's comical story, I heard this message: everyone messes up at times. And not only do we make mistakes, but if we're patient, God can even use our messy stories to bless others.

Lord, help me to extend kindness and grace toward myself, believing that You can use my mess-ups to bring lessons—and even laughter—to others.
—Carla Hendricks

Digging Deeper: Psalm 126:2; Isaiah 43:18–19; 2 Peter 3:18

There is neither Jew nor Gentile, neither slave nor free, nor is there male and female, for you are all one in Christ Jesus. —Galatians 3:28 (NIV)

The Reverend Dr. Martin Luther King, Jr., once said, "I think it is one of the tragedies of our nation, one of the shameful tragedies, that eleven o'clock on Sunday morning is one of the most segregated hours—if not the most segregated hour—in Christian America. I definitely think the Christian church should be integrated, and any church that stands against integration, and that has a segregated body, is standing against the spirit and the teachings of Jesus Christ, and it fails to be a true witness" (from *Meet the Press*, April 17, 1960).

Whenever I think of those words, it takes me back to an experience I had twenty-five years ago that let me know we are all truly the same in God's eyes. The day after my first son was born, I remained in the hospital, and my visitors were limited to family members. But my friend Barbara was determined to see me and meet my newborn. Nothing was going to stop her.

"Miss?" the nurse tried to stop Barbara as she stepped toward my room. "You can't visit her—only family."

"I know. I'm her sister," Barbara said, as she walked past the nurse into my room.

As a white woman, Barbara didn't look much like my sister, since I'm black. She announced our "sistership" with such conviction, the nurse was left speechless.

Barbara and I laughed about how she fooled the nurses, but then we realized this wasn't funny at all. The two of us, close friends for more than a decade, did indeed love each other as sisters, despite our lack of a shared bloodline and skin of different hues.

Father, I thank You for all the people of the world,
Your creations who show that beauty comes in all shades.
May we come together as one, in Your sight.
—Gayle T. Williams

Digging Deeper: John 7:24; Romans 10:12

Tuesday, January 21

Teach me knowledge and good judgment, for I trust your commands.
—Psalm 119:66 (NIV)

I have a temporary job delivering supplies for a medical lab. It made sense to hire me—a lifelong Pittsburgher who's familiar with this city's awkward topography and wayward streets. I was, in fact, the perfect candidate, except for one small and off-putting personality trait: road rage.

I'm the guy gesticulating in a traffic jam, tossing random critiques out of the open window: Who doesn't turn right on red? Oh, *now* you put your signal on. Did you buy your license online, or actually take the test? What is *wrong* with you?

This leads to the self-reflexive follow-up question: What is wrong with *me*? Needless to say, I was concerned that my poor citizenship behind the wheel might lead to incidents, which might lead to accidents, which might lead to unemployment.

Instead, the opposite happened: I became uncharacteristically calm. I witnessed so much bad driving that I became sympathetic. Instead of anger, I found compassion, mostly out of curiosity: What would make ordinary people abandon all reason and barrel through an intersection? Selfishness? Possibly—or perhaps they're having a horrible day (or week or year), or maybe the kids' school bus was late and now they're late, and their cold-hearted boss will fire them on the spot, or maybe they're distracted, waiting for the biopsy results…

Sure, I still have my moments, but I'm happy with my decision to spike my morning coffee with sympathy instead of spite, with kindness instead of revenge, with love instead of rage.

Lord, I changed my heart as a driver; help me change my heart
as I walk (or drive) with Your people every day.
—Mark Collins

Digging Deeper: Psalm 46:10; Matthew 11:28

We all, with open face beholding as in a glass the glory of the Lord, are changed into the same image from glory to glory, even as by the Spirit of the Lord. —2 Corinthians 3:18 (KJV)

I sagged deeper into my recliner as yet another youthful celebrity on television touted her flawless skin and one of those face creams that never seems to work so well for me. In an era where physical beauty drives much of what our minds consciously or subconsciously absorb, the relentless offers to maintain youthful looks by ridding ourselves of worn-out skin and unsightly wrinkles can be both tempting and disheartening.

But what if we were promised a continuous, priceless makeover, without charge and without appointment, all day long sloughing off layers that strip us of our vitality and cause us to shrivel in discontent?

I love the imagery and metaphor often used in the Scriptures, so recently, when a Bible class member compared the act of looking at Jesus to a facial, a light went off reminding me of the passage from 2 Corinthians describing the believer as "beholding as in a glass the glory of the Lord." What if there were a daily means to reduce the ever-deepening wrinkles of worry, anger, greed, and bitterness? According to Apostle Paul, there is!

The more we look into the face of Christ, the more the world's troublesome wrinkles are smoothed as we are changed into the Lord's image. But although there is no cost to us, there is a requirement: keeping our eyes on Him.

Often as Christ-followers, we are lured from His face, forgetting that focusing on our Savior not only protects us, it causes us to reflect more of His splendor. Not only does resting in the Lord make us "dwell in safety" (Psalm 4:8, KJV) when we gaze upon Him—in prayer, meditation, and Scripture reading—we actually become more beautiful.

> *Father, in a world filled with glamorous distractions,*
> *help me to keep my eyes on Your splendor.*
> —Jacqueline F. Wheelock

Digging Deeper: James 1:23–25; 1 Peter 3:3

Thursday, January 23

Fools show their annoyance at once.... —Proverbs 12:16 (NIV)

The vet had been nice enough to squeeze me in at day's end to see our dog, Sage, who wasn't feeling well. We'd been escorted promptly into the examining room, where an assistant wrote down my summary of the problem. But now we'd been sitting in that austere tiled space for nearly forty-five minutes, waiting. I wanted to run to the post office and grocery store and fit in a workout before dinner. I didn't need this delay.

"Sorry," the assistant stuck her head into the room. "It's taking a little longer than we thought. The doctor will be in soon." I took a not-too-subtle look at my watch, commenting that if they were running late, it would have been helpful to call and let me know before I arrived. "Sometimes things don't go as we'd hoped," she said softly, and shut the door. I scratched Sage's fluffy neck. She panted up at me and then settled onto the floor, obviously feeling more patient than I did.

The vet came in just over an hour after we had. "Well, how's Sage feeling today?" He stroked her head. I reviewed her problems with him, trying to ignore my annoyance at the wait.

As Sage and I got in the car to leave, the back door of the vet's building opened. The assistant was rolling out a gurney on which lay something large, covered by a blanket. An older woman followed. My heart sank as the woman opened her car trunk and the assistant gently lifted the lifeless bundle inside.

I pulled out of the parking lot, my petty irritation replaced by tears.

*Lord, when I feel impatient, help me realize that others have
burdens much heavier than mine.*
—Kim Taylor Henry

Digging Deeper: Proverbs 2:11, 14:29

He said, "Look! I see four men walking around in the fire, unbound and unharmed, and the fourth looks like a son of the gods."—Daniel 3:25 (NIV)

Beau, our new baby, slept well, ate ferociously, laughed easily, and hated the car seat. Unfortunately, car time was unavoidable. I tried to limit it, but school drop-off, pick-up, and the grocery store still had to happen.

Before car trips with the family, I fed him, changed his diaper, and placed his lovey toy right beside his cheek. Then my husband, Brian, would start the engine and the wailing began.

The big kids sang and talked to Beau, but his screaming only intensified. The one thing that calmed my heart was knowing he was full, clean, and safe—he was just mad!

Often I look at my children and wonder how God must feel about us. I know He'd take away every heartache if He could, but then what kind of people would we grow up to be?

One day, I looked Beau in the eyes from my spot in the backseat. "I wish I could take you out of this," I told him. "But I can't. Instead, I'm going to sit right here beside you while we both endure it."

A nine-week-old baby can't comprehend those words, but I said them for two reasons: to allow my other children to hear them and to remind myself what to do when I beg God to take me out of a difficult situation. In the Bible, Shadrach had to endure the fire. Daniel withstood the lions. I needed to remember not to get caught up in my current situation and instead focus on Who was in it with me!

Beau turned four months old and, just like that, the car-seat crying vanished. He just had to grow a little bit to understand how safe and loved he was, in every situation.

> *Lord, help me remember that You are with me.*
> *You will never leave or forsake me.*
> —Ashley Kappel

Digging Deeper: Daniel 6:22; 1 Corinthians 10:13; 1 Peter 5:10

Saturday, January 25

My heart was grieved.... —Psalm 73:21 (NKJV)

"You have to come right now," my niece, Michele, sobbed. Standing in the mall, I held my phone tightly and hung the shirt back on the rack. "What's wrong, Michele?" But I knew, though my heart was begging me not to know. My brother was dying.

We had been with him three days before. He seemed on the way back from a terrible bout with cancer. He and my husband, David, were talking of fishing; a trip to Tellico, our father's birthplace; and, best of all, his reconciliation and anticipated remarriage to his first wife, Carol, mother of his daughters, Kristi and Michele.

I had always adored my big brother Davey. He was the smartest student in every class, gentle and sweet, every teacher's favorite. He loved baseball, especially the Chattanooga Lookouts and always had his glove primed, ready to catch that elusive fly ball at game time.

Recently I had texted him: "I can see us at our little table, eating alphabet soup or peanut butter and banana mixed for lunch. Safe and happy and cared for. I've never met anyone who had a better childhood. Nothing on this earth can touch it."

"I think about that too," he texted back, "and I totally agree. I never realized at the time just how unique and perfect it was."

Davey never caught the fly ball. His most recent plans didn't happen. But he had gone to God in peace with his family reunited around him.

At the end of our last visit, Davey had pulled me close and, totally out of character, he had whispered in my ear, "I love you."

"I love you back," I said.

I'll always grieve for Davey. But the happy times make it easy to let go of regrets. His last gift of "I love you" moves me toward tomorrow with joy.

Father, in our grief, help us remember love in
whatever way it has been offered to us.
—Pam Kidd

Digging Deeper: Psalm 30:5; Isaiah 53:4

Many waters cannot quench love; rivers cannot sweep it away. If one were to give all the wealth of one's house for love, it would be utterly scorned. —Song of Songs 8:7 (NIV)

Recently, I received a letter from Julie, a former member of the church in Carmel, New York, where I served as a pastor. After retirement, she and her husband, Marty, moved to Pennsylvania, but thankfully, she continued to stay in touch. Over the years, after reading my devotionals, Julie would send me notes of encouragement; however, this letter was not like the others. When I began reading, my heart sank as I learned of her husband's passing. A few weeks after his birthday, Marty had suffered a massive cerebral hemorrhage and passed away three weeks later. In the letter, Julie wrote about the "great love affair" they had shared for fifty-three years. I could feel her love for Marty and her deep sadness with his passing pouring through the letter. She wrote about how thankful to God she is for the wonderful years she had with him and for the legacy he has left behind, "the memory of love," and their wonderful sons.

In the letter, Julie also wrote, "I want to tell you how much he loved you. We both loved you! As you know, I am a *Daily Guideposts* reader and have been since the second edition. When Marty would see me coming to the breakfast nook with the book in hand, he'd ask, 'Did Pablo write something? Read it to me, please!' We enjoyed your inspiration together."

The day I met Julie and Marty, we bonded instantly. We would chat every Sunday after service and would always find something to laugh about. They were and continue to be a true blessing in my life. Although Marty is no longer with us, we have the memory of his love—it will never die.

Lord, thank You for the gift of love and friendship.
—Pablo Diaz

Digging Deeper: 1 Corinthians 13:1–3; 1 John 4:7

Monday, January 27

... I call to you, Lord, every day; I spread out my hands to you.
—Psalm 88:9 (NIV)

This morning I quietly entered my office and sank down in my old easy chair. I did not turn on the lights. I wanted to fade into shadows, close my eyes, and be silent. I was tired. Eight good hours of sleep each night evades me. And, the pace of life does not slow down. In the midst of many people, I often grow lonely.

After a moment of stillness, my lips moved and I subliminally intoned the words of a hymn by Charles Wesley: "Father, I stretch my hands to Thee, no other help I know; If Thou withdraw Thyself from me, Ah! whither shall I go?"

What I need most from God is the realization of His presence with me. And, what God needs most from me is my desire to live in close relationship with Him. I love theology and Bible study and rich devotional literature. But I yearn most for an intuitive awareness of God within me. John Wesley, the charismatic founder of the Methodist church, prayed for this same presence. And, Jesus did too.

There is a rest that only God can bring to a weary soul. And there is a joy that warms the heart of God when we lift our hands and spirits toward Him.

Father, I stretch my hands to You. No other help I know. Amen.
—Scott Walker

Digging Deeper: Psalm 42:1–2, 7–8; James 4:8

Return, my soul, to your rest; the Lord has been very good to you.
—Psalm 116:7 (NABRE)

Six years ago, when I took my first quilting class, I burned with such enthusiasm and joy that I was sure I would finish the quilt within a year. The instructor had suggested I start small, with a quilt for a crib or a twin bed, but I set out to make a queen-size quilt. I didn't like being a beginner and figured that a big project would catapult me into the realm of "expert." I bought a fancy sewing machine. I purchased yards of fabrics, cut them into pieces, and started sewing them together into quilt blocks.

And then, overwhelmed, I stopped. *This is tedious and hard*, I thought.

I told this story to Beth. She and seven other women had booked our bed-and-breakfast for a quilting weekend. I watched them at work, in awe of their skill and speed. They made more headway on their projects in three days than I had made on mine in six years.

I finally showed Beth the fabric pieces, cut and sorted and collecting dust.

Showing her my fabric pieces, I said glumly, "I'll never get this done. I should throw everything out. Who'd want this fabric, already cut up like this?"

"I can see how much time and effort you've put into this," Beth said with compassion. "Give them to me. I'll sew them together for you."

I was stunned and delighted by her generous offer. In my mess she saw something valuable and worth salvaging.

Weeks later, Beth texted me. "I've finished your quilt blocks." I could see from the photo she sent that Beth had made sense of my bits and pieces of fabric. My quilt—our quilt—is going to be beautiful.

> *God, sometimes I don't see the value of my struggles and I get discouraged. Deepen my trust in Your way of making all of my mess into a thing of beauty.*
> —Amy Eddings

Digging Deeper: Isaiah 30:18, 61:3

Wednesday, January 29

"I am the Lord, the God of all mankind. Is anything too hard for me?"
—Jeremiah 32:27 (NIV)

My friend Maryanne loves to dance. When a movie ends, she will spring from her seat to dance through the credits. There will be a disco ball at her fiftieth birthday party. And today, because her son and daughter-in-law live across the street from us, and because she was visiting them when I walked my Labrador, I saw her dancing with her grandchildren. She twirled across the patio, babe in arms, as her long, dark hair swooshed behind her. Stunning.

Like everyone under God's great lights, Maryanne has struggles. We'd texted just that morning, and I knew her struggles. But there she was. Dancing with abandon, joy, and what looked like trust and hope. When had I last been that free?

My home was once a place of dance. I cradled my sons and swayed. I danced with toddlers on my feet and taught my boys to slow dance. My husband Lonny and I weren't strangers to the worn-rug living-room dance floor either. But lately I'd been weighted with worry over a family circumstance. The situation spiraled downward, and I felt helpless. I was disappointed. Hurt. I wondered where God was in the wild mess. But watching Maryanne reminded me of powerful truths.

God never promised we wouldn't struggle. He did promise He'd never leave.

As I paused for a moment and savored the scene, something in my spirit shifted. I realized I'd lost my focus. My eyes had been fixed on the chains that seemed to bind us and not on the One Who would set us free. In Him, there is hope.

Maryanne swooped to gather another grand-girl to her arms. She saw me and waved as my dog tugged his leash. My friend would stop over later. For now, it was time to go. I was changed. I'd dance again.

Lord, You are my hope.
—Shawnelle Eliasen

Digging Deeper: Psalm 9:10; Daniel 6:23

Don't run up debts, except for the huge debt of love you owe each other...
—Romans 13:8 (MSG)

Dishes clattered as I washed and stacked them in the drain rack to dry. It was a Sunday evening before service and I'd volunteered to help in the church's kitchen. The monotony of doing dishes was a welcome relief after the last couple of emotionally draining weeks. I really wanted to hide in the solitude of the kitchen all night.

Then I heard from the doorway, "Rebecca, I'd like you to meet my mother."

I sighed, dried my hands and turned to see Susan guiding her elderly mother toward me. Her mother's blank stare and the uncertainty of each step revealed the progression of her dementia. Compassion for my friend swept over me. *Oh, Lord, what can I possibly say to encourage them?*

Susan lovingly patted her mother's hand. "Mom, I'd like you to meet Rebecca."

Although her mother's eyes stayed blank, they almost twinkled as she turned toward me and with a delicate voice, she said, "I love you."

Shocked, I leaned back, just as her mother repeated, "I love you."

Susan heartily chuckled and explained that for years her mother had worked in a local grocery store as a cashier. She'd always greeted everyone in her line, whether a stranger or a friend, with an "I love you." Many times all the other checkout lines were empty, but her mom's line brimmed with people who longed to hear those three special words.

Warmth flooded my heart and erased the stress of the previous weeks. I glanced at the wisps of gray hair and the curl of her back. She was merely a shadow of the woman she once had been, but she still spoke those three transforming words. I gently grasped her hand, "I love you too."

Thank You, Lord, for showing me that a great way to encourage others, and to be emotionally recharged, is by reaching out and saying, "I love you."
—Rebecca Ondov

Digging Deeper: John 13:34; Romans 12:10

Friday, January 31

Therefore, do not throw away your confidence, which has a great reward.
—Hebrews 10:35 (NASB)

January is often a difficult month for us northerners. Snow and ice, cold and dark. This year I hated the fog; usually I love it. It's like being carried in a cozy pouch. I call a foggy day a "marsupial" day.

This time it made me almost claustrophobic. A nameless anxiety filled me. When my husband, Terry, intended to drive a few miles into town on an errand, I asked him not to go. I didn't want to be alone. Instead, we lay side by side and he held my hand.

A family road trip song from my childhood came back to me—"I Believe the Answer's on the Way." I found myself humming a line repeatedly about holding on to our confidence. Encouragement wrapped around me, dissipating the fog. The next line about faith was equally reassuring. Slowly I felt strength return to my spirit.

January had slipped from the calendar before I began to see beyond the fog and understand why I'd been uneasy. The previous spring, Terry had had a kidney removed because of cancer. Then in the fall, he'd been airlifted to a medical center while suffering a heart attack.

These were major life events. We had both seemed to roll through them at the time. But once a new year began, deep down I wondered what would happen next. I felt afraid to walk into the unseen days ahead.

The Holy Spirit brought to mind a simple song from childhood to refresh my trust in the God Who has been with me from day one—and continues with me year after year.

Lord of my confidence, You clearly promise that You are with me always,
"even to the end of the age" (Matthew 28:20, NASB).
—Carol Knapp

Digging Deeper: Joshua 1:9; Jeremiah 17:7–8

HE PERFORMS WONDERS

1 _____

2 _____

3 _____

4 _____

5 _____

6 _____

7 _____

8 _____

9 _____

10 _____

11 _____

12 _____

13 _____

14 _____

15 _____

January

16 _____

17 _____

18 _____

19 _____

20 _____

21 _____

22 _____

23 _____

24 _____

25 _____

26 _____

27 _____

28 _____

29 _____

30 _____

31 _____

FEBRUARY

*Make sure that nobody pays back
wrong for wrong, but always strive
to do what is good for each other and
for everyone else.*

—1 Thessalonians 5:15 (NIV)

Saturday, February 1

FIRSTS: Winter

He casts forth his ice like morsels; who can stand before his cold?
—Psalm 147:17 (RSV)

Most "first-times," of course, we can't remember. Our first breath. Our first sight of a human face. Every now and then, though, we're given a wondrous chance to rediscover even these earliest things.

Such an opportunity came for me when John and I were living in Uganda. Three mornings a week, I taught ninety bright, inquisitive teenagers at a wall-less school overlooking Lake Victoria. One day I was asked about a baffling phrase in the book the headmaster was reading aloud. How to explain "change of season" on the equator? *Summer* was hot, I began. That was easy for these young students; eighty degrees was a chilly day for them. *Spring* with its flowering trees they could imagine; Uganda is a land of flowers. Leaves falling in *autumn* sounded feasible.

But *winter?* I tried to come up with something they'd understand. I mimicked shivering, putting on boots and a coat. Uncomprehending stares. "In winter," I said, "water becomes like stone." The stares became dubious. "If Lake Victoria were near my home in New York State, the surface would be stiff enough to walk on." With that, I'd lost all credibility. Then I thought of the ice cube tray in our refrigerator.

Two days later, I wrapped twenty-four ice cubes in layers of newspaper and drove faster than I'd ever dared on the corrugated red-earth road. "Pass them around!" I urged. There were many more outstretched hands than ice cubes. And then! The swell of astonished cries as these bright minds registered their first experience of *cold*.

And in the gasps, the laughter, the murmurs of wonder as the ice disappeared and their hands dripped with water, I caught the excitement of my own long-forgotten first-time.

> *Lord, Who makes all things new, Your change-of-season gives me the chance to experience Your world anew four times a year.*
> —Elizabeth Sherrill

Digging Deeper: Genesis 8:22; Ecclesiastes 3:1–22; Daniel 2:21

Pray in the Spirit on all occasions with all kinds of prayers and requests.
—Ephesians 6:18 (NIV)

When my rector asked me to serve as the spiritual emphasis coordinator for the upcoming capital campaign and to compose a campaign prayer, my first impulse was to wiggle out of it. *Attend meetings? Raise money? Write prayers? "Why me?"*

She replied, "You have a way with words and can be counted on...I know you are someone who will take seriously the needs and challenges...and pray through them."

Well, I admire Reverend Kate and respect her judgment, and as I've written for genres other than prayer for thirty years, I agreed to trust the Holy Spirit and give it a go. After all, the church was in dire need of both a new elevator and a new roof, and I could offer only modest financial support. I could, however, contribute significantly in writing.

Within two or three days, divinely guided, I'm sure, I wrote the prayer, which praised 200 years of church stewardship and asked for the wisdom and vision to continue this ministry. The prayer was distributed on card stock and spoken at services. Many parishioners found it moving. About four months later, our church achieved its financial goal.

Did my prayer alone make this happen? Hardly. Dozens of volunteers—accountants, architects, pledge workers, vestry, and one writer—worked together using our special gifts for a common good. I was blessed that my pastor recognized my latent talent and invited me to use it. Now the choir director wants prayers for rehearsals too!

Lord, I love when we talk together, whether the words are written or not.
—Gail Schilling

Digging Deeper: Philippians 4:13; 1 Timothy 4:14

Monday, February 3

Love each other as if your life depended on it. —1 Peter 4:8 (MSG)

Unthinkable. Jaw-dropping. The underdog Philadelphia Eagles were Super Bowl champions for the first time. I was winding down South Second Street, trying to make my way to the City of Brotherly Love's Dock Street. Post-victory parade revelers made driving difficult. Yet, I couldn't help but catch their celebratory spirit.

I was in Philadelphia for the annual Chapel of the Four Chaplains awards dinner, commemorating the seventy-fifth anniversary of the sinking of the United States American Troop transport ship *Dorchester*. In the early morning of February 3, 1943, an enemy submarine torpedoed the USAT *Dorchester* in frigid North Atlantic waters just off Greenland. The troop ship, transporting army personnel, sank in less than twenty minutes. Of the 902 soldiers aboard ship, 672 died.

The exceptional story of the *Dorchester* is about its four chaplains. According to eyewitnesses, Chaplains George Fox (Methodist), Alexander Goode (Jewish), John Washington (Catholic), and Clark Poling (Dutch Reformed) calmed the frightened, tended the wounded, guided the disoriented to safety, and handed out life jackets. When life jackets ran out, the chaplains gave away theirs. Private William Bednar, floating in the icy oil-smeared water, recalled, "I could hear the chaplains preaching courage.... Their voices were the only thing that kept me going."

As the ship went down, those in nearby rafts could see the chaplains—arms linked and braced against the slanting deck—their voices offering prayers and singing hymns. Today we remember these leaders of faith, their sacrificial action, and their selfless love. Through them, we're reconnected to our larger humanity, and so are blessed.

All of us who attended the banquet were freshly inspired by the valor of these four chaplains. We left the dinner, celebrating not with team colors and a parade, but with hearts encouraged.

Generous God, enable me to reach out to help others this day.
—Ken Sampson

Digging Deeper: John 15:13; 1 Peter 4:9–10

God is our refuge and strength, a very present help in trouble.
—Psalm 46:1 (NKJV)

Time to downsize.
Anybody who has ever tried this has wished desperately that he or she had never upsized in the first place. Margi, my wife, and I looked at our big house and our two children nearing college age, and decided it was time. We sold our dream house, bought a place half the size, and got ready to move.

Immediately, we were struck by two problems: How would we ever get rid of our mountain of stuff? And who's going to help us move it all? Getting rid of stuff was relatively easy—a moving sale. We sold the best stuff at the cheapest prices anybody had ever seen. We were "highly motivated sellers." Even so, we still had a huge load to move.

Family lived half a country away. Our furniture was heavy, and we had lots and lots of stuff. The task seemed almost impossible, and I felt overwhelmed. We had many friends, but they were older, and we didn't feel we could prevail upon them. I am a pastor, but didn't feel right asking people in our church. We were shopping around for professional movers, when a good friend came up to me at church.

"Hey Bill, I have a bunch of people lined up to help you move. When do you want us to come?"

Problem solved before I even asked. What surprising grace!

Margi and I were beyond grateful.

Our move was a mixture of gratitude and humility. God's love was on display in the willing hands, the laughter, and labor of His people. I'm still humbled when I think about it. I'm even more humbled that God used a friend to gather help before I even asked.

Gracious Father, thank You for surprising me with grace,
meeting my needs, and surrounding me with friends who care.
—Bill Giovannetti

Digging Deeper: Ruth 1:16; Proverbs 17:17

Wednesday, February 5

He said to them, "Go into all the world and preach the gospel to every creature." —Mark 16:15 (NKJV)

Said to be the oldest newsboy statue in the country, the one in Great Barrington, Massachusetts, is a five-foot bronze rendering of a classic nineteenth century newsboy hawking his papers, holding the latest edition aloft with one hand and a bundle more under his arm.

Old-fashioned newsboys are, of course, old news, and newspapers themselves are now endangered. We get our news on our various devices these days, as fast as it happens, until almost nothing registers substantively. I'm as bad as anyone is; I expect to know everything instantly.

I'm a former newspaper boy myself. We were the successors to the newsboys. I remember the thud of a bundle of the *Detroit Free Press* in our suburban driveway at 4:30 in the morning, sleepily rolling the papers with rubber bands, and then delivering them door-to-door. I was relentlessly reminded—by the driver, by my parents, by every Tigers fan who couldn't stay up to get the final score the night before—that the papers must be delivered at the crack of dawn to everyone with a subscription. No excuses. The toughest mornings of all were when I had to follow up my paper route with serving morning Mass as an altar boy. Yet that was another way of delivering the news—the good news—wasn't it? I didn't recognize it at the time. I was just trying to stay awake.

The newsboy statue, however old school, reinforces the fact that we are information-craving, information-devouring, information-hoarding, and information-sharing life-forms. What we share and don't share matters a lot. But without the honest and free flow of information, ideas, and beliefs, we could no longer be who we are. And we certainly couldn't share the beliefs that are most important to us.

> *Lord, let my words today be for good. Help me remain*
> *truthful and true to Your Word.*
> —Edward Grinnan

Digging Deeper: Proverbs 15:23, 25:11;
Matthew 28:19–20; 1 Peter 3:15

You will make known to me the path of life; in Your presence is fullness of joy; in Your right hand there are pleasures forever. —Psalm 16:11 (NASB)

*U*phill both ways…

Remember your grandfather's sob story? Walking to school through the snow? I think every grandfather in America must have attended the same place—certainly they all walked the same route.

As a youngster, I highly suspected my old Grand-pop was stretching the truth, at least about the snow, since he was from Tempe, Arizona. Now, with a few (okay, more than a few) gray hairs of my own, I'm rethinking. You see, my wife and I spend a lot of time cycling, and on this morning's ride, I began to wonder if there might have been more than a little truth to Grandpa's tale. It certainly felt uphill—both ways. Cycling is like that. Ten minutes of climbing, thirty seconds of zooming down, and then straight back to the grind.

It hit me, about halfway up what felt like my eight-hundredth hill: Isn't this exactly like life? I zip through the peaceful stretches without a thought—they're often short-lived—then, legs aching, I'm climbing again, feeling sure I have an invisible plow chained behind my bike.

But there's a funny thing about hills—they get easier the more we ride them. As our tires reel in miles, our faith, like our legs, gets stronger. Because it's on those impossible life-climbs, the ones where we can't see the top, that our miraculous God shows Himself strong. Cheering, coaching, He loves us to the top. And if we take the time to pause and look back, we usually see we weren't the ones doing the pedaling at all.

Life's path gets dark and steep, certainly. But every crank of the pedal builds faith. And faith is measured in one of those beautiful God-equations—the bigger it gets, the lighter it is to carry.

Thank You, Lord, for the wind at my back. I am weak,
but You are strong!
—Buck Storm

Digging Deeper: Deuteronomy 31:6; Psalm 91:14–16

Friday, February 7

FRIENDSHIP OF WOMEN: Disappointment

Bread of deceit is sweet to a man; but afterwards his mouth shall be filled with gravel. —Proverbs 20:17 (KJV)

I purchased a lovely paper punch sampler for my collection from a respected antiques dealer. "It's from the Victorian era," she told me. "Don't you just love the colors they chose for the needlework?"

Love it, I did. It was absolutely precious. I adored the green and russet palette, but it had the look of a print that had been reproduced only a few years ago.

"Are you sure this is truly old?" I pressed.

The dealer affirmed that it was, saying that she had taken the frame job apart and noticed that the perforated paper of the sampler had become brittle with age. "I'd leave it as is," she said as her eyes dropped. "I wouldn't try to reframe it or anything. It's really fragile."

Once I had it home, though, the color of the mat didn't go with my decor. So I visited my favorite framing shop. Marty, the proprietor, was uncertain about the sampler as well. Once she pried the nails out of the frame and removed the wooden backing, our suspicions were confirmed. The promised "Victorian" paper punch sampler was instead a pristine ten-dollar print, secured to the mat with a shiny strip of Scotch tape.

I'd blown nearly a hundred dollars on a dud. Was I disappointed? Sure. I hated to waste the money. But my biggest disappointment was that the dealer was a treasured friend.

I picked up the phone with plans to rant to a mutual friend, but something stopped me—the words of Carole, a dear confidante, now in heaven. In her typical wisdom, she had once told me, "Whenever you have a friendship foible, Roberta, don't lash out in anger. Instead, let it be your teacher."

> *Help me, Lord, always to speak truthfully and*
> *to deal honestly in every situation.*
> —Roberta Messner

Digging Deeper: Proverbs 12:17; Zechariah 8:16; Ephesians 4:15

By faith Abraham, when called to go to a place he would later receive as his inheritance, obeyed and went, even though he did not know where he was going. —Hebrews 11:8 (NIV)

After several years of living in an apartment complex in Florida, my mother-in-law, Neredia, received a phone call letting her know of an opening in a fifty-five and older community nearby. She had expressed great interest in the community and was thankful that God had answered her prayer. The new community was only five minutes from where she currently lived, and the rent would be much less; however, when my wife and I were helping her clean and pack for the move, she appeared nervous. Sensing her uneasiness, I asked her, "How are you feeling?" She responded, "I don't want to move." She went on to explain that she was having second thoughts about leaving her community and friends. Yes, she knew that this was a good move for her, but the fear of the unknown was making her doubt her decision.

Several months later, I visited my mother-in-law for the first time in her new home and was delighted to see how happy she was with her new neighbors and apartment. Neredia's new place is much larger than the last and she now has a small porch where she tends to her plants and parakeets. She's thankful to God for her new apartment and friends, and doesn't have any regrets about the move. She was nervous about the move before she made it, but once she did, she realized it was a positive change for her. Often, we see the purpose of life's transitions *after* we have gone through them, not in the midst of them. This being said, we must not let our fears hold us back.

Lord, give us the courage to trust Your guiding hand.
—Pablo Diaz

Digging Deeper: Proverbs 16:9; 2 Corinthians 5:1

Sunday, February 9

"They are like a man building a house, who dug down deep and laid the foundation on rock. When a flood came, the torrent struck that house but could not shake it, because it was well built." —Luke 6:48 (NIV)

A week ago, I showed an acquaintance a kindness, and she robbed me: physically, stealing my wallet, and emotionally, shaking my equilibrium. I confronted her, and she lied to me. "That's not how I was brought up...I would never..." But she had, and her betrayal made me distrustful, of my community and me. *Could I, or should I, have been more watchful, more guarded, more careful?*

Heeding concerns from friends, I grew more wary. (Hadn't I already been reasonably cautious?) But anticipating malfeasance in every casual encounter takes its own wearisome toll.

This morning I walked slowly toward my church's entrance to attend the service, desperately needing the refuge represented by its red door. A friend even inquired, "You okay? Need a hand?"

The red-door church relies on a big, blue traditional hymnbook. So what was this supplemental insert in the bulletin? Oh my—I smiled to recognize the familiar words and music to one of my father's favorite gospel songs. Its title: "My Hope Is Built." I hadn't heard it in years. The tune is simple and satisfying. The lyrics were written by Edward Mote, a pastor and a respected builder of cabinets. More than a century later, his Spirit-inspired song still builds hope. Midway through the service, we sang a rousing rendition, repeating its refrain: "On Christ, the solid Rock, I stand, / All other ground is sinking sand."

I later walked out of church with a straighter stance and surer gait, my whole being buttressed by one key line: "When all around my soul gives way/He then is all my hope and stay."

Lord Jesus, on You I build my hope. This week, help me claim the reality of Your solid foundation.
—Evelyn Bence

Digging Deeper: Psalm 18:1–3; Matthew 7:24–28

From the Lord comes deliverance. May your blessing be on your people.
—Psalm 3:8 (NIV)

As my father approached his ninetieth birthday a few years ago, I recalled how much he loved to receive cards. But I realized that as a widower, the last surviving sibling, a person with few friends alive, and the father of just one child, he wasn't likely to receive many cards at all.

Social media to the rescue! I sent a quick message to my contacts, asking them to send my dad a card—even if they had never met him—with a simple note wishing him a happy birthday. Within a few days, more than a hundred people asked for his address.

I was thrilled, and I knew my dad would love the extra mail and attention. What I didn't realize is how this would be a "God moment" for so many folks. One friend told me that buying a card for Dad was more difficult than she imagined, because she had not purchased a card for a father since her own dad had passed nearly twenty years earlier. In this challenge, she was able to find comfort, for she realized that despite her loss, she was able to provide a blessing to someone else. She sent my father a beautiful card, telling him how she and I met as work colleagues and wishing him many more birthdays.

Another friend, who lost his own father just six months earlier, sent a card with a note telling my dad, a Korean War army air corps vet, about his own father, who served with the navy during World War II. Sending a card to my father was difficult for him to do, too, but he did it, simply because he wanted to bless someone else.

> *Father God, thank You for friends who know You and*
> *who realize that sometimes we have to tread through difficulties*
> *in order to be a blessing to someone else.*
> —Gayle T. Williams

Digging Deeper: Psalm 27:13; Romans 15:14

Tuesday, February 11

Have we not all one Father? —Malachi 2:10 (NKJV)

Returning to Zimbabwe with our daughter Keri and her children, Abby and Charles, we could hardly wait to see our new school at Village Hope farm, a daring adventure being built grade by grade.

The farm was first a home for AIDS orphans, but under the leadership of our Zimbabwean partners, Paddington and Alice, it served hundreds of people in this rural area. Innovative projects offered food, farming techniques, animals, empowerment programs, and more.

Now, a school that went from preschool to second grade!

"Charles," I asked our grandson, "would you like to visit the school?" His yes was a bit uncertain.

When we arrived at Village Hope, Paddington whisked Charles away and returned him dressed in a required, scratchy wool, school uniform. *Oh my goodness,* I thought. *I'm not sure how this will play out with our somewhat picky first-grader.* Paddington led Charles to the school where a group of children stood, singing their welcome with gusto.

Charles took his seat. "We'll pick you up in an hour," Keri called. Later, on cue, we returned to school and peeped in. Charles was totally engaged with the children. He refused to leave. As the day passed, the children marched to the thatched pavilion for tea and bread. Charles fit naturally with these children who live in mud huts and who count on the school for their meals. He made no complaints as he ate his bread, crust and all. There were no computers, the lessons were written on the blackboard, and the children might be seen by others as the "least of these" (Matthew 25:40), but our Charles was happy and content.

The next morning, Charles was dressed in his uniform by 6:00 AM, waiting to catch a ride to school with Paddington. It was a beautiful sight.

> *Father, how beautiful it is that Your children love*
> *without condition. Let us follow.*
> —Pam Kidd

Digging Deeper: Proverbs 22:2; 1 John 3:18

*When I am afraid, I put my trust in you. In God, whose word I praise—
in God I trust and am not afraid.* —Psalm 56:3–4 (NIV)

I wake up scared some nights with a painful gnawing in my stomach.
Then I remember. I'm facing a seemingly impossible writing deadline that feels too big and too complicated. Instead of making progress,
I'm getting increasingly tangled in the process. In the darkness, my
fears start growing beyond the writing project. What if my brain can't
handle hard challenges? What if I don't have what it takes? What if I
can't meet this deadline?"

I wrote these words in my journal several months ago. Rereading them
now, I'm surprised by the depth of my doubts. The writing project—a
book manuscript—was one of the hardest things I've ever tackled but
it is finished. Now, I want to remember how I got from *doubts* to *done*.

I told a friend about this and she reminded me of Joshua and the
stone memorial. God told Joshua to lead the Israelites across the Jordan
River into the land He wanted to give them. As they camped on the
shore of the rushing, flood-stage waters, they must have tried to fall
asleep, fearing the seemingly impossible task ahead of them. Were they
capable? Did they trust God to provide what they needed? The next
morning as they stepped into the water, the river stopped flowing and
they crossed over on dry ground. God then told them to take stones
from the river and build a memorial to remind them that He provides
what is needed when it is needed.

Joshua's story reminds me that God didn't give me what I needed in
the middle of the night but in the morning when I sat down to write.
Page by page, I met my deadline. Now, the finished book will be my
stone memorial, a reminder of God's power and faithfulness.

Lord, help us trust Your faithfulness, even in the dark.
—Carol Kuykendall

Digging Deeper: Joshua 3:4; 2 Corinthians 12:9; Philippians 1:6

Thursday, February 13

*Let marriage be held in honor among all.... —*Hebrews 13:4 (ESV)

I got a ninety-one on my Latin exam!" my husband crowed. I smiled, quietly grateful that Andrew was pleased with his work. He has been auditing two classes at City College this year, and it's done us both good. The classes get him out of the house three days a week (yay!), interacting with other people (yay!), and engaging his brain (yay!). Activation—interacting with something other than one's own dark thoughts—is a pivotal strategy in breaking the dark grip of depression.

It took nearly a decade of therapy and medication for Andrew to begin to step out into the world again. His illness isolated him, made him unable to work, and nearly destroyed our marriage. The *worse* in "for better or worse" was evident every day. In the midst of that much pain—both Andrew's and mine—it became hard to honor the *we* more than the *me*. It was hard to remember more than that we each were hurting.

Amo, amas, amat: I love, you love, he/she loves. It's been a long slog. Even now, it's possible Andrew's darkness could return. We walk this road of marriage putting one foot in front of the other, one prayer after the next, with no assurance that things will work out. I know I may need to do the bulk of the walking and praying. That's okay. My Latin lesson for today is this:

Amo: I love you, Andrew, in whatever imperfect way I can.

Amas: You, Andrew, love me in every imperfect way you are able.

Amat: The good Lord loves us both perfectly, eternally, unselfishly.

There's nothing about the distribution of the work of love that's equal or fair. It's all mostly God's.

> *Father, when I feel unloved or unappreciated, remind me that*
> *when I give to others I am always also giving back to You.*
> —Julia Attaway

Digging Deeper: Song of Songs 8:6–7; Matthew 19:6; John 13:34

"Set your affairs in order...."—Isaiah 38:1 (TLB)

Dad got a pacemaker at age ninety-eight—making him his heart surgeon's oldest patient ever to receive one. Despite Dad's spirit and mental alertness, it was obvious that Dad and his wife Bev could not continue to live alone in their big house in northern Illinois. Since my brother lives in Kentucky and my sister and I live in Florida, I wrote down six options for them that day in the hospital:

1. Move to an assisted-living facility.

2. Stay in your home alone and depend on your nieces and nephews to buy your groceries and take you to doctors' appointments.

3. Stay in your home with additional hired help, and agree to use the county transportation system for the elderly.

4. Move to Kentucky or Florida, and let us (your children) care for you in our homes.

5. Hire someone to be in your home three to five hours a day to do anything you need.

6. Let us (your children and in-laws) rotate staying for one or two months at a time to care for you in your home.

We (Dad's children and our spouses) left the room and let Dad and Bev discuss it. A half hour later, the verdict was in. They chose number six, much to our delight. I said, "Let's make a pact that one of us will be with you 24–7 in your own home for as long you need." I put my hand out over Dad's lap in his hospital bed, and we all joined together by stacking our hands. We called it "The Pact." From that day on, we vowed to care for the two most important people in our lives.

Sadly, Dad died, peacefully, just two months after we made The Pact, but living that pact brought more joy than anything I've ever done.

Heavenly Father, You made a pact when You created me.
Thank You for helping me see how to pay Your gift forward.
—Patricia Lorenz

Digging Deeper: Philippians 4:10–14; James 2:14–17

"Worthy are You, our Lord and our God, to receive glory and honor and power; for You created all things, and because of Your will they existed, and were created."—Revelation 4:11 (NASB)

About twenty years ago, a friend who is a few years older than I said that eventually my eyesight would fail and I'd need glasses to read. *Not me!* I thought. I'd always had better than twenty-twenty vision, and I took for granted that I always would.

Time has a way of changing things, though. In my forties, I noticed words on the page getting blurrier. A lady at church joked that my arms needed to grow longer. "It happens to us all!" she assured me.

I bought a pair of reading glasses at the drugstore and took it all in stride, thinking about how lucky I am to live in a time when such an easy, painless fix exists. But when I became annoyed with taking the glasses on and off to see up close and then far away, someone suggested I try monovision: wearing one contact lens so that one eye handles close-up vision while the other handles distance. No way! Could something like that really work?

The answer is yes! It's amazing, really. When the ophthalmologist's assistant put the lens in my left eye and had me read small text, I couldn't help but exclaim the words of Psalm 139:14: "I praise you because I am fearfully and wonderfully made" (NIV). The very idea that my Creator had wired my brain with the complexity to perform such a feat—and perform it instantaneously—filled me with awe and appreciation.

What a blessing to see clearly the wondrous works of God, both up close and far away!

> *Thank You, God and Father, for taking the dust of the earth*
> *and making such marvels of engineering.*
> —Ginger Rue

Digging Deeper: Nehemiah 9:6; Psalm 19:1; Romans 1:20

The righteous live with integrity; happy are their children who come after them. —Proverbs 20:7 (CEB)

Mom wasn't a great pianist nor was she much of a singer, but she knew how much I loved music. When I was a youngster she would sit me next to her on the piano bench, open the score to Rodgers and Hammerstein's *The Sound of Music*, and play our favorites. I can still hear her reedy voice proclaim "Climb Every Mountain," "Do-Re-Mi," and "My Favorite Things."

I marvel now at how she ever found the time. I was the third of four children, each of us some two years apart, and in those early years Dad was often away for work. And yet somehow the food appeared on the table, our clothes got washed, there were books for bedtime stories, and we managed to get to church on Sunday mornings. Tempers were surely frayed at times and budgets had to be strictly adhered to, but I never once wondered if I was loved. It never occurred to me to ask the question.

Having brought up two children with a wife who is a master at planning and balancing the constant demands of work and home, I know only too well the challenging logistics that come with raising a family. What I hope I provided in the midst of it all were moments when I was sharing with our boys their favorite things—not to mention sitting with them on the piano bench, playing their favorite songs. To show someone how much you love them by doing what they love to do is an extraordinary gift. You teach them just how they can climb every mountain.

Lord, never let me miss an opportunity to show my love.
—Rick Hamlin

Digging Deeper: Song of Songs 8:3;
Romans 12:9–10; 1 Peter 4:8

Monday, February 17

Pray especially for rulers and their governments to rule well....
—1 Timothy 2:2 (MSG)

I have a confession.

For most of my life, I haven't prayed for men and women serving in government positions as often as I should have. Maybe because I didn't feel a strong emotional connection to them.

History classes bored me as a kid. I recall staring disinterestedly at our presidents' faces in textbooks. After I became an adult and started to vote, I still felt disconnected from our elected officials.

But everything changed one rainy evening in 2018.

Settling down on the couch with the February issue of *Guideposts*, I spotted Abraham Lincoln's face—a black-and-white photograph that covered the entire page. His solemn, deep-set eyes peered right at me, as though I'd never seen the infamous expression. I looked closer.

Glittering tears gathered near his lower lids, and his mouth formed a sad, tired line. The story written about him, "A Sorrow So Deep," by Elizabeth Sherrill, was part of a "Living with Depression" series.

Mr. Lincoln's face held the terror and sadness of clinical depression. *That's what's he's feeling,* I thought. *I've been there. Twice. I didn't think I'd survive. Mr. President, despite the terrifying shadow nipping at your heels, you led our country with great strength and courage!*

I read each word carefully. Elizabeth Sherrill struggled with depression too. "When depression incapacitated me," she said, "reading about Lincoln's life was a way back to the functioning world."

When I connected the dots between my heart and soul, the Lord filled me with compassion. Our country's presidents have struggles, and they experience fear—sometimes quite similar to my own.

Father, forgive me. It's a high calling to pray for those in office,
particularly the President of the United States.
—Julie Garmon

Digging Deeper: Proverbs 21:1; 1 Peter 2:17

A friend owes loyalty.... —Job 6:14 (JPS)

After my husband, Keith, died, our friend Dawn, who had visited every day when Keith was housebound, kept coming over. She had been Keith's friend more than mine—we had both met her at our exercise class, but when the cost of the class went up, only one of us could continue. Keith had balance problems, and I did not, so we chose to have him be the one to keep attending.

Dawn had known Keith and liked him; he had told me she warned the other women in the class that he was one of the good guys and not to tease him. She often expressed regret to me that she hadn't had more opportunity to know me before he died, to see us as a couple, to see how we "were with each other."

While Dawn's visits continued, I was often tempted to refuse any invitations and just sink into my melancholy. She was quietly firm about my doing things with her: watching TV, going to the movies, sitting with her in doctors' offices, celebrating birthdays, talking about current events. She always made it seem as if she needed me to do these things with her. It didn't fill all the empty spaces in my life that the absence of Keith's companionship had left, but it seemed to fill just enough of them to give me some equanimity and comfort. It took me more than a year to figure out how much more I needed her company than she—with a consulting job, several volunteer stints, and two daughters—must have needed mine.

> *When I might have withdrawn from life, Lord of all that's good,*
> *You offered a beautiful way to keep me engaged with the world.*
> —Rhoda Blecker

Digging Deeper: Proverbs 8:1; Isaiah 60:20

Wednesday, February 19

I have fought the good fight, I have finished the race, I have kept the faith. —2 Timothy 4:7 (ESV)

It was piano recital night. Eleven-year-old Gabriel and nine-year-old Isaiah sat, spiffed and shined, on folding chairs. They'd gelled their hair. Matched shoes to belts. Ironed shirts and braved the mountain of men's socks for matchers. They'd also practiced for weeks.

"Isaiah will now play 'Tarantella,'" announced Mr. Benevides.

My son headed for the piano, music tucked under his arm. I sat with my husband, Lonny, a band of brothers, and two pairs of grandparents. When Isaiah's hands hovered above the keys, my heart hammered.

Let him do well, Lord, I prayed. My boys were passionate about playing and adored their teacher—a gentleman whose own love of music fueled their fire. But recitals weren't their thing. They were nervous. They didn't care for neckties. An audience made their tummies twist. They'd rather play for pleasure on our ancient piano that their teacher joked belonged in a saloon. But there we were.

Isaiah began to play. I'd heard the piece a half-million times, and it was easy to know when he missed a note. He squirmed and kept playing. *Plink.* He opted to finish fast, and he hit more wrong keys. Then the worst happened. He stopped still. His shoulders curled. His head hung.

There was silence. A fight-or-flight moment. My son breathed deeply and looked back to where his teacher sat. Isaiah nodded and Mr. Benevides came forward, whispered, and pointed to a place on the page. Isaiah began again. The notes came steady and smooth and his music carried the rhythm of strength—the melody of picking up and pressing on through something tough. Isaiah played a song of perseverance when things toppled and didn't happen the way he'd hoped.

The Lord had heard my prayer. My son had done well.

Father, You are the giver of strength and courage and bravery.
—Shawnelle Eliasen

Digging Deeper: Galatians 6:9; Philippians 3:14

"Even to your old age and gray hairs I am he, I am he who will sustain you. I have made you and I will carry you; I will sustain you and I will rescue you."—Isaiah 46:4 (NIV)

On a recent trip home during my daughter's school break, I was reminded that moments of beauty are sometimes found in things that seem unbeautiful.

We had the blessing of celebrating the fourth birthday of my son, Jacques, with a small family gathering. It was a great birthday; in fact, it was the first birthday Jacques spent with family since military life keeps us away from home. We gathered at Aunt Nanny's home, which allowed us to celebrate with my grandfather PawPaw, who lives with Nanny and her husband.

Jacques's birthday was a great opportunity for us all to spend time together with PawPaw. I was jarred to see my grandfather aging quickly and needing constant care due to failing health. Knowing that caregiving for a parent can be emotionally and physically challenging, I helped with my PawPaw's bedtime routine. I cried the entire time; it was a beautiful experience to be blessed with the opportunity to care for a man who cared for our family with such love. I was humbled by the love that my uncle, Nanny, and Mom bestowed on PawPaw with simple, unbeautiful tasks such as showering, dressing, and bathroom visits.

Seeing such love in action reminded me, poignantly, how beauty is often birthed from service to others. I will strive to serve and care for my parents in the same way my family cares for PawPaw. Having such a selfless example of love to follow is indeed a blessing.

Father of my heart, create in me a dedication to service and a heart of love outwardly witnessed through the care and love that I show to others. May I be Your faithful servant here on earth.
—Jolynda Strandberg

Digging Deeper: Genesis 49:26; Ruth 4:15; Psalm 71:9

Friday, February 21

A merry heart doeth good like a medicine.... —Proverbs 17:22 (KJV)

B rock, Wanda—line two," my assistant, Jeannine, said. "She sounds upset."

Wanda is one of my favorite clients. Now in her nineties, she was the first licensed female stockbroker in Tennessee. She is also a phenomenal cook who often invites me over for made-from-scratch lunches.

"Wanda, what's wrong?"

She seems stressed as she says my name. She clears her throat, "Oh, honey, bad, bad news. The foundation of my house is cracking. It's going to cost a fortune to get it fixed. Can you come over Friday and help me figure out how to raise the funds?"

Anticipating our meeting, I found myself sending out quick prayers: *Help me solve Wanda's problem in the easiest way possible. Give Wanda peace from worry.*

And then it was Friday. Our appointment was at 11:30 AM. When I drove up to her house, my heart sank. There was a yellow ribbon stretched across her drive with a sign attached. "Danger," it said.

"Oh, this is worse than I thought," I said out loud. "Her entire house might be sinking into the ground. Oh Father, take care of poor Wanda."

I knocked tentatively and noticed a note on the knob. "Come on in."

I stepped into the living room. "Wanda?" I called.

I heard laughter, followed by Wanda, carrying a big birthday cake with the candles lit—a couple of colleagues from my office in tow.

"Gotcha!" she said merrily.

She had made up the foundation story and even stretched the warning tape across her drive, all as part of a clever birthday surprise.

A delicious lunch waited. But it's the laughter I'll remember most.

Later, sending off a quick prayer of thanks, I laughed some more, realizing that God had surely been in on the joke, and He was laughing too.

> *Father, thank You for friends, for laughter, for love.*
> —Brock Kidd

Digging Deeper: Proverbs 15:15; Ecclesiastes 9:7

"In Your hand is power and might; in Your hand it is to make great and to give strength to all." —1 Chronicles 29:12 (NKJV)

My husband, Randy, calls at 9:05 AM. "A lineman has been burned on the 500kV transmission line. I don't know how badly. He needs prayers. They're flying him to the burn center in Portland."

Calls like this are a kick in the gut, another opportunity for fear to whisper: *This could be Randy.* My husband is a lineman with the power company. I pray fervently for his safety every day. My hands shake as I type a message to my battalion of prayer warriors.

The phone rings before I hit send. "Two men were involved," Randy says. "Up the prayers." Electrical burns are devastating. Extremities are most vulnerable. They can even affect one's personality permanently.

Lord, be merciful. Envelop them in your love. Give them hope and healing. It's not just the linemen I pray for; it's their wives and children. It takes a special kind of person to be a line worker. Risking their lives is their everyday job. It isn't easy being a lineman's wife either. Coping with the danger affects the whole family. All we can do for our loved ones is pray they make it home each day. Often, that doesn't feel like enough.

Two somber days pass. Randy calls again in midmorning. This time he's ecstatic. "Your prayers worked! The lineman has been released. He has feeling in both hands and can use his legs. The burn center can't explain it. He took a direct hit and fell a long way, but his injuries are minor. The second man wasn't hurt at all. They said Someone was looking out for them."

I hang up and text my prayer warriors, praising God. That same Someone is looking out for my Randy too.

Please, Lord, bless the line workers who risk their lives every day. Keep
their hands steady and bring them home safely. Comfort their families;
You are protecting their loved ones on the line.
—Erika Bentsen

Digging Deeper: Deuteronomy 31:6; Psalm 86:5; Philippians 4:7

Sunday, February 23

Christ has made peace between Jews and Gentiles, and he has united us by breaking down the wall of hatred that separated us. —Ephesians 2:14 (CEV)

The weathered sign read: *Church of the Holy Rude.* Cue laughter. Who could blame us? Four friends stuffed into two tiny cruise cabins for fourteen days were bound to get a bit punchy along the way. Besides, having been involved in the relational ups and downs of the local church for over forty years, I wasn't just amused. I was impressed with a church body that was transparent about its humanity!

To our disappointment, my friends and I soon discovered that the word "rude" (or "rood") was actually the Old English equivalent of the word "cross." However, after stepping inside the stone walls of the fifteenth-century church, we learned our first impression wasn't that far from the truth. Adjacent to Scotland's famous Stirling Castle, the Holy Rude is known for two things: for being the site of James VI's coronation, and for the wall built to divide a feuding church into two separate congregations.

Apparently, back in 1656, Rev. James Guthrie was known for being more of a rabble-rouser than a peacemaker. When he and a colleague disagreed about how the worship service should be conducted, they "solved" their problem by erecting a wall between the nave and the choir area. It remained standing for almost three hundred years.

The more I pondered the Holy Rude's legacy of division, the more relevant it seemed. Today, the walls that divide so many of us as God's children aren't built of wood or stone, but of political or theological disagreements, racial and denominational differences, and the mentality of wanting everything our way.

Back in the early days of the Church, Jesus accomplished what was once thought impossible. He broke down the walls between the Jews and Gentiles. What walls does He want us to help dismantle today?

Dear Lord, humble my heart. Show me how to foster unity both inside and outside Your Church.
—Vicki Kuyper

Digging Deeper: 1 Corinthians 1:10; Colossians 3:12–14

Think about things that are pure and lovely, and dwell on the fine, good things in others. Think about all you can praise God for and be glad about. —Philippians 4:8 (TLB)

My husband Don and I bought a new car. We'd intended to wait another year before trading, but we were intrigued by the safety features on the shiny model in the dealer's showroom. As older drivers who log lots of miles, we decided that a safer car was a good investment. And it was, mostly. The automatic braking system kept Don from backing into a pickup that seemed to appear out of nowhere. The wide-angle backup camera was a huge help when I navigated busy parking lots. We appreciated the warning light that signaled when a vehicle was in our car's blind spot.

There was one problem, though, and I considered it huge. The second time I drove the car, a piece on the front bumper broke. The dealer insisted the damage was my fault and refused to replace the bumper. Then a clip holding the mud flap to the fender fell off. Same story. Don replaced the clip and superglued the bumper so that the damage was hardly visible, but that didn't keep me from brooding about my "plastic car" every time I started the ignition.

I shared lots of angry words about it too. Finally, Don had heard enough. "We bought this car for the safety features, and they are as good as promised. The car is comfortable and it drives like a dream. Could you please concentrate on the positives instead of broken bits of plastic?"

Good advice about my car—and about how to live my life.

Dear Jesus, help me concentrate on the abundant good that is in everyone I meet and to overlook the imperfections and tiny flaws.
—Penney Schwab

Digging Deeper: Proverbs 15:4; Romans 14:10–13; James 3:2

Tuesday, February 25

She sets about her work vigorously; her arms are strong for her tasks.
—Proverbs 31:17 (NIV)

The lady selling the giant used shelf unit stared in disbelief at my little cart. "Is this what you're going to use to transport the shelf?" she chuckled.

I walked through the door smiling. "It's stronger than it looks."

My foldable cart came with an infant car seat ten years ago, which I'd click on top and stroll my son through the city. When he outgrew the car seat, I continued to use the rolling basket for everything else. "Trust me," I continued, "this amazing thing has carried me through years of laundry, shopping hauls, and transporting all kinds of stuff."

She led me to the shelf, towering sixty-plus inches over my head, with the same measurement in width. She did not look convinced. "You'll see," I said.

Together we lifted the shelf and fit it between the stroller handles. It looked like a tiny ant carrying a giant leaf. She laughed in amazement as I carefully guided it through the door, into the elevator, and out the front entrance. Slowly and carefully, I rolled it on the bumpy sidewalks, uphill and downhill as I headed home. I was quite the spectacle, like a circus act parading through the city streets.

"Whoa! You are Superwoman!" one lady shouted.

"How is that even possible?" a man asked.

Comment after comment, I smiled with gratitude for my little-cart-that-could, with a strong sense of connection to its unexpected might. As a single mother with no family where I live to depend on, I've had to become everything this cart has been—little but tough, unphased by the seemingly impossible, and unbending under the heaviest of burdens.

Life at times may look impossible. But I've come to know with experience, certainly, nothing is impossible with God.

Father, thank You for the reward of strength through a journey of struggle.
—Karen Valentin

Digging Deeper: Luke 1:37; Philippians 4:13

PRAYING IN PUBLIC: A Reminder of Lent

"Beware of practicing your piety before others in order to be seen by them;..."—Matthew 6:1 (NRSV)

I always struggle on this day to know what Jesus wants from me," That Ash Wednesday, the pastor seemed more somber than usual as he spoke these words. He went on to say that he keenly felt the conflict between Jesus's admonition to pray privately and the fact that he wore ashes shaped in a cross on his broad forehead all day. Was he "showing off" his piety, or was he modeling humility?

I'd wondered the same thing. When it comes to public displays of prayer, I've always felt a little squeamish, although, I must admit, not only because of Jesus's teaching that we should pray privately. I'm a private person, not given to attracting attention. I picked this up from my mother, who had always warned my sister and me to avoid the limelight. But as I listened to the pastor I also remembered that my mom would never let us wash our faces until the end of the day. This was even more unusual coming from a woman who made a high priority of cleanliness.

"It's the first day of Lent," she'd say, "It's a day for everyone who sees you to know you are with Jesus."

Late that Ash Wednesday night, I was finishing some grocery shopping, not thinking at all about the black cross still on my forehead. The young woman working the cash register looked at me once, then looked again. "Oh, wow!" she exclaimed, "It's Ash Wednesday. Thanks for reminding me."

Thanks, Lord, for reminding me. And, thanks, Mom.

Jesus, please give me the courage to show others that
I am with You, so that I might help them to be with You too.
—Marci Alborghetti

Digging Deeper: Psalms 2, 9:1, 11; Matthew 6:5–8

"He himself bore our sins" in his body on the cross, so that we might die to sins and live for righteousness; "by his wounds you have been healed."
—1 Peter 2:24 (NIV)

*S*crunch, *scrunch, scrunch.* Packed snow gave beneath my boots as I made my way down a wooded path near our cabin. I placed my feet carefully. One wrong step, and I'd post-hole down into a winter's worth of hip-deep snow. Wan light filtered through the trees, matching my mood. How many days had it been since I'd felt bright sunshine on my face? Too many, I thought, glancing up. A thick blanket of leaden clouds covered the February sky.

I stopped in front of a slender spruce, bent nearly double beneath a heavy load of snow that was frozen fast to its branches. I passed this tree every day on my walk, and I'd come to feel a deep sense of sympathy for it. Lately, a series of mistakes had me feeling the same way: stooped over by the weight of my own stubborn flaws. The harder I tried to struggle free from them—to be the person I thought God wanted me to be, the person *I* wanted to be—the tighter they seemed to cling.

"Just a little longer now," I said aloud to the tree. Despite all the snow, spring really was just around the corner.

I thought then about Easter, just under forty days away from this wintry afternoon. Soon the little tree's icy burden would melt. Not because it had earned it or proved itself worthy. But because spring's warmth is a gift God gives the world, as He also gave us His only Son. A perfect sacrifice made for a world of flawed, mistake-prone, imperfect people—like me.

I am humbled, Lord, and so very grateful for the reminder that even though I am—and will always be—deeply flawed, through the sacrifice of Your perfect Son, my burdens are lifted.
—Erin Janoso

Digging Deeper: Psalm 68:19; 1 John 4:10

*Jesus replied, "Truly I tell you, if you have faith and do not doubt...
you can say to this mountain, 'Go, throw yourself into the sea,'
and it will be done."* —Matthew 21:21 (NIV)

It is painful to watch a friend make the same mistake over and over again. My friend across the street, Jim, built a retaining wall ten years ago, designed to protect his backyard from flooding every spring when the creek expands. It seemed like a good idea at the time until that first spring when the wall broke in half. Jim fixed it. The next spring, the wall leaked in about eighteen places. Jim patched it. This went on for a decade—until last year.

Last winter, I watched as Jim worked again at shoring up his retaining wall. He added cement and even painted it, as if it was becoming something even more than a dubiously useful flood deterrent. When the snow melted, the rains came, and the creek began to rise and flood its banks, Jim's lovely ever-new wall did the trick. It actually worked.

I kept believing that Jim was making a mistake all those times he was outside fixing that stubborn wall. "Forget the wall. It doesn't work," I used to say to him. But I was wrong. Now I see that Jim was practicing faith.

*Guide me, Lord, to know You better, to serve You better, and to put
my faith and hope into practice in the world around me. Amen.*
—Jon M. Sweeney

Digging Deeper: Matthew 21:22; Hebrews 11:1–2

Saturday, February 29

I can do all this through him who gives me strength. —Philippians 4:13 (NIV)

The call to service, military or otherwise, is not negated by youth. Often I am struck by how young our soldiers are today; this is probably magnified by the fact that I am getting older. Nonetheless, I notice their young faces, bright eyes, and joyful spirit, which inspire feelings of awe and gratitude for their sacrifice and service to our great nation. At such a young age, they have volunteered to answer the call to defend our freedoms, a weighty decision.

Many of our young soldiers are younger than my oldest son, and military enlistment is often their first adult experience. Sometimes I catch myself referring to them as "kids." And when I do, I remind myself that those willing to sacrifice themselves for others are not children, nor should they be treated as such. It's a slip I make from time to time, and one I instantly regret.

The truth is, we were all young once and many times we feel unworthy for the tasks at hand. The path of our life's calling takes unique and unexpected twists. Indeed, the young are called to live out great purpose and give great witness with their lives.

Our young soldiers remind me that the Lord calls us all to serve Him without bounds, often in spite of youth, in spite of inexperience, and in spite of circumstance. There are times in my own life when I feel ill-equipped for the challenges I face. I must constantly remember that the Lord is my strength, and I will not falter as I keep my vision and soul directed toward Him.

*Dear Lord, when we are weak, You are strong. May I continually
open my heart and mind to Your will and Your work, even when
I feel unprepared for the challenges and path You have set before me.*
—Jolynda Strandberg

Digging Deeper: Exodus 15:13; Isaiah 40:29

HE PERFORMS WONDERS

1 _____

2 _____

3 _____

4 _____

5 _____

6 _____

7 _____

8 _____

9 _____

10 _____

11 _____

12 _____

13 _____

14 _____

February

15 _____

16 _____

17 _____

18 _____

19 _____

20 _____

21 _____

22 _____

23 _____

24 _____

25 _____

26 _____

27 _____

28 _____

29 _____

MARCH

Let us eat, and be merry.

—Luke 15:23 (KJV)

Sunday, March 1

FIRSTS: The Opera

He put a new song in my mouth.... —Psalm 40:3 (RSV)

How well I remember my first opera! A wealthy client of my father's had offered my parents his box that evening, and they'd decided that I was old enough, at age eleven, to go with them. Mother made some hurried alterations to one of her evening dresses for me, and a trip to the hairdresser transformed my pigtails into a "coiffure" that I hoped made me as elegant as that word sounded.

We went to New York's old Metropolitan Opera on Broadway and Thirty-Ninth Street. I climbed the staircase deliciously aware of a long skirt swishing at my ankles. We stepped into the box—and a fairy-tale world. Tiers of boxes rose above us. Chandeliers glittered. Below us, down the aisles, women paraded in fabulous furs and men in top hats. Our box was in the "Diamond Horseshoe," nicknamed for the glimmering jewels on display. There were tiaras, emerald necklaces, loops of pearls.

Entranced by the sparkling setting, I remember nothing of the performance except that it was very loud. Only years later did I come upon the program from 1939 and realize that I'd heard—or failed to hear—Richard Wagner's *Gotterdammerung*, sung by Lauritz Melchior and Helen Traubel, whose names today bring sighs in reverence.

I had another first-time just as thrilling when I first went to Europe. Gothic cathedrals—the vast naves, the soaring arches, the brilliant stained glass! I bought books, followed guides from crypt to tower, and learned words like *gargoyle* and *flying buttress*.

Again, long afterward, I realized that, as I'd missed the music at the opera, I'd missed the point of these great churches. Only when I became a Christian did I grasp the message of that glowing glass, those heaven-aspiring arches. Once again, dazzled by the gorgeous wrapping, I'd missed the gift itself.

> *Lord, Who makes all things new, never let me stop at mere novelty.*
> —Elizabeth Sherrill

Digging Deeper: Lamentations 3:22–24; 2 Corinthians 5:17

Jesus looked at them and said, "With man this is impossible, but with God all things are possible."—Matthew 19:26 (ESV)

I think I can go to Japanese class on my own," Elizabeth offered, tentatively. Eighteen months into recovery from anorexia, half a year after becoming weight restored, my daughter's mind was finally finding its clarity. After eons of apathy and deep depression, the first thing she wanted to do was to learn Japanese. Okay, then. Let's do it!

For nine months I accompanied her to classes, which are, by Manhattan geography, as far away as traveling to Asia. Her malnutrition-induced anxiety eliminated the possibility of traveling alone. At the start, I had to accompany her on the seventy-five-minute subway ride, stay to encourage her while she ate lunch, wait through the two-hour class, and then bring her home. The next step was to trek across town, sit with her while she had her meal, and let her go to class and return home alone.

For her to propose traveling *and eating* on her own was both scary and exhilarating. Could she really do it?

She could. She arrived home utterly exhausted, unable to do anything other than listen to music and podcasts the rest of the day. *But she did it.* She did it. Rejoicing, once again I prayed:

> *Good Jesus, grant us the courage to do the simple,*
> *impossible things that move us forward.*
> —Julia Attaway

Digging Deeper: 2 Corinthians 6:2; Philippians 4:13

Tuesday, March 3

PRAYING IN PUBLIC: At the Gym

Pray for us, so that the word of the Lord may spread rapidly and be glorified everywhere.... —2 Thessalonians 3:1 (NRSV)

One of the most challenging things I've done in my efforts to pray publicly is to pray in the tiny gym in my building. I've always prayed during and after my workouts, but when I was in the gym, I'd offer my prayers silently or wait until I was alone. I didn't feel embarrassed to pray in front of others, but I worried about making people uncomfortable. Gyms are odd spaces that combine blatantly public activity with extreme personalized zones. Many times, I've worked out next to people who don't say a word, even though we are in close physical proximity.

The first time I prayed aloud softly on the treadmill next to a man on a StairMaster, he looked straight ahead, pretending he couldn't hear me. I felt sorry for both of us: him for being uncomfortable, and me for making him feel that way. That experience made me feel shy about praying in the gym again. I decided that I would only pray if I was alone working out, or I'd wait until I was back home.

One afternoon I was by myself when I finished on the treadmill. I knelt beside the weight machine and closed my eyes. In the middle of quietly praising God for a great workout and my good health, I heard the door open. I took a breath and kept praying. After a few moments, a male voice said softly, "Say a prayer for me too."

I looked up at a muscled young man, who'd just moved into the building, and I smiled and said, "I will."

Then he started riding an exercise bike.

And I had something else for which to praise the Lord.

Powerful Father, give me the courage to pray at all times,
with all people, for all people.
—Marci Alborghetti

Digging Deeper: 1 Kings 8:22–23; Psalm 17:6

"The Lord does not see as man sees; for man looks at the outward appearance, but the Lord looks at the heart."—1 Samuel 16:7 (NKJV)

On the new indoor studio cycling bikes at my gym, a digital display tells us our RPM, MPH, wattage output, distance in miles, and calorie burn. We get both real-time data and running averages, a much more sophisticated analysis than the old bikes had. The more numbers the better, right?

Maybe not. Now when I ride I rarely take my eyes off the display. Am I maintaining my average watts? Are they high enough? Am I on track to hit my mileage goal? What are my miles per hour? Am I putting up better numbers than my last ride? When the numbers aren't good, I'm really bummed. I feel like I haven't succeeded. I haven't beaten the numbers.

A few minutes into a class the other day, Gregg, the instructor, came over to my bike, covered the display with a towel and said, "Stop looking at your numbers. Just ride. Listen to your body." I tried to peek, but Gregg gave me a stern look.

It was a strange experience. When Gregg said to add resistance or increase the RPM, I had to do it according to how my body felt and not what the numbers told me. I was sweating just as much and breathing just as hard, but I felt better, like I wasn't in a live-or-die competition with the data. Gregg let me see my numbers at the end of the class. They weren't great, but they weren't bad either. And I felt better. Invigorated, not exhausted. Successful.

"See?" Gregg said. "You have to listen to your body, not the numbers. That's the lesson."

Yes, and for more than cycling.

Lord, so often I judge myself by external factors. Yet it is the inner workings of the heart that really matter. Teach me that by being true to myself I am being true to You and who You made me to be.
—Edward Grinnan

Digging Deeper: Proverbs 16:2; Jeremiah 17:10

Thursday, March 5

Before the mountains were born, and before you created the earth and the world, you are God. You have always been, and you will always be.
—Psalm 90:2 (ICB)

Optometrist appointment? Check. Now all I had to do was drop off the taxes, get my hair cut, find a local doctor accepting new patients, meet with my Bible study group, and rendezvous with my granddaughters to celebrate their first day at a new child center. My day felt overwhelming, and it wasn't even 9 AM.

I was sailing through one green light after another on the way to my next appointment, when a red light finally forced me to a complete stop. Then, I did something I hadn't done all morning. I looked up.

Straight ahead of me was the rocky grandeur of Pikes Peak frosted with new-fallen snow—over fourteen thousand feet of it! I drank in the beauty, like a freshly brewed cup of tea. If I could overlook a mountain like this, I was undoubtedly missing the wonder of any molehills God might bring my way throughout the day.

When I'd first moved back to Colorado a year earlier, I had checked out the mountain every morning. Some days, like today, it wore white. On others, its granite landscape was a barren brown patchwork of shadow and light. Occasionally, only the highest summit would be visible above a sea of early morning fog. My children and I used to call this the "floating mountain." How soon after I moved back had I stopped noticing the majesty, which overshadowed the entire western horizon, of the summit that inspired Katharine Lee Bates to pen "America the Beautiful"?

Too soon. When busyness and routine dig a rut so deep that I forget to peer up over the top of it, leave it to God to provide a wonder so immense that it reminds me to look up—and live. There's so much more to life than what's on my to-do list.

Dear Creator, thank You for the art gallery of wonder I get to call home.
—Vicki Kuyper

Digging Deeper: Psalm 95:6–7; Isaiah 54:10

"I am the good shepherd; I know my sheep and my sheep know me."
—John 10:14 (NIV)

While touring New Zealand, my wife and I enjoyed an excursion to a sheep farm. The farmer showed us his barn while explaining the various aspects of managing the farm. He also talked about the different types of sheep and let us pet some lambs. But the highlight for me was a demonstration by Susie, a sheepdog, of her skills herding and guiding the sheep.

As we stood in light rain outside the barn, the farmer pointed to a flock of sheep—tiny specks in pastureland high in the foothills of the Southern Alps bordering his farm. The farmer said, "As I get older, I depend more and more on sheepdogs to make the five or six daily treks up the mountain to fetch the sheep." Using a small whistle, he sent Susie to the sheep. Directing her left or right with different whistle sounds, she rounded up the scattered sheep and skillfully guided them down a mountain path to the area where we were waiting.

We watched Susie line up the sheep in front of the farmer, barking and nipping them into place. The precision with which she did her job and the obedience of the sheep held our attention but was not the most astonishing thing. As the sheep stood side by side, their heads remained still with all eyes intently focused not on the dog, but on the farmer—their shepherd. The sheep never took their eyes off the farmer, even with the distractions surrounding them, a barking guide dog and two busloads of spectators.

Jesus said, "I know my sheep and my sheep know me." The sheep knew their shepherd from their guide—obedient to both, intent on one!

Lord, help us to keep an unbroken focus on You our Shepherd, even in the midst of all the distractions that get in our way.
—John Dilworth

Digging Deeper: Psalm 100:3; John 10:4, 16; Hebrews 13:20

Saturday, March 7

Good people leave memories that bless us.... —Proverbs 10:7 (ERV)

Today, March 7, is my mother's birthday, the first one she will not celebrate here on earth. I'm uncertain how to honor her. It seems callous to let the day pass by like just another ordinary day—to go grocery shopping, tackle the laundry, scrub the tub, write, and then go to sleep and start all over again. If my mother's passing has taught me anything, it's that an "ordinary" day is anything but ordinary. It's a once-in-a-lifetime gift.

So, I head out to my favorite restaurant and pick up a peach cobbler, my mother's favorite. I rent the movie she and I had planned to see at the theater before her unexpected passing. I look at the photo album of the transatlantic cruise we took a few years back, the one where we laughed and explored, ate, read, relaxed, and simply enjoyed being together. I take time to remember...

To remember is a blessing. It's our God-given ticket to time travel. As we reminisce, we celebrate the best, learn from the worst, and glean a deeper understanding of what it means to be alive right here, right now.

My mother was there for my first breath. I was there for her last. She and I remain bound together by more than biology, family ties, or even a shared history. We're bound by threads of memory woven into a unique tapestry of love. Imperfect love, certainly. But she was my first true love. She showed me what it means to sacrifice all you have for someone who cannot return the favor. Thanks to God's gift of memory, that love continues to speak into my life, long after my mother's voice has gone silent.

Dear Father, teach me how to use Your gift of memory in a positive way. Remind me to live in the present, but to visit the past just long enough to learn from it, savor its gifts, and take away what will help me live this moment to the fullest.
—Vicki Kuyper

Digging Deeper: Psalms 63:5–6, 77:11; Isaiah 49:15

The Lord himself shall descend from heaven with a shout... and the dead in Christ shall rise first: Then we which are alive and remain shall be caught up together with them... so shall we ever be with the Lord.
—1 Thessalonians 4:16–17 (KJV)

Living fourteen hours away, I get to see my four-year-old grand-daughter only several times a year. I cherish the moment I see the light in her eyes and hear her exclaim, "Grand!" Dangerously close to feeling proud, I laugh when my daughter reminds me never to mention to my granddaughter exactly when I will arrive because the excitement in the house borders on overwhelming.

Though pride might play a small part, in truth, what most warms my heart is my granddaughter's trust in my return and the thought of the fun that will ensue. She knows that sooner or later her "Grand" will be back, and with my arrival will come a continuous round of play.

I am left to wonder: What if believers always felt that type of unwavering certainty about our Lord's return, knowing that, unlike grandparents, He will never leave us.

Paul must have felt that kind of surety when he said, "I am torn between the two" (Philippians 1:23, NIV), *two* referring to the choice between remaining on earth in order to make disciples or departing to enter the eternal glory of King Jesus.

Sometimes as believers, we become battle weary, and our joyful anticipation wanes. The relentless cares of this world dull that initial happiness of looking forward to what our Savior has promised, leaving us drained of enthusiasm about the mansions the Lord has prepared for us and the unimaginable eternity that awaits every true believer.

Only when we reach back to the trust of a preschooler—that Jesus will ultimately show up again in person—can our forward-looking continue to wax lively, molding our days into the expectation of never-ending joy.

Lord, restore the joy I had when my world with You was new.
—Jacqueline F. Wheelock

Digging Deeper: John 14:3; Philippians 1:22–23

Monday, March 9

This is the confidence that we have toward him, that if we ask anything according to his will he hears us. —1 John 5:14 (ESV)

On Saturday, my young neighbor-friend fretted: "My mom changed her mind and says she can't go on the Monday field trip. She won't give me permission to go without her. What can I do?"

Hmm. "Let's pray about it now. Then later, ask your mom again and say 'please,' with respect."

My Thy-will-be-done prayer covered a lot of territory: May Mom get on the bus. If not, may she allow her daughter to go. If not, help us to be sad, not angry. Amen.

On Monday, mother and daughter enjoyed a warm, blustery field day with teachers and classmates.

On Monday I faced my own problems. Car trouble. After it was fixed, I walked to the mechanic's, but I had to keep fetching my wind-blown hat. As I went to pay, I grimaced. "I'm sure I had my glasses when I left home."

"They're not here," the mechanic and I agreed. Not on his desk or in my small purse. Not pushed back on my head or hanging from my shirt collar. And they weren't at home either.

What can I do? I set out, retracing my steps. My eyes scanned. My spirit prayed. "Lord, if my glasses fell between here and there, please help me find them." Halfway down the street, I heard an almost imperceptible click. Several steps farther along, I stopped. Had my toe kicked something? Is this where I leaned over to pick up my hat? *Look again.* Yes, I'd walked right past my glasses, intact, not even askew, at the edge of the sidewalk.

I later told my friend about my day and heard highlights of hers. "And now what can we—should we—do?" I asked. I continued, "We'll pause and say, 'Thank You, Jesus,' for answering our prayers."

Father, I ask for Your help as I look for solutions to today's challenges.
—Evelyn Bence

Digging Deeper: Matthew 7:8–11

Wait for the Lord; be strong and take heart and wait for the Lord.
—Psalm 27:14 (NIV)

I will never forget the day my son, Paul, was born. It was one of the
happiest days of my life, but also one of the scariest. Sadly, Paul was
born with medical complications that damaged his kidneys. In his first
year, his right kidney was removed and the other one has been functioning at fifty percent for most of his life. He is now in his early thir-
ties and his kidney function is declining. When Paul's doctor advised
that he begin the process of getting on the kidney transplant list, my
wife and I were disheartened by the news. We always knew this day
would come, but still we weren't prepared.

In taking the first step to be put on the list, Paul was scheduled for
a four-hour orientation and exam at Henry Ford Hospital in Detroit.
My wife, daughter, son-in-law, and I traveled to be with him for the
appointment and we all agreed to be his kidney donor if we met the
criteria. On the way to the hospital, I could sense my son was uneasy.

After several hours of meeting with doctors, a social worker and others,
we finally met with the doctor who runs the transplant department. She
was warm, witty, and caring. She said to Paul, "The results of your test
indicate that your kidney is functioning at twenty-four percent. This is
good news. You need to be at twenty percent to get on the kidney transplant list and begin the process." Paul was relieved and so were we. Our
prayer was answered; his kidney would hold up a little longer. He must
continue to see his doctor quarterly as the level of his kidney function is
being tracked. We know that it's only a matter of time; yet, we trust the
Lord to be with him and us when the time comes.

Lord, teach us to keep our trust in You for good outcomes.
—Pablo Diaz

Digging Deeper: Psalm 56:3; Philippians 4:7

Wednesday, March 11

He said to me, "My grace is enough for you, because power is made perfect in weakness...."—2 Corinthians 12:9 (CEB)

Last year I spent several days in a Houston hotel with my friend Susan. She was receiving follow-up treatment at an adjoining medical facility after extensive, difficult surgery. Susan has a special talent for helping others. Despite her illness, she tutored a boy struggling with math homework, played cards with a man attached to a feeding tube, and complimented the medical staff on their dedication. Since I don't view myself as a talented helper, my ministry was making sure we had lots of snacks.

In fact, we had too many snacks, so we decided to eat them for supper the night before we left. For dessert, we'd share a jar of luscious-looking pears. Because we couldn't get the jar open, I started walking to the bell desk for help. Ten steps down the hall, a young Catholic priest stepped out of his room and saw me carrying the pears. "Problems?" he asked. "Arthritis," I said, showing my swollen joints. Despite his frail appearance, he opened the jar with ease.

The next morning we saw the priest in the hotel restaurant. "The pears were delicious," I said, "and we are leaving today. How about you?" He managed a weak smile. "My cancer is inoperable and terminal," he said. Remembering Susan's example, I asked, "Would you allow Methodists to pray for you?" He nodded, so Susan and I put our hands on his shoulders and prayed simply: "Lord Jesus, please strengthen Your faithful servant for the journey ahead. Amen."

I don't know how his story ended. But I do know that God can use all of our weaknesses, from Susan's illness to my arthritic hands, to share a bit of friendship, a moment of kindness, or a prayer with someone in need.

> *Lord God, may I always be willing to let Your power be*
> *shown through my weakness.*
> —Penney Schwab

Digging Deeper: Isaiah 35:3–4; 1 Corinthians 2:3–5;
2 Corinthians 12:8–10

Those who hope in the Lord will renew their strength. They will soar on wings like eagles; they will run and not grow weary, they will walk and not be faint. —Isaiah 40:31 (NIV)

Nana's toy closet is full of wonder. Organized shelves offer toys from my childhood, a vintage menagerie of cars, trains, dolls, and games that seem to call out to my children.

One day, Olivia noticed a box tucked in the corner. Inside, she discovered something that made her four-year-old heart squeal with joy—costumes!

Quickly, she became a dancer, then a cowgirl, and then at long last, a fairy. Dressing up is a big deal in our house!

Olivia shimmied into the pink-and-green sequined fairy outfit, then ran over to me as I held the wings. I helped her into the shoulder straps. Olivia spun around, scrunched up her eyes, and waited—but for what?

She opened one eye slowly and then the other. Looking up at me with tears glittering on her lashes, she asked, "I can't fly?"

Oh, to believe with the heart of a child! For Olivia, the only thing holding her back from flying was that she was missing her own set of sparkly wings.

She was crushed, and, frankly, so was I. I saw then her capacity for belief, for faith, and her complete immersion in the stories she read.

Gently, I reminded her that fairies are not real, but that mommy believes that angels are real. One day in heaven, she will meet the most glorious, sparkly-winged beings she could imagine. And that yes, on that day, she'll definitely be able to fly.

> *Lord, help me remember that my hope,*
> *my eternal life, and my victory are in You.*
> —Ashley Kappel

Digging Deeper: Matthew 18:3, 10; Mark 9:23–25

Friday, March 13

*Whatever you do, whether in word or deed, do it all in the name
of the Lord Jesus, giving thanks to God the Father through him.*
—Colossians 3:17 (NIV)

"A re you all in?" I watched my daughter's basketball coach shout
from the hardwood as the team huddled around him. He swirled
a pointed finger as he turned around the circle. "I need everyone to be
all in if we're gonna win!"

"All in" has become a popular buzz phrase these days, but I first heard
it as a youth, when my dad and I would play poker. All in for Daddy
was his putting his proverbial cards on the line with betting-the-farm
confidence and giving his best. When Dad was all in, he usually succeeded whatever the task.

All in is a decision—whether out of arrogance, recklessness, ignorance,
or desperation—in which players bet all of their chips on a single hand.
It's being willing to win it all or lose it all, to experience the consequences,
not looking back, being fully committed, and giving it your best.

Still, I'm not really all in on many things. It's exhausting to try my
hardest on everything all of the time. I want a pajama day every now
and then. But it's deeper than that, really. At midlife, I've become content to hang my hat on who I used to be: former news reporter and
anchor, former radio talk show host, former executive director, and former public relations manager. I traded it all, almost two decades ago,
to be a stay-at-home mom. Now, my high school daughter graduates
soon. Surely, there's more for me to do.

I'm laying down my metaphorical cards, even though God already
knows what's in my hand. I'm ready to come off the sidelines. I want
to be a player. I want to go all in.

> *You went all in for me and I want to be all in for You,*
> *Lord, whatever the game. Use me for Your glory.*
> —Stephanie Thompson

Digging Deeper: Isaiah 6:8; Hebrews 12:1–2

He makes me to lie down in green pastures; He leads me beside the still waters. He restores my soul; He leads me in the paths of righteousness for His name's sake. —Psalm 23:2–3 (NKJV)

I'm usually a steady guy, but panic was setting in. We'd sold our house, were under contract, and the deadline loomed for us to move out. But we couldn't find a house for sale that we both loved. Realtors had warned us: "There's no inventory. It's hard to find a house." They were right.

Now, we were visiting what few open houses we could locate, and contemplating increasing the budget we'd determined with such care.

One Sunday, after I finished preaching in our church, my wife, Margi, and I were driving down an unfamiliar street. We had been told of a house coming on the market and wanted to see it first.

"There's something weird about this street," I said.

"I seem to recall that too," Margi replied. "Wasn't there a problem with that house?" She gestured toward the home directly across the street. A man was washing his car in the front driveway. As I drove past, I heard the words, "Is that Bill?"

I stopped.

The man said, "I heard you preach this morning. Great job!"

He and his wife came out to the car and visited with us. "The people who lived here before us were doing shady things. But they're long gone."

They told us about the lovely neighborhood and mentioned that many of the neighbors attended our church. This community offered everything we were looking for.

My burgeoning panic turned out to be another case of needless drama before the God Who leads me so well.

Three months later, we moved into that house, into a neighborhood that welcomed our family with open arms.

*Lord, thank You for leading me day by day, even when
I can't see around the next turn.*
    —Bill Giovannetti

Digging Deeper: Psalm 32:8; Isaiah 28:29

Sunday, March 15

Satisfy us in the morning with your unfailing love, that we may sing for joy and be glad all our days. —Psalm 90:14 (NIV)

It was the morning after, and I walked through the house, gathering stuff to go back in the dress-up box, picking up pieces of popped balloons, and washing spots off the kitchen stools.

Last night, eighteen people came to dinner—ten grandchildren, ages four to fifteen; their parents; and us, Oma and Opa. It started with a spontaneous Friday afternoon text message from my daughter-in-law: "We miss you all! Any free pockets of time to get together this weekend?" A flurry of messages followed. A "pocket" was found, potluck assignments made, and a late Saturday afternoon plan put in place.

We live in the house where our children grew up, so it's often the most logical place to gather. Plenty of room outside to run around, climb trees, even ride horses. And time inside to spill apple juice, lose small toys in the couch, and make a game of throwing popcorn into each other's mouths.

I used to pray that God would allow us to live our grandparent season in a home that welcomed our children, their children, and dogs. Yes, even dogs. I'm now incredibly blessed that that happened. Yet sometimes I sit in the midst of my answer-to-prayer chaos and fixate on the growing mess around me, which makes me annoyed at my small-thinking self. Other times I start cleaning in the midst of it all and miss joining in with what is going on.

Have I forgotten that years ago we used to live in the morning-after-look all the time? Now that we live alone, I've grown used to our orderly surroundings. But that's no reason to worry about a messy kitchen when I'm in the middle of what I've wanted most of all.

Gifts from the Giver, I remind myself as I pick up each popcorn piece.

> *Forgive me, Lord, for focusing on what matters least*
> *when I'm surrounded by what matters most.*
> —Carol Kuykendall

Digging Deeper: Psalm 16:11; Ephesians 4:2

"Choose this day whom you will serve...."—Joshua 24:15 (RSV)

It started innocently. One tiny thought. A Pinterest idea.

My husband and I lead a small group from church in our home. We gather to study the Bible and pray. The ladies always put their purses on our bed, but our bedroom didn't resemble the ones on Pinterest. Ours looked dreary. Dark-stained log walls and an outdated floral bedspread.

Decorating isn't easy for me, but I thought that if I could redecorate my bedroom, the women would be impressed. My daughter, Katie, agreed to be my virtual decorator. I'd text pictures for her approval.

Racing around town, I found dozens of possibilities. Each time I thought I saw the perfect comforter, Katie texted "NO!" or "I can't tell."

Nothing worked. The green curtains clashed. Patterns were too busy.

A week later, my sheets and pillows were piled on the floor—along with another terrible comforter that looked gorgeous in the store. My bedroom was totally out of control. Just like me.

Hoping for praise from my friends, I'd allowed decorating to consume my thoughts. My peace. Even my prayer time.

The next morning, Katie suggested a coverlet and Euro shams. I'd never heard of either.

I approached the saleswoman in the bedding department and explained the situation. "I have no idea what I'm doing," I said. "I'm praying you can help me." She smiled and calmly led me to an embroidered quilt and scarlet Euro shams. "This'll look homey in your cabin."

Back home, I remade the bed with the new quilt and shams and discovered it wasn't my bedroom that needed a makeover. It was my heart.

The night my friends put their purses on the embroidered quilt, I confessed. We laughed. None of them noticed the changes in my bedroom. Only the ones in my heart.

Lord, forgive me. I made my bedroom an idol.
—Julie Garmon

Digging Deeper: Matthew 6:21, 33–34

St. Patrick's Day, Tuesday, March 17

"For who has known the mind of the Lord so as to instruct him?" But we have the mind of Christ. —1 Corinthians 2:16 (RSV)

I was determined to learn the prayer attributed to St. Patrick and sing it from memory on St. Patrick's Day. At least to myself. But the lyrics to the hymn kept tripping me up. "Christ be with me, Christ within me, Christ behind me, Christ before me, Christ beside me…" All those words, all those different locations.

Patrick, as you may know, wasn't born in Ireland but was kidnapped from England and taken there, enslaved, and forced to work as a shepherd in the brutal Irish climate. I picture him praying these words attributed to him, "Christ beneath me, Christ above me…" while shivering in wind, sleet, snow, and darkness. He didn't have a portable heater or down parka. All he had was prayer.

Finally he escaped from his captors, went back to England, studied on the European continent, and then returned to Ireland where he brought Christ's love to the people, an amazing turnabout. As I mulled over the words of his prayer, I considered his remarkable success. Maybe it was just what was tripping me up. The Christ Patrick could bring to the people was the Christ Patrick knew on all sides and in all people: "Christ in hearts of all that love me, Christ in mouth of friend and stranger."

The only way I could remember the lyrics was by pointing: behind me, above me, beside me, around me, within me. Doing so, I finally got the message of the prayer. Christ is indeed everywhere.

Christ in hearts of all that love me,
Christ in mouth of friend and stranger.
—Rick Hamlin

Digging Deeper: John 14:9–11; Romans 8:9

*After Job had prayed for his friends, the Lord restored his fortunes and gave him twice as much as he had before. —*Job 42:10 (NIV)

We have a bedtime routine at our house: jammies, teeth brushed, bathroom, three books, hugs, kisses, prayer, and song.

Now that we have three children, my husband, Brian, decided to change the classic "Jesus Loves Me" ending to, "Yes, Jesus loves Olivia. Yes, Jesus loves James. Yes, Jesus loves Beau baby, the Bible tells me so."

Every night we sing that song, rubbing their backs when we sing their names, then tucking them into bed and turning out the lights.

James, ever the gatherer, often cons me into snuggling with him for a few minutes after lights out. We watch the stars from his nightlight dance on his ceiling and, almost without fail, he'll roll over and say, "Mommy. You forgot someone."

"Who?" I'll ask.

"Colby," he begins, mentioning our dog. "And Daddy. And you. And Nana, KK, and Poppa. And my cousins. And my school friends." As he names them, yes, all of them, including twelve cousins, ten aunts and uncles, and eleven friends from school, this wild man with all the passion and energy only a three-year-old can have, settles and calms until he's drifted almost to sleep.

Someone once told me to imagine if everything you didn't pray for today was gone tomorrow. What would you have left? Their intention was to remind me to be thankful for even the smallest things in my life. Leave it to James, though, to show me that the biggest, most wonderful things in our lives, our friends and family, are worth mentioning every night.

We don't sing the refrain for everyone; if we did, bedtime would last an hour! But now when I lay down with James, I remember to name all of his friends in the list of people Jesus loves.

> *Lord, thank You for the blessing of friends and family.*
> *Watch over them today and always.*
> —Ashley Kappel

Digging Deeper: Romans 8:26; 1 Timothy 2:1; James 5:16

Thursday, March 19

Every good and perfect gift is from above, coming down from the
Father of the heavenly lights, who does not change like shifting shadows.
—James 1:17 (NIV)

Sorry, we can't come."

Another "no." Would anyone be at Mam Ma's ninetieth birthday? I'd started planning last March, right after my husband's grandmother turned eighty-nine.

"What about a big birthday celebration next year?" I asked.

"That would be wonderful," she said. "I've never had a birthday party."

What? I decided to give her the best party ever! My goal was to have ninety birthday cards.

I reserved her church's fellowship hall, ordered decorations, a full sheet cake, specialty cookies, punch, and fruit trays. I sent a media release to the newspaper and wrote an invitation for the church bulletin. I e-mailed, texted, and posted on social media.

The day before the party, I called Mam Ma. She'd had an upset stomach. "I'm going to the emergency room."

I notified everyone and arranged for a sign on the fellowship hall door. Mam Ma spent her ninetieth birthday at the hospital.

Three weeks later, she was back to her spry self. On Monday we decided to have the party on Saturday—not a lot of notice. Thirty-four people had sent cards. I was sweating it; ninety seemed out of reach.

That Saturday, I pinned a pink corsage on Mam Ma. The party started at 2:00 PM. By 2:05, there was a line out the door. She worked the room like a politician running for reelection. Dozens of people showed up with gifts. At the end of the party, we counted the cards—103! It might have been belated, but Mam Ma agreed, it was her best birthday ever.

Thank You, God, for Mam Ma and for the gifts of health,
friendship, fellowship, and 103 cards.
—Stephanie Thompson

Digging Deeper: Proverbs 9:11; Song of Songs 2:11–12

Be content with what you have.... —Hebrews 13:5 (NIV)

Getting our dog, Cookie, wasn't my idea. The children found her on a rescue site and promised they'd take care of her if we'd please, please, please, bring her home. So we did.

To their credit, my daughter and stepson did their part. And my husband, Dwight, was a rock, as always. But while he was at work and the kids were at school, there was little question as to who would clean up messes and deal with Cookie's barking, whining, and incessant need for attention. The first few weeks, I complained to Dwight, "This dog is taking over my life!"

I found that if I took her for a long walk/run or two each day, Cookie's energy had someplace to go, and she was much easier to handle. With work and family responsibilities, it wasn't as though I had time for this. But my options were either a hyper puppy or daily walks—not much of a choice.

Just before we'd gotten Cookie from the shelter, I'd gone in for my annual checkup. I was a few pounds heavier than I'd like, and my cholesterol numbers were iffy too. There just never seemed to be enough time to exercise. But now, here I was, every single day, making the time. And with such lovable company too. Seeing Cookie's exuberance when I took her for a run made me forget all my stress for a while.

Six months after Cookie's arrival, she was thriving at thirty-four pounds, and I was thriving too—at five pounds lighter and with lower cholesterol numbers. When my doctor asked what healthy changes I'd made, I thought of all those daily walks and runs with my energetic little pup.

"I have a thirty-four-pound Cookie every day," I explained.

> *Lord, I'm sorry I don't always see Your blessings for what they are.*
> *Please forgive me when my attitude is wrong.*
> —Ginger Rue

Digging Deeper: Proverbs 12:10; Philippians 4:12

The Spirit of God moved upon the face of the waters. And God said, Let there be light: and there was light. And God saw the light, that it was good: and God divided the light from the darkness. —Genesis 1:2–4 (KJV)

An icy breeze blew across Rock Lake at Chena Hot Springs. Already submerged shoulder-deep, I sank a little lower into the hot water. Snow blanketed the boulders and trees at the lake's edge. It had been a long winter, my first one in Alaska, and the warmth was a soothing balm. The wind-whipped steam billowing and rolling its way into the sky made it easy to believe I was the only one there, and I was happy to be alone with my thoughts. So much in my life was in transition, and there was a lot to ponder.

But then the wind and steam stilled just as the sun came out from behind a cloud, bathing half of the lake in its rich afternoon glow. I was still sitting in shadow, but as I looked up, a beam of sunlight appeared, passing through a small hole in the rock just above me. Like a laser, it bounced from one airborne water droplet to the next, creating gossamer threads of light that traveled ever downward, until they met the liquid silver of the water's surface. There, forming a flawless golden *V*, they reflected heavenward again.

I stared, transfixed. I was familiar with the law of reflection—that light hits and reflects off of smooth surfaces at equal angles—but I'd never seen it so breathtakingly demonstrated. I couldn't help feeling I'd just witnessed something divine. After all, if God could so perfectly bend light to His will, the structure and design of my life—even when I could not see it—must be beautiful as well.

Lord God, help me remember—even when my limited human eyes and heart cannot see the order You bring to the world—it is there, all around me, all the time.
—Erin Janoso

Digging Deeper: Psalms 119:89–91, 148:4–5

JOURNEY TO THE HOLY LAND: Jerusalem

As he approached Jerusalem and saw the city, he wept over it and said,
"If you, even you, had only known on this day what would bring you
peace—but now it is hidden from your eyes."—Luke 19:41–42 (NIV)

I'd seen photos of modern-day Jerusalem, yet clung to images of mud-walled homes, a sleepy town. I was unprepared for how large the city of Jerusalem is—crammed with people, cars, buses, and tightly packed buildings. In its midst is Old Jerusalem, somewhat more in tune but still at odds with my Bible-reading imaginings.

Today's Jerusalem conveys a grandeur, yet an air of indifference rather than reverence. I'd expected to feel immediate awe as I explored God's special city. Instead, I was saddened by the scurrying, and aghast at trash-strewn hillsides. Then I realized that two thousand years ago, no garbage trucks picked up the trash, and probably the ancient hillsides looked similar to today's. Yet even then, Jerusalem was, no doubt, consumed with its own goings-on, its masses largely ignoring or rejecting God, even as Jesus walked among them.

Later, as I stood on the Mount of Olives, soaking in Jerusalem's expanse below, I wanted to cry out, "Stop, everyone! This is holy ground! Bow down. Worship. Give praise." But the city bustled on. I thought of the words of Jesus. "Jerusalem, Jerusalem...how often I have longed to gather your children together, as a hen gathers her chicks under her wings, and you were not willing" (Matthew 23:37, NIV).

In Jerusalem, I had expected to feel connected to God through tranquility. Instead, worldly hustle helped me to understand His heart.

Lord, thank You for helping me to comprehend Your pain.
When I become so consumed by my daily activities that
I fail to think of You, remind me of Jerusalem.
—Kim Taylor Henry

Digging Deeper: Jeremiah 2:32; Malachi 3:7

Monday, March 23

JOURNEY TO THE HOLY LAND: Gethsemane

"They may be ever seeing but never perceiving, and ever hearing but never understanding...."—Mark 4:12 (NIV)

I had looked forward to the Garden of Gethsemane as a hushed highlight of our trip to Israel, a spot where I would reflect on our Savior's suffering, a place of pain, yet serenity.

Instead, I saw a fenced-off grouping of knobby olive trees, with the word *peace* spelled out in rocks within the enclosure. It didn't feel peaceful. A cattle-drive of tourists encircled the fencing, chatting, bumping into each other, taking grinning selfies. Hawkers shoved scarves in my face, trying to make a sale. The tone was anything but reverent. I was especially upset by raucous laughter of two sightseers boasting over their bartering. They barely glanced at the olive trees. One bragged he'd gotten the price on a set of coins down to two dollars from twenty. I remembered the words Jesus spoke as he scattered the coins of the money changers and overturned their tables in the temple: "Get these out of here! Stop turning my Father's house into a market!" (John 2:16, NIV).

With its gnarled ancient trees, Gethsemane gave me a glimpse of where Jesus prayed the night he was betrayed. Perhaps that was the key—He was *betrayed* at that spot by a world who refused to see and believe, a world who stubbornly clung to their self-centered blindness. No, Gethsemane didn't provide me with the repose I'd anticipated; it imparted something more vital—insight into the outrage Jesus felt over greed and self-focus. He sought solace beneath trees in an area likely larger and more peaceful than it is now, yet still pierced by a world that failed to recognize and respect God and His glory in their midst.

> *Lord, I'm sorry I so often focus on the things of this world*
> *and neglect what truly matters. Help me not to just see and hear*
> *but to perceive and understand.*
> —Kim Taylor Henry

Digging Deeper: Mark 11:15–17, 14:32, 37, 38

JOURNEY TO THE HOLY LAND: Calvary

But they shouted, "Take him away! Take him away! Crucify him!"…
—John 19:15 (NIV)

Opinions differ as to where in Jerusalem Christ was crucified and buried. Some believe it was at the site of the Church of the Holy Sepulchre; others think that it was on a hillside outside the city walls. The Via Dolorosa, a narrow, stone lane within those walls, leads to both. It's thought to be the very route Jesus took to His crucifixion.

Walking the Via Dolorosa, I felt irritated by what I viewed as near-oblivion to the sanctity of this path. Crass crowds and the array of souvenir shops disturbed me. Yet, I realized, this was a glimpse into how it was in Jesus's day—the clamor of busy markets with hordes of noisy people.

The atmosphere I experienced changed at the Church of the Holy Sepulchre, ornate and lavishly decorated, and Calvary, stark and simple, each reverent in its own way. The tones of those at both locations were hushed and respectful, silently waiting to kneel by, touch, and experience the holy spaces. The awareness that our Savior had suffered, died, and risen was palpable.

Why is the Via Dolorosa bustling with indifference and commercialism, while the sites of death and resurrection are worshipful? Perhaps it's a reminder that I, like so many, get too wrapped up in the world, succumb to peer pressure, realize my errors too late, and how down after the fact—when crisis has already struck.

My visit to Calvary was, appropriately, on a day of icy rain. I stared at the empty tomb, then huddled with others under umbrellas, absorbing the magnitude of the place. With them, I took Communion, grateful for our forgiving God.

Lord God, may I never wait until crisis strikes to turn to You.
—Kim Taylor Henry

Digging Deeper: Zephaniah 1:11–12; Matthew 27:54

JOURNEY TO THE HOLY LAND: Sea of Galilee

"Peace I leave with you; my peace I give you...." —John 14:27 (NIV)

There's a bench on a hillside by my home where I go, especially when I'm seeking comfort and peace, to talk to Jesus. I call it my "special place." From that spot I can see Pikes Peak in the distance, stately behind rolling hills, expanse of fields, and groves of trees. Sitting with Him, surrounded by nature, I feel peace.

The greatest delight of my trip to Israel was when I felt Jesus showing me His "special place" by the Sea of Galilee. Surely, this locale where Jesus chose to concentrate his ministry must have brought Him peace as well. It is called a sea, so I don't know why I pictured it as a small lake, but when I saw its size, its intense-green rock-strewn hillsides splattered with canary-yellow mustard plants, its surrounding mountain silhouettes, I was mesmerized.

By the rocky shoreline is where it's said Jesus appeared to His disciples after His resurrection. I wandered from our tour group to a place of solitude on a rock by the edge of the sea. Sunlight shimmered on its surface. Transparent water lapped its shoreline. I understood why Christ selected this spot to appear to them. It was, no doubt, part of His "special place"—the sea, the hillsides, the land, the mountains, the peace. After the torture of His execution and the miracle of His resurrection, Christ didn't choose to return to the masses in Jerusalem or to the barrenness of the desert, but to this familiar spot. I could picture His tender smile as He stood watching His hapless disciples, telling them where to cast their nets, calmly cooking fish as they returned with their huge catch and recognized their Lord.

During and following times of trial, I choose to go to my special place. It felt good to know that Jesus had one too.

Lord Jesus, thank You for the peace of special places.
—Kim Taylor Henry

Digging Deeper: Matthew 4:18–19; 15:29, John 21:4

JOURNEY TO THE HOLY LAND: Armageddon

Then they gathered the kings together to the place that in Hebrew is called Armageddon ... And out of the temple came a loud voice from the throne, saying, "It is done!" —Revelation 16:16–17 (NIV)

I approached the Valley of Armageddon in Israel with trepidation, envisioning an ominous, desolate, desert place—the location where "the battle on the great day of God Almighty" will occur (Revelation 16:14, NIV). But again, God surprised me. Though this valley has hosted battle after battle through the centuries, it is far from bleak and barren. Rather, it is a huge stretch of rich green fields, encircled by mountains and wooded hillsides, interspersed with towns and buildings. Fascinatingly, two of Israel's most strategic military bases already lie squarely within its bounds.

As I stood on a mountaintop observing the valley, I breathed deeply of a wind of fresh, clear air. The fertile plains below were capped by an azure-blue sky. The vastness and beauty filled me with awe. I was amazed to feel no fear, no dread, only a quietude that I was seeing the very spot that would usher in the beginning of the end of this earth as we know it. There, in this valley of battles, the location of the most significant of all battles to come, God filled me with His calm assurance that life is unfolding according to His perfect plan.

Father God, when I face battles of all kinds, may I remember the unexpected peace of Armageddon, a reminder that You have it all under control.
—Kim Taylor Henry

Digging Deeper: Psalm 33:11; Matthew 28:20

Friday, March 27

*"Ask the Lord your God for a sign, whether in the deepest depths
or in the highest heights."* —Isaiah 7:11 (NIV)

God," I said, "show me something so I know You're here." I don't
know why I said it. The words just came as I struggled to find
my stride running on the road. Spring had officially sprung, yet this
morning my sons' school had a two-hour snow delay.

I hadn't jogged since autumn, and it was hard to get going. I went
down the first hill and then around the bend looking for an answer to
my prayer. I looked at the road ahead but nothing stood out. Approaching a monster hill that takes some training to master, I slowed down
to a quick walk. That's when I saw a cute little fuzzy brown and black
woolly bear caterpillar just bumping along on the side of the road.
When I was growing up, woolly bears were my favorite.

"Oh, thank You," I said.

I picked up the pace, ran into town and then back over the bridge
toward home. The distance made me question the significance of
the woolly bear. "If that was really for me, I want to see him again."

How crazy would that be? It had been at least a half hour, and he
was moving pretty fast. I looked down at the shoulder for the fuzzy
little guy. Nope. No sign. And then, I saw him, a few feet in front of
me zooming up the massive hill.

"All right," I said, "Three's a charm! If these are signs, show me something *really* good!"

The words were just out of my mouth when a heron appeared from the
tree line right above my head. A heron! I'd never seen one near my house.

My eyes filled with tears as the heron hovered right above me longer
than seemed possible. Though anything—no, everything—is possible
with God.

*Heavenly Father, thank You for showing me signs that erase
any doubt that You are here with me.*
—Sabra Ciancanelli

Digging Deeper: Genesis 18:14; Matthew 19:26

I have learned to be content whatever the circumstances.
—Philippians 4:11 (NIV)

The Apostle Paul's encouragement to be content whatever the circumstances was my devotional lesson for the day. I grimace at the thermometer. Minus ten degrees? This is going to be hard. My breath puffs into clouds as I trudge through the snow with a larger-than-usual armload of hay for my horse. Jack thrusts his frosty muzzle into the hay. At least *he* looks content. I grab the ax to chop ice on the water trough. A few whacks and I open a small hole in the ice. One hearty swing to widen the hole and—*Ping! Splash!* The spacer holding the ax together shoots off into the hole. I reach for the ax head, but too late. It scuds harmlessly along the bottom of the trough, but I'm not sticking my arm in three feet of ice water to retrieve it.

Wanting to lower the power bill, I'd put the electric tank heater away a week before during an unseasonable warm-up. It had been easy to be content then. I shake my wet glove. Contentment in this? Impossible! *Why, God?* I break trail to the pump house and kick snow away from the door just enough to reach the tank heater on the shelf. *Why is the pump running? Is that water dripping?* The pressure valve is broken; water pours from the tank. I stretch from the door jamb to shut off the power to the well. At least it's a cement building. Standing water would have destroyed wood.

I kneel in inches of water to remove the broken valve. I laugh suddenly when it hits me. *That's why, God.* Content with minus ten? I'm rejoicing in it instead! Praise God for minus ten, and praise God for the broken ax—otherwise I wouldn't have opened the pump house door until June!

> *Praise You, Lord, for broken things that guide us toward*
> *unexpected blessings. Yes, in this we can be more than content.*
> —Erika Bentsen

Digging Deeper: Romans 12:12; 1 Corinthians 13:7

Sunday, March 29

He is your praise. He is your God, who has done for you these great and terrifying things that your eyes have seen. —Deuteronomy 10:21 (ESV)

My friend Bill is one of the more forgetful people you will ever meet. When he's heading out the door to walk the dog or to pick up his daughter at school, it often takes him five minutes to search for keys or wallet or you-name-it.

One day recently, Bill was out doing errands in the car. He had several stops to make: visit his great-aunt in the hospital, go to the grocery for some basics, put gas in the car, and then stop at the hardware store. The problem was once he got to the hardware store where they know him well, Bill went to the checkout with his can of paint and discovered his wallet was missing. He searched the store, thinking he had dropped it. No wallet. So he left the paint can on the counter, ran out to the car, determined to double-back and drive to each of his previous stops to look for the wallet.

When he still couldn't find it, Bill frantically headed back to the hardware store, thinking perhaps he had missed the wallet somewhere inside. As he pulled into the parking lot, into the same spot where he'd been only fifteen minutes earlier, Bill noticed his wallet tucked under the windshield wiper on the passenger side. It had been there since he'd dropped it upon exiting his car the first time to go into the hardware store. Someone had noticed it beside his car and attached a note: "Bill: Yours?"

He'd been frantically racing around town looking for something that was right in front of his nose the entire time.

You, God, are my hope today. You are right here beside me.
—Jon M. Sweeney

Digging Deeper: Psalms 119:151, 145:18

Even youths grow tired and weary, and young men stumble and fall;
but those who hope in the Lord will renew their strength....
—Isaiah 40:30–31 (NIV)

Over a cup of oolong tea, my friend Alyssa suddenly reached for a nearby napkin. I thought she was going to sneeze.

Nope. She was going to cry, and had no plan to stop.

In a quaking voice, she revealed that her troubled relationship with her brother now seemed beyond repair. She couldn't understand how her brother—ordinarily a nice guy—could suddenly blow up at her for the slightest slight. Alyssa told me, in painful detail, exactly what he said and how he said it.

When she was done, I reached for a nearby napkin. I was not going to sneeze.

"Oh, I'm so sorry," Alyssa said. "I didn't mean to upset you."

She had no idea.

Her brother's harsh diatribe, barbed with sarcasm, was familiar to me, because I had unleashed similar verbal cannonades toward my wife. You would think that a seemingly nice guy like me—writing for a publication such as this—would never weaponize his words. Not so. Alyssa had unintentionally held a mirror to my transgressions and I was forced to stare back, unable to blink or turn away.

Before we parted, I mumbled some advice to Alyssa. It was heartfelt and earnest but probably ineffective. (Failing twice in one afternoon—a new record, even for me.) I then went home and mumbled an apology to Sandee, my voice quaking with shame and regret. My only solace: We are not beyond repair.

Lord, help us heal our troubled relationships in our troubled world—
and keep Alyssa and her brother in Your loving hands.
—Mark Collins

Digging Deeper: Genesis 50:17; Luke 17:2–4

Tuesday, March 31

When day came, Jesus left and went to a secluded place; and the crowds were searching for Him.... —Luke 4:42 (NASB)

The one bedroom in our apartment has always belonged to my sons. I made it the perfect room for two little boys. I painted the wooden loft bed to look like a tree house and hung Christmas tree lights and a swing underneath. Every inch of the room was dedicated to them as a sanctuary of childhood, to play and grow. At night, I'd lie down for the night on the couch or the extra futon in their room. I didn't have a space of my own but convinced myself it wasn't necessary.

Years later, I had an extra room built. It was mainly for my parents during their extended visits. The builders came and up went the walls. I walked into the room, shut the door, and sat in the middle of the floor. There was silence. I couldn't remember the last time I felt this peaceful in my home. I moved the extra futon into the new room, painted the walls a soothing grayish blue, put up expensive curtains, and painted a white Moroccan decal on the walls. I bought beautiful flowers and scented candles.

"Go to your own room," I'd tell the boys when I'd find them playing on my bed with the fluffy, new quilt. When my parents came for their visit, they were content to sleep on the pullout in the living room. I was content not to argue.

I didn't realize how much I needed a place to retreat, breathe, and recharge, but I'm grateful I discovered the importance of sanctuary within those four wonderful walls.

Lord, as I serve others and live out my purpose, help me to
find sanctuary and rest in You.
—Karen Valentin

Digging Deeper: Matthew 6:6; Mark 1:35

HE PERFORMS WONDERS

1 _____

2 _____

3 _____

4 _____

5 _____

6 _____

7 _____

8 _____

9 _____

10 _____

11 _____

12 _____

13 _____

14 _____

15 _____

March

16 _____

17 _____

18 _____

19 _____

20 _____

21 _____

22 _____

23 _____

24 _____

25 _____

26 _____

27 _____

28 _____

29 _____

30 _____

31 _____

APRIL

I will praise thee;
for I am fearfully and
wonderfully made....

—Psalm 139:14 (KJV)

Wednesday, April 1

FIRSTS: Cleaning Service
Open my eyes that I may see.... —Psalm 119:18 (NIV)

This is the day, each month, when a cleaning lady comes, and for an hour and a half she scours floors and fixtures and countertops. With my focus this year on first-times, I'm thinking back, some fifty years, to the first time I hired household help.

It was April 1969. Our son Scott and three college friends from overseas had been home for Easter. Donn and Liz, still in high school, had had friends over too. They'd gone back to school, and I stood in the living room looking at the unmade sofa bed, someone's baseball cap on a lampshade, and the remains of some food in the fireplace.

In the yellow pages, I found Handy Andy Cleaning Service. The woman on the telephone said, "Before the team arrives, remove all bric-a-brac from surfaces." *Bric-a-brac!* I thought, offended. I didn't have any bric-a-brac! I hated rooms cluttered with doodads.

An hour later, I was still removing picture frames, carved wooden animals, grandmother's teacups, ceramic sculptures, and hand-stitched samplers. And who knew what I'd find in the next room? Bric-a-brac, I decided, were other people's mementos. These were *treasures* that I or someone in the family had placed where we could see them.

Except, I thought, as I lifted a birthday card from my dresser top, I'd stopped seeing them. Things that are "always there" become background. When Handy Andy left that afternoon, I found new spots for our precious possessions, or put out different ones.

So when the cleaning lady leaves today, I won't put things back where they were. I'll bring out some long-forgotten treasures and, for a while, see them again for the very first time.

> *Lord, Who makes all things new, what I fail to see,*
> *I fail to thank You for. Keep my vision ever new!*
> —Elizabeth Sherrill

Digging Deeper: 1 Chronicles 16:34; Proverbs 20:12

THE FRIENDSHIP OF WOMEN: Prayer Warrior

Bear one another's burdens.... —Galatians 6:2 (NKJV)

My friend Karen is a true prayer warrior. Every morning at 6:30, she heads out in her Alpharetta, Georgia, neighborhood for a two-and-a-half-mile prayer walk during which she prays for specific people at certain stops. My stop occurs about 7:30, in front of ever-blooming red roses. Every day, she talks to God about various creative projects I'm engaged in, my work, my finances, and my struggle with a painful, chronic illness. For years, I've celebrated answers to her prayers for everything except pain control.

This past spring around Easter, a miracle occurred. A new doctor who specializes in pain management recommended a new drug that's sometimes used for diabetic peripheral neuropathy. "This drug will specifically target your tumors' nerve cells," he told me. You'll be amazed at the results, and you'll be more alert and vibrant as well."

He was right. I now no longer experience the horrendous burning, pressure nerve pain behind my eyes and all over my face. When I telephoned Karen with the good news, she was delighted but not surprised. For unlike me, she had never given up hope and anticipated God's intervention. "That's answer number 2,118, Roberta," she announced. I could hear the smile in her voice across the miles.

Years ago, Karen started out walking for exercise; then she decided she could do a bit of praying along the way. "It's not elaborate," she maintains. "I just remember my friends and family and church before God." Some people, I might add, she doesn't even know.

Do you have friends who pray for you? Thank them today. Better yet, return the loving gesture.

Where would I be without my friend Karen, Lord?
She bears my burdens every single day.
—Roberta Messner

Digging Deeper: 1 Chronicles 16:11; 2 Chronicles 7:14;
1 John 5:14

Friday, April 3

May He grant you according to your heart's desire, and fulfill
all your purpose. —Psalm 20:4 (NKJV)

My husband, Terry, and I once road-tripped from north Idaho to Texas to visit our son, Phil; his wife, Ashley; and their two children. They were expecting another child.

I took a big box of juicy gleaner peaches. A hit right away. And lots of grandma toys. We joked that Terry finally got his "toy hauler."

What a fine time we had during our two weeks there. But as we drove off, I became practically undone: the family stood in a row on the front porch waving goodbye in the morning sun. I stuck my head out the window to catch that last glimpse.

Ashley had tested positive for an autoimmune disease. I wondered how they would manage. I longed to be nearer to them.

The next spring I received a "Guess what?" call. They were moving to a community only an hour away! A year later, it got even better. I answered the phone to "Your son would like to rent my house in town. He's listed you as a reference." They were going to be only ten minutes away!

They moved into the rental on the very same street where I had lived as a teenager. It seemed a dream. What wasn't a dream was Ashley's struggle with lupus nephritis. Her medications came with serious side effects. She had a port placed for infusions. She was, and is, often ill.

I have been called upon many times to help care for the children— now ages two, five, and six. My longing for our Texas family to be near comes with responsibility. God has shown me that desires of the heart are made of opportunity. When He answers those desires, it's not only for my own satisfaction. It also benefits others. He entrusts me with His heart's desire for the greater good.

> *A heart's desire shaped by You, Lord, is a bountiful thing.*
> —Carol Knapp

Digging Deeper: Psalm 37:4–5; Isaiah 58:10–11; Ephesians 2:10

Put on the full armor of God, so that when the day of evil comes, you may be able to stand your ground, and after you have done everything, to stand. —Ephesians 6:13 (NIV)

For a generation, aprons slipped out of fashion, rotting in rag bags or hanging limply in closets. But they're back, on display in shops and protecting cooks' shirts. After I'd written a book chapter touting the benefits of aprons, friends gifted me with their finds: colorful photos of artful boutique displays, and wrapped packages containing functional examples, which I placed alongside a few I'd made by hand.

I wear aprons often, when cooking or eating informally, hoping to shield a favored outfit from drips and splashes. I also try to foist them on a young neighbor friend who comes by on Saturday mornings to cook breakfast and bake sweets. "Here, this will protect your clothes," I say.

She often resists. "I don't want it. I don't need it."

But sometimes my friend listens, follows my lead, and throws on an apron. For example, this past weekend before mixing banana-bread dough, she said okay to a chef's bib apron, a no-nonsense handmade gray-and-white-striped one that would cover her well. As I tied the strings behind her back, I envisioned it as a layer of spiritual "chain mail." She had seen the value of protection and agreed to wear a sturdy style. As a mentor, I helped her secure its placement. As I tightened the bow, I silently prayed a prayer that never goes out of fashion:

Lord, shield us and those in our care from evil and its harms.
—Evelyn Bence

Digging Deeper: Ephesians 6:10–19; Colossians 3:12

Palm Sunday, April 5

A great multitude... took branches of palm trees and went out to meet Him.... —John 12:12–13 (NKJV)

In the East, the palm tree is known as the queen of trees, and in ancient times, its feathery fronds were symbols of victory, used to honor military heroes and Olympic champions.

Jesus's triumphal entry into Jerusalem was an advance celebration of his triumph over death. First, he'd face rejection, humiliation, and torture before being nailed to a cross until he expired. Only after rising from the dead would He become our Champion.

My wife, Sharon, was watching the Winter Olympics. She is not athletic, unless you count living with me as a marathon, so she was mesmerized by the artistry of the ice skaters. Her face was a slide show of emotions: excitement, admiration, anxiety, and more than a touch of envy.

"How can people do these things on ice?" she wondered aloud.

At last, there was the presentation of gold. I saw moisture in her eyes.

After the event, there was a series of flashbacks to the skater's childhood. Sharon gaped in disbelief at the grueling exercises the young skater endured—scolding from her coach, the falls, the injuries, and the pain.

"I can hardly believe what these skaters go through," she responded.

It was a reality check for both of us. Frankly, I prefer victory without all the suffering, but as I looked at my to-do list for the upcoming month, I could see that it was grim. So, I tried to envision the joy I would feel at the end of this month of misery. With God's help, I would go for the gold. Or the bronze. Okay, I would settle for a couple of palm branches to hang on my wall.

> *You showed us how to turn suffering into gold, Lord. Now,*
> *if You could just give me the courage to begin.*
> —Daniel Schantz

Digging Deeper: Psalm 92:12; Revelation 7:9

*Now in the morning, as He returned to the city, He was hungry.
And seeing a fig tree by the road, He came to it and found nothing on
it but leaves, and said to it, "Let no fruit grow on you ever again...."*
—Matthew 21:18–19 (NKJV)

On Monday morning, when Jesus came upon a fig tree growing by the road, he saw that it bore only leaves. His face fell. He was greatly disappointed.

In a way, this tree was symbolic of the many disappointments Jesus endured in His ministry: the clumsy misunderstandings of His disciples, rejection by the religious leaders, betrayal by Judas. Even on the cross, Jesus said that His own Father in heaven had let him down.

Through no fault of my own, I recently found myself in a tempting situation. My good angel and my bad angel were engaged in a spirited debate, and, frankly, my bad angel was winning. I muttered a prayer for help, and soon the words of an old hymn came to mind. I remembered only a couple of lines: "I would be true, for there are those who trust me; I would be pure, for there are those who care...."*

I thought of all the people who love me and look up to me: family, friends, students. How could I disappoint them by yielding to temptation? Then I thought about Jesus, Who paid dearly for my freedom. The thought of disappointing Him was too much for me to bear, and that gave me the strength to walk away.

When Jesus checks me over at the end of each day, I don't want to see disappointment in His eyes. I want Him to be proud of me. I want Him to find in me the Fruit of the Spirit.

Be patient with me, Lord, as I learn to produce fruit, and not just leaves.
—Daniel Schantz

Digging Deeper: Matthew 7:19; John 15:1

*("I Would Be True," lyrics by H.A. Walter.)

Tuesday of Holy Week, April 7

"As the branch cannot bear fruit of itself, unless it abides in the vine, neither can you, unless you abide in Me." —John 15:4 (NKJV)

O n Tuesday, Jesus—Who was always teaching—told his disciples a parable about some vinedressers. The "vine" was a favorite analogy of his, and some of his most serious admonitions were about vines: "I am the vine, you are the branches.... without Me you can do nothing" (John 15:5, NKJV).

I thought of this passage recently, when I was preparing a commencement speech. The harder I worked on it, the more frustrated I became.

One night, I had a flashback to one of my first days in the classroom as a college professor, when I went to class unprepared. I had worked hard on the lesson but had only enough material for about ten minutes. I shuffled into class, resigned to failure.

Five minutes into the lecture, a student asked a question. While I pondered it, another student answered his fellow classmate. Soon the whole class was crackling with discussion on the topic I had introduced. I just tweaked the discussion, and it turned out to be one of the best classes of the semester. It was good for me to learn, early on, that teaching is not all up to me. It's a partnership with God and students.

The next day I looked at my commencement notes and realized that I was overpreparing. I had not allowed any room for the Spirit to work. I put the notes away. On the night of commencement, I dusted them off, talked to God about my fears and hopes, and then delivered a speech that was "ours," not "mine."

When facing such frustrations, I need to remember that I am just a branch. God is the vine, my secret source of nourishment.

Thank you, Father, for the peace of mind that comes from
realizing that success is not all up to me.
—Daniel Schantz

Digging Deeper: Proverbs 11:28, 28:26

He cast down the pieces of silver in the temple, and departed,
and went and hanged himself. —Matthew 27:5 (KJV)

Legend says that Judas Iscariot hanged himself on a redbud tree, a common ornamental tree in Palestine, often referred to as the "Judas Tree."

It was a rash and irreversible decision Judas made in a state of grief and remorse.

I have lived long enough to be wary of impulsive decisions. How quickly life can turn around, if I am patient. In as little as a day, a week, a month, everything can look very different.

I am writing this on March 14. It has been a long and bitter winter for Missouri, and it has often made me feel trapped indoors and depressed. Outside my study window, I see no signs of life. Black cottonwood limbs claw at a dull aluminum sky. The lawn is brown and brittle. Even the evergreens are bronze. It seems impossible that any form of life could emerge from this landscape.

Yet, just seven days from now is the official first day of spring. My willows will green up first, then the Saskatoon bushes and plum trees will turn brilliant white, followed by a row of golden forsythias and red quinces, down by the road. Soon I will be outdoors, standing barefoot on a lime-green carpet of fur, letting the warm breezes play with my hair.

I sometimes wonder how many workable marriages have ended a month too soon. How many good jobs were abruptly left behind because of an oppressive boss who would soon be replaced by a congenial one? Thinking of this reminds me that if I can just hold on during the darkest of times, brighter days are coming soon.

Help me not to be rash, Lord, when things go horribly wrong.
Give me the strength just to hold on, until I can get over the hump.
—Daniel Schantz

Digging Deeper: Psalm 130:6; Ecclesiastes 7:8

Maundy Thursday, April 9

As they were eating, Jesus took bread, blessed and broke it, and gave it to the disciples and said, "Take, eat; this is My body." —Matthew 26:26 (NKJV)

With just six words, Jesus transformed a common grain into a symbol of our salvation. On that Thursday night, Jesus was like soft dough, about to be kneaded—squeezed and stretched, pounded and pummeled, then finally, baked in the hot sun until He became the Bread of Life.

What He needed at this Last Supper was not food but comfort from the twelve men He loved, before His sufferings began.

"Let's do lunch," my colleague Richard said recently, as he began a new semester of teaching.

I smiled at the pop phrase, "Do lunch," but I really didn't want to do lunch. I wasn't hungry, I am not a great conversationalist, and I hate to spend good money on something that will be gone in fifteen minutes. But I sensed that Richard was not so much hungry as needy.

We met at the Chinese buffet, piled our plates high, and sat near a window. Richard prayed a meaningful table grace, and then we plunged into egg drop soup and chicken-fried rice.

Soon we were laughing at all the crazy things husbands and wives do, and bragging shamelessly about our children.

Sitting across from him, I could see lines of tension on his face as he described a difficult new class coming up this semester. I nodded my head in sympathy.

Then he listened as I rehearsed the unforeseen trials of retirement. It felt good to get those feelings out in the open.

All too soon it was over, and I was reminded that there is more to lunch than food—there is comfort. Lunch is not just something I eat; it's something I "do" with friends.

Father, I thank You for friends, who double my joys and halve my sorrows.
—Daniel Schantz

Digging Deeper: Proverbs 18:20, 24

Who Himself bore our sins in His own body on the tree, that we . . . might live for righteousness. . . . —1 Peter 2:24 (NKJV)

Jesus was crucified on a man-made tree, which well-known legend asserts was made of dogwood. The crucifixion process is thought to have been invented by the ancient Persians and tweaked by the Romans to create additional pain.

It would be hard to devise a more excruciating way to die. In fact, the English word *excruciating* in its Latin form is derived from the Latin for *crucifixion.*

Physical pain: Jesus experienced just about every kind of wound known to medical science, from bruises and punctures to lacerations and contusions.

Social pain: Hanging naked in public is more than awkward. Being watched by family, friends, and enemies while writhing in agony would be unimaginable.

Emotional pain: To be punished for doing only good is the ultimate injustice.

Recently I experienced some unusual pain when I had a growth removed from my tongue. It swelled up, large and black, and pain pills didn't help. Worst of all, I was wondering if I would be able to speak again, not a fun thing for a teacher to contemplate. (Good news: I can!)

Suffering is a language, a "tongue." I used to tell my Christian college students, "You can get by in ministry without knowledge of Latin, Greek, or Hebrew, but you had better understand the language of suffering, because you will be ministering to people in pain."

No picture I've ever seen affects me the way the crucifixion does. It's like Jesus is speaking to me personally, saying, "This is how much I love you, Dan." It makes me want to live in a way worthy of that price.

*Lord, teach me the language of suffering, so that I might be
useful to those in pain.*
—Daniel Schantz

Digging Deeper: Romans 8:22; 2 Corinthians 2:4

Nicodemus... also came, bringing a mixture of myrrh and aloes, about a hundred pounds. Then they took the body of Jesus, and bound it in strips of linen with the spices, as the custom of the Jews is to bury.
—John 19:39–40 (NKJV)

Saturday of Holy Week was a time of despair for the disciples, who were in hiding, bewildered, and disillusioned.

Jesus's body was in the tomb, but it had been generously treated with spices, filling the musty cavern with the aroma of hope.

Spices—such as cassia, cinnamon, saffron, and spikenard—were costly and fragile, but indispensable in a time when people had no running water, no showers, no bathtubs. Moreover, spices were used to express friendship and respect, as we do now with flowers. Even prayers were sent aloft on the wings of incense.

One Sunday evening at church, I said something that wounded my wife. All the way home Sharon was silent, and she went to bed early.

That night I slept fitfully, praying for wisdom. In the darkness of early morning, I had a revelation. I drove to a 24-hour store and bought a bouquet of roses. Back home, I made breakfast for my wife, her favorite meal, and I put the roses in the middle of the table.

When she came to breakfast, Sharon still looked miserable. But when she smelled the coffee, the biscuits, and the roses, her face softened into a smile.

I think Easter season would be a good time for me to spread some aromatic sunshine to a friend: a scented candle, some lilies of the valley, or a freshly baked loaf of bread might do the trick. Nothing says "I love you" like a fine fragrance.

You gave us five senses, Lord, but sometimes I forget the power of one that's right in front of my nose.
—Daniel Schantz

Digging Deeper: Psalm 141:2; Proverbs 27:9

Now in the place where He was crucified there was a garden, and in the garden a new tomb in which no one had yet been laid. —John 19:41 (NKJV)

Life on earth began in the Garden of Eden. How fitting that it began afresh in the Garden of the Resurrection. A Jerusalem garden would typically feature flowers—such as anemones, poppies, phlox, and daffodils—plus small trees, such as fig, acacia, almond, and tamarisk. There would be a cistern for water, some stone benches to sit on, and maybe a potting shed for the gardener's tools.

When the resurrected Jesus appeared to Mary Magdalene, she thought He was the gardener; in a way she was right, for we are all "transplanted into the Lord's own garden and are under his personal care" (Psalm 92:13, TLB).

As I look back over this year, I can see that the Master Gardener has been at work in my life, and it makes me feel secure to know that I am being tended by a wise and watchful Gardener.

When I was overwhelmed with busywork, he pulled some of the weeds that were crowding me. When retirement caused me to become a bit lazy, he cultivated around me and pruned me sharply for more fruit-bearing. And, during a dry spell, I found refreshment in His Word and in some recorded hymns inspired by that Word.

Someday, perhaps soon, the Heavenly Gardener will harvest me and take me into His house.

For now, on Easter morning, I am content to know that the tomb of Christ opened into a garden, for "one is nearer God's heart in a garden than anywhere else on earth."*

> *Lord, I pray that the garden of my life will bring you the kind of pleasure my garden brings to me.*
> —Daniel Schantz

Digging Deeper: Isaiah 58:11, 61:11

*Dorothy Frances Gurney, London, Country Life, 1913

Monday, April 13

PRAYING IN PUBLIC: Stepping Out of My Privacy Zone

We declare to you what we have seen and heard so that you also may have fellowship with us; and truly our fellowship is with the Father and with his Son Jesus Christ. —1 John 1:3 (NRSV)

Every year after Easter I feel let down. I wonder how to sustain the spiritual intensity following Lent and Holy Week.

This year was different. On Good Friday, after a moving service at St. Paul's in Concord, New Hampshire, I remained seated in the back of the church. I thought I was alone until I noticed an elderly woman standing in front of me. She waited patiently for me to notice her. When I looked up, she asked, "May I hug you?"

Hug me? A complete stranger? But something in her face caused me not to refuse her. Sensing my hesitation, she added, "I see that you need to be held." I stepped into her arms, understanding that God had sent her not only to comfort me on this bleak Good Friday, but for all the times in the last weeks and months I'd needed comfort.

After Easter, I knew I wanted to do for others what she'd done for me, even if it meant stepping out of my privacy zone.

Finishing my walk one evening, I passed a normally bubbly neighbor. She was on her phone, sobbing. I walked on, assuming she wanted privacy, but then turned, and went back. Without pausing or speaking, I wrapped my arms around her, phone, tears, and all. Instantly she put her arms around me. I held her for about fifteen seconds as she continued to listen on the phone and cling to me. When we let go, she looked into my eyes and nodded gratefully.

I've seen her since; we've never spoken about that evening. We'd said all that needed saying.

> *Lord, help me step out of my comfort zone and*
> *into the arms of whoever You send me.*
> —Marci Alborghetti

Digging Deeper: Luke 6:21; John 17:20–24

"Truly, I say to you, as you did it to one of the least of these my brethren, you did it to me."—Matthew 25:40 (RSV)

I was climbing out of the subway tunnel and an earnest woman in a tattered sweatshirt and jeans stood there with an empty cup, soliciting donations. With the words of Jesus about "the least of these" echoing in my ears, I dug into a pocket and pulled out a buck, putting it in her paper cup, and then hurried off. "Sir, sir," she called after me. I turned around. "Here's a bracelet. I want to give you something for your donation." She thrust a string of blue-and-white twined yarn into my hand. "Thanks," I muttered.

What am I going to do with this? I thought. I don't wear bracelets. I have barely gotten into the habit of wearing a watch. I thrust it into my pocket and only thought of it again later that night when I was taking stuff out of my pocket. The bracelet. I left it on my bureau.

It's still there, next to a dish that fills up too fast with loose change and a loose cufflink and an extra key ring—excess baggage of a life that is rich and blessed. Any day now, my wife, Carol, is going to ask, "What's that for?" I can tell her it's a bracelet that I never intend to wear, or better yet, that it's a reminder to never forget how Jesus told us where to look to see the face of God. We can see Him in a tattered sweatshirt and jeans.

> *Help me serve those who need God most: the poor,*
> *the hungry, the sick, the stranger.*
> —Rick Hamlin

> *Digging Deeper:* Deuteronomy 15:11;
> Proverbs 19:17; Matthew 5:16

A merry heart makes a cheerful countenance.... —Proverbs 15:13 (NKJV)

Lots of movies and television shows are shot in Manhattan, and we New Yorkers have come to accept that sometimes the activities of the industry make things inconvenient for us. The other day as I was rushing home from work, I was detained on the corner of my block by a hand placed gently on my chest. "Sorry, we're filming. You'll have to wait a minute, please." There were mobile trailers with stars on the doors, food trucks, and klieg lights lining the block. There was a time when I would have been starstruck. Today I was annoyed. "Look, I have a dog to walk," I snapped.

Shortly thereafter, I was let through and asked politely to hurry along because they were doing another take. Worse, the action was happening in the lobby of my building. I shouldered my way past a couple of actors whom I recognized. *Not these guys again*, I thought. Another variant of the franchise had shot in my building a year before. I guess we look like a good crime-scene location.

Upstairs I broke the news to Gracie. "No park tonight," I said. "We'll go out later." She gave me a puzzled look and wagged her tail. I flipped on the television and that's when it struck me: there's only a thin membrane between make-believe and reality. Yes, once I would have been thrilled to watch a hit television show being filmed in my building. Was I becoming just another jaded New Yorker? Was I taking a pretty cool thing about the city I live in for granted? And if so, what else about my life, or even my faith, was I taking for granted? I turned off the television and pulled open the window. Why not watch the real thing?

Lord, do not let me become hardened to the things that once thrilled me.
Let me see afresh each day the world You have blessed me with.
—Edward Grinnan

Digging Deeper: Lamentations 3:22–23; Philippians 2:14–15

I have spoken, but did not understand; things too marvelous for me,
which I did not know. —Job 42:3 (NABRE)

There is a For Sale sign in front of our beautiful house. It pains me
to see it. I hadn't expected to be leaving my adopted rural Ohio
community after only four years. In fact, I hadn't expected to leave at
all. My husband, Mark, and I thought this would be our forever home.

The only thing that's forever is eternity.

It feels like a death, this sale. It's not only a death of a dream to live
more simply, more slowly, after nearly thirty years of living in New York
City and working in fast-paced media jobs there. It's the death of the
confidence I had in my ability to discern God's plan for my life.

I had been so certain that moving here to this old Victorian home
and opening a bed-and-breakfast was the next right thing to do. I
remember how the thought of it had rung me like a bell, shaking me to
my core, as my husband and I walked through the empty house with a
realtor. I'd had a vision of welcoming strangers and sharing the house's
history and beauty with them. I had even burst into tears in the entryway, crying out, "I've got to live in this house!" We threw ourselves into
our little hospitality business and delighted in our guests. But we've
found that new friends have been hard to come by and so has a livable
income.

So when the opportunity came for me to return to broadcast journal-
ism and city living Cleveland, this time—I took it. With that move,
there were no tears and there was no emotional earthquake. There was
just a knife blade of sadness and a haunting notion that this, too, was
the next right thing to do.

God, I have no idea what You want for me, or from me, today.
Help me stay faithful to You anyway.
—Amy Eddings

Digging Deeper: Proverbs 16:9; Jeremiah 29:11

Friday, April 17

You, therefore, have no excuse, you who pass judgment on someone else,
for at whatever point you judge another, you are condemning yourself,
because you who pass judgment do the same things. —Romans 2:1 (NIV)

On a recent trip to the grocery store, I found myself purchasing
a single brand of organic products. After a little metacognitive
analysis, I discovered my gravitation to this particular brand stemmed
from its attractive label. Full of regret for my shallow choice criteria
while such adages as "never judge a book by its cover" and "looks can
be deceiving" flooded my mind, I realized that my days are filled with
judgments based on appearances.

While the judgments I made about groceries can be innocent, often I
make more serious judgments. Given my propensity to judge, I started to
evaluate how often I made snap decisions based on personal presentation.
Too often, I have judged a person based on appearance. Does the person
look nice, honest, or trustworthy? Packaging, whether of grocery-store
products or a person's appearance, does not reveal the whole truth about
what's inside. Jesus, for instance, was not fully revealed in appearance
nor in the circumstance of His earthly life; He was the Son of a carpenter
from humble origins. Indeed, Jesus was judged on appearances.

Despite Jesus's experience of judgments against Him, He offers the
ultimate example in looking past appearances and into people's hearts.
His public ministry was filled with outcasts, marginalized individuals,
and the untouchables of society. As a follower of Christ, I am called to
daily conversion, to follow His example, and to preach the Word with
my actions. While I fall short, I, as is every believer, am redeemed in
Him. Following His example requires that my actions demonstrate the
Word and honor the dignity of every life.

Father, help me to reflect Your love to others through my thoughts, words,
and actions. Guide me to look past appearances and to see the hearts of others.
—Jolynda Strandberg

Digging Deeper: 1 Samuel 16:7; Matthew 7:1–5; Luke 6:37

Don't you know that the runners in a stadium all race, but only one receives the prize? Run in such a way to win the prize.
—1 Corinthians 9:24 (CSB)

I t's freezing!" I said to my husband, Zach. We were standing near the start line, ready to run our first 5K race in downtown Kansas City, enveloped in some 7,000 participants.

The countdown began; then a loud horn blared. We all moved forward. In that first half-mile, many people were sprinting—burning through their energy too soon. Others had already slowed down to walk.

Even though we were all strangers, we were still in this race together. Much like we are in life too. Paul's words ran through my head: "Only one receives the prize."

Zach and I weren't looking to beat anybody. In fact, we were looking for something else. A new way to experience Jesus. To physically feel the endurance for Christ that is often mentioned in Scripture.

As we jogged the rest of the race, I noticed each person that we passed. I wondered why each one was in this race today. What were the runners racing for?

Toward the last mile, my legs ached with exhaustion. How often this happens to us in our lives. At some point, we all start to feel an ache in our bodies. A feeling that makes us want to stop, pull back, and find an easier way. But Jesus never stopped or pulled back, despite the pain at the Cross. He knew what the prize meant for us.

I wondered how many others in this race were also experiencing the sting in their bodies. And I wondered how much harder it was to run this race—or live this life—if you weren't in it for the prize: Jesus.

> *Papa God, You've suffered more than enough to give us life and freedom. When my mind wonders if it's worth it to endure for Your love, whisper Jesus's name again in my ear.*
> —Desiree Cole

Digging Deeper: Luke 21:19; Romans 15:4; Philippians 3:12–14

Sunday, April 19

When they were discouraged, I smiled and that encouraged them and lightened their spirits. —Job 29:24 (TLB)

Nearly everyone who lives in Florida has experienced, at one time or another, some sort of precancerous or cancerous skin condition caused by the sun. Thank goodness, modern medical advancements are amazing when it comes to taking care of these various scares.

When my husband, Jack, was diagnosed with melanoma on top of his head, he had to undergo general anesthesia and the removal of the offending piece of scalp, along with a skin graft of his thigh to close the wound on his head. When I walked into his hospital room after he was released from recovery I was shocked to see Jack's entire head, cheeks, jaw, and neck wrapped in gauze bandages. Gauze covered everything including the spot where they'd taken a lymph node from under his ear. The giant turban that stuck up five inches above his head was so funny looking I couldn't help but laugh. He looked just like one of the Coneheads from the *Saturday Night Live* skits years earlier.

When I shared with our friends that they had to graft skin from his leg, everyone had comments like, "Make sure they take it from the part of his leg with the most hair. Maybe he'll have hair on his head then." Later, when friends and neighbors saw his ridiculous Conehead bandages, the jokes became even funnier. My cousin suggested a game of ring toss using Jack's head as the goal. The more we all laughed, the less anxious Jack and I became about his condition.

The thousands of prayers before, during, and after the surgery were certainly the healing balm that calmed us the most; but those laughs, oh my goodness, those laughs eased the stress, dissolved the worries, and gave us something wonderful to do as the healing process unfolded.

> *Gracious Father, thank You so much for the gift of laughter*
> *that heals hearts and heads alike.*
> —Patricia Lorenz

Digging Deeper: Psalm 126:1–6; Luke 6:21

We have received, not the spirit of the world, but the Spirit who is from God, that we might know the things that have been freely given to us by God. —1 Corinthians 2:12 (NKJV)

I thought my car would hit the young man, but it didn't. I was pulling into an oil change place, and the mechanic was guiding me in. My car crept forward, tires straddling the open bay below. He stood front and center, waving me in. I idled forward. I thought for sure he would tell me to stop, but he still waved me in.

Inch by inch, my car rolled toward the mechanic. I was surprised I hadn't hit him already. I just figured as long as he was waving me on, I'd keep moving forward.

This guy had a lot of faith in me.

As soon as the thought crossed my mind, I pictured God waving me forward. There were areas of life where He had been beckoning me to step out in faith. I was nervous. Overcautious. Foot on the brakes.

But God trusted me better than I trusted myself, just like the mechanic that day. Finally, he held up his hand, telling me to stop.

"You have a lot of faith in me," I said.

A smile lit up his face. "I knew I could trust you," he said.

I waited in the car while workers topped off fluids and checked my tires. I thought of all the blessings God had poured into my life. A great family. A thriving ministry. The confidence of His presence and grace.

A mechanic with greasy hands had banked his life on me. My holy and loving God had entrusted me with riches and resources more than words can tell. If He believed in me enough to do that, I could believe in myself.

The mechanic shut the hood and waved me out. "Have a good day," he said.

"I'm sure I will."

Father, help me to believe in myself as much as You believe in me.
—Bill Giovannetti

Digging Deeper: Judges 6:11–16; Romans 8:15–16

Tuesday, April 21

My life is deprived of peace, I have forgotten what happiness is;
my enduring hope, I said, has perished before the Lord.
—Lamentations 3:17–18 (NABRE)

My husband, Mark, is inventorying all his losses in our upcoming move. He is not happy. "I have to sell my home and my car. I'm losing my motorcycle and my friends," he says.

We argue over what furniture to take with us. The list will be small. We're downsizing from a spacious Victorian home with a yard, a gazebo, and a garden to an apartment on the fourth floor of a converted warehouse in Cleveland. We will be getting rid of nearly everything we'd invested in over the last three years for our bed-and-breakfast. I think of what it will be like to listen to the country auctioneer taking low-ball bids for the beds, the beautiful china, the rugs, the linens, the antique marble-topped dresser, and the vintage sideboard.

I feel like the prophet: "He has made me eat gravel, trampled me into the dust" (Lamentations 3:16, NABRE).

We're not just shedding material things. I'm losing a sense of myself as someone who can make something out of nothing, who can dream up opportunities and reinvent herself at will. My deepest nature is less pliable than I had thought. I'm not who I thought I wanted to be. My husband is heartbroken, and I feel responsible. He liked my dream of being a country girl and an entrepreneur.

The prophet advises me to stop dwelling on the losses. It's the main reason my soul is deprived of peace. There's a list to be made of the opportunities too. They're there, if I get honest. "To put one's mouth in the dust—there may yet be hope" (Lamentations 3:29, NABRE).

There is hope, along with the peace that always comes when I stop worrying and start trusting.

> *God, this experience is stripping me bare. May it*
> *make room in my life for more faith in You.*
> —Amy Eddings

Digging Deeper: Proverbs 3:1–8; 2 Corinthians 1:3–4

Love cares more for others than for self...doesn't fly off the handle,...always looks for the best,...keeps going to the end. —1 Corinthians 13:4–7 (MSG)

In fifty years of marriage, you'd think we would have learned how to argue maturely. Yet here my husband, Lynn, and I were crawling around under my desk, arguing like children.

We were untangling a mess of electrical cords, while listening to a voice on my cell phone, telling us how to unplug these cords from our old modem and into a new one. Neither of us understands this stuff, so we felt stupid and began taking out our frustrations on each other.

We had no dial tone on our landline, which was connected to our old modem. The new modem didn't look anything like the old one, so everything the voice said sounded confusing.

Voice: "See the blue plug?"

Lynn: "It's that one."

Me: "That's not blue. It's this one."

Voice: "Plug it in on the right side of the new modem."

Lynn: "That's the wrong side."

Me: "It's *my* right side!"

Lynn: "But you're not *right.*"

Me: "You aren't either. Let me do it!"

Lynn: "You think I can't do it?"

Voice: "Have you got it plugged in?"

Silence, as we exchanged mean looks.

By the time we finally got all the plugs in the right places and revived the dial tone, we were exhausted. The voice signed off, surely thankful to be done with us. We crawled out, stood up, and looked at each other.

"That was terrible," Lynn said. "I'm sorry."

"Horrible," I nodded. "I'm sorry too." And that was the end of that. Maybe arguing maturely means knowing how to end right. Maybe?

> *Lord, help me remember the power of "I'm sorry."*
> —Carol Kuykendall

Digging Deeper: Luke 6:37; Ephesians 4:29–32

She extends her hands to the needy. She is not afraid for her household when it snows, for all in her household are doubly clothed.
—Proverbs 31:20–21 (CSB)

Be generous, I learned from Sunday school. Plan for the future, I learned from my parents' well-stocked pantry shelves. It's still hard for me to make peace with the tension. Aren't *both* characteristics, which seem to be opposites, praised in Proverbs?

I think of friends who are neighbors to each other. Every few years, one or the other orders a truckload of inexpensive leaf mulch. It's dumped near their respective driveways, and they "share the wealth."

One spring I asked one of the friends if she could spare several shovelsful for my porch boxes. "Sure. Take some. Here are a few grocery bags for you. Double-ply, they should be strong enough."

This year I similarly asked a friend if I could have a few gallons of the *mucho* mulch sitting out front, on her side of the street. She hesitated. "I still have to mulch two trees. I'm not sure I'll have enough…And you'd have to bring your own container, of course."

Two friends. Two disparate outlooks. One optimistically convinced there'll be plenty more. The other wanting to hedge her household against a shortage; be prepared.

A neighbor friend is learning about opposites. Yesterday we played a game: What's the opposite of…loud? Long? However, her question of "What's the opposite of rainbow?" stumped me. My laughter ended the game, but her query led me to clarity.

A rainbow—God's colorful prism is evident only in the presence of opposites, sunshine and rain. Mindful of that promising image, I head to my kitchen to make a pot of soup. Some to keep. Some to give.

Lord, give me a generous spirit, even as I provide for my own household.
—Evelyn Bence

Digging Deeper: Proverbs 31:10–31; Luke 6:38

Therefore, if anyone is in Christ, the new creation has come:
The old has gone, the new is here! —2 Corinthians 5:17 (NIV)

What's under all that paint?

My son and daughter-in-law pulled into our driveway with one new-to-them *very* vintage Jeep CJ7 and two big smiles.

"What do you think?" my son asked.

"Pretty cool."

"It's a project," my daughter-in-law said.

I poked at a large rust spot. "Your work's cut out for you."

Grinders and sandpaper came out, and the pair began working through layers and layers of paint jobs and repairs. Their smiles remained.

A week later, the whine of electric grinders still filling the air, I checked out the progress. Sarah, my daughter-in-law, took a step back and considered. "We need to think of a name for it."

"How about '*Rusty*'?" I said. I'm nothing if not helpful.

They didn't think Rusty was funny.

But the thing was, the more they sanded and the more paint came off, the more rust emerged. Frustration reared more than a few times.

But, I have to say, those two never gave up.

Isn't that the miraculous hand of our loving God? He takes us into His arms with a smile and He gets to work, no matter how "rusty" we are. Sometimes the heavenly sanding hurts. But—bit by bit—off come decades of old paint and self-administered patch jobs. Stripped away are the rust-pockets of sin, self, and pain—things we never knew we had.

The old has gone, the new is here!

I'm proud of that young couple. That old Jeep looks pretty good now. Solid and shiny—restored with willing hands, hard work, and love.

I'm a little vintage myself. Maybe you are too. Aren't you glad our God isn't only the God of the past but the God of What Will Be?

Restore me, Lord. I need Your touch daily! —Buck Storm

Digging Deeper: Isaiah 41:18; Revelation 21:5

Saturday, April 25

The Lord is good to all: and his tender mercies are over all his works.
—Psalm 145:9 (KJV)

I packed my grandmother's picnic basket to the brim. Our oldest son, Logan, had called and asked if we'd visit. He was one week from his final finals. Then he'd graduate from law school. "I don't have much free time," he said. "But I'm tired, and I'd love to see my family."

The sun was bright, and I prayed as I loaded the basket. Homemade triple berry cobbler on the bottom. Artisan breads next. Logan's favorite healthy chips on top. I pulled a pretty tablecloth from the buffet drawer and rooted around until I found paper plates and napkins too.

My husband, Lonny, four sons, and I crammed in the van.

An hour later, we met Logan at a park near his apartment. There were hugs all around. My fifteen-year-old Samuel elbowed Logan. "Better feed this guy," he said. "He's thin." Sam popped open the back of the van. There sat the cooler. But no basket.

"We left it on the porch?" I asked. Six men felt the loss. I did too. The planning. The special foods. The perfect vintage tablecloth.

"There's a gas station right off the bike path," Logan said. "I'm sure they have bread."

Together we walked, spring sun on shoulders, to the station and back. Then we shared simple sandwiches. Chatter was a sweet song. The boys ribbed each other, and laughter was rich. We even played Frisbee.

I was grateful for a God Who reminds me that what we have is never as important as who we have. That from a great bounty, His blessings flow. That the greatest joy bubbles from breaks in our own plans.

"Thanks, Mom," Logan said as my men and I left. "Today was perfect." I could only agree.

Thank You, God. Your gifts exceed my plans.
—Shawnelle Eliasen

Digging Deeper: Psalm 135:3; Jeremiah 31:14

PACKING LIGHT

"Blessed are the merciful, for they will be shown mercy."
—Matthew 5:7 (NIV)

I had the privilege of traveling to Lebanon and Jordan with a team from World Vision to visit the Syrian refugee camps. Viewing life inside these camps was an eye-opening experience: the poverty, the hopelessness, and the inability to dream were everywhere. Refugees are the least wanted people in the world, and the lack of welcome in these host countries had worn them down. Those who had fled to escape death and torture don't want to stay in these countries—their biggest desire is to go home.

Seeing their plight firsthand had a strong impact on me. Meeting them face-to-face and hearing their stories tugged at my heart. The highlight of the trip was bringing the knitted items many of you had contributed to the World Vision's Knit for Kids program, an initiative that originated at Guideposts. How I wish all of you who furiously knitted and crocheted to bring warmth and love to these precious ones could have seen the happiness that lit up their faces as we handed out the sweaters, hats, mittens, blankets, and scarves. They squealed with delight to have something special just for them. Knitting seems like such a little thing to us, but to these children, it was loving out loud.

Father, bless each of these children. Give them hope and a future.
Heal our broken world, so they can return to where they long to be.
—Debbie Macomber

Digging Deeper: Ephesians 4:32; Hebrews 6:10

Monday, April 27

The Spirit of God was hovering over the face of the waters.
—Genesis 1:2 (ESV)

Pier 66 was filled with chattering teens and parents and sailing instructors for the "Back to the River" celebration of my son's after-school program. The sun was shining, the waters of the Hudson gleaming. It was the initiation of the spring season, when students launched the small craft they'd built during the long winter months.

The good news was that no one's boat sank. The better news was that each Monday from now on the youngsters would be sailing again. Putting teens in boats isn't what people normally think of when they imagine what public school in New York City is like. But my Manhattan-born and bred fourteen-year-old, who used to be familiar only with navigating crowded subways, has taken to the water with surprising ease. He arrives home exhausted each Monday after maneuvering around cruise ships, through tides, and in the wake of speed-boats. His sailing friends are almost all from different countries, neighborhoods, and ethnic backgrounds. The river—and a nonprofit called Hudson River Community Sailing—bring them together.

I chose an empanada from the potluck table and steered myself and my cup of lemonade toward a bench at the end of the pier. This was Stephen's territory, not mine. I wondered if I was supposed to talk to people, and decided that for today it was fine to let someone else take the initiative. I would rest in the sunshine, enjoy my spicy meal, and observe my son. He and his buddies clustered nearby, chatting in their newly deep voices and eating vast quantities of pizza. Periodically Stephen glanced my way as if to say, *I'm glad you are here, even if I'm hanging out with my friends.* That was enough. I was near the water, near my son, and a light wind blew in contentment like the breath of the Spirit. What more could I ask?

Holy Spirit, move over my heart and stir up love within it.
—Julia Attaway

Digging Deeper: Deuteronomy 6:4–9; John 3:5

The Lord replied, "My Presence will go with you, and I will give you rest."
—Exodus 33:14 (NIV)

I have a thousand things to do: reading assignments, notes to review, a spin class in an hour. I walk down the path that runs from the law school to the parking lot. I'm wearing headphones, listening to an audio recording of a lecture. I hate how rushed I am, but this is the life stage I'm in right now. Next month I'll graduate; I'm hoping that things will slow down.

I look up and see a ceiling of thin, new leaves covering the path. A week ago, the trees were just budding. In the intervening days of gray and rain, the leaves had surreptitiously unfolded.

I reach the edge of the parking lot, and my eyes are drawn to two trees. They are ten feet apart, straight and strong. In the past, I used them to hang my portable hammock. I wish I had time to do that now, but I have to keep moving.

When I reach my car, I swing my backpack off my shoulder and into the trunk. I open the driver's door, then look at my watch: fifteen minutes to spare. So instead of sliding into the seat, I reach under it and pull out a tightly wrapped bundle. My hammock is right where I left it last fall.

I return to the twin oaks and wrap a strap around each one. Then I clip my hammock into place and wriggle into a cocoon of parachute fabric.

The hammock sways back and forth. I take off my headphones and listen to the branches creaking in the breeze. I still have a list of things to do, and, in a moment, I will return to it.

But today there is sunshine. And I would be a fool to let the day slip by without soaking up just a few minutes of the beauty and rest that God provided.

Father, thank You for giving us sunshine and reprieve.
—Logan Eliasen

Digging Deeper: Psalm 23:1–3; Mark 6:31

Wednesday, April 29

"Be still, and know that I am God. I will be exalted among the nations, I will be exalted in the earth!" —Psalm 46:10 (ESV)

It was one of those crazy busy days.

My son had a poetry presentation, right before my meeting with the principal about the PTA committee. Then I had to take my car to the shop to fix that scratch, and then go to swim practice, a soccer scrimmage, and church youth group. Somehow, in the midst of it all, I would have to figure out dinner and pick up a bottle of laundry detergent.

My mind began to race. *How was I going to get it all done?* I didn't have ten minutes to spare in my entire day. I grabbed my purse and my travel mug of coffee and hopped in the car, my heart beating fast, my adrenaline pumping.

I bit my lip and prayed. "Lord, I'm feeling so frantic. Please give me a little bit of peace today." Five minutes later, my prayer was answered. But not with a wave of indescribable peace, a little cheer-me-on pep talk from God, or a sense of calm in the midst of the chaos. Instead, God answered in the way I least expected.

My mom called: My grandmother had fallen, broken her hip, her surgery was scheduled. Instead of off to the school, I turned right toward the hospital. The scratch on the car could wait, swim practice, the scrimmage, and church youth group would have to be missed. Dinner would be in the hospital cafeteria. I would be spending my day in the quiet of a hospital room, holding my grandma's hand, reading psalms, praying, singing, and being still.

Finding peace. Doing nothing but being exactly where I needed to be.

Father God, You answer prayers in the ways that we least expect. Yet, You always know precisely what we need. Help me to hear Your voice and be willing to respond to whatever it is You need me to do today.
—Erin MacPherson

Digging Deeper: Matthew 11:28–30; John 16:33

"Blessed is the one who trusts in the Lord, whose confidence is in him."
—Jeremiah 17:7 (NIV)

The store employee squinted as she surveyed the wall of laptop chargers. I drummed my fingers on my jeans. The final paper for my labor law class was due tomorrow, and I hadn't anticipated replacing a fried computer charger. I had already wasted an hour.

That's when the storm sirens started—loud and mournful. They were accompanied by an announcement over the loudspeaker.

"Attention, customers. A tornado warning has been issued. The store is now closed. Please seek shelter in the back of the store."

"You're kidding me," I said. The employee shook her head.

I followed a line of customers to a break room. The sirens continued their death knell to any plans of finishing my paper.

As I sat with the crowd of people, I couldn't stop thinking about the paper. My heart beat faster, seeming to match the pace of the rain on the roof. The woman next to me stared at her phone. The weather radar on her screen blipped as she twisted and untwisted a lock of hair. She was also nervous, but her fear was focused on the weather.

The weather didn't bother me. I trusted that I'd come out safely.

Why could I be so sure of God's power over a tornado but unwilling to trust that He would help me complete a paper? I was comfortable relinquishing my physical safety to God, but not my GPA. But the God Who calmed storms also cared about the intimate details of my life. I needed to learn to entrust those details to Him.

"Good news," the store manager said. "The tornado is passing, and the store will be reopening soon."

I was glad to be free to leave, finally. But there was even greater freedom in remembering to trust God.

> *Lord, help me to entrust all areas of my life to You.*
> —Logan Eliasen

> *Digging Deeper:* Psalm 143:8; Proverbs 3:5–6

April

HE PERFORMS WONDERS

1 _____

2 _____

3 _____

4 _____

5 _____

6 _____

7 _____

8 _____

9 _____

10 _____

11 _____

12 _____

13 _____

14 _____

15 _____

16 _____

17 _____

18 _____

19 _____

20 _____

21 _____

22 _____

23 _____

24 _____

25 _____

26 _____

27 _____

28 _____

29 _____

30 _____

MAY

"Six days you shall labor and do all your work, but the seventh day is a sabbath to the Lord your God." ...

—Exodus 20:9–10 (NIV)

His anger lasts only a moment, but his favor lasts a lifetime; weeping may stay for the night, but rejoicing comes in the morning. —Psalm 30:5 (NIV)

My best friend, I'll call her Jean, died suddenly on May 1, 2002, at age forty. It was such a shock to all of us—her husband, young children, family, and friends. Since then, I've always thought the days of spring—my favorite season of the year—were destined to be full of sadness. But as the years pass, I realize that during the spring season I am completely surrounded by happy memories of my dear friend.

In late April, a friend of Jean's and mine texted me a photo of a tree planted in Jean's honor, which beautifully blossoms each year right around the anniversary of her death. While this could be a sad reminder, it now assures us that our friend's spirit lives on.

Ironically, the day that I received the text message happened to be Jean's wedding anniversary—a day that always brought her such joy. The day after her anniversary is her daughter's birthday. When I think about the waves of love—agape love—that have surrounded her and her younger brother for their whole lives, I simply thank God for His mercy.

A few days later at an art show, I came upon Jean's favorite Henri Matisse print. After that, a string of songs that reminded me of her streamed through my earbuds as I walked to work one morning. I realized that while I miss my friend Jean, God has made it so that her memory lives on and on. And He has made it possible that the days around the anniversary of her death are no longer for weeping, but for celebrating the joy of having known her.

> *Dear Lord, thank You for placing joyful memories in my view,*
> *which allow the beauty of my friend's life to eclipse any sadness.*
> —Gayle T. Williams

Digging Deeper: Philippians 1:3; Philemon 1:4

Saturday, May 2

FIRSTS: Sensory Adventures

They pressed upon him for to touch him.... —Mark 3:10 (KJV)

There's one first-time so basic that I would never have thought of it if not for Becky. She was eleven months when her grandmother, our neighbor Sue, welcomed Becky and her parents into her home.

Becky was blind. I paid my first visit to the expanded household for her first birthday party, a cheerful affair with lots of singing from Becky's favorite records. Over the following months and years, especially after Becky's parents returned to full-time jobs, I visited often. The reason I gave for my visits was to give Sue a break, but both of us knew I came for the sheer delight of watching Becky explore her world.

Becky talked early, but it was her sense of touch that was exceptional. When you held her on your lap, her small hands were everywhere, swiftly, gently getting acquainted. Your face, your hair, your hands—wristwatches and rings got rapt attention. "She knows my wardrobe better than I do," Sue told me. Becky could identify my outfits too. Sweaters that were identical to my touch had subtle differences for Becky.

It wasn't just her hands that touched. Her whole body reveled in the feel of upholstery on armchairs, fabric of curtains, and texture of rugs. She had an ever-growing collection of nail and toothbrushes, each with a name and a place among her dolls and shape-puzzles. Her very first word was "b'ush." Smooth and lumpy, hard and soft, these simplistic descriptions that I'd considered adequate were for Becky broken into an infinite variety of sensory adventures.

And for a while after each visit, I too would feel the slippery solidity of my kitchen sink, the hard chill roundness of a door handle, and the fuzzy tickling of my bathrobe.

> *Lord Who makes all things new, what will I touch today*
> *with fresh awareness?*
> —Elizabeth Sherrill

Digging Deeper: Psalm 94:9; 1 Corinthians 12:18

Love is patient.... —1 Corinthians 13:4 (NIV)

I'm sitting at the round table in our bedroom, trying to find words to describe my feelings as I look out the window. Down the hill, I see the fields and our old barn where our two daughters kept their horses when they were growing up. Caring for horses together had been a bonding part of our mother-daughter connection. Sadly, for me, when the girls left home for school and adventures and independence, our horse season ended. After we found new homes for their horses, the pasture and barn became lifeless, and I rarely gazed out that window. Maybe because it reminded me of what I'd lost. The years of separating and seeking independence brought some broken places in my relationship with my daughter Lindsay. We endured some misunderstandings that grieved me.

It's springtime now and this year feels different; the pasture is greening up, the trees are leafing out. And two horses are once again grazing in our field, a sight that heals a sadness buried inside me.

Here's the surprising turn in the story. In our bumpy years, I assumed that Lindsay would choose to live far away when she went to college, married, and began a family of her own. Yet several years ago, she and her family moved back to Colorado and—can you believe this—they bought a house right next to us! Soon, her seven-year-old daughter became interested in horses, so they repaired the fences, cleaned out the barn, and found two horses that needed a new home.

Looking out my window today, I watch a mother and daughter, working side by side as they brush and feed their horses and clean the stalls. When they see me in the window, they wave. I'm suddenly overwhelmed with gratitude for this full-circle blessing, because Lindsay and I are now living a new story in a new season.

> *Lord, in a painful season, may I remember that my story is not yet over and that Your redeeming love can shape every new season.*
> —Carol Kuykendall

Digging Deeper: Psalm 119:50; Jeremiah 31:13

Monday, May 4

The word of God is quick, and powerful, and sharper than any two-edged sword.... —Hebrews 4:12 (KJV)

I'm not sure how our prayer group got started. There were six of us: four battling cancer, one who'd been healed from stage-four melanoma, and me. I have a couple of autoimmune illnesses and felt blessed to be included.

The faith of these ladies was like nothing I'd ever experienced. They walked the balance between life on earth and life in heaven gracefully. I wanted to be more like them. More like Jesus.

One night we prayed and the Holy Spirit joined us, His presence so sweet that I could hardly breathe.

Afterward, Denise, fighting stage-four colon cancer, recounted a childhood story. She picked up her Bible. "One Sunday at our little country church, the pastor—who was really old—waved his Bible above his head. With a gravelly voice, he said, 'This ain't no play-pretty. It's quick and powerful, sharper than a two-edged sword. Don't ever forget it!' Scared me at the time," Denise said. "But he was right."

We laughed, but her memory stuck with me. For Denise, the Bible wasn't a toy. You could see it in her eyes, her faith, her sense of humor— even when she prayed with her chemo pack attached to her waist.

Moved by her story, I came home that night and jotted the pastor's words on a pink sticky note. *This ain't no play-pretty.* I stuck the reminder on the cover of my Bible and decided to leave it on, forever.

Six months later, Denise went to heaven. The family asked me to share a few words about our friendship at her funeral.

All across the packed room, saints of God dabbed their shining eyes as I showed them my Bible and shared Denise's truth.

> *Father, thank You for a lesson in how to live and*
> *how to die—clinging to Your words.*
> —Julie Garmon

Digging Deeper: 1 Corinthians 4:20; Ephesians 6:10

Let us not lose heart in doing good, for in due time we will reap if we do not grow weary. —Galatians 6:9 (NASB)

It seems impossible, but I am now old enough to fully retire. While I do not intend to retire soon, it has caused me to ask, "What does retirement mean?"

Sometimes I do grow tired of long days of work and responsibility. I am aware of fatigue and the delight of falling asleep in my favorite chair long past midnight. And, with age, I relish freedom and wistfully gaze at my bucket list. I know I will choose retirement one day.

However, there is never a time to stop loving, to cease helping your neighbor, or to take your hand off the plow (see Luke 9:62). My wife, Beth, retired two years ago from Mercer University. Now she teaches English as a Second Language to international women. She is a deacon in our church. Beth visits my mother at a senior adult center, babysits our grandchildren, and even keeps our "grand-dogs" from time to time. She is modeling healthy retirement for me.

For each of us, retirement will come in our own time and with consideration of our uniqueness and our health. But the commandment to love God with all of our heart and to love our neighbor as much as we love ourselves knows no end.

Father, may all our years be filled with love, generosity, and service to others. Amen.
—Scott Walker

Digging Deeper: Psalm 92:12–14;
Matthew 22:37–39; Luke 9:62

Wednesday, May 6

*Through you we push back our enemies; through your name
we trample our foes.* —Psalm 44:5 (NIV)

I didn't want to make the phone call. The last time I'd spoken with
our landlord things had not gone well. Despite the time sensitivity of
what I needed to discuss, I avoided dialing the number.

All morning I reminded myself to make the call. All morning I didn't
do it.

What's going on? I finally asked myself after lunch. *Why are you avoiding this? You've made plenty of uncomfortable calls in your life.*

The answer came promptly: *I'm afraid.*

Startled by what should have been obvious, I was astonished at how
adroitly fear had wafted into my heart. But giving my amorphous dis-
comfort a name made it easier to address.

"I see you, Fear," I said to his wispy face, "and now that I do, I need
you to step aside." Caught, he floated off a bit, sulking at being called
out. I took a deep breath. I took another.

Then I dialed my landlord's number, still mildly uncomfortable but
thinking more clearly. I was not unhappy that the call went to voice-
mail. I left a message.

By the time I hung up, Fear had vanished.

> *Lord, help me to see and name my fears, so that I can push
> them back in Your name.*
> —Julia Attaway

Digging Deeper: Joshua 1:9; Psalm 118:6; John 14:27

Sing praises to the Lord with the lyre, with the lyre and the sound of melody! —Psalm 98:5 (RSV)

When I was a child, I loved listening to music. Records I played on a little turntable. I'd never heard a live orchestra, but I knew something about it from "Peter and the Wolf." Then one day I was invited to a real concert. Our next-door neighbor was a violinist for the Pasadena Symphony. Her husband asked my parents if I wanted to hear them perform.

Did I ever.

Our seats were in the balcony of Pasadena's venerable Civic Auditorium. I stared with fascination at the musicians on stage. There were violinists, trumpeters, clarinetists, and drummers, some of them tuning up, creating a cacophony. Finally, the conductor stepped onstage. He turned to the orchestra and everything went quiet. Then he raised his baton.

I was stunned. The music was like what came out of my record player. Only better. Infinitely better. Richer, fuller, melodic, captivating.

So that's where the sound comes from, I thought. That luscious orchestral sound came from dozens of musicians playing together, the string players sawing away with their bows, the brass blowing into glistening horns, the timpanist drumming. Nothing could have prepared me for it. Except that my records *had* prepared me.

I think reading the Bible is like this. What a rich collection of stories, poems, laws, history, theology, and wisdom. It's demanding, absorbing, and sometimes the concepts feel beyond my limited understanding. *Will I ever really get it?*

Then I picture a moment when a celestial conductor raises a baton and something magisterial unfolds. Like hearing an orchestra—a real orchestra—for the first time.

> *Lord, help me understand the music of the spheres,*
> *the music of life and being.*
> —Rick Hamlin

Digging Deeper: 1 Chronicles 23:5; Colossians 3:16

Friday, May 8

I will sing to the Lord, for He has been good to me. Psalm 13:6 (JPS)

The e-mail was from someone I didn't know, and it took me completely by surprise. "Our family is new to the congregation," the sender, the family's mom, wrote. "Our oldest son is going to be bar mitzvahed in the fall, and he doesn't have any grandparents. We've heard you speak, and we love the stories you tell. Would you consider joining us on the bimah for the part of the service where the Torah is passed down from generation to generation?"

I thought about it for a couple of days. Then I e-mailed her: "I am honored by your request, but I would need to have a relationship with the family, so that you would know who I am and I would know all of you." And there were a lot of people for me to get to know: In addition to the mom and dad, there were five children—two girls and three boys. This was a little overwhelming and presented a challenge I was leery about. I didn't really understand why they would ask a complete stranger to play such an important role in their family.

We met for the first time a week or so later. They asked me to tell them a story, and I did. Then we talked for a time and arranged another date to meet. In late April, the mom asked if they could take me out for breakfast on Mother's Day. I was stunned. Since I have no children of my own, I had never been part of a Mother's Day celebration, and it felt as if they were offering me the opportunity to become someone I had never been before.

As we were waiting to be seated at breakfast, Mom leaned over and said softly, "My children have been so excited about having a Jewish grandmother." I waited to feel doubtful, but this time it just didn't happen.

Dear God, thank You so much!
—Rhoda Blecker

Digging Deeper: Judges 13:17; Isaiah 60:4

THE FRIENDSHIP OF WOMEN

A friend loves at all times.... —Proverbs 17:17 (NIV)

I still miss her even today, and it's been over two decades. She was the kind of friend I adored from the moment she entered my life. She was a wonderful nurse on one of the floors of the hospital where I worked, and she and I shared the same interests—nursing, fashion, home decor, writing for healthcare publications, and faith.

Early in our friendship, my friend's mother was dying. We went out to eat at favorite diners and cafes to discuss how much our mothers meant to us. I mentored her in writing, recommending her for a prestigious scholarship, which she won. She showered me with thoughtful words and gifts to show her appreciation.

The Mother's Day shortly after her mother passed away, my own mother insisted I spend the holiday with my friend in a town several hours away, helping her clean out her mother's apartment. "Nothing would honor me more than for you to help a friend," Mom insisted. So I did.

Throughout our time together, we often talked about how we would be friends for life. "We'll be at the same nursing home," she said.

That's not likely to happen now. After my friend left our hospital, I never heard from her again. Phone calls and notes went unanswered. Mutual friends didn't know anything either. Finally, with no explanation, I had to face that our friendship was over.

Having this friend no longer in my life broke my heart. I asked myself a thousand questions. Did I do something to offend her? Was she ill? Did her husband not like me? Had family obligations consumed her?

It's hard when a friendship ends. You simply have to release the person to God, and thank Him for the season He gave you together.

*Lord, help me to trust Your timing and Your ways in all of
my friendships. Help me also to be a good friend to others.*
—Roberta Messner

Digging Deeper: Ruth 1:16–17; Proverbs 18:24

Mother's Day, Sunday, May 10

He makes the barren woman abide in the house as a joyful mother of children...—Psalm 113:9 (NASB)

I'm a mother of four and grandmother of twenty. I had a wonderful mother who didn't leave my life until I was sixty-two and she was nearly ninety-two. So for me Mother's Day is a joyous time.

This isn't the case for everyone. Some friends have lost young children. Others longed to be mothers, but it didn't happen. There are those whose mothers were (or are) mentally ill or troubled with substance abuse, while others were abandoned by them. Some have recently lost their mother, or are about to. Others have a thorny relationship with a child or mother.

There was a year when I didn't welcome this day either. In fact, the bond my children shared with me was so damaged that I told them I'd never felt less like a mother and let's skip Mother's Day. Thankfully, that listing ship was righted. It took time, effort, prayer, and faith from all of us.

What encouragement is to be found for a wide array of mother-daughter experiences? I find it in the Bible's story of Jesus in Luke 8: 19–21. Jesus had been traveling and preaching the kingdom of God. When His mother and brothers showed up, the crowd was so large they couldn't get near Him. Someone let Him know His family was standing outside, wanting to see Him. Jesus replied, "My mother and My brothers are these who hear the word of God and do it" (8:21, NASB).

Jesus wasn't disrespecting His birth mother. He was inviting all who respond to Him—Savior for the world—to join His family. To hold the honored place of mother. To be regarded deeply as daughter.

When Mother's Day hurts—for whatever reason—Jesus is telling a different story. A kingdom story of family.

> *Jesus, in motherhood and in daughterhood,*
> *my hope is fulfilled in You.*
> —Carol Knapp

Digging Deeper: Isaiah 49:15; Romans 15:13; 1 John 3:1

May she who gave you birth be joyful! —Proverbs 23:25 (NIV)

"Mom, we can't all get together on Mother's Day, so can we take you out for Mexican Monday night?" My eldest, Jason, sounded frustrated, a sign he'd tried to coordinate plans with his brothers.

"Oh? Where's everyone going to be?" I tried to hide my disappointment. I live close to my three grown sons, but we seldom get together. I'd looked forward to the gourmet dinner my middle son had promised to cook for me on Mother's Day, and seeing my sons in church as well.

Jason explained that they each had different commitments. "So I thought Monday would be the best option."

I mulled over his suggestion. "Okay. Sure."

But when I got off the phone, I wasn't satisfied. Much as I appreciated the fact that they wanted to do something for me, eating wasn't the most important thing. I just wanted to be with them.

Although we only live fifteen miles from the beach, Chuck and I don't go there. We always have too much to do at home. With our grandson Logan's schedule of school, soccer, and Scouts, the beach might as well be a hundred miles away.

But separately, my sons often go the beach. After working hard all week, the beach is their getaway. And who started that custom of theirs? Yours truly. When they were children and we lived in another state, we'd go to the beach on vacation. Wasn't it time I joined them there again?

"I want to go to the beach for Mother's Day," I told my husband, Chuck. "Since we can't get together on Sunday, let's bring a picnic and meet there on Saturday."

"I'll check with them," Chuck said.

That Saturday, my heart was filled as I watched my boys laughing together like old times. For me, that was the perfect Mother's Day.

Lord, thank You for giving me the gift of motherhood.
—Marilyn Turk

Digging Deeper: Proverbs 4:3; Luke 2:51

Tuesday, May 12

PRAYING IN PUBLIC: A Show of Remorse

The tax collector, standing far off, would not even look up to heaven, but was beating his breast and saying, "God, be merciful to me, a sinner!"
—Luke 18:13 (NRSV)

The older I get, the more I feel my need for forgiveness when my actions contradict the spirit of Jesus's teachings. Well into the second half of my life, I am more able to admit my failings to God—and to myself.

Could I admit them to others?

Christianity has a history of public confession. Indeed, some believed it to be the only path to forgiveness. Public confession expressed true humility.

How could I show public remorse without frightening people or being perceived as crazy? When I seek forgiveness privately or at church, I softly beat my fist against my chest, quietly repeating the words of Jesus's sinful tax collector. I'd try this during my daily walk.

It was terrifying! I didn't make an extravagant display of myself, but I knew that passersby could see my lips and fist moving. I sought to express humility, but I didn't realize I was also expressing empathy until I noticed the reaction of some students from a college on my route. In the past, the young people with visible or public manifestations of their disabilities would avoid me when I passed. But as a few noticed my forgiveness prayer, they stopped scurrying away and drifted closer. Some met my eyes for the first time. In the past, I'd respectfully not engaged them; now I gazed back fully, smiling. We were alike, wearing our vulnerabilities on our sleeves. The Lord had given us common ground.

> *Father, thank You for the capacity to recognize and*
> *help heal each other's hurts.*
> —Marci Alborghetti

Digging Deeper: Matthew 5:3–5, 7–8; 9:9–13

See, I am the Lord, the God of all flesh; is anything too hard for me?
—Jeremiah 32:27 (NRSV)

Just the other day, this was the conversation I had over breakfast with my six-year-old:

"Daddy, did you know some people dance before they walk?"

"No. How's that?" I said.

"I heard it in a song," she said. Then, she quoted from an old song that talks about someone's mother singing about her being a dancer before she could walk. How she learned ABBA lyrics, I'll never know for sure.

"Well, maybe that's just a fun way of saying something in a song, but it's not really true?" I suggested to her. But clearly, my avoidance technique was not going to satisfy.

"No way," she said, "if a mother said it was true, then it's true."

Oh, the wonderful, simple faith of children! No wonder Jesus loved them as He did, and encouraged us to model ourselves after them.

Even deeper, I believe, what subtle truth my little one had intuited! Her mother, my wife, has surely, unlike George Washington, told a lie at some point in her life. But when she advises our children, she is always in the realm of truth. No good parent would do otherwise. A loving mother or father does not intentionally lead their children astray. How much more, then, does God our Father love and care for us?

Thank You, God, for loving me. "Our Father which art in heaven..."
—Jon M. Sweeney

Digging Deeper: Psalm 77:14–15; Matthew 7:9–11, 19:26

Thursday, May 14

I pray that out of his glorious riches he may strengthen you with power through his Spirit in your inner being, so that Christ may dwell in your hearts through faith.... —Ephesians 3:16–17 (NIV)

It was a double whammy. A major move *and* a major remodel. We tore up our new house before we moved in. We ripped out floors, gutted the kitchen, tore up two bathrooms, and then moved in, in the middle of the chaos.

The next three months saw a steady stream of workers invading our sanctuary. They pounded and painted and sawed. My family dodged tools and debris. Boxes sat unopened, piled high in the garage. Furniture waited for flooring. Boxes waited for furniture. Our only stove was the grill outside. Our only refrigerator was an old clunker in the garage. Fast food became a reluctant blessing. Chaos reigned.

We endured paint fumes, early-morning hammering, daily disruption, dust, displacement, and disorder. My wife selected light fixtures and countertops. We built new walls, installed new floors, and constructed an essentially new house.

All of this to take somebody else's plan and transform it into a home that reflected our style, our personality, and our plan.

During the middle of the mess, I drove home one day and sat in the driveway. Contractors' pickup trucks flanked me. I was tired of the chaos. As I lingered in the quiet car, I felt God's whisper. "Your heart is My home. I'm using these stresses to create in you something beautiful. One that reflects My style. My grace. My plan."

Peace flooded in. God was doing in me what we were doing in our house. The results in our home were spectacular. My wife's tasteful eye turned a house I dreaded into a home I love. I hope God says the same about the dwelling place He's crafting in my soul.

Lord, make my heart a dwelling place where You truly feel at home.
—Bill Giovannetti

Digging Deeper: Matthew 7:24–25; 1 Corinthians 3:16;
2 Timothy 2:15, 21

Lord, You have been our dwelling place in all generations.
—Psalm 90:1 (NKJV)

After my parents died decades ago, I brought home a few of their books, including the King James Bible my dad had read in his late teens. This morning, with nostalgic curiosity, I pulled the dusty volume from my shelf. *Would its pages reveal anything about my dad's youth that might be relevant to me today?*

Pages of the Psalms were well worn. I examined the few that had fallen loose from the sewn binding and noted his fountain-pen underlining: Psalm 137:1, "By the rivers of Babylon, there we sat down, yea, we wept when we remembered Zion." At the margin edge, alongside some torn-away, illegible script, I deciphered one distinct cursive word: *remembering.*

Why did this verse resonate with a Depression-era teen? Maybe he was a homesick freshman in a riverside college town, trying to bridge his past to his present and future. I myself have traversed the territory. But that's not where I am now, facing challenges—shorter breath, stronger eyewear—that present themselves downstream, closer to the great, wide sea.

On the same page, my dad—before he was my dad—had underlined a second verse, even accentuating it with a check mark. "If I ascend up into heaven, thou art there: if I make my bed in hell, behold, thou art there" (Psalm 139:8, KJV).

I set aside the loose page to ponder later. As I closed the Bible, its black leather binding disintegrated in my lap. The book itself has fallen apart, but the words endure. From generation to generation, for the psalmist, for my dad, and for me—from a decade past to a decade future—our God assures us that He is present.

> *Lord, help me understand the eternal truth that*
> *You are with us at every turn.*
> —Evelyn Bence

Digging Deeper: Psalm 91

Saturday, May 16

He has committed to us the message of reconciliation.
—2 Corinthians 5:19 (NIV)

Sorry Sir, the seats are taken," mentioned one of the six marine captains sitting at a table for eight. Located at Kaneohe Bay's Marine Air Station, the expansive Officer/Senior Noncommissioned Officer Club provided a majestic view of the Pacific Ocean, exotic craters, and Oahu's Ko'olau Mountains. I was in Hawaii on a Guideposts military outreach ministry visit, seeing navy religious support teams who'd gathered for training.

Feeling somewhat out of place, I leaned in to my sense of unease, and spotted two marine captains at a table for eight. Again, no available seats.

Finally, practicing my "grow-through-discomfort" maxim, I shot up a desperate prayer, and saw a lone marine at a table for three. With a look of hesitant disinterest, the iPhone-engaged chief warrant officer III indicated that he was awaiting a sergeant major friend but space was available.

After a few awkward moments, the iPhone went away, and I introduced myself. Rather quickly, we became engaged in a significant discussion, focused on life after retirement from the military.

When the sergeant major arrived, looking like a recruiting poster of what every marine ought to be, I felt fortunate to be sitting with these leaders. Before long, we had a sense of connection, healthy pride, and ease as our discussion turned to profession-building mentoring.

I got up to leave and told my tablemates how honored I was to share the meal with them. It was the highlight of my week in Kaneohe Bay, eating with a marine chief warrant officer III and a sergeant major. Indeed, the fact that I write about it for Armed Forces Day shows the long-term impact of this bridge-building experience.

> *God, our Healer, empower me to bring peace*
> *and reconciliation to others today.*
> —Ken Sampson

Digging Deeper: 2 Corinthians 5:16–20; Ephesians 3:12

*Blessed are your eyes because they see, and your ears because they hear.
For truly I tell you, many prophets and righteous people longed to see
what you see but did not see it, and to hear what you hear but did not
hear it.* —Matthew 13:16–17 (NIV)

*U*gh, I thought, glancing out at my garden.

It was already late spring, and the weeds were taking over, competing with last year's dead plants still waiting to be cleared away. At this rate, my tomatoes and peppers would never make it into the ground on time. Why was everything I did always behind schedule?

My five-year-old daughter Aurora joined me at the screen door. She stood there for only a second before starting to point, excitedly. "Look Mom, look!" she exclaimed, as she burst through the door, running barefoot through the garden. I followed her. "Your flowers are blooming!" she said, crouching down for a closer look.

Sure enough, beneath the bric-a-brac of last year's growth and amid the weeds, a carpet of anemone flowers had opened—their brilliant white mingling with dozens of fragrant lilies-of-the-valley. Yellow daffodils danced just above them, and iris buds, filled to nearly bursting with their purple petals, would soon join the show. How had I missed this?

I had longed for this floral performance all winter long; yet when it was in full swing, I'd looked right at it and registered only work, weeds, and missed deadlines. I smiled at my daughter, her nose buried in the lilies-of-the valley. Sometimes I just need a little help remembering to look at the beauty of God's handiwork with eyes that really see.

*Thank You, God, for reminding me to put worldly worries aside so that
my eyes and my heart can see the glory of Your creation.*
—Erin Janoso

Digging Deeper: Song of Songs 2:12; John 9:25

Monday, May 18

He will take care of the helpless and poor when they cry to him;
for they have no one else to defend them. —Psalm 72:12 (TLB)

When my friend Heidi and I returned home from our week-long adventure in Tuscany, Italy, we were exhausted. I'd had two knee replacements, and extensive walking was difficult. Plus, the morning we were to fly home I had a horrible bout of food poisoning. Heidi had an ankle replacement the year before, and after all our walking in museums and on uneven cobblestone streets in Italy, we felt like we were in our nineties rather than spirited seventy-somethings.

With my stomach in an uproar I had no choice but to ask for wheelchair assistance. Heidi opted for it as well to take the pressure off her hurting ankle.

Our wheelchair pushers whisked us around for what seemed like miles in both the Milan airport and JFK in New York. They took us up and down elevators, down sloping corridors, through security, more elevators, through customs and baggage claim.

I started thinking of other times I've asked for help. Every year when I can't figure out my taxes, I ask our tax professional for help. I asked my husband, Jack, for help lugging suitcases up or down stairs. Whenever I get a new electronic device, I ask my brother-in-law for help. Figuring out how to work my new TV, I had to call the provider and ask for help.

I wish I were more self-sufficient, but that airport wheelchair experience reminded me that help is always available. And so is Jesus.

I just need to come to Him more often when I'm troubled, afraid, confused, disillusioned, angry, lonely, and especially when I'm grateful for His blessings. I learned at the airport that asking for help is a beautiful, comforting thing. Since then I try to set aside a little time every day to simply thank Jesus for all the help He provides.

Jesus, thank You for being my rock, my helper, my problem solver.
Thank You for never turning Your back on me.
—Patricia Lorenz

Digging Deeper: Romans 8:26–28; Hebrews 4:14–16

"Blessed are the peacemakers, for they will be called children of God."
—Matthew 5:9 (NIV)

It's not every day that you get to be a princess. My granddaughter, Shea, was determined to make the most of it. She looked as regal as any three-year-old at the theme park, dressed in a gown embroidered with silver snowflakes. A cameo of Princess Elsa (from Disney's animated film *Frozen*) adorned her bodice. Unfortunately, the layers of tulle hid a battery pack that not only turned the dress into a flashing light show but also played a rousing chorus of "Let It Go." Mercifully, the gown was a thrift store find and its soundtrack, sporadic.

But Shea had more on her mind than dressing the part of Elsa, whose frosty fictional powers almost proved to be her younger sister Anna's demise. Shea's true objective that day appeared to be clearing Elsa's name.

"Elsa didn't mean to hurt her sister," she explained to everyone—cashiers, ride operators, and even Anna herself. (Or, at least, the young woman dressed as Anna who was signing autographs.) When Little Elsa (Shea) finally met Big Elsa (theme park employee), Shea made sure the princess understood that Anna was okay. All was forgiven.

Shea was a pint-size peacemaker that day. Her tenacity in making certain that everyone, including Elsa, understood that Elsa's heart was good, even when the princess's actions seemed to prove otherwise, filled my grandmother's heart with pride. Perhaps it was Shea's way of reassuring herself that sometimes her own wayward actions don't reflect the amazing little girl she really is. All I know for sure is that with or without the light-up dress, Shea's heart already reflects some of the royal qualities of her heavenly Father, the King.

> *Dear Lord, show me how to be a peacemaker and grace extender.*
> *As Your child, help me mature into a woman worthy of being*
> *called the daughter of the King.*
> —Vicki Kuyper

Digging Deeper: Romans 12:9–18, Romans 14:19;
2 Corinthians 13:11

Wednesday, May 20

Unless the Lord builds the house, those who build it labor in vain....
—Psalm 127:1 (ESV)

Something's not right, I thought as I inspected my once-lovely double knockout rose bushes. The thick, dark canes had a scarlet hue. There were ten times as many thorns as last year. Each branch was gnarled. The once generous buds wilted before they bloomed. I snapped a photo on my smartphone and headed to the garden store.

My roses were the envy of the neighborhood. They flowered April to October. Neighbors stopped to inquire about them. They were low maintenance, I rarely pruned them, and they bloomed like mad. Our house even won "Yard of the Month." I was sure it was because of those red and pink show-offs.

At the garden center, I showed a salesperson my screen. She shook her head. "Rose rosette disease, more commonly called witches' broom. It's an incurable virus—best to remove the bush and destroy it."

Ugh! Five bushes in the front yard and three in the back. I decided to purchase replacement rose bushes while I was here.

"Oh no," said the salesperson. "The virus is insidious. You'll have to wait three years before planting more roses."

A lump formed in my throat and sadness enveloped me. Driving to my house, I couldn't shake my melancholy mood. It felt like grief.

Back home, I pushed a shovel into the hard ground as I sniffed back tears. Why was I taking this so hard? I was so proud of those bushes!

Maybe a little too proud.

Three years of rose-free landscapes would remind me that I was not the Botanist who was responsible for such beauty.

> *Lord, eradicate rose disease from my yard and pride from*
> *my heart. Plant humility—may it bloom profusely.*
> —Stephanie Thompson

Digging Deeper: Proverbs 31:30; Ecclesiastes 2:11

Do not forget to entertain strangers, for by so doing some have unwittingly entertained angels. —Hebrews 13:2 (NKJV)

Having lived in New York City for many years, I've earned the right to call the city home. I've also developed a New Yorker's sense of impatience, especially with crowds, particularly slow-moving tourist groups near my office downtown. One of which I got trapped in this morning just as I was about to cross Broadway in front of historic Trinity Church.

When the light turned green, I found myself engulfed in a throng of tourists. A man at the head of the crowd held a yellow pennant aloft and spoke about the church through a microphone. Undoubtedly, he told them in their language that this was where many people took refuge on 9/11. I tried to extricate myself from the crowd without actually pushing anyone out of the way but couldn't. I counted the minutes while people took selfies and shot video.

As we entered Wall Street, the guide pointed out old Federal Hall, where George Washington took the oath of office. I glanced at my watch. He then turned everyone's attention across the street to the New York Stock Exchange, epicenter of the world's financial markets. He gestured up Nassau Street to the bastion-like Federal Reserve. Finally, they turned in that direction, toward Ground Zero and the Twin Towers memorial, presumably. Finally, I broke free.

Free from what? I suddenly asked myself. From the false urgency of time? Here were people who had traveled across the world to visit my city, my home to see its amazing sights. Couldn't I be more generous in my feelings to spare a few minutes to stand in wonder with them, to commune with them? A few minutes that I could more than afford to spare?

*Lord, You gave me this place as my home where lots of people visit.
Let me always remember that Your Word teaches me to welcome
strangers. After all, I was once one myself.*
—Edward Grinnan

Digging Deeper: Matthew 25:35–40; Ephesians 2:12, 19

Friday, May 22

The steadfast love of the Lord never ceases; his mercies never come to an end. —Lamentations 3:22 (ESV)

It's the day our oldest son Logan graduates from law school. It's also the day we put an offer on a new home. Emotion is deep and wide.

My row of men sit and watch their brother receive his diploma. Logan stands, humble and strong, six feet one with a red beard. But I see my mop-headed little boy. The one I pushed on the swing while we sang. The one I read to. Built castles from the edge of a sandbox. My mom understands and she squeezes my hand.

As Logan walks across the platform, pride and joy swell in my soul. We'd given him roots and wings, and this tension fills me. Watching our boy step into life, into who God made him to be, brings peace. But this is the final launch: He'll move away. We'll move into our new home.

Soon we're in a sea of celebration, searching for our son. When we finally see him, we rush over. The brothers cuff him on the back. Hug him tight. Logan scoops our youngest right off the floor. When a friend stops to congratulate Logan, Isaiah's feet go back to the ground.

Suddenly my dad is by my side. "Precious," he says. He nods toward my boys. "Logan's hand."

While Logan talks, he runs his fingers over the bristly softness of Isaiah's freshly cut hair. This simple, quiet tenderness runs rich with God's mercy. It flows through my family.

It's stronger than change.

It's mightier than letting go.

All of my sons will stretch and grow toward God's plan, and today Logan paves the way. The home we'll launch them from won't be the same one we brought them home to.

But I'm mindful of mercy, and all will be well.

Lord, Your mercy offers safety and strength.
—Shawnelle Eliasen

Digging Deeper: Psalm 116:5; Hebrews 4:16

When Moses' hands grew tired, they took a stone and put it under him
and he sat on it. Aaron and Hur held his hands up—one on one side,
one on the other—so that his hands remained steady till sunset.
—Exodus 17:12 (NIV)

I ran my fingers through my beard, and then fidgeted with my graduation cap. Three more names, and I would walk onstage.

Logan Eliasen, Juris Doctor.

I didn't know if it was the thought of acquiring that title or the fact
I was wearing three layers of clothing that made me break out into a
sweat. Was I ready to practice law—to carry the weight of defending
other people's rights and livelihoods?

The line moved forward, but I was looking backward. I wanted to
return to being a student, where the only person I was responsible for
was myself. The past looked easier, more comfortable. For a moment, I
stood in the dark. My robes blended into the backstage shadows.

"Logan Eliasen," the announcer called, breaking me from my thoughts.
I stepped tentatively onto the bright stage. I looked out over the crowd.
The jumble of faces made my throat tighten. I didn't recognize anybody.

Then a whistle pierced through the silence and broke through my
uncertainty. My mom's whistle. The same one that had cheered me
on since Little League. And that whistle was followed by cheers and
shouts—the rest of my family.

I knew that I was going to be all right, because people who loved me
were on my side. And they would continue to strengthen and support
me as I moved forward into my career as a lawyer.

The shouts and clapping continued as I received my diploma and
shook hands with the dean. And as I exited the other side of the stage,
my mom's whistle followed me.

> *Father, thank You for providing people to hold me up*
> *when I am unsteady.*
> —Logan Eliasen

Digging Deeper: Ecclesiastes 4:9–10; 1 Thessalonians 5:11

Sunday, May 24

"I will send down the showers in their season; they shall be showers of blessing."—Ezekiel 34:26 (ESV)

I called my friend Anne. "Are you going to the cemetery this weekend?"
"Yes, Sunday."

"Would you like me to go with you?" I knew Anne pretty well. If she wanted privacy, she'd say so.

"That would be great." After church, despite raindrops and storm clouds, we drove to Arlington National Cemetery to visit the grave of her husband, Dick, a career army officer. Earlier in the week, soldiers had posted small flags one boot-length in front of every tombstone. Today civilians fanned out along the roads, hauling totes full of long-stemmed roses to lay alongside the flags. I pointed to a volunteer approaching Dick's sector, just behind the Tomb of the Unknown Soldier. "May I ask him to give us a rose, so we can 'have the honor'?"

As I said, Anne isn't shy with her opinions. "No," she said, giving a reason—something about the simplicity of the flag itself—that I didn't quite understand. With rainwater, we washed the marker. With bare hands, we trimmed several blades of grass. We prayed in silence and quietly reminisced. I asked again about the rose. No, she said.

We watched the end of the guard-changing ceremony—with a holiday-weekend bonus: a wreath-laying and a bugler playing "Taps" twice. Returning to the car, I noted a stem-broken rose blossom on the walkway. A stranger saw it also. "Is this yours?" he asked.

"No, but…" I picked it up and handed it to Anne. We both smiled. It seemed this floral remembrance was mysteriously meant for her to enjoy at her home table, rather than for strangers to place at Dick's grave. As we left the cemetery, a Sunday afternoon shower blessed us all.

Lord, show special grace to those who this weekend mourn
and memorialize their loved ones.
—Evelyn Bence

Digging Deeper: Psalms 4:1, 13:1–6

"Greater love has no one than this: to lay down one's life for one's friends."
—John 15:13 (NIV)

In the crowd of red, white, and blue outfits, the woman stood out in her khaki uniform, but her clothing wasn't the reason I noticed her.

"Are you the bugle player for the Memorial Day service?" I asked, pointing to the silver instrument in her hands.

"Yes. Although it's technically a trumpet."

"How long have you played?"

"Sixty years. I started when I was ten."

Behind us, people settled into folding chairs under a temporary structure as we chatted for a few more minutes before I took my seat.

Motorcycle riders from American Legion Posts 35 and 91 brought in Old Glory to start the program, followed by prayers, patriotic songs, speeches, and stories of sacrifices for freedom. After the benediction, we stood for three rifle volleys and the playing of "Taps."

The bugle player stepped off the stage and stood apart from the dignitaries as she raised her instrument to her lips. Military personnel stood at attention as the first notes went out over the crowd.

"I played "Taps" for my grandfather's and my father's funerals," the woman had told me. "Both veterans." Her eyes had gone to the 2,800 flags waving all around us on veterans' graves.

"I also played at my son's," she added as her eyes had swung back to mine. "My son served as a medic with the National Guard in Iraq. He died in the line of duty as a police officer when he returned home. He's buried in this cemetery."

She played the tribute with precision. Unwavering. I listened as she held out the last of the twenty-four notes, before lowering her horn. She stood a moment longer. Remembering.

> *Jesus, on this Memorial Day, may we be sensitive to those*
> *who have given so much for the freedoms we enjoy.*
> —Lynne Hartke

Digging Deeper: 1 John 3:16, 4:7–11

Tuesday, May 26

We do not want you to be uninformed, brothers, about those who
are asleep, that you may not grieve as others do who have no hope.
—1 Thessalonians 4:13 (ESV)

This Memorial Day my husband, Anthony, and I sat in the pew
of a beautiful Baptist church for my goddaughter's high school
graduation. I waited in anticipation for the moment she would stride
across the stage, extend her right hand, and receive her diploma. She had
worked hard, earned great grades, and excelled in dance and volleyball
as a student athlete. I looked forward to celebrating her achievements.

I also looked forward to my goddaughter's commencement speech.
Each year the graduating class nominated two student speakers, and
she was one of the chosen. I could hardly wait to hear the words of
inspiration and hope she would impart to her fellow graduates.

After a beautiful processional and opening words of welcome,
the school headmaster directed us to pay tribute to members of the
military. We shared a moment of silence for those who had lost their
lives in service to our country. Then we clapped, as individuals who
had served in the armed forces stood for recognition.

Lastly, guests with a family member who had served in the armed
forces were asked to stand. I stood, honoring my late father who served
in the army as a young man. As I took my seat, I was surprised by the
tears that streamed down my face. I was undone for a while afterward.

In the aftermath of my parents' passing, I've experienced many
unanticipated moments of grief. Each time, I'm reminded that grief
is a flame that never dies. Over the years, God has sprinkled showers
of blessing over this flame, lessening its glow, but it will continue to
flicker within my heart until the day I see my parents again.

Heavenly Father, help me grieve with hope, anticipating
the joy of seeing my loved ones again in glory.
—Carla Hendricks

Digging Deeper: 2 Corinthians 5:1–8; 1 Thessalonians 4:14

And the Lord God said, "It isn't good for a man to be alone; I will make a companion for him, a helper suited to his needs." —Genesis 2:18 (TLB)

After Dad died at age ninety-eight, our stepmother, Bev, went to live with her daughter in Maryland. So the task of getting rid of all of Dad's papers, furniture, tools, and various collections in their large northern Illinois home, barn, attic, garage, and apartment above the barn fell to my brother, sister, and me. On our first trip, my brother Joe and his wife, Linda, and I spent five days going through everything he'd stored in the attic during the seventy years he lived in the house he built and died in. We were shocked to discover that he had saved every card he had ever received.

As we were tossing the cards into large trash bins, a note on five-by-seven-inch lined paper appeared. In perfect Palmer Method cursive writing I had written, "I hereby state that I will not get married. Not Ever! Signed: Patricia Kobbeman, June 10, 1957. A TRUE STATEMENT."

I have no idea why, at age eleven, I had written such a thing. My parents and all their friends were happily married. Perhaps it was my silly response to Dad's teasing me about boys.

When I saw that paper I laughed because not only did I get married at age twenty-two, but I had a second and now a third marriage, the happiest one by far to Jack, my hunka hunka burnin' love. When I got home, I framed that "never getting married" declaration of mine to remind me that my plans are not always what God has intended for me. My first two broken marriages taught me valuable life lessons and prepared me for other life struggles. But I wouldn't change a thing about the way it all turned out because I trust God's plan for my life.

Father, keep my bullheadedness in check and remind me to always appreciate and learn from the gentle way You guide my life.
—Patricia Lorenz

Digging Deeper: Luke 20:34–36; Romans 7:1–3; Hebrews 13:4

Thursday, May 28

A word spoken in due season, how good it is! —Proverbs 15:23 (NKJV)

It's not that people don't care about you," I tried to convey to a friend who had lost an only child in a horrible accident, "it's just that they don't know what to say."

How often over the years I've had this same conversation. People in grief frequently find themselves alienated from others. Their friends avoid the subject of their loss. "No one speaks my loved one's name," they say.

The truth: It's awkward, difficult, painful to approach someone who is grieving. We want to bring comfort, but we don't know how. Trying to avoid being trite, saying something vacuous, or embarrassing ourselves, we say nothing at all.

After my brother, Davey, died, I got flowers, cards, and other expressions of sympathy. All were nice and appreciated. But there's one gesture that I will never forget, because it hit me directly in the heart.

It came from Lawrence, a man I know on social media. He is a donor to our work with AIDS orphans in Zimbabwe, and most likely we will never meet face to face. His message was simple, but it taught me something important. "I'll come and hold your hand," he wrote.

That was it. Nothing more. Six words. But the sincerity of the message was clear. Like the rest of us, he didn't know exactly what to say. But he didn't hesitate. He reached out with a few words and said everything someone who's hurting needs to hear: I care about you. My heart is with you. "I'll come and hold your hand."

There are so many ways I can be better than I am. When someone's grieving, I hope I can always remember to start with those six simple words, and go from there.

> *Father, give me the words that others need to hear.*
> —Pam Kidd

Digging Deeper: Proverbs 3:27; Romans 12:15

Train up a child in the way he should go, and when he is old he will not depart from it. —Proverbs 22:6 (NKJV)

My grandma Ruth watched my brother, Trey, hop off the school bus and run as fast as his legs could carry him. We met him at the back porch and for the first time noticed what he held—a plant inside of a small Styrofoam cup. I peeked over my grandma's shoulder as he excitedly explained how his teacher had sent one home with all of his second-grade classmates.

We rushed through an after-school snack; then Trey convinced Grandma to plant what she'd said wasn't a plant but a tree. My sister and I followed them to the far end of the backyard and watched excitedly as Grandma dug a hole. Then she set the tree in its new home. We dutifully checked its growth for about two months, but when it seemed stagnant and not as exciting as we'd wished, we quickly found interests in other things. And life moved on.

Years passed before I thought of that tree again—more than twenty years actually, and even then, it was only when my grandmother recounted the story. She's in her nineties now and my siblings and I have our own families. Now when we gather, our children run under the tree that once came home in a Styrofoam cup. At least three times a year I make a point of returning to my grandmother's house with my family so they have the opportunity to make memories in the same place where my family and faith roots were established. And I pray that my children will do the same.

> *God, thank You for a family that's rooted in Your Word.*
> *May we always remember the sacrifices we make for*
> *each other and the love that binds us together.*
> —Tia McCollors

Digging Deeper: Jeremiah 17:8; John 15:5; 1 Corinthians 15:58

Saturday, May 30

Cast all your care upon Him, because He cares for you. —1 Peter 5:7 (MEV)

M y son, Jonathan, and I had driven two hours for his high school tennis match. We joined his team, saw the schedule, and realized he wouldn't play for another hour. I left to pick up coffee. When I returned, I was directed to courts on the other side of the campus for my son's game. I drove over and enjoyed his match.

When it was time to head home, he realized his phone was missing. We retraced his steps. We asked other players. We called his number. We searched the grass and the courts. No success. Our worry grew. Had someone stolen it?

Jonathan borrowed my phone and looked up a Web site to help locate it. We had not done this before for his phone, and we weren't sure we could log in. My son persisted and finally produced a map with a dot representing his phone. But the dot was in a strange place, well off the street, and nowhere near the tennis courts. An older couple pointed the direction, and we walked down the block, anxiety growing with every step.

The dot was inside the high school's main office. It was after-hours, and the doors were locked. My son knocked. After an eternity, a door opened. A lady popped her head out. "Are you looking for your phone?"

A huge smile spread across Jonathan's face. "Yes, I am."

"Come on in."

A gentleman opened a drawer and pulled out the phone. "Somebody turned it in a while ago. It probably dropped out of your bag." I breathed a prayer of thanks. We shook hands and said thank you.

On the ride home, Jonathan said, "I'm glad there are still a lot of good people in the world."

"Me too," I said. "I'm more glad there's a really good God in heaven."

Gracious Father, I cast all my cares upon You, for You care for me.
—Bill Giovannetti

Digging Deeper: Psalm 34:8; Nahum 1:7; Philippians 4:6–7

He gives families to the lonely.... —Psalm 68:6 (TLB)

Last spring a friend and I were discussing a difficult family situation when she said, "Be grateful you have siblings that care about you. Not all of us are so fortunate."

I am fortunate! My sister and brother have supported me through every twist and turn of my life. They and their families have driven countless miles to attend happy events—my retirement celebration and grandson's commissioning as a marine officer—and sad ones like the funeral for two of my grandchildren's father. My sister sat with me during the long hours of my husband Don's cancer surgery. For my birthday this year, my brother treated me to a catfish dinner (my favorite) and a pink "cake" made entirely of cotton candy!

I am abundantly blessed by my siblings, children, and all of my family members. But here's the thing about blessings: they are meant to be passed on. Was there a call to action in my friend's remarks? I thought of the old rhyme my grandma would recite when I complained that life wasn't fair: "Dear God, Bless me and my wife, my son, John, and his wife. Us four, no more." Shouldn't I be sharing my blessings with a wider circle? I could include people who are alone at Sunday dinners at a local café. I could visit friends in nursing homes regularly instead of regularly being too busy. I could pray for and with people who are lonely. I could try to be "family" for those without close relationships.

It's been months since that conversation. Often my good intentions are just that: good intentions. But more and more, I'm actively trying to bless others with my presence, time, and prayers, just as my family blesses me. Those blessings are passed on and sometimes, more often than not, returned to me.

> *Thank You, Lord, for my caring family.*
> *Help me care for those who long for that same blessing.*
> —Penney Schwab

Digging Deeper: Matthew 12:46–50; Romans 12:10; Ephesians 1:5

HE PERFORMS WONDERS

1 _____

2 _____

3 _____

4 _____

5 _____

6 _____

7 _____

8 _____

9 _____

10 _____

11 _____

12 _____

13 _____

14 _____

15 _____

16 _____

17 _____

18 _____

19 _____

20 _____

21 _____

22 _____

23 _____

24 _____

25 _____

26 _____

27 _____

28 _____

29 _____

30 _____

31 _____

JUNE

*We have different gifts, according
to the grace given to each of us....*

—Romans 12:6 (NIV)

FIRSTS: Play Ball

"Man looks at the outward appearance, but the Lord looks at the heart."
—1 Samuel 16:7 (NKJV)

I was eight when my grandfather took me to my first baseball game. Papa lived in Miami Beach and brought his wardrobe of white linen suits, white shoes, and white Stetson hat with him for summers with us in New York. Aside from his clothes and his beloved Packard car, Papa lived frugally. He'd bought us the cheapest seats at Yankee Stadium, the bleachers in full sun behind the outfield.

Whistles and hoots greeted us. The other men had stripped down to their sweat-soaked undershirts. "Hey, Fauntleroy, whacha doin' in the slums?" When Papa, who was deaf, failed to respond, the jeers and catcalls grew angry. "Too full'a y'self to talk to us?"

A pushcart with beer and soft drinks distracted the crowd until Papa called out, "Two orange tonics, please." Howls of laughter: "Ever hear of soda pop, Pop?" And as they handed up the bottles: "Which one of you is the little girl?"

Then Papa opened his program and in the overloud voice of the deaf, shared his encyclopedic knowledge of baseball. "This man had played four years ago for Detroit and then was sold to Chicago. That one had batted 350 for New York last season but had a wrist strain in training. The next one was in his first year in the majors...."

"Excuse me, sir," said he who'd called him Fauntleroy, "Can you tell me..."

"He's deaf," I said.

For the rest of the afternoon, the seats on either side of us were seized by one man after another, shouting their eager questions into Papa's ear. We were drowned in orange soda and lavished with praise of which Papa was as calmly unaware as he'd been of the mockery.

Lord Who makes all things new, never let me judge by mere appearance.
—Elizabeth Sherrill

Digging Deeper: Psalm 139:1–4; Matthew 7:1

Tuesday, June 2

"You pity the plant, for which you did not labor, nor did you make it grow, which came into being in a night and perished in a night. And should not I pity Nineveh, that great city, in which there are more than 120,000 persons who do not know their right hand from their left...?"
—Jonah 4:10–11 (ESV)

I hadn't been able to sleep a wink.

My mind had been racing about my daughter's swimming relay. Even as I type, I realize how crazy this sounds. My daughter Kate swam about two-tenths of a second slower than her teammate Madilyn, and because of this, Kate was moved to a different relay team. I was so worried that she would be devastated that I spent an entire night fretting about it.

The next morning when Kate got up, I broke the news. She shrugged and said, "Wow. Madilyn swam really fast. That's okay. I like swimming with the girls on the other relay too."

I sat there in shock for a few minutes. She hadn't been devastated. She had been happy for her teammate.

I had to stop my whirring mind.

I turned to God, and the story of Jonah came to mind. Jonah had been fretting about a plant that had died. A tiny, insignificant plant. While God's concern was for so much more—for a great city full of desperately lost people who needed Him.

In the same way, I had to turn my worries away from tiny plants of things—things like who swam on which relay—and allow my heart to grieve over the things that pain God. Great "cities" of things like my daughter's character. Like kindness and patience and humility. Like people who need His love.

Things that are eternally significant, instead of things that last for mere moments and then are forgotten.

Father God, give me insight into the things that matter most to
You, so I can focus my time and attention on those.
—Erin MacPherson

Digging Deeper: Proverbs 17:22; 1 Peter 5:8

I urge... that petitions, prayers, intercession and thanksgiving be made for all people—for kings and all those in authority, that we may live peaceful and quiet lives in all godliness and holiness.
—1 Timothy 2:1–2 (NIV)

I'd never "trampled territory" for God and had no idea what to expect. I attend a ladies' small group. Last summer, our leader suggested that from June through August we forgo our indoor prayer meetings and have prayer walks in nearby communities.

Seven of us met on a June afternoon. A friend suggested we circle the police station seven times, just as the Israelites had circled the walls of Jericho. "If we spot any officers, let's ask if they have prayer requests," she said.

Won't that be intrusive? They probably don't have time for nonemergency-type questions. What if they don't believe in prayer?

Sure enough, on our first lap around the building, two officers headed toward their patrol car. My bold friend approached them and explained what we were doing. She asked if they had prayer requests.

"Yes, ma'am," one said. "We have financial needs. Marital struggles. There's unrest in our community. Officers are entering dangerous situations."

"We're not the only ones who need prayer," his partner said. "Pray for the people we're arresting. So much is going wrong in their lives."

"Pray for peace," the other added. "Wisdom. Discernment. God's mercy."

Oh, me of little faith. Their honesty melted all my doubts.

Before we said our goodbyes, our leader told the officers we'd be lifting their requests to God aloud as we walked around the police station. Beaming, they shook our hands with gratitude. Off we went.

During our final lap, we praised the Lord, calling out His names in thanksgiving—"Abba, Father, King of Kings, Jehovah..."

Father, when we prayed as the officers requested,
I felt such peace. You walked with us.
—Julie Garmon

Digging Deeper: Philippians 4:6; 1 Thessalonians 5:17

Thursday, June 4

To seek one's own glory is not glory. —Proverbs 25:27 (NKJV)

I don't think I can do this anymore," I whine to my husband, David. "I'm not sure it means anything. No one ever thanks me."

Once again, I have jumped into the middle of something I think is important. I've worked hard to make it happen. At this moment, it's organizing monthly meetings for people who want to learn about local issues. Finding meeting places is a hassle. Someone is always eager to tell me how I might do it better. I get little thanks.

I stop myself midsentence. Ego, I remind myself once again, is not my friend. I realize that I'm trying to accomplish something I believe in, but I'm mixing it up with selfish motives like recognition and self-enhancement. I forget that living my beliefs without static from the past or the future should always be my goal. In other words, now is all that matters. I am doing what I set out to do. Outside praise or criticism shouldn't matter, unless I invite in that mean old ego to react.

God spent considerable time warning us against egotism, conceit, and pride. Jesus was a walking, talking advertisement for living to serve and not expecting adulation in return. He told us to study the flowers and learn from them.

I think of the faces of people who come to our meetings, eager to learn. I think of our speakers, gratified that people care about what they are trying to accomplish. I finish working on the schedule, which had stressed me a few hours earlier. I send off the last e-mail and go to sit on the porch. The day is warm and breezy. The birds are singing. Life is now. Life is good.

Father, keep me in the present. Keep me simple. Keep me humble.
—Pam Kidd

Digging Deeper: Isaiah 5:21; Matthew 23:12

Cast all your anxiety on Him because He cares for you.
—1 Peter 5:7 (NIV)

I was the very first to hold her.

She cried the first day she went to kindergarten. *I* cried the first day she went to college.

And now I was just a few weeks away from handing off my little girl to the man who was to be her husband. *Where did the years go?*

Plans finalized. Dress bought. Meals planned. DJ hired. The wedding would be held in my in-law's backyard. Even the flowers planted in the spring would match the wedding's color scheme.

"Are you really ready for this?" I asked her.

Of course she was. But was *I* ready? Absolutely not. It wasn't that her fiancé wasn't a great guy; he was. It was just that this was my daughter—my pal.

It's hard to let go, isn't it? Still, time marches. The sun rises and sets, planets spin, and seasons change. I hold on to my daughter with a white-knuckled grip, but God gently reaches down and begins to pry my fingers loose, one by one.

Two things I know without a doubt—I love her, and God loves her more.

I don't think anyone likes change, especially when it takes us into unfamiliar territory. But, like it or not, change is a constant companion on this earthly journey. Life is a series of learning to let go—learning to *trust*. Sometimes it's a relief. Sometimes it hurts.

But when we trust Him completely with our lives, it's always *right*.

Come to think of it, there's one more thing I know—I'll cry again on her wedding day.

But that's okay. We'll both be cradled in the arms of the One Who *never* changes!

Lord, help me to walk boldly on the path You lay before me.
—Buck Storm

Digging Deeper: Deuteronomy 31:6; Hebrews 13:8

Saturday, June 6

Teach us to number our days, that we may gain a heart of wisdom.
—Psalm 90:12 (NIV)

"I wish we could go fishing together again," I said to my husband, Chuck.

"We will, soon," he responded.

I never thought I'd utter those words. Fishing was not an interest of mine before I met Chuck. But when Chuck and I started dating, ten years ago, he took me fishing and opened my eyes to the beauty of the experience. Leaving at dawn, we'd be on the water in time to see the sun peek over the horizon and slowly paint a black-and-white world with a palette of colors. As the gray sky turned light blue, the birds began to herald the new day with their variety of songs. The moment was magical, and even more special sharing it with Chuck.

For the first five years of our marriage, we went fishing almost every weekend, and I hate to admit it, but I became bored. The experience was no longer exciting and new, but mundane.

Then our grandson Logan moved in with us at age three, and those early fishing days were set aside as we adjusted to his schedule. For the last five years, the main activities are church, school, soccer, and Scouts.

Now I longed for that quiet, peaceful time when it was just Chuck and me out on the water. I felt like I was being chastised for not appreciating what we'd been able to do when we had the freedom.

"Logan's dad has changed his schedule, and now he'll be off on Friday nights and Saturdays, so Logan can spend that time at his dad's house. And we can go fishing again!" Chuck explained.

I jumped into Chuck's arms, vowing to always appreciate our time together.

Please forgive me, Lord, for not appreciating each moment
You've given me.
—Marilyn Turk

Digging Deeper: Psalm 39:4–5; Ephesians 5:15–16

PACKING LIGHT

These were his instructions: "Take nothing for the journey except a staff—no bread, no bag, no money in your belts. Wear sandals but not an extra shirt."—Mark 6:8–9 (NIV)

I have a friend who can pack for a three-week cruise using nothing more than a carry-on. I'm not kidding you. She has packing down to a science. To her, it's an art form, and to the rest of us, it's a marvel. Wayne reminded me of this as we started to pack for our anniversary cruise. My husband knows me. I need an entire suitcase for my shoes alone. I've never been able to pack light. You can forget about me traveling with a carry-on. There are things I need, items I can't be without, and a few of those are bulky and take up a lot of room. I can't help myself.

Wouldn't you know, the Sunday before our departure, with our bags half-packed, the sermon was on the sixth chapter of Mark where Jesus sends out His disciples and tells them to take only their staff and their sandals. Wayne's eyes caught mine, his message to me loud and clear: Pare it down. Get everything into a single suitcase.

So I did my best. As I thought over what I had planned to take, I began to understand what Jesus was trying to impress upon His followers: *He* is all we need. *He* is more than enough. We don't need all those extras that we tend to stuff into our suitcases of life. Scale back, reduce, and eliminate unnecessary items, like pettiness, resentments, and jealousy. Leave behind fear, worry, and pride. No need to cart around those burdens. Jesus wants us to pack light, learn from Him, and lean on Him.

Lord, I'm doing my best to get everything into a single suitcase.
Help me to remove the things that dishonor You.
—Debbie Macomber

Digging Deeper: 2 Corinthians 12:9; 2 Peter 1:3

Monday, June 8

His invisible attributes, namely, his eternal power and divine nature,
have been clearly perceived, ever since the creation of the world, in the
things that have been made.... —Romans 1:20 (ESV)

It was a tense meeting, as meetings tend to be at select soccer tryouts. We had just found out that certain teams were being divided, others were being formed, players were being moved, and coaches were being rearranged. People were upset and worried for their sons and daughters, and things began to get a bit more emotional than any of us had expected. Raised voices echoed across the fields. Angry feelings rose.

Then the coach stopped midsentence and pointed behind us. A brilliant orange full moon was rising over the tree line.

A collective gasp rippled through the crowd as the moon came fully into view. It's hard to describe that moment—the sunlight trickling away as streaks of moonlight burst into the sky. Every man, woman, and child standing there felt it. We were witnessing a moment of glory, a moment so beautiful and so inspiring that all else was momentarily forgotten.

We all stood there silently for a few minutes watching the sky light up. Lightning bugs floated around us as the moon rose and stars began to appear. Each of us seemed to breathe in the beauty and soak up the peace that came from what will be remembered as a magical moment.

I'm not sure if it was seconds or minutes later, but as if on cue, we all turned back to the coach and he began to speak again. Only now, the arguments and anger from before felt petty and insignificant. Worries about who would be on which soccer team, who would coach each team, and who would play which position suddenly felt silly.

It was soccer we were talking about. Youth soccer.

We had just witnessed the glory of God.

Jesus, when I start to worry about things that do not matter,
pull my heart back to You.
—Erin MacPherson

Digging Deeper: Exodus 34:10; Psalm 8:1–9

"Go and tell this people: 'Be ever hearing, but never understanding; be ever seeing, but never perceiving.'"—Isaiah 6:9 (NIV)

My earliest memories of the Catholic mass are…confused. I was very young, and our local church had yet to switch from Latin to English. Needless to say, I misheard a multitude of prayers and proverbs. For instance, the proper response to *Dominus vobiscum* ("The Lord be with you") is *et cum spiritu tuo* ("And also with you"). Me? I thought it was the Pope's postal code at the Vatican: et cum spiri 2 2 0, like Chicago 6 0 6, Illinois. Made sense to me—a handy address if you wanted to drop a line to the Pontiff in Rome 2 2 0, Italy.

Problem is, I continue to mishear prayers and proverbs. Oh, I clearly understand the words, but I butcher their intent. For the scripture: "Love others as you wish to be loved," I instead hear, "Love others when it's convenient." When I hear, "Remember the widow, the orphan, and the prisoner," I hear, "Give five bucks to a random charity at Christmas so you can feel good about yourself." And, my favorite: We're supposed to "Forgive those who trespass against us." Yeah, right.

My mistranslation of Latin at a tender age is understandable. My current deafness regarding clear commands is both willful and woeful. I have no excuse. It's not mere cherry-picking of biblical verse; it's out-and-out self-deceit, aimed at avoiding the hard work of faithful witness.

I've decided on my next step: Get my hearing tested. I'm not sure what procedures my health insurance policy will cover, but maybe there's a way to open both my ears and my heart.

Anyone know the Latin word for "co-pay?" I may need it.

Lord, let me clearly hear—and understand—Your Word.
—Mark Collins

Digging Deeper: Psalm 119:105; Acts 2:4

Wednesday, June 10

They began telling each other how their hearts had felt strangely warm as he talked with them and explained the Scriptures during the walk down the road. —Luke 24:32 (TLB)

I read once that, on average, women speak 20,000 words a day and men utter only 7,000 words. This information became the basis for a talk I give to women's groups: "Celebrating the Wild, Wonderful Side of Women's Friendships." I like to point out that one reason it's crucial for women to have close women friends is that men generally do not want to listen to our 20,000 words every day. But get a group of women together and we can chatter, exclaim, compare, complain, solve, reason, suggest, explain, advise, and sympathize while we all get our 20,000 words out.

One day, out of curiosity, I looked on the Internet to see how many words there are in the Bible. It said 789,650 words in my preferred translation. If I used every one of my 20,000 words a day to read the Bible aloud, it would take nearly forty days. That said, I have to admit that one of my favorite discoveries was the poem "The Bible in Fifty Words." Whenever I'm stuck for a way to begin my daily prayers I start with these fifty words:

"God made, Adam bit, Noah arked, Abraham split. Joseph ruled, Jacob fooled. Bush talked, Moses balked. Pharaoh plagued, people walked, sea divided, tablets guided. Promise landed, Saul freaked, David peeked, prophets warned, Jesus born. God walked, love talked, anger crucified, hope died. Love rose, spirit flamed, Word spread, God remained."

That pretty much covers it, right?

At the least, I've learned that words, whether a few or many, have a tremendous impact on the hearts and minds of those who hear them.

*Lord, when I'm upset or angry, help me keep my words
to a minimum. When I'm complimenting someone,
help me say as many of the right ones as possible.*
—Patricia Lorenz

Digging Deeper: Isaiah 50:4; Colossians 4:6

"Give, and you will receive...."—Luke 6:38 (NLT)

Every spring I teach a creative writing workshop in which students read and discuss one another's writing. Giving feedback is delicate. What writers really want to hear is that their writing is wonderful. Mostly it's not, though, and even the best writing can be improved.

I take steps to preempt hurt feelings by monitoring students' language. "Don't say 'I like' this or 'I don't like' that," I advise. "It's not about what you like. It's about what works and what doesn't."

I also nurture among them a writerly, convivial community. To that end, we sit face-to-face around a table and drink tea, and I regularly bring muffins, cookies, or some other baked treat.

The baking part got difficult this semester. Fully a third of my students were gluten-free. Despite recipes and advice from gluten-free friends, I couldn't get into gluten-free baking. It was expensive. I hated working with the sticky doughs. And the results were never as good as my baking usually is. My students' lukewarm reactions also hurt my pride. *They think of me as a bad cook!* I secretly lamented. By week three, I regretted my commitment to bake weekly.

Then I googled a simple recipe for luxurious chocolate cookies that amazed everyone—even me, though I'm no chocolate fan. Later I came up with a terrific cornmeal cake with rhubarb. I've since baked both gluten-free treats for friends and family, and everyone wants the recipes. And the gluten-free students said they felt uncommonly included through my efforts, which was, after all, the goal of my baking in the first place.

Serving others—even reluctantly—always rewards me.

> *Lord, help me remember the inevitable delight of giving.*
> —Patty Kirk

Digging Deeper: Proverbs 11:24–25; 1 Peter 4:10

Friday, June 12

Since the day we heard about you, we have not stopped praying for you. We continually ask God to fill you with the knowledge of his will through all the wisdom and understanding that the Spirit gives. —Colossians 1:9 (NIV)

Road trip with Mom, and I was psyched! I had a workshop in Santa Fe, and I wanted a traveling companion. Commitments kept my family homebound. Life was so busy that I rarely had time for important conversations. I looked forward to connecting with her.

Cruising down I-40, Mom mentioned an evangelical seminar she'd recently attended. The speaker explained how, while dining out, he would ask servers if they had prayer requests.

"That's awfully bold," I said.

"Half the time they'd share with him." Mom added with conviction. "Many people need prayer desperately."

Hours later, we stopped for dinner. A young waitress brought water while we waited. I took a chance, mostly to humor Mom and said, "We always pray before our meal. Could we pray on your behalf?"

She hesitated. "No...well...I guess. I'm pregnant."

We congratulated her. I was pleased with my little experiment.

The waitress returned with platters of steaks. "There's something else. I'm not married. My baby's father and I aren't getting along."

Mom nodded. The joy we felt earlier turned somber. Mom blessed our food and prayed for the waitress. She was within earshot of our table.

When she brought the check, she had tears in her eyes. "I was raised in a Christian home. My parents are in ministry. I haven't talked to them in ages. I sang on the worship team. Now I don't go to church."

Mom and I tried to comfort her. The rest of the trip we prayed for that troubled young woman each morning, evening, and mealtime.

Mom was right. People are desperate for prayer.

> *Lord, may I never be too timid to offer the gift of*
> *prayer to friends, family, and strangers.*
> —Stephanie Thompson

Digging Deeper: 1 Timothy 2:1–2; James 5:16

Jesus said to him, "If you can believe, all things are possible to him who believes." —Mark 9:23 (NKJV)

Have you ever watched as a young child begins a new, imaginative project? A fort in the living room. A tunnel in the garden. Teaching the dog to jump puddles on the sidewalk. It is astonishing how he or she believes it will work. Sometimes it *does* work.

I watched my first-grader on a rainy day recently as she built a castle out of cardboard boxes in her bedroom. It became an all-day project involving the box from a recently delivered refrigerator, black and red magic markers, a roll of packing tape, a variety of stuffed animals, and, for a time, our dog, Max, who was supposed to be the alligator in the moat surrounding the castle.

This dramatic creativity went on for hours until finally, the time came to construct the castle's roof. I continued to watch from the next room while my daughter gingerly placed cardboard pieces into position and then used books from my shelves to hold them there. She'd run out of tape.

But then, all at once, the whole thing collapsed. I held my breath. She screamed (so much assembled so carefully, suddenly fallen), but here's what surprised me: her scream lasted only for a second. A moment later, her face was popping out from a hole in the cardboard rubble. She looked at me and said, "Let's do it again!"

I want to find that kind of faith and determination again in my life.

With You, God, I can do it.
—Jon M. Sweeney

Digging Deeper: Mark 9:24; Philippians 4:13

Sunday, June 14

Let not loyalty and faithfulness forsake you; bind them about your neck, write them on the tablet of your heart. —Proverbs 3:3 (RSV)

It was a warm Sunday afternoon, and I was walking across 125th Street from the train station to the subway that would take me back to our apartment in upper Manhattan. The sidewalks were busy with a mix of tourists, churchgoers, and shoppers. I paused at an intersection where a man with a walker was trying to get up onto the curb. "Can I help you?" I asked.

"Yes," he said. He gestured toward the walker. Together we pushed and he got up on the sidewalk. Good deed accomplished. I was ready to head on my way, but then he asked, "Can you push me to the supermarket?"

"I'm going the other direction..." I started to say until my better nature got the better of me. "Sure."

He maneuvered around to sit in the seat of the walker and I pushed, trying to avoid the bumps in the uneven sidewalk (who knew there were so many?). We got to the supermarket. I pushed him up a slight ramp and in the door. Couldn't have been easier. "Thank you," he said, shaking my hand. "Can I buy you something?...I can use my food stamps."

I stood there stumped. That he would want to use his limited means to help me was beyond belief. I stumbled around for the right words, probably not grabbing them, and then headed home.

"Sometimes," I said to my wife, Carol, trying to explain the whole thing, "the kind thing you think you are doing is nothing compared to the kindness that comes back."

Lord, let me be always open to the opportunities to serve.
—Rick Hamlin

Digging Deeper: Acts 9:36; Galatians 5:22–23

Out of the mouth of babes...thou hast perfected praise.
—Matthew 21:16 (KJV)

Okay, I love my children, but let's be honest. Traveling with four little ones, from a toddler on up, is not material for a happy television commercial. You know, the ones where unrumpled children sit quietly, read their books, and smile sweetly at fellow travelers.

First, four children, at least ours, are very noisy. And one of them is always thirsty or hungry, or needing to "go," while another is grabbing a shared toy and yelling, "Mine!" You get the picture.

Today, as we sit in the airport waiting for a delayed flight, our youngest, David, will not hush. His vocabulary pretty much revolves around the nonword, *BaBa*. He has so far said it at least a hundred times. He points at the seat and says, "BaBa." He looks out the window. "BaBa."

He watches a man walking by, "BaBa."

Each one is louder than the one before: "BaBa." "BaBa." *"BaBa!"*

I'm ready to stand on a table to offer an apology for the racket to the poor souls around us, when a lady in a flowing sari approaches us. She looks straight at me and says, "My family is from Nepal. There, *BaBa* means "father." Maybe he sees our Father in everything?"

I'm not sure about Nepali customs, so I restrain myself from throwing my arms around her and planting a big kiss on her cheek. "Wow," I say. "Thank you."

I look to see what David's pointing to now. "BaBa," he says to a man being rolled down the concourse in a wheelchair.

And suddenly I see Him too. I see our Father, in the man in the wheelchair, in his caregiver, in the lady hurrying for her plane.

"BaBa," I say to David. "Thanks for the reminder."

> *Father, give me the eyes of a child so that I might see*
> *and offer You my perfect praise.*
> —Brock Kidd

Digging Deeper: Proverbs 17:6; 1 Corinthians 13:11

Tuesday, June 16

There are "friends" who pretend to be friends, but there is a friend who sticks closer than a brother. —Proverbs 18:24 (TLB)

Jack and I would have celebrated eight years of marriage today if he hadn't died last year. I was in my sixties when we married and he in his seventies, and although I knew we'd never make fifty years together, I was hoping for at least twenty-five. So imagine my delight when my dear friend Heidi and I traveled to Italy and I figured out that we'd known each other for exactly fifty years that month. We met when I was just out of college, and she was a ski instructor. We roomed together for a few months; then she was maid of honor at my first wedding and I was matron of honor at hers. We've lived in different states but managed to see each other every few years.

In Italy, I kept thinking about the power of fifty years of friendship. I'd watched her grow from a wild twenty-something playgirl to a devout Catholic, with a master's degree, who leads pilgrimages to the Holy Land and is a professional tour guide.

As Heidi did all the driving in Italy, sailing through at least 500 harrowing roundabouts that Europe is famous for, I thought about the gifts she'd brought to my life: her take-charge personality (so I could sit back and relax); her insistence on visiting every church we saw (so I could ponder my faith and appreciate the artwork); and her compassion when I got food poisoning on the last day (so I could rest easy while she managed to get us to the airport).

I may not celebrate fifty years with my husband, but my fifty years of friendship with Heidi has a backbone that will surely last until our days on earth are over.

Jesus, thank You for this special friend whose friendship can always be counted on and whose devotion to her faith has inspired and strengthened mine.
—Patricia Lorenz

Digging Deeper: 1 Samuel 18:1–4; Proverbs 17:17

Amazement seized them all, and they glorified God and were filled with awe, saying, "We have seen extraordinary things today."—Luke 5:26 (ESV)

It was a moment so precious, so divine, that I almost felt guilty listening in.

As a gift to the parents in the class, my son's first-grade teacher had recorded her class's morning meeting on the last day of school. We got to listen in as our precious children recited the date, their ABCs, their addition tables, their memory verse, and then shared prayer requests.

The teacher began to pray for their day. "Dear Jesus," she began. "You are so wonderful. You are Almighty God." Then a tiny voice chimed in. "You are love."

Another voice. "You are holy."

"You are good. You are kind. You are truth. You are hope. You are light. You are everything we need. You are friendship. You are joy."

Voice after cherished voice chimed in, each one sharing another attribute of our all-powerful and all-knowing God.

Tears sprang to my eyes as I heard these children worshiping God. The truths of our God rolled easily off their tongues, one after another, each one just as true, just as magnificent as the next.

Each child was full of wonder, full of awe as the words seemed to come in a divine rush.

I rewound the recording and listened again and again, my heart bolstered, my soul thankful.

In an ordinary day, I heard something extraordinary. I heard tiny voices, tiny hearts turned as one to the God who daily performs wonders.

*Thank You, Jesus, for the extraordinary ways You work in
my life. Fill my heart with praise and my tongue with words
to express the wonderful things You have done. Amen.*
—Erin MacPherson

Digging Deeper: Isaiah 66:2; Acts 2:43

Thursday, June 18

"While the earth remains, seedtime and harvest, cold and heat, winter and summer, and day and night shall not cease." —Genesis 8:22 (NKJV)

My husband, Don, and I live on a farm, so our family is familiar with the cycle of planting and harvesting crops using modern tractors, planters, combines, and huge trucks. We didn't know much about how people farmed on the Kansas plains eighty or one hundred years ago, but when our grandson Caden visited, he asked about farming "in olden days."

So last June we took Caden to an Old Fashioned Harvest Day, hosted by a Mennonite family in our community. It was like watching pictures from history books spring to life! A 1930s model tractor pulled a side rake that cut wheat so it could be piled by hand into stacks, or shocks. A horse-drawn wagon carried the shocks to a large stationary thresher that separated the grain from the straw and chaff. Antique farm trucks, planters, and tractors on display were from as far back as the 1920s.

"Farmers have it easier today," Caden remarked as he enjoyed a cup of ice cream from a hand-cranked freezer, "but I think the main thing is still growing enough food so that everyone gets enough to eat."

He was spot-on. Farm equipment and farming practices today are more efficient. The United States Department of Agriculture estimates that in the 1930s one farmer grew enough to feed four people. Today an average farmer grows enough to feed 155 people. There is also increased emphasis on soil and water conservation and preservation of wildlife habitat. But the primary goal remains the same: bountiful crops to share with our families and all of God's children.

> *Lord of the harvest, let me keep the main thing*
> *the main thing, in all areas of my life.*
> —Penney Schwab

Digging Deeper: Deuteronomy 24:19–22;
Psalm 126:5–6; Mark 6:39–44

"Be still, and know that I am God...."—Psalm 46:10 (NIV)

Would you like to go on an artists' retreat?" a woman from church asked me. My experience with retreats was not a positive one. They often included lengthy indoor workshops and speakers that left me wanting to jump out of my skin.

I politely declined the invitation, saying it was too expensive.

Days later, she called to say they could offer me a scholarship. I still didn't want to go, but as she continued to speak, my excitement grew. I would spend five days with a group of talented women in a beautiful island mansion on Alexandria Bay. It sounded more like a vacation than a retreat—something I desperately needed with the stresses in my life.

Everything came together. The boys would stay with their father, and I was able to rearrange my work schedule.

I could feel the tension leave my body on the boat as we neared the island. We settled into our rooms and had a feast for our first meal together. Every day would be a feast. The immediate connection I felt with these women was indescribable. Each day my only responsibility was to make art. I sat by the water and wrote, painted on the spacious porch, and lounged on the hammock with my guitar. I listened to the ripple of the water, stared at the clouds in the sky, and breathed in deeply the life that was mine.

That week I was reminded of the talents God had given me and the importance of sharing them. I realized how desperately I'd needed this time for myself and for my art and to sit quietly at God's feet. I'm just grateful God knew it too, because as reluctant as I was at first, He made a way.

> *Lord, thank You for knowing and meeting my needs*
> *before I even recognize what they are.*
> —Karen Valentin

Digging Deeper: Matthew 6:8; Philippians 4:19

Saturday, June 20

To everything there is a season, a time for every purpose under heaven.
—Ecclesiastes 3:1 (NKJV)

Our family knew summer had arrived when the big hearty mulberry tree in our backyard produced berries. Some berries could be tart, but the sweet ones were incredible. Mom said the tree was a gift to us from God. She would pick the berries off the tree right into a big colander, rinse and serve.

My dad viewed the tree as a mixed blessing. Mulberry trees are messy and birds love them (one reason we rinsed our take), so we had to put up with a lot of avian squabbling. The mulberries that made it to the ground stained our shoes. Our shoes stained the linoleum in Mom's kitchen when we neglected to take them off, which was often.

One winter when I was about six I was having a tough time with my asthma. "I'm sure that mulberry tree doesn't help," Dr. Volk, who still made house calls, said. "They give off a lot of pollen. Maybe you should consider taking it out before spring comes."

I'm sure my father was tempted to follow the doctor's orders, but getting rid of the mulberry tree would be like canceling summer. We just couldn't do it. I wheezed my way through the spring. It was worth it—for the tree, for Mom, for the birds, for everyone.

That year for the first time, the tree did not flower, did not produce fruit, and, presumably, did not produce pollen. And my asthma got better.

I have no idea if taking a season off is normal fruit tree behavior. I've learned since that only the male tree gives off all that pollen. Females don't. And mulberry trees can change their gender, which would have baffled me as a child. One thing I do know is that the tree went right back to producing big fat berries the next season. Our shoes were purple all summer long.

Father, thank You for all the wonders of nature whose secrets only You know.
—Edward Grinnan

Digging Deeper: Psalms 95:4–5, 96:11–12

"It shall come to pass that before they call, I will answer; and while they are still speaking, I will hear." —Isaiah 65:24 (NKJV)

Josie, my teenage daughter, was calm, though worry marked her face. Josie was driving to the DMV for that huge rite of passage, her driver's test. We had an hour's ride to the dreaded facility.

Anxiety creased Josie's eyes. "What if I fail? How long will it take? What if I don't hear an instruction?" We chatted and reviewed the rules of the road. I even got her to laugh. It seemed as if I had blinked, and my curly-headed baby had become a radiant young woman.

Pulling into town, Josie made a horrible discovery. She'd forgotten her contact lenses and her glasses. She could not take the test without them. Her permit would expire before we could get another appointment. We'd have to start the whole process over. My daughter was defeated.

I kicked into dad-mode. First, we prayed. Then I started calling optometrists. Maybe somebody local could help. Josie held back tears. The first two places couldn't help, but the third asked if I had her prescription. It was stored in my phone. Dad-victory! We found the doctor's office. A friendly receptionist greeted us. I brought up the prescription and handed her the phone. She disappeared into the back. Josie and I fidgeted on office chairs. I squeezed her hand and prayed.

After an eternity, we heard, "You're in luck," as the doctor handed Josie a box of contact lenses. I don't ever recall a smile that big.

"How much?" I said.

"No charge."

My heart overflowed for multiple victories. For Josie, as a new driver. For me as a scrappy dad. But most of all for our Heavenly Father, Who provided for His children's need before we knew we had One.

Father, Your abundant kindness and constant care make
my life a joy. I praise You as the ideal Father. Amen.
—Bill Giovannetti

Digging Deeper: Psalm 91:15; 1 Peter 5:7

Monday, June 22

"As one whom his mother comforts, so I will comfort you..."
—Isaiah 66:13 (ESV)

I sighed as I scrubbed the dinner dishes. Nothing was wrong; I was just in a melancholy mood of wishing I was anywhere except in my little kitchen, my elbows in suds, with a pile of dishes more to go. On a whim, I turned on the radio.

Tom Petty's "American Girl" filled the room, and I was taken back to almost a lifetime ago, when I was a high school exchange student in Corsica. I was on the dance floor of a mansion owned by my host family's friend of a friend.

Nearly sixteen, I couldn't believe the vastness of the world, the warmth of the Mediterranean Sea, or the fact that I was standing on a blinking dance floor that pulsed to the beat of the music. I'd been in Europe for a few weeks. Long enough to make friends that I danced and danced with, without a care in the world—until, amid the grandeur of it all, I suddenly realized that a huge something was missing. I had to get outside, away from the booming music and blinking lights. On the lawn, the starry sky stretched endlessly over the sea. I tried to figure out what time it was in my hometown. What was my mom doing right now? How could I ever explain all of this? I focused on the brightest star and wished for nothing more than to be home.

"Why are you so sad, American girl?" a new friend asked. I shrugged. I had no words.

The song ended and I sighed, a happy sigh of relief, of being home in my kitchen.

Heavenly Father, thank You for moments like this, when
everything comes full circle and life is beautiful—and the
only thing that's changed is my perspective.
—Sabra Ciancanelli

Digging Deeper: Matthew 28:20; Colossians 3:2

. . . but the greatest of these is love. —1 Corinthians 13:13 (NIV)

Our two vans, stuffed with ten children, eight adults, and lots of luggage, turned down a steep driveway in Bucerias, Mexico. Doors flew open and children spilled out, giddy-excited to explore this villa perched on a hillside overlooking the beach. Adults followed, equally as excited. This vacation was more than a year in the planning and unlike any we'd ever experienced as a family. My husband, Lynn, and I meant it to be a pure family celebration for our fifty years of marriage.

We'd all replayed the promo video of the setting countless times, building our anticipation. Finally, here we were, and the dreamed-about vacation was a reality. We toured the house, settled on who would sleep where, and then ventured out on the patio. Everywhere we looked was beautiful. A pool. The ocean. Bougainvillea and palm trees.

Then I saw it. One long table with many chairs. In the video, small tables had been scattered around the patio but now they formed a single table. Quickly I counted. Exactly eighteen chairs. Everyone had a place to sit. All together at every meal.

So the fun began. We had lots of water and beach adventures, many wet towels, and a few squabbles among little ones. A sacred re-reciting of our wedding vows, and a formal dinner around the table with many toasts. It was a glorious week, packed with memories. It flew by all too quickly.

As we waited with our luggage for the vans to take us back to the airport, our daughter Lindsay spoke up. "Let's thank Oma and Opa by naming our favorite things about our vacation." Words flowed: Pool. Sand castles. Surfing. Water olympics. Flea market. Beach games.

"The table," I said, tears surprising me. "I realized that every person here had a seat at the table because we got married fifty years ago. This family is the greatest testimony of our love."

I praise You, Lord, for the generations that have grown out of our love.
—Carol Kuykendall

Digging Deeper: Deuteronomy 4:9; 1 Corinthians 13:1–13

Wednesday, June 24

Beloved, let us love one another, for love is from God, and whoever loves has been born of God and knows God. —1 John 4:7 (ESV)

We spent the day of our twenty-fifth wedding anniversary packing. The movers were arriving in two days to transport us out of our too-small, too-expensive, and repeatedly bedbug-infested apartment to a larger, less-costly, and cleaner place. My husband, Andrew, packed his books. I took care of the kids' rooms, the kitchen, logistics. We ate takeout Dominican-style chicken and collapsed, exhausted, long past our bedtime.

It was far from romantic, but it was an apt summary of the lessons learned in a quarter-century of marriage. As Andrew filled yet another box with seemingly random items and labeled it "Miscellaneous #6," I bit my tongue. Andrew, in turn, sighed but didn't sputter when I ramped up into relentless efficiency mode. His ways are far from my ways, and my ways are alien to him. Yet if we had been perfectly compatible, we'd never have had to learn to set aside our preferences or to work through inconveniences.

Still, I did begin to hyperventilate when my husband spread books out on the floor of our new home to sort through them. But just then, Andrew looked up and said softly, "We should still go out for that fancy dinner sometime."

Startled, I took a slow breath. My practical mind raced to the money we'd spent moving, the expenses still coming due. I took another slow breath and sent up a prayer to the Holy Spirit to give me the words I needed. Marriage teaches one to do this.

I replied, choosing to look at my spouse instead of my worries, "we should do that."

Jesus, inconvenience isn't a sin. Use it to teach me the limits of my patience so that I know how and where I need to grow in love.
—Julia Attaway

Digging Deeper: 1 Corinthians 13:1–7; James 1:2–8

*"When you stand praying, if you hold anything against anyone,
forgive them, so that your Father in heaven may forgive you your sins."*
—Mark 11:25 (NIV)

During my son's first few months of his freshman year of college, he ran afoul of a roommate who maligned my son's reputation. As a result, school officials suspended my son for a semester.

That kind of setback would've been detrimental to my eighteen-year-old self, but it seemed to invigorate my son. He attended a local college for six months, worked diligently, earned a 3.9 GPA, and was steadfast about returning to his original college. The following fall, he was back.

My son put his energies into his studies. I grappled with negative emotions targeted at the roommate: anger and, I'm ashamed to say, hatred.

Sometime during this period, I rehearsed a piece with the liturgical dance ministry at my church, to the song "A Heart That Forgives" by Kevin LeVar. As I danced, the lyrics served as a balm, eventually easing my strong feelings against the roommate.

Fast forward to the end of my son's sophomore year: He succeeded in school and had great roommates and friends. My husband and I drove to move him out of the dorm for the summer, and while they were loading the car, I had a few moments alone in my son's room. That's when "A Heart That Forgives" started playing from my phone.

I stopped packing my son's clothes and listened. I thought about how pained I was when I first heard this song and how it quietly reminded me that in order to move on, it was necessary for me to forgive. I realized that over the past eighteen months, I had not just obliterated the bad memories but had also removed the hate from my heart.

*Lord, thank You for teaching me that forgiveness,
always and forevermore, trumps hate.*
—Gayle T. Williams

Digging Deeper: Ephesians 4:32; Colossians 3:13

Friday, June 26

"My thoughts are not your thoughts, nor are your ways My ways," says the Lord. —Isaiah 55:8 (NKJV)

W hat's wrong, Babe?" My husband can always pinpoint my mood by my countenance. "I'm good," I said, shrugging him away. It's a sunny, summer day but I'm in a gloomy mood. It's all because I'm having an internal battle with the "what ifs."

The questions never announce their arrival, but they sneak into my mind at the slightest hint of disappointment. They seek an open door and slip in quietly. This time it came on the tail of a family financial decision. *What if I'd continued to work in the corporate arena after having my first child?* We'd probably have fewer times of financial stress.

Another time, the "what if" came after the death of my paternal grandmother. *What if I had visited her one last time instead of only praying that she'd be healed?*

There was the time my son's nearly failing math grade was the only subject that kept him from the honor roll achievement he'd been working toward. *What if I'd hired a tutor instead of enduring the stressful weeknights when both of us were in tears wading through fractions and word problems at the kitchen table?*

Then my mind was flooded with other thoughts. Of the countless times God has supplied all of our family's needs. I was reminded of my son's academic growth and how he'd grown in confidence. I was grateful that the trench between my brother's and father's relationship had been repaired at my grandmother's funeral. It was the exact thing she'd prayed for, even until her last breath. God is faithful and does all things well.

Although we can turn back our clocks, we can never truly turn back time. So instead of worrying about a past I couldn't change, I headed outside. Because the Son was still shining.

> *Lord, help me to see the imprint of Your hand on my life.*
> *Thank You for ordering my steps according to Your plan.*
> —Tia McCollors

Digging Deeper: Romans 8:28; Philippians 4:8

"The King will reply, 'Truly I tell you, whatever you did for one of the least of these brothers and sisters of mine, you did for me.'"—Matthew 25:40 (NIV)

A s adoptive parents, my husband, Anthony, and I have often considered fostering a child or sibling group. My sister Lori has inspired this desire, having fostered multiple children over the years and currently fostering two young girls. Yet for one reason or another—work obligations; my husband's master's degree program; the daily responsibilities of raising our four children, ranging from elementary school to college—the time has never felt right.

I've spent several years involved in ministries focused on caring for orphans and vulnerable children in my community and around the world. Recently, my heart has made a slight shift. I feel drawn to helping not only children in need, but families in need. I wasn't sure how this change in focus would connect to my wanting to foster, but my heart was open.

Then one day I received a call from a friend. She and her husband had recently separated and were disagreeing over their children's care while she was out of town. In desperation, she asked if I would consider taking in the children for a few days.

I had many reasons to say no to her request. Anthony and I were both facing a very busy workweek. My kids had just gotten out of school for summer break, and I was already struggling to keep them entertained daily. I was also on deadline for a publication, having procrastinated for months.

Then I remembered my newly birthed desire to support families in crisis. My decision was clear. This was an opportunity from God to help a mom in need, helping her children as well.

In spite of the many reasons to say no to my friend's request, I quickly came to my senses and responded, "Yes, Lord. Yes."

Lord, help me to say "Yes, Lord," when You call me
to support others in their times of need.
—Carla Hendricks

Digging Deeper: Proverbs 14:31; Matthew 10:42, 25:34–40

Sunday, June 28

Let everyone bless God and sing his praises; for he holds our lives in his hands, and he holds our feet to the path. —Psalm 66:8–9 (TLB)

I always wondered why my prayer life perks up when I'm at the beach, finding it easier sometimes to pray there than at church. My beach on the Gulf of Mexico is near my home, just a mile-and-a-half away. When I'm there for four hours, I am in the water for three. The rest of the time, I'm walking barefoot in the warm sand looking for interesting shells, chatting with other beachgoers, or saying my prayers.

One day I read about a study providing evidence that the beach is the best place to recharge and unwind because it promotes good health, physically and mentally. Sea air is charged with negative ions that produce antidepressant effects and help balance serotonin levels, which help greatly with seasonal affective disorder. The repetitive sound of the waves crashing on the shore can calm your mind. Even the blue color of the water is psychologically soothing. The high levels of magnesium, potassium, and iodine, the minerals in sea water, help fight infection, heal the body of minor cuts and scrapes, and detoxify. Walking barefoot in the sand strengthens foot muscles too.

I cherish all those benefits of going to the beach, but the one I like the most is how easy the prayers come when I'm totally relaxed and floating in salt water. Every time I'm at the beach, whether I'm swimming, snorkeling, jumping the waves, floating, or kicking around, I'm in such a relaxed state that meditation, prayer, and counting my blessings just come naturally. You may not have easy access to a beach, but God wants to meet you wherever you pray.

Heavenly Father, maker of the oceans, lakes, rivers, and seas, keep giving me the grace to use my beach time as prayer time. Thank You for such a perfect outdoor cathedral.
—Patricia Lorenz

Digging Deeper: Psalm 107:29; Jeremiah 29:12; Colossians 4:2

Many, Lord my God, are the wonders you have done, the things you planned for us.... —Psalm 40:5 (NIV)

A month away, and I was in the last stages of planning a writers' retreat. Anxiety threatened to engulf me, but I held onto the belief that God had led me to direct the event. I have to admit, I was a little worried. What if no one heard about it or registered? What if I couldn't pay all the expenses? Daily I went to the Lord praying for His help and direction, trusting Him that everything would go well.

Never mind that I had never done this before. But I had been to such events, so I had an idea of how they should function—the schedule, the faculty, and the classes. First, I asked several well-known Christian authors I'd met at other, larger writers' conferences to be on the faculty of our small foundling one. Their agreement to participate was miraculous.

As each item was checked off my to-do list, I prayed that nothing would be left undone. Had I remembered everything?

Finally, the day arrived for the retreat, and as people began arriving, I began to relax. But then I realized there were a few things I hadn't covered. For one, I'm not techy, and someone needed to run the audiovisual equipment. The first night, when my own attempts failed, one of the attendees offered to handle it for the entire retreat.

Another thing I'd forgotten to do was arrange for pictures to be taken. But it just so happened that one of the attendees had brought his new camera, and he gladly offered to photograph the retreat.

Lastly, we needed a designated "prayer person" to pray for any requests that attendees had. Without my asking, a woman stepped forward and said she'd be happy to pray for and with anyone who desired prayer.

One by one, everything was taken care of. God provided as only He can.

Lord, forgive me for doubting Your provision.
—Marilyn Turk

Digging Deeper: Psalms 65:8, 111:4; Jeremiah 29:11

Tuesday, June 30

"Do not judge by appearances, but judge with right judgment."
—John 7:24 (ESV)

I used to teach middle and high school English. Part of my job was to teach grammar, so frequently my former students post their "grammar pet peeves" to my social media account.

I always thank my students, but inside I cringe every time I get one of these messages. While I think correct communication is certainly valuable, I also think that kindness is much more important than being right. I try not to delight in pointing out others' mistakes.

This past summer, my husband, Dwight, and I were out-of-state in a small town to visit his family. We stopped off at a locally owned doughnut shop. No one was at the counter when we walked in, but there was a whiteboard sign near the register, with the day's flavors written in marker: "strawburry" and "blueburry."

A veteran of the red pen, of course, I noticed right away. And I admit I rushed to judgment, wondering why someone hadn't caught this mistake. Simple spelling errors are, after all, unprofessional.

But when the owner of the store emerged from the back to take our order, she spoke in broken—but extremely polite and sweet—English. She was an immigrant.

I tried to imagine myself writing anything in her language, let alone moving to her native country and attempting to run a business. Would I be able to pull off a feat like that and have such a warm and welcoming smile on my face as well?

So while I may have caught a couple of misspelled words on a sign, it's safe to say I was not the smartest person in the room.

My husband ordered doughnuts and coffee.

I had a bagel—and a slice of humble pie.

Father, help me not to jump to conclusions, but to extend grace
just as You have taught me.
—Ginger Rue

Digging Deeper: Proverbs 25:8; James 1:19

HE PERFORMS WONDERS

1 _____

2 _____

3 _____

4 _____

5 _____

6 _____

7 _____

8 _____

9 _____

10 _____

11 _____

12 _____

13 _____

14 _____

15 _____

June

16 _____

17 _____

18 _____

19 _____

20 _____

21 _____

22 _____

23 _____

24 _____

25 _____

26 _____

27 _____

28 _____

29 _____

30 _____

JULY

When he hath tried me,
I shall come forth as gold.

—Job 23:10 (KJV)

Wednesday, July 1

FIRSTS: Computers

The old has gone, the new is here! —2 Corinthians 5:17 (NIV)

What if a first time is negative? My mother's mother was pushing her baby in a carriage, when the first automobile huffed down the unpaved main street of Ipswich, South Dakota.

"I was terrified," Grandmother remembered. "I snatched the baby and covered her face so the fumes wouldn't poison her." It was 1901 as the alarming machine bumped along a road rutted with the iron wheels of farm wagons. Most frightening to my grandmother: there was no horse. No visible explanation for why the thing was moving at all.

Grandmother never got over her distrust of cars. She and my grandfather settled eventually in Miami Beach, where each Saturday Papa lovingly polished his black Packard, but Grandmother refused to learn to drive. To visit us in New York each summer Papa drove for six days on two-lane US 1 with his wife beside him, informing him of every approaching southbound car.

I had the same distrustful reaction to new technology when computers first appeared. My move from an upright Royal to an IBM Selectric typewriter was enough. In 1981, I flew to visit our son, John Scott, and his wife. They met me at the airport—but where was three-year-old Kerlin?

"Oh," they said, "she's at computer playschool."

If a toddler could use one, I reasoned, a computer couldn't be that difficult. Yes, it was! My first experience was as traumatic as Grandmother's introductions to cars when three weeks of work disappeared into an electronic abyss, never to be found. I still have a wary relationship with cyberspace.

What if we were to take unhappy first-times to God, confessing our reluctance and resistance? Wouldn't He give us a brand-new beginning?

> *Lord, Who makes all things new, help me begin*
> *again with my hand in Yours.*
> —Elizabeth Sherrill

Digging Deeper: Isaiah 65:17; Ezekiel 11:19

Point your kids in the right direction—when they're old they won't be lost. —Proverbs 22:6 (MSG)

My phone pinged, and my heart gave a skip: it was nineteen-year-old Mary, messaging me from Italy. Photos of Lake Como streamed through, each more splendid than the one before. She told me about the ferry ride from Lecco to Varenna, and trivia about how parts of *Star Wars 2* were filmed nearby.

Aside from the joy of vicarious travel (and the keen thrill of hearing from my daughter daily), I've had nothing to do with Mary's trip except encourage it. Since she left the dance world last year, Mary has been attending college and working in a restaurant four nights a week. She has her own apartment, own income, and own ideas about where she wants to go. I am proud of her.

"We've stopped in every church we've passed!" she messaged, "They are all so gorgeous!" A gentle hope grew in my heart that the Holy Spirit will ping upon my girl's soul in one of those sacred spaces. Early adulthood is a tenuous age for faith, and my daughter has grown ambivalent about her beliefs. It is good that she can see others have built beautiful things for God. Someday she may do beautiful things for Him too.

In the meantime, I pray for her. I trust that when the day comes that her heart yearns for truth rather than adventure, she will return to the faith she was taught as a child. And—*shhh!* Don't tell! Can we all be happy that my young adult walked into a church *voluntarily?*

Jesus, Your love for my child—like my love for her—does not fade when she forgets about us. I entrust her to You.
—Julia Attaway

Digging Deeper: Deuteronomy 7:9; Psalm 86:5; Isaiah 54:13

Friday, July 3

"The Lord does not look at the things people look at. People look at the outward appearance, but the Lord looks at the heart." —1 Samuel 16:7 (NIV)

W e should get T-shirts that read "I survived Arthur!" a faculty member at the writers' retreat said.

Everyone laughed as they recounted their experiences when Arthur showed up in their classes.

Arthur is an old codger who lives near the retreat center and has a reputation for showing up at meetings in the area just to cause problems. He likes to start arguments and disrupt whatever setting he's in, whether it's a town hall meeting or a church. As a result, many people have shunned him and uninvited him from their events.

As the director of the event, I, too, didn't appreciate his rude attitude and the way he went about changing peaceful, informative classes into debates. Listening to the way each instructor handled the situation, I was angry that Arthur had caused such disruption and wanted to cheer for the way they'd put him in his place.

While the faculty made jokes about Arthur and his challenge, I was in full agreement and wondered what I could have done to stop him. But I hadn't spent any time getting to know him. He had arrived late for the retreat saying he got lost trying to find it, something I found odd since he lived in the area. I had quickly ushered him into a classroom so he wouldn't miss any more of the event.

But when Kim spoke up, the laughing stopped. "What a lonely man he must be to try to gain attention in such a negative way."

Kim's comment humbled me because I had not seen the pain, only the facade. Arthur was reaching out, but in a way that created negative results. Suddenly I saw a sad old man instead of a belligerent one. Kim had seen him through God's loving eyes, the way I should have.

> *Lord, please forgive me for looking on the outside instead of trying to see a person's heart within.*
> —Marilyn Turk

Digging Deeper: Proverbs 15:1; 1 Corinthians 13:1–13

Our citizenship is in heaven, from which also we eagerly wait for a Savior, the Lord Jesus Christ. —Philippians 3:20 (NASB)

Over the years, I'd often thought about my family tree. I'd heard stories, but with time a precious commodity, I'd never really looked into the subject. I was glad when a cousin told me he'd done just that. And I was amazed when he sent me the information his research had uncovered—a genealogical record tracing our family name all the way back to the 1400s.

What a thrill to see my direct ancestor on a copy of an original ship's manifest. I'd never known the first *Storm* made his home in the Americas all the way back in 1728—*forty-eight years* before our country declared independence!

John "Patriot" Storm and his son fought for freedom in the Revolutionary War. Laun Lee Storm went down with the USS *Arizona* and rests with his brothers-in-arms at the bottom of Pearl Harbor. A rich and proud history.

I'd always loved my country but somehow I'd never really felt *part* of it. These names, speaking to me from the past, changed everything. I belonged to something much bigger than "me."

A few short days later, I sat with my family watching a barrage of Independence Day fireworks. I've always celebrated the Fourth of July, but this year was different. Every flash and boom spoke of a life lived. That long line of men and women—my family—who helped shape this great nation.

And then to think it's just a taste—a tiny taste!—of what's to come. That beautiful day when I'll breathe even sweeter air and get to see so many of those whose names I share, face-to-face. That day—down by the riverside—when sword and shield rust in the dew of a new and glorious dawn.

Jesus, bless and keep this great country until all of Your children sing in the presence of our forever King!
—Buck Storm

Digging Deeper: Psalm 33:12–22; 1 Peter 2:17

Sunday, July 5

"When you pray, do not be like the hypocrites, for they love to pray standing in the synagogues and on the street corners to be seen by others. Truly I tell you, they have received their reward in full."—Matthew 6:5 (NIV)

This morning, in my daily read-through of online news headlines, I succumbed to one of those lists called "Ten Most Annoying Things People Do on Social Media." I agreed with most—baby spam, cliché quotes, selfies with animal-face filters (especially annoying!), gym selfies, selfies in general—but not with the weather, sky, and nature posts.

Who gets annoyed looking at a picture of a gorgeous sunrise or snow-covered field? I wondered. (Those were the only egregious posts on the list I was prone to post.) But really, how can someone not find photos of clouds, wildflowers, beagles, even bugs and snakes interesting, if not awe-inspiring? As Paul writes, it takes a dark heart to look at the created world—the very expression of God's divine personality—and not be overwhelmed with gratitude.

It must be social media itself that sours viewers. After all, posting an Instagram of nature (or a daughter, even a Bible verse) can be an act of pride. Pride has a way of sullying our best offerings. For me it does anyway. I'm not just saying *Isn't this beautiful?* but *Am I not a great photographer?*—or worse *Am I not a fine person for drawing this to your attention?*

How much better it would be for me to take a walk with a lonely person than to merely show her—and the rest of the world—the beauties I'd seen while off by myself. This is why I think God repeatedly tells us, "I desire mercy, not sacrifice" (Hosea 6:6, Matthew 9:13, 12:7, NIV). He wants genuine beauty of spirit, not show-offy pictures of our holiness.

Father, make me love the way You love.
—Patty Kirk

Digging Deeper: Luke 18:9–14; James 4:6

Do not be deceived: "Evil company corrupts good habits."
—1 Corinthians 15:33 (NKJV)

The college campus was empty, the summer offered triple-digit heat, and the parking lot was far away. So, when I taught a one-week intensive class at our local seminary, I parked right in front of the building. The No Parking on Campus Streets signs didn't deter me. That's not because I'm a scofflaw, but because the head of security had told me that the parking rule didn't apply during the summer break. The sign was there for student safety but there were hardly any students to protect. My small class was the only one on campus that week.

On the first day of class, my car was the only vehicle on an empty street, steps away from the front door. Students had dutifully parked in the lot and trudged a quarter mile in blistering heat to the classroom.

On the second day of class, another car joined mine. By day three, there were three cars. By the end of the week, the whole campus street was full of cars, right in front of the sign that prohibited parking there.

It was a sobering realization for me. The example I set mattered. Those around me would follow my lead, for good or for bad.

God whispered to my spirit the importance of being faithful. My family, children, friends, church—needed to see God's grace lived out.

On the last day of class, I pulled up to park as a student was getting out of his car. I greeted him and asked, "Why did you park here?"

"Because everyone else was," he said.

"What about the no-parking sign?"

"I figured nobody cared," he said.

I felt convicted. In the grand scheme of things, parking isn't a big deal. But setting a good example *is*, and God was calling me higher.

Father, lead me in ways that lead others to Your grace.
—Bill Giovannetti

Digging Deeper: Psalm 139:23–24; 1 Timothy 4:12; James 4:17

Tuesday, July 7

The Lord knows the days of the blameless, and their heritage will remain forever. —Psalm 37:18 (ESV)

When my dad passed away in 2015, I had one regret. I'd never completed the memoir he had asked me to help him write. I was a daddy's girl, and my memories of him are fond. And yet, I have this one regret.

During the Fourth of July weekend this year, my husband, Anthony, our four children, and I ventured a few hours away from our Tennessee home to Atlanta, Georgia. We spent our time there learning and revisiting our nation's history at the Center for Civil and Human Rights Museum, visiting historically Black universities, and watching an amazing holiday fireworks show.

My most memorable time there was our visit with my dad's cousin Donald, who is more like an uncle to me. When my parents passed away, my phone calls to Donald were filled with memories of my folks and many shared tears. During my visit, we caught up on family news and quickly segued to stories of his childhood memories. Having grown up in a house next door to my father, he had memories of my dad as a little boy and a teenager.

He spoke of working the farm, collecting unique coins, and dabbling in mischief, and shared a huge part of the family's history that I had never heard. My grandparents were sharecroppers, farming the land they lived on in exchange for the house they rented from the landowners. I had read multiple books about sharecropping, but had no idea this common way of life in the South fit into my own ancestors' story.

I left Cousin Donald's home with renewed inspiration to share my dad's story, and I've been telling it ever since. One day I hope to share it in written form. I relish the joy of a promise kept.

> *Lord, thank You for the sacrifices my ancestors made so*
> *I might enjoy a life of freedom.*
> —Carla Hendricks

Digging Deeper: Proverbs 13:22, 20:7; Hebrews 12:1

"How can you say to your neighbor, 'Let me take the speck out of your eye,' while the log is in your own eye?" —Matthew 7:4 (NRSV)

The woman, late and dressed in a brightly flowered dress and fuchsia jacket, strode up the church aisle and settled in a front pew. Head high, she sat, her attention focused on the minister. My attention was on her.

"I can't believe her," I grumbled to my husband, Charlie. "Ten minutes late, and she has to walk to the front? In front of everyone?"

Charlie gave me a look. We've been married long enough for me to know his looks. This one meant *As if you're never late?*

Okay, I'm always late. But usually just a few minutes, and when I am late, I creep into the back of the church, and slip into the last seat. I don't parade down the center aisle, heels clicking, making sure I'm the center of attention.

As the service continued, I noticed that the woman seemed to be intent on the minister's sermon. She often nodded as if to encourage him. When a deacon asked for help bringing the gifts, she leapt up immediately. During the Peace Greeting, she went down the aisle greeting everyone, especially those sitting alone. After church, I saw her shake the minister's hand enthusiastically and hug his wife. Then she helped an older woman go down the steps, so the woman didn't have to use the disability ramp alone at the other end of the building.

I felt ashamed that I had been judgmental. I was witnessing one of the best modelers of Christian conduct I'd ever seen, and I'd been too critical to realize it.

I wasn't the only one who noticed. As we walked to the car, Charlie gave me another look. And I knew what that one meant too.

Lord, remove the log in my eye so I can see the examples You give me.
—Marci Alborghetti

Digging Deeper: Psalms 141:3; James 4:11–12

Thursday, July 9

Take away the disgrace I dread.... —Psalm 119:39 (NIV)

L ast summer, I was preparing for a rare trip to visit one of my nieces when I found myself putting too much equity into what I would wear while there. I always know when the scale is tipping away from excitement toward frustration, and as I scurried around the house readying myself for the flight, I felt my anxieties skyrocketing.

"Why," I asked myself, "am I turning an event I have so looked forward to into a veritable chore?" I was reshaping a potential joy into a near-dread, and deep down, I understood the reason: fear of facing the inevitability of aging.

I'm slower and they'll know it. I'm fatter and they'll see it.

I was dreading the reality of my loved ones seeing the person I had become.

Then I read Psalm 119, which prodded me to seek the ageless One. "Take away the disgrace," it read, which I was unwittingly allowing my golden years to become. I began to reset my priorities. I saw myself not for who I was in the flesh but who I am in the Spirit: a blessed woman of God who has been given the gift of maturity. What the enemy of my peace, through the culture I live in, had insidiously suggested was *dis*grace, was, in truth, *grace.*

Whether the psalmist suffered reproach from his own sins or from anticipation of what lay ahead from his mocking enemies, without God's grace the result was the same: dread. But through prayer and supplication we are able to turn situational anxiety into confident peace.

Lord, thank You for access to the Holy of Holies,
where dread can be turned into rest.
—Jacqueline F. Wheelock

Digging Deeper: 2 Corinthians 4:16; Hebrews 4:15–16

Open thou mine eyes, that I may behold wondrous things....
—Psalm 119:18 (KJV)

I have a sort of satellite office at our Alabama cabin. There, I have the finance channels and the intricate workings of the stock market at my fingertips. So, occasionally, I hole up there to work without interruption. At home, my assistant is waiting for anything I need to pass on to her. It's a great way to work through an overload.

Except for the *cabin rule.*

There is a sacred time of day on this rural island, which has been in place since the cabin was built. It approaches now, as the sky takes on a pinkish hue. I leave my work, push my chair under the desk, and walk outside. The golden hour has come. It's sunset time!

Family lore says that my grandfather chose this very spot to build the cabin with the perfect sunset in mind.

It's been a family rite ever since: "Stop what you're doing, and watch the sun set."

The cabin rule has taught me that people can find the deeper things they long for if they stop to see the sunset, take in the night stars, or delight in rain showers, budding trees, the leaves of fall, and the crunch of snow.

Why? Because God waits there.

We can show up broken, flawed, lonely, and discouraged, and there He is, amid His unfathomable creation. We can't understand it. We can't deny it. In a way, it's His most clever rendition of "I Am."

Now, as the sun sinks beyond the distant mountain, I offer a prayer of thanks for the golden hour. The cabin rule, you see, is just a simple invitation to stop and let our eyes linger on God's wondrous world. "Come, sit a while, enjoy My view," He seems to say.

*Father, open my eyes that I may see You in Your creation and hear
You in the language of the world.*
—Brock Kidd

Digging Deeper: Psalm 139:14; Daniel 4:3

"See! I stand at the door and knock. If anyone hears my voice and opens the door, I will come in to him...." —Revelation 3:20 (CSB)

Things weren't going according to plan. It had been four months since my husband, Zach, and I left New York City to move back to my hometown in Kansas. I thought by now I'd have a job. Maybe a new house. But there'd been one roadblock after another.

Instead of locking eyes with Jesus, I was getting distracted by fear. It was getting harder to hear His voice as time went on.

One morning at church, our pastor called a small prayer team to the front. The lights dimmed, leaving the room bathed in only candlelight. The worship band's melody saturated the room with God's Spirit. Then, a whisper in the air dug its way down into my heart. God wanted me to go forward to be prayed for. But I resisted moving. I was afraid that I didn't know what to ask the team members to pray for me.

When I got up there, no one on the prayer team was available. Others had followed their nudges before I did. So I stood there, alone. Humiliated! People in the front rows stared at me.

I was about to go back to my seat when something caught my attention. A middle-aged man on the prayer team had emerged from a dark corner of the room. He walked toward me, smiling, motioning to come to him. The scene gripped my heart.

I realized that Jesus does this for me every day, especially when I feel lost or misplaced. He walks toward me, waving me closer. His attention is only on me. "Come to Me," I hear from Him. "I'll talk to Father about what you need."

> *Jesus, You always find a way to catch my eye at just the right time, and offer to do what I can't.*
> —Desiree Cole

Digging Deeper: Zephaniah 3:17; Romans 8:38–39

"I demand that you love each other as much as I love you."—John 15:12 (TLB)

For some reason my dad often commented about what he perceived to be my overactive social life. "I don't need all that socializing like you do. I'm a homebody," he'd grumble. But he was mistaken. Dad was the most social person I have ever known. For seventy years, he socialized with people he went to high school with. He organized parties in the barn he had built behind his house. He took hundreds of people for rides in the airboat and pontoon boats that he built. Dad socialized with people from his job as a rural mail carrier, from his church, and with fellow pilots from World War II. He socialized with all sorts of people from the various groups he joined like the library board, his American Austin car club, and the Rock River Development Authority. And, of course, there were the Barn Owls, a group of men who came to his house every Wednesday morning for fourteen years for coffee and doughnuts in the barn. Then they would play horseshoes, corn hole, or just gab until they all went out for lunch. Dad loved being around people even if he wouldn't admit it.

Shortly after his death at age ninety-eight, I heard a talk by a professional woman who listed the top ten ways to live to be one hundred. They included clean air, taking care of your heart, exercise, cardiac rehab if you do have heart problems, little drinking, no smoking, and having a close relationship. But the number-one thing was to have plenty of social interaction with your friends.

I picture Jesus out there walking from town to town, interacting with everyone He met. And now I also picture Dad laughing and telling stories with his many friends, especially his Barn Owls. No wonder he almost made it to one hundred.

Lord, don't let me get complacent. Remind me to walk this journey side by side with acquaintances, neighbors, church members, friends, and family.
—Patricia Lorenz

Digging Deeper: Luke 15:3–6; Acts 27:3

Monday, July 13

"What is impossible with man is possible with God."—Luke 18:27 (NIV)

Life is full of coincidences, some friends tell me. I try not to make too much of them. I try to think logically. After all, there are more than 300 million people in the United States. That means that every single day something with a one-in-a-million chance occurs about three hundred times. No big deal, right?

Except when it happens to you or someone you know. Like today when I called my wife, Julee, who was spending time at our vacation house in Massachusetts, with Gracie, our golden retriever. When she heard my voice, Julee said frantically, "Call me later, okay?"

"Wait..."

She hung up. I knew why she was so frantic so I called right back.

"What?" she shouted so loud that Gracie started barking in the background. "Edward, I can't find my wallet! It has everything in it!"

Everything except her contact information in the Berkshires, that is. So I explained. A few minutes earlier, my colleague, Rick, had rushed into my office in Manhattan and said, "My wife got the strangest e-mail from our upstairs neighbor who says she has Julee's wallet."

"What? How?"

"Our neighbor is vacationing in the Berkshires. She saw the wallet in a parking lot. There was no local information for Julee inside, only your business card. She knew I worked with you, so she contacted Carol to see if she knew Julee."

That's why I was calling Julee. Incredulous, she said, "So this lady contacted Carol, who called Rick, who told you, and you called me? Thank God! No way that's coincidence!"

I was tempted to tell her what people say about coincidences and the odds of a one-in-a-million occurrence. I knew she wouldn't believe it.

Loving God, You watch over us in so many ways, sometimes big and sometimes small. Well, sometimes a coincidence is a miracle in disguise.
—Edward Grinnan

Digging Deeper: Deuteronomy 10:21; Jeremiah 32:27

I saw a light from heaven, brighter than the sun, blazing around me and my companions. —Acts 26:13 (NIV)

I am at a convention, surrounded by strangers and feeling about as comfortable as a broken toe in a pointy cowboy boot. Everyone seems to know everyone else. *Why did I come? Lord, let me hide.*

"Where's the craziest place you've eaten?" someone asks me as an ice-breaker.

"On the roof of a ranch house," I blurt out. Eyebrows rise at the table-ful of people around me. I blush furiously, but it's too late to take it back.

I was the new kid, working for the summer on a family ranch. They were strangers too. Haying that day had been plagued with breakdowns. The sun had set hours before. I was too tired to eat. I trooped in behind the others and plunked into my seat. Ranch wife Virginia set out our supper, but as we took turns dishing up—*poof*—the lights went out. Virginia produced candles and matches. "A romantic dinner for five," she said, her cheerfulness sounding a bit forced. Everyone was exhausted, inside and out. I decided to skip dinner after all. I stood up to leave.

Light flashed in the window behind us. Then again. And again.

"Look! It's a meteor shower," Bruce said. His eight- and six-year-old children had never seen one before. "Come on, I'm eating on the roof."

"Let's all go," Virginia said.

One by one, we carried our plates up the ladder and balanced them on our knees. I stole glances at the family while we marveled together at the splendor in the cool night air, our faces lit from without, our hearts lifted from within.

"That's when I knew. God let me see them better in the dark. I wanted to belong there. I stayed almost twenty years," I finish. I look at the faces around me. Smiles and nods have replaced the dubious looks. Somehow, we're not strangers anymore.

Lord, light up the world so I can see others through Your eyes.
—Erika Bentsen

Digging Deeper: Psalm 55:14; 1 John 1:7

Wednesday, July 15

Then they would return home. —1 Samuel 2:20 (JPS)

It felt like a tragedy when the Web site that hosted our online newsgroups announced that we were a very minor part of their business, and they could no longer subsidize us. We were a group of science fiction and fantasy authors who'd been offered a place to gather online, and we had jumped at the chance. Now our hosts needed all their resources to keep themselves going. We all offered to pay more in order to stay together, but the owners of the Web site reluctantly refused— they were simply spending too much time on us.

I had lived for more than ten years in this community, where we endlessly discussed writing and publishing, shared our concerns and life events, prayed for one another in hard times, and celebrated together when things were good. I had never met in person many of the people I considered my really good friends; they were scattered over the country, and some were overseas. This community had been one of my strongest supports during my husband's illness and after his death. The thought of losing them all filled me with unhappiness.

The Web site gave us some time to find other places to congregate, but many of my friends chose to set up their own groups, and instead of a central place for all of us, it looked like there would be a lot of different destinations. Since I was not going to set up a site of my own, I got more and more depressed.

Then most of the people I was closest to chose a single destination, so I followed them into the world of social media, which I'd been able to avoid up to that point.

Despite my ongoing misgivings, soon there was another community developing—not the same, but not so different either.

You know how much I hate and fear change, Lord. Keep showing
me it can work out, and someday maybe I'll learn.
—Rhoda Blecker

Digging Deeper: Isaiah 43:19

When I am afraid, I put my trust in you. —Psalm 56:3 (NIV)

"Did your sister marry that man?" my father asked as we packed for a weekend at her new house. "Yes, Papi," I answered, "Remember? We went to her wedding last month."

"Ah yes, that's right, I danced with her." He shook his head and laughed, "I'm getting too old."

My father has dementia, but until that moment, I had excused his forgetfulness as being like things that would slip my own mind—where I put the hairbrush, forgetting why I walked into the kitchen, calling someone by the wrong name. That small conversation made my stomach nauseated. *It's getting worse,* I thought.

I spoke with my sister and mother about my fears, and they felt the same way.

"We have to talk about what we're going to do if it gets really bad," my sister said.

"They'll stay with me," I answered quickly. "I'm going to take care of him."

"What if you can't?" she argued. "What if it's too much for you to handle?"

"I'll get a nurse!" I said, starting to get upset. "He's never going to a nursing home."

The next few days I could barely sleep. I'd wake up feeling sick, just thinking about my father in a nursing home.

One beautiful day, my father asked, "Do you want to go with me for a walk around the reservoir?" I was tired, but I went anyway.

We talked and laughed and even jogged a bit. It seemed he had more energy than I did. I wasn't sad or worried as we walked together. I don't know what the next few years will bring, or if he'll remember my name on his next visit to the city. But I'm not going to allow my fear of the future to steal away the precious moments we can enjoy right now.

Lord, help me to live in the moment, not in my fears about tomorrow.
—Karen Valentin

Digging Deeper: Lamentations 3:21–23; Matthew 6:27

Friday, July 17

"It is the living who give thanks to You, as I do today; a father tells his sons about Your faithfulness."—Isaiah 38:19 (NASB)

Through the great prophet Isaiah, we learn that King Hezekiah of Judah was very ill and near death. In addition, it was a depressing and dangerous time for Hezekiah and the people because of the powerful Assyrians who were threatening to defeat them.

Hezekiah, encouraged by God's Word through Isaiah, prays to God, focusing his thoughts on thanksgiving instead of despair. Hezekiah's spirit rebounds and his perspective becomes positive. Hezekiah recovers. He praises God and encourages the people to communicate His goodness to their children: "A father tells his sons about Your faithfulness."

Tomorrow my wife, Beth, and I will be driving to my oldest son's lake house in South Carolina for a vacation with our three children, our two daughters-in-law, and our grandchildren. As we gather, I know that I will assume my role as the family storyteller. I am also known for great exaggeration, frequent inaccuracy of memory, and telling a grand tale whether it is completely true or not. I do not believe in ruining an epic story for the sake of correctness!

However, Isaiah has convinced me that I also need to share with my family the moments when our clan has been upheld by the faithfulness of God. Such recounting of thanksgiving is crucial to family tradition and spiritual health.

Dear God, may I tell my children the stories of Your faithfulness
in our life together. Amen.
—Scott Walker

Digging Deeper: Deuteronomy 6:6–7; Psalm 78:5–6;
Lamentations 3:23

He is the Maker of heaven and earth, the sea, and everything in them—he remains faithful forever. —Psalm 146:6 (NIV)

My young adult son and I stand in the ocean, neck deep. Warm water rolls in, lifts our feet, and moves us like grains of sand. He's struggled long, this boy. But here, in the vastness of this place, I see him smile. My own soul lurches. I want to grab this quiet-gentle moment and hold it with both hands.

A wave suddenly comes high. Looking into the curve of it is like looking at glass. There are fish in the wave—a great school. I've never seen anything like it and neither has my son. We're used to green Illinois fields, and this steals my breath. The wave peaks, curls, and melts to the rumbling surface of the ocean. Before I can say a word, fish shoot from the water and arc in the space between my son and me. There are fifty or more, moving together. We laugh out loud and words I want to speak fill my chest.

Do you see it, Son? God's glory? Do you see His grace in the glory of creation? Look! Don't miss this. See this, Son, for what it is.

But I don't say a word.

Instead, I look at the wonder in my boy's bright blue eyes. I see something in his expression that washes over the worry that seems, at times, to be a fiber of my spirit. I'm filled with hope. I understand that what I've witnessed is God revealing Himself to my son, but He's revealing Himself to me too. And it's like a whisper to my mother-heart. *I'm here. I'm with your son. I'm close and I'm showing him who I am. I haven't forgotten this boy. I'm pursuing him. Day by day. I won't stop. You can rest, daughter. Hold your words. I am here. He's my child too.*

> Lord, thank You for revealing Yourself to us.
> What a loving Father You are!
> —Shawnelle Eliasen

Digging Deeper: Psalm 107:24; Jeremiah 31:35;
Matthew 8:27

Sunday, July 19

I have not stopped giving thanks for you, remembering you in my prayers.
—Ephesians 1:16 (NIV)

The savory smell of chicken breasts sautéing filled the kitchen as I tossed a salad. Pulling open the silverware drawer, I smiled when my eyes fell on Kate's silver spoon. *I need to return it next time we get together.*

The previous week, at a time when I needed some encouragement, Kate and Mary brought over a basket with tea and cookies for a tea party and prayer. Kate even brought her dainty china cups and silver spoons. We lived miles apart and our lives were incredibly busy, so we cherished the rare moments we shared as sisters in Christ. When they packed up the basket to leave, one spoon was forgotten.

I picked up the spoon. *I'd like to give Kate and Mary something as a thank-you. But what can I give them?* Holding it, I prayed, *Lord, please bless them and watch over them.*

Over the next few weeks, warmth flooded my heart when I clasped that spoon. It was a reminder of their kindness. *What can I give them? Lord, I ask that You bless their families and everything they do today.* Soon weeks turned into months. I'd lost the desire to give them a present, but my prayers had grown lengthier.

A year later, we finally scheduled lunch at a local café. Gathering my things to go out the door, I pulled open the silverware drawer and gently grasped the spoon. For a year, that silly spoon had reminded me of the kindness of my friends and inspired me to pray for them. And, methodically, that spoon had slowly transformed my heart from wanting to give them a physical gift, to giving them the extraordinary gift of consistent prayer.

When I shared the story and presented Kate with the spoon, both of their hearts were touched.

> *Thank You, Lord, for revealing to me that consistent prayer*
> *for a friend is one of the best gifts of all.*
> —Rebecca Ondov

Digging Deeper: Ephesians 6:18; Colossians 1:9

The Lord is my strength and my shield.... —Psalm 28:7 (NIV)

"Look, Mama, look!" my five-year-old daughter called from beneath a tree. She was poking at an oblong, furry object. "There are BONES in it!"

"Bones?" I bent down for a closer look. Indeed there *were* bones—of the small rodent variety—peeking out from the fluff. My mind flashed back to eighth-grade biology. "Wow, Aurora! You've found an owl pellet!"

At home, with an Internet PDF serving as our guide, we got busy examining her find.

Owls don't have teeth, so they often swallow their food whole. Because of this, they end up eating things like feathers and fur that are indigestible, and some stuff—like bones—that could puncture their tender digestive systems. Lucky for the owl, it has a gizzard that acts as a shield of sorts, sifting what is nourishing from what's not. Inedible or harmful materials get compacted by the gizzard into pellets, passed back up the owl's esophagus and ejected from its mouth.

I thought suddenly about the silly quarrel I'd had with my husband, Jim, the night before. And the time I'd burned on social media that morning. And the unforgiveness I harbored toward a friend who had hurt me. Were any of these things good for me? Not at all. Harmful to my heart? Absolutely. I realized that, like the owl, I too had a shield: God. But, unlike the owl, whose body acts involuntarily, I can forget how desperately I need God's help sorting what's nourishing from what's not.

I looked again at the gray mass lying on the table. If an owl's gizzard could put such an end to the things that would harm it, imagine what God could do for me, if only I remembered to ask.

Lord, help me eject from my heart the things that are indigestible,
things that harm me and separate me from You.
—Erin Janoso

Digging Deeper: Ephesians 6:16; Philippians 4:8

Tuesday, July 21

How beautiful on the mountains are the feet of those who bring good news, who proclaim peace, who bring good tidings, who proclaim salvation, who say to Zion, "Your God reigns!" —Isaiah 52:7 (NIV)

As a freelance writer for almost three decades, I've enjoyed working from the comfort of home. But when money's tight, you do what you have to do. That's how I found myself with a sales job that involved standing in front of more than 250 pairs of designer shoes.

Good thing I like people—and shoes. My own closet sports polka-dot oxfords, faux snakeskin sandals, and Italian newsprint booties. Understated, I'm not. However, the Great Wall of Chanel was both out of my budget and out of my area of expertise. I didn't know anything about Zanotti, Manolo, Louboutin, or Gucci. But customers came in asking for them by name, like old friends.

First, I judged those clients. *Those boots cost as much as my rent!* Then, I envied them. *I could rock those rose-gold Mary Janes, if only I had the good fortune of marrying a doctor....* Eventually, I realized my customers and I were exactly the same. We were all "branding" ourselves, albeit in different ways. Whether it's with Prada pumps, the car we drive, the hours we put in at the gym, what we post on social media, or the tattoos emblazoned on our ankles, we're all trying to announce to the world who we are. *This is me! I matter! I'm successful, beautiful, unique, a survivor, rebellious, loved...* or whatever descriptor best fits our insecure little hearts.

I only worked in shoe sales for a season, but I'm still reaping the benefits. I learned that just because a shoe is expensive doesn't mean it's comfortable—and that becoming comfortable in my own skin means allowing my loving actions to be the "brand" by which I long to be known.

Dear Lord, remind me that it's how I live that reveals who I really am.
—Vicki Kuyper

Digging Deeper: Matthew 6:28–33; Galatians 1:10; Colossians 3:12–14

THE FRIENDSHIP OF WOMEN: Letting Go of Hurt

Do not let any unwholesome talk come out of your mouths, but only what is helpful for building others up.... —Ephesians 4:29 (NIV)

When I arrived home from shopping, my answering machine light was blinking, alerting me to a message from my friend Pat. We'd just taken a weekend antiquing trip together and had a marvelous time. Pat just probably wanted to tell me what her daughter-in-law had thought of the treasures she'd found.

Pat had gone through a rough time recently so I'd tried to pamper her on the trip—driving her to the hotel entrance, delivering coffee and a pastry to her bedside, offering her first dibs on vintage goods we discovered.

So imagine my shock when I played her telephone message. First was a cheery, "What's going on, Roberta?" But then, I heard Pat talking to the lady who cleans house for both of us. "That Roberta is *soooo* selfish. It's Roberta, Roberta, Roberta!" Obviously, Pat thought she had ended the call.

I was so hurt. First, I cried. Then I thought I'd terminate the friendship. Then I dialed another friend to tattle, thought better of it, and hung up. Finally, I made a list of all the things I honestly valued about Pat.

In most situations, she is incredibly kind and considerate. The day of my divorce hearing, for instance, she was the one friend who insisted that I not be alone. The day of my magazine photo shoot, she was the person who cleaned up messy props afterward. A social worker, Pat always rooted for the underdog too.

In the end, I let it pass. And on Pat's deathbed, when I was one of three friends she asked to see, I was grateful to have focused on her many good qualities instead of one negative experience.

Dear Lord, we are never sorry when we extend love and grace to others.
—Roberta Messner

Digging Deeper: Proverbs 15:1–2; Colossians 4:6; 1 Peter 4:8

Thursday, July 23

"The Lord searches every mind, and understands every plan and thought. If you seek him, he will be found by you...."—1 Chronicles 28:9 (NRSV)

Every summer for the past twenty-plus years, I've taught technical writing at a camp for aspiring teen engineers. I love showing them how different technical writing is from what they've learned in English classes: make it as concise as possible, and don't try to make it sound pretty. High fives and fist bumps are a common occurrence when STEM*-inclined young people find out they've been set free from "artistic" writing!

Another difference I teach my students is that sometimes it's acceptable, or maybe even preferable, to use passive voice in tech writing. Instead of writing *I measured the acidity of the solution*, it might be better to write *The acidity was measured* to keep the focus on the acidity instead of who measured it.

This past summer, a student asked if there would ever be an occasion in real life when passive voice might be preferred. "Hmm," I said. "Maybe if you wreck your dad's car, you might want to open with, 'The car was wrecked' instead of 'I wrecked your car.'" The students laughed, but when I got home, I happened upon the perfect example in my Bible reading.

First Chronicles 28:9 in the New Revised Standard Version doesn't say *If you seek him, you will find him*. Instead, it uses the passive construction, "he will be found by you." The emphasis is exactly where it should be—on God, not on us. We do not find God on our own; rather, through His grace, He allows us to encounter Him. How often I'm guilty of putting the emphasis on myself instead of on the Lord! What a nice reminder at just the right time.

> *Thanks, Lord, for my own private lesson.*
> *You always have so much to teach me!*
> —Ginger Rue

Digging Deeper: Proverbs 8:17; Acts 17:26–27

*STEM: Acronym for science, technology, engineering, and math

Blessed be the Lord, who daily loadeth us with benefits, even the God of our salvation. Selah. —Psalm 68:19 (KJV)

I live a two-day drive from my son, so in order to find out how his talk went at a prestigious university recently, I was forced to dig a bit. In the past, he would have immediately given me a report—good or bad. Now that he has a wife to share with, however, my adult "child" no longer views me as his number one, go-to person. At the time of my self-imposed sleuthing, what was actually a benefit looked like a concern. But oh, how many times in the past had I sought God for that wife! Then I had a "Selah" moment.

Like many of us, I confess to not knowing a definitive meaning of the biblical word *Selah*. One term I knew to be associated with it is "pause," or what some twenty-first century Christians call a "praise break"—a time when one stops and offers a deliberate outbreak of praise either internally or externally.

Suddenly, it occurred to me that I might be taking God's gift of my son's caring mate for granted, placing it on the shelf of countless other answered prayers I had forgotten. When I took a moment to pray, I remembered the many years I had sought God for what was now staring me in the face: someone geographically close to love and listen to my son.

Unchecked, our thoughts can convince us that life is a series of nothing but hurriedness and troubles. But, in truth, we are daily loaded with benefits. Sometimes it takes only a pause—a closer look at something as simple as a red bird in the snow or as divine as a son taking a wife—to declare a mandate for deliberate praise. Selah!

Today, Lord, I make a conscious effort to recall and give thanks for a portion of the forgotten blessings that You have consistently poured out upon me and mine.
—Jacqueline F. Wheelock

Digging Deeper: 2 Corinthians 9:8; Deuteronomy 26:11

Saturday, July 25

PACKING LIGHT

If any of you lacks wisdom, you should ask God, who gives generously to all without finding fault, and it will be given to you. —James 1:5 (NIV)

I have a terrible sense of direction. Few things in life upset my husband more than my reading a map and giving him directions while we are taking road trips. Wayne knows that I don't have a clue where we are, in what direction we're headed, or how to get there. Invariably, he needs to pull off to the side of the road and read the map himself. Thankfully, with the advent of GPS, I can find my way around now, although the shrill voice that says *"recalculating, recalculating"* is still heard far too often.

Recently I was muttering to God that I wished He'd given me a GPS when it came to answering some tricky life questions. The fact is, we all need help finding our way through the twists and turns of decision-making, relationships, and responsibilities. He reminded me that He *has* given us what we all need for guidance: the Bible is our GPS, and the more time we spend with Him, reading and studying His Word, the more direction we receive. He has promised to provide us with the wisdom and the directions we need to navigate through life, and He is able to set us back on course when we are lost. God is in the business of recalculating too.

Father, without You I am lost, both figuratively and spiritually.
—Debbie Macomber

Digging Deeper: Psalm 119:105; John 16:13

Children's children are a crown to the aged.... —Proverbs 17:6 (NIV)

Want to go driving on Sunday, Gabi?" I texted my granddaughter. Sounds ridiculous, I know. What teenager wants to go driving with her grandmother on a Sunday afternoon? One who is almost sixteen. One who needs to accumulate fifty hours of driving with another adult family member before she can get her driver's license.

"Sure!" Gabi answered within minutes. Her family was coming to our house for Sunday dinner, so we could sneak out for a drive.

Soon after they arrived, we climbed into my car, with Gabi behind the wheel. Off we went. Very slowly. We turned into an empty church parking lot. Testing the brakes. Backing up. Going in circles. Until she gained some confidence. Then we ventured out onto the main road.

"You can go a little faster," I encouraged her. Cautiously, she stepped on the gas, getting closer to the speed limit. We talked about going too fast or too slow and watching out for other drivers. I also told stories about the stress of teaching her daddy and his sisters to drive.

"They told me I was overreacting when they stopped quickly and I complained about getting whiplash. They didn't like my loud-teacher voice when I told them they were driving too close to people's mailboxes. I kind of wanted them to hit one, just so I could say, 'I told you so.'"

She laughed and we had a good time driving around.

"How did it go?" her mother asked when we returned.

"She was great!" I reported.

"Much easier than driving with you!" Gabi told her mom with a smile and exaggerated eye roll that reminded me of my own teenagers.

Her mom smiled too. "I totally get that."

I did too.

What a blessing, Lord, to be a grandparent with a whole new generation to enjoy in a whole new way.
—Carol Kuykendall

Digging Deeper: Psalm 145:13; Ephesians 3:20–21

Monday, July 27

Jesus wept. Then the Jews said, "See how he loved him!"
—John 11:35–36 (NIV)

M y office sits off the lobby of a large army chapel. One of the truly humbling aspects of its location is that sometimes memorial ceremonies take place a few feet away. I don't believe I will ever grow accustomed to roll call or the playing of "Taps." Frankly, I hope I never do.

Memorial ceremonies are solemn and reverent. Soldiers may shed a tear during a service, but only occasionally will one or two have to leave the service in order to contain emotions. Outward showing of grief is rare, for reasons I don't even begin to understand.

On a recent occasion, I sat tending to administrative duties, and I noticed a slight commotion outside my office during a memorial ceremony. My door was shut, so before I opened it, I said a little prayer. A weeping soldier stood there, unable to rein in his grief over losing a battle buddy. He was surrounded by peers and a chaplain offering support, so I immediately turned back to give them privacy, praying for God to comfort him.

Witnessing such grief stirs my soul, the place where God rests within me. I was reminded that strength does not equal lack of emotion or lack of grief. It takes strength to love and to care for others; soldiers are no exception. This young soldier wept for the loss of a brother in arms, just as Jesus wept for the loss of His beloved Lazarus. Like Jesus, this soldier's weeping was a tangible sign of love, an earthly sign of God's great love for us all.

Lord, be with those who weep and with those filled with grief. May they know Your eternal comfort and peace in all things and in all ways.
—Jolynda Strandberg

Digging Deeper: Psalm 35:14; Matthew 17:23

Now you are the body of Christ, and each one of you is a part of it.
—1 Corinthians 12:27 (NIV)

I was done with my day. Not finished, mind you, just *done*. Nothing was going right, no one was on time, and I was at my worst. I took a quick break to check my phone. *"I'm at the hospital for my child's latest round of chemo and we noticed that there aren't any coloring books left in the family area. Can anyone help?"* The request came over a social media network.

I saw the post while sitting at my desk. Specific and tangible, the call for coloring books was something I could definitely help with.

I posted on my social media wall that I was grabbing coloring books and that if anyone else wanted to donate books or send money, I'd be happy to pick up extras.

For the next hour, my phone kept buzzing. Joanna sent $20. Mary Beth sent $25. Caleb sent $25. Within a few hours, I had $200 and lots of posts from friends thanking me for the chance to help.

When my husband, Brian, got home that night, we loaded up and headed for the store. We told our children who we were buying the books for and why they needed them. Then we let the children go wild.

The next day, Brian delivered fifty pounds of coloring books. I had to load them into a rolling suitcase!

While the kids received dozens of new books, I can honestly say the often-repeated message is true: I got the bigger blessing. Because of my friends' generosity, I was able to show my children that we can be God's hands and feet.

My day started off being all about me, but ended up being about my community. The next time I feel *done*, I'm going to stop looking at my own actions and start looking at how I can help others.

> *Lord, thank You for calling me to greater things*
> *than I could have ever imagined.*
> —Ashley Kappel

Digging Deeper: Acts 20:35; 1 Corinthians 15:58; Galatians 5:13

Wednesday, July 29

For the sake of your name, Lord, forgive my iniquity, though it is great.
—Psalm 25:11 (NIV)

A widow I knew recently passed away. Gloria's greatest desire, next to making as many disciples for Christ as she could, was that her two sons wholly give themselves over to the Lord. Though she didn't live to see them experience the depth of relationship she enjoyed with the Savior, I still pray it comes to pass.

As I remember and relish her fierce love for God, I find myself praying, "For the sake of Gloria, Lord, please draw her beloved offspring to Yourself." While I have often struggled with other doubts, I always feel hopeful about that particular prayer because Gloria and her husband, Freddie, were such Christian warriors.

Then I ask myself, "If I believe that God might be open to honoring a prayer based on the life and name of earthly servants, how much more will He honor prayers consistently prayed, first and foremost, to edify His Name?

In Psalm 25, David coveted forgiveness for the shocking sins he committed, but not solely for his peace. Above all else, he wanted to glorify the Name. As a king, he would understand better than most the importance of an official title. But even more, relationship caused him to understand the absolute sovereignty of *the* Name above all names. In another revered psalm, he says, "He leads me in the paths of righteousness for His name's sake" (Psalm 23:3, NKJV). He guides us simply because of Who He is.

When I need immediate help, I hear myself say, "In the name of Jesus," failing to fully grasp the treasured name I invoke. What if we take a moment each day to remind ourselves that whatever we ask for must first bring glory to His name? Otherwise, our request is ultimately in vain.

Lord, help me to keep the light of Your Name ever before me
as a pure and worthy reason for my life choices.
—Jacqueline F. Wheelock

Digging Deeper: Psalms 23:3, 91:14

This slight momentary affliction is preparing us for an eternal weight of glory beyond all measure. —2 Corinthians 4:17 (NRSV)

Charlotte is my tough daughter. Unlike her sister Lulu, who's something of a hypochondriac and worries about any sickness in our family, Charlotte's always been skeptical of suffering or weakness—others' as well as her own. Rarely seeing herself as sick enough to go to a doctor, Charlotte rolls her eyes when my posttraumatic stress disorder overwhelms me with panic and inability to focus, sending me off to my therapist. She must have somehow inherited the similar attitudes of my father, who, throughout my childhood, scoffed at my friends' allergies, most mental illnesses, my sisters' and my menstrual cramps—all ailments that, having never suffered them, he considered imaginary.

"It's only pain," he'd say if one of his six kids got hurt. "Ten years from now you won't even remember it!"

Charlotte is much the same, though not as vocal. This spring, after slipping while playing Frisbee, she spent a weekend unable to walk on her swollen, purple ankle before reluctantly going to the doctor. Even after the X-rays, she struggled to believe it was broken in two places.

The ensuing months of crutches and a boot nurtured in her a newfound interest in others' struggles. She zealously addressed the inadequate handicapped entrances in her dorm even after her own need passed. And when I reported suffering from a pinched nerve in my shoulder that made it just about impossible for me to sit for more than a minute, she was unexpectedly concerned and attentive.

The one, beautiful thing about any struggle is that it makes you recognize and empathize with the similar struggles of other people. Suffering softens our hearts.

Dear Lord, I love how You use everything, even our suffering,
for our good and Yours!
—Patty Kirk

Digging Deeper: Psalm 119:17; Galatians 6:2

Friday, July 31

"Love your neighbor as yourself." . . . —Mark 12:31 (NIV)

I smiled as I walked downstairs singing along with the familiar theme song, "Won't You Be My Neighbor?" We'd recently discovered that the beloved show, *Mister. Rogers' Neighborhood,* was on Amazon, and my daughter would sometimes turn on an episode if she was the first one awake in the morning.

As I snuggled in beside her on the couch, I watched as Daniel Tiger, Henrietta Pussycat, and the other puppets in the Neighborhood of Make-Believe worked through "the mad" that one of the characters felt.

Before long, though, it was time for Mr. Rogers to go. Singing his goodbye song, he switched his sweater for his jacket, his tennis shoes for his dress shoes, and headed for the door. But before he walked through it, he turned toward us, his "television neighbors," and said, so sincerely: "You always make each day such a special day by just your being you. There's only one person in the whole world like you, and I like you just the way you are."

My heart lodged in my throat, and tears pricked the backs of my eyelids. Aurora and I had watched dozens of episodes together, but no matter how many times I heard it, this message never failed to choke me up. How thirsty my heart apparently was to hear that I was enough, likeable just the way I was.

I looked over at my daughter. How blessed I was to have her as one of my "neighbors" in life. I got up to make the coffee, determined that, no matter what this day in our neighborhood brought our way, I would remember how God loves her, others—and even me—exactly as we are.

Lord, thank You for loving me just as I am. Help me, please, as I strive to love my neighbors, and myself, as You would have me love them.
—Erin Janoso

Digging Deeper: John 13:34; Romans 15:7

HE PERFORMS WONDERS

1 _____

2 _____

3 _____

4 _____

5 _____

6 _____

7 _____

8 _____

9 _____

10 _____

11 _____

12 _____

13 _____

14 _____

15 _____

July

16 _____

17 _____

18 _____

19 _____

20 _____

21 _____

22 _____

23 _____

24 _____

25 _____

26 _____

27 _____

28 _____

29 _____

30 _____

31 _____

AUGUST

Remember, O Lord, thy tender mercies and thy lovingkindnesses; for they have been ever of old.

—Psalm 25:6 (KJV)

Listen, my son, to your father's instruction and do not forsake your mother's teaching. They are a garland to grace your head and a chain to adorn your neck. —Proverbs 1:8–9 (NIV)

Today is my father's birthday. His name was William; he claimed that his parents called him Bill "because I came on the first of the month, like all the other bills." Apparently my dad was telling Dad-jokes even before he was a dad.

His birthday brings back memories, not all of them good. The final ten years of his life were rough for both of us. After he passed, my mind stubbornly moored itself in that last difficult decade.

But not this year.

Recently I helped a friend of mine install a new washing machine. I spied his old washer, an ancient Norge, in a lonely corner of his basement…and suddenly I was ten years old again. It was the era of moonshots and astronauts, and I longed to be a NASA engineer (*Apollo, this is Houston, do you read?*)—but what I needed was a control panel with switches and knobs and stuff like I saw on TV. I asked my father (a real engineer) to build one, and he agreed—provided that I helped.

So we built a NASA dashboard out of the control knobs from our old Norge; he even let me borrow the microphone and headphones from the reel-to-reel tape player. I spent hours guiding astronauts through their missions.

I grow misty as I write this; the memories of those last awful years fade away. I so desperately want to whisper a message to him on those reel-to-reel tapes:

> *Dear Dad: I am so sorry that things deteriorated between us. I put my pride first—I should have put you first, not because you came on the first of the month but because you always came when I needed you. Your mission is over now; maybe my control-panel prayers can guide your eternal spaceship to its final splashdown in the welcoming waters of heaven.*
> —Mark Collins

Digging Deeper: Proverbs 23:22; Ephesians 6:1–2

*"Teaching them to obey everything I have commanded you. And surely
I am with you always, to the very end of the age."* —Matthew 28:20 (NIV)

Recently, I received the sort of phone call that would bring any
parent to his or her knees. Justin, my twenty-five-year-old son,
said, "Mom, I want to kill myself. I just want to die." In that moment, I
felt panic, fear, sadness, helplessness, and loneliness all at the same time.

Justin has struggled with major depressive disorder since the age of
twelve. We have had many crises, but I thought he was doing better. As
I spoke to my son, trying with every part of myself to save this child I
love so purely, my prayer was, "Jesus, please, please be with him."

As a parent it was excruciating to hear how painful life is for my
child. There was nothing I could do or say to make a difference in
Justin's thoughts to end his life. The only hope was for Jesus to be with
us. I prayed the most sincere prayers of my life that day, imploring
Jesus to take control. In our desperate situation, indeed Jesus came.

Jesus walked with Justin and me that day. He was the voice of a
family member who helped locate a hospital for my son. Jesus was the
steady and reassuring manner of the nurse who took Justin to his room
there. He was with me as I sat in the waiting room crying uncontrol-
lably. Through this trying time in our family, Jesus faithfully walked
alongside us and kept Justin safe not only that day, but every day since.

*Jesus, thank You for Your faithfulness, for Your steadfast love, and for
Your eternal presence. May I always honor Your presence in my care for
others, and may I honor the sanctity of life wherever it is found.*
—Jolynda Strandberg

Digging Deeper: Luke 24; 1 Thessalonians 3:13

You have delivered my soul from death, yes, my feet from falling, that I may walk before God in the light of life. —Psalm 56:13 (ESV)

My grandmother broke her hip. She fell on her way to the bathroom and shattered her entire left pelvis. She was rushed to surgery, where the break was repaired and secured with pins. Two days later, the physical therapist helped her to stand up and begin some basic strengthening exercises. Three days after her surgery, the doctor felt she was well enough to go home. Oh, the marvels of modern medicine and a stubborn Finnish personality.

One problem: My grandmother also has Alzheimer's and promptly forgot everything. She hopped out of her wheelchair and ran.

Before I go on, I feel the need to reassure you that she's fine. We caught her on her way out the front door, and aside from a bit of pain and swelling in her leg, she made it through without a new scratch. But those of us who care for her? We feel constantly panicked that she'll forget about her injury again and take a dive out of her wheelchair.

It has become a constant vigil: Who has eyes on Grandma so she won't try to run?

It could be a bit funny considering that we are struggling to keep a ninety-two-year-old woman with a broken hip from running away from us, but that's what we have to do to keep her safe.

I imagine God often feels the same way about me: "What? Erin is trying to run again? Doesn't she remember what happened last time she ran from Me? Doesn't she feel the pain?"

Yet, like my grandmother, I forget. I run. And my heavenly Father always chases me down and brings me back to Him—the only place where I am truly safe.

> *Father God, never stop chasing me. I need You,*
> *even in those moments when I forget.*
> —Erin MacPherson

Digging Deeper: Psalm 139:7–10; Romans 8:35–39

PRAYING IN PUBLIC: Wearing the Word
Jesus wept. —John 11:35 (NKJV)

Wherever I've lived, I've walked every day. San Francisco, Oakland, Key West, Fort Lauderdale, Baltimore, New Hampshire, Maine, Washington, DC; whether I've been on a short visit or a months-long stay, I walk. And because I develop a route, people soon recognize me. I am most public, most visible, when I walk; and while I walk, I pray.

I pray visibly by writing Scripture with an indelible marker on the back of my jackets. One of my favorites, given the state of our world, is "Jesus wept." It's also the Bible's shortest passage, so it can be written in large letters on my jacket.

People notice. One couple asked if they could take a photo for their social media. I obliged, happy that the Scripture would appear while my face would not. Those seeing it could imagine anyone wearing God's Word, including, maybe, themselves.

One day a homeless man in Baltimore asked, "Why did Jesus weep?"

"For his friends, for the city he loved," I answered, "for Lazarus, for Himself, maybe, because He knew He would soon suffer and die."

The man gazed at me, "So Jesus wept for the same reasons as I do."

This reminds me of the time my young godson studied my jacket and asked me, "What's *wept*?"

"It means to cry."

"Was Jesus sad?" he wondered.

"Yes, he was sad that people hurt each other," I explained.

"I'm sad when someone hurts my feelings."

"But Jesus was sad when *anyone's* feelings got hurt."

He looked at me with just one word, "Wow."

Wow, indeed.

> *Jesus, help my tears to water the seeds of love for You.*
> —Marci Alborghetti

Digging Deeper: Luke 6:21–25, 19:41–44

Wednesday, August 5

Now to Him who is able to do exceedingly abundantly above all that we ask or think, according to the power that works in us. —Ephesians 3:20 (NKJV)

A stressful season of moving and remodeling had taken its toll on me. Looking at a mountain of boxes and looking forward to seemingly endless projects, made me wonder if I could handle it. I was doubting God's provision and worrying as a result.

About that time, I saw a news report that grabbed my attention. The reporter explained that each state has an office to store unclaimed treasures. These include forgotten bank accounts and other unclaimed assets. Just for fun, I went online and checked. To my surprise, I found an unclaimed bank account from forty-three years ago, owned by my mom and dad. I remember going to that bank as a child. When my parents moved to a different state, they must have forgotten that account. It wasn't a life-changing amount, but it certainly would help my octogenarian mom.

I called. "Mom, guess what! You're richer than you think!" We had a fun conversation, and soon, she would have some surprise cash in hand.

As our conversation ended, I began to realize it was true of me too. I'm richer than I think. I was letting my mountain of work obscure the even bigger mountain of my blessings. God had been faithful. He had provided strength, helpers, finances, and encouragement along the way. I had the power of prayer and the Word of God. I possessed spiritual blessings beyond comparison. His provision was perfect. My worry was wasted in light of a God Who provides.

I'm glad I found some unclaimed treasure for my mom. Now it was my turn to reclaim the treasures I found when I found Christ.

> *Father, teach me to enjoy*
> *my inheritance as a child of the King.*
> —Bill Giovannetti

Digging Deeper: Ephesians 1:7, 2:7

You created my inmost being; you knit me together in my mother's womb. I praise you because I am fearfully and wonderfully made; your works are wonderful, I know that full well. —Psalm 139:13–14 (NIV)

In the mountains of Vermont, where I lived for twenty years, we saw lots of large animals and birds that don't often appear in more populated areas.

One morning, I was walking my dog, Max, up the mountain behind our house, when Max suddenly stopped in his tracks. It was strange that he didn't bark. He didn't even move. Max just stared to the right, at something.

"Come on, Buddy, let's go!" I said enthusiastically, tugging on Max's leash. He did not move.

I went two steps ahead of Max on the path and tugged again on the leash. "Come on," I said. Still, he just stood there. Then I stopped too. A dog can be far more aware than his master. I looked where Max was staring.

Standing there in a birch grove, also perfectly still, was an eight-foot-tall bull moose, in profile. He must have known we were there (who wouldn't have heard my chattering?), but he paid us no attention. What a creature it was! A giant, his head was high up, eating leaves from a tree. Max's awe and respect were just right.

You are beautiful, God. Everything You make is beautiful.
—Jon M. Sweeney

Digging Deeper: Ecclesiastes 3:11

Friday, August 7

The barrel of meal shall not waste, neither shall the cruse of oil fail....
—1 Kings 17:14 (KJV)

My wife, Corinne, and I slipped away for a quiet dinner and a chance to hash out some looming decisions.

We wanted to commit both time and money to my family's project in Zimbabwe. Adding a new grade to our Village Hope school each year was our goal, and a worthy cause. But at home commitments were mounting.

Our son Harrison's college bills were sizable, as were flights to visit him. Both Corinne and I were working on projects for inner-city children, and with three little ones at home, our plate was overflowing.

"Well, so much for a quiet dinner," I said to Corinne, nodding toward two noisy children seated near us at the restaurant.

Their grandparents seemed unprepared to deal with them, and efforts to calm the melee were not working.

Instinctively, Corinne pulled out a package of goldfish crackers, smiled and offered them to the grandmother.

The grandchildren grew still—until the crackers disappeared.

Corinne dug into her bag, and pulled out a box of pencils with matching activity tablets.

"Corrine," I whispered, grudgingly, "we need those."

Ignoring me, she shared her bounty with the children. We didn't hear another peep. The grandparents were all smiles.

We returned to weighing the pros and cons of a gift to Zimbabwe.

I'm familiar with God's promises to replenish our offerings, but the gift would be a risk. "If only God would send a sign," I groaned as the waiter appeared.

"Excuse me, sir, the couple who just left covered your bill."

"That's the sign," Corrine answered, flashing her biggest smile.

Father, let me hold to Your promise to replenish the widow's
meal and step forward in faith.
—Brock Kidd

Digging Deeper: Luke 6:38; Hebrews 10:24

Ascribe to the Lord the glory due his name; worship the Lord in the splendor of his holiness. —Psalm 29:2 (NIV)

"Mom, push me in the tire swing?" eleven-year-old Gabriel asked. He was still small enough to curl in the curve of the swing.

"Sure thing," I said. I began to push, but despite the sunshine, I felt unsettled. My parents were struggling with their health. A son was working through a tough circumstance. My marriage was on the back burner because Lonny and I ran endlessly in opposite directions and meeting in the middle seemed impossible.

"Lord, I'm worried," I whispered as I pushed. "Show me how to trust."

My son's toes nearly touched a low branch of the tree overhead. Then my fingers caught the warm, black tire and I pushed again. As I did, words came from somewhere deep inside.

"Lord, You are faithful."

The swing arced back. I pushed again. "Lord, You're compassionate." To and fro. "Lord, You're in control."

Higher and higher. "Lord, You are gracious."

As I pushed that swing, praise for the Lord pulsed. God shifted my focus. He heard my prayer, and the Holy Spirit prompted praise. When God's character and kindness is the heartbeat of my soul, every circumstance looks different. Every circumstance *is* different.

Acknowledging God's powerful presence changes our perspective.

"Hey, Mom, look at me!" Gabriel called. Safe in the curve of the swing, he let go of the tire rims and waved his arms in the air. He tilted his face toward the sky.

My spirit felt unencumbered. I'd once read that worship and worry cannot occupy the same space. Worship brings freedom from worry; and like my son, I could fly free.

Lord, when I worship You, worry flees! Thank You, God.
—Shawnelle Eliasen

Digging Deeper: Psalms 63:1, 103:1; Isaiah 25:1

Sunday, August 9

Thou hast brought a vine out of Egypt: thou hast cast out the heathen, and planted it.... Return, we beseech thee... and visit this vine.
—Psalm 80:8, 14 (KJV)

From time to time, I run into people I once taught. The latest such experience occurred while I pumped gas at a busy convenience store. I startled momentarily as a thirty-something left the door of her car open and flew toward me laughing and shouting my name. While I treasure the occasional positive recounting of my limited influence on someone's life, I cannot help but think how much teachers need those words while still on the job.

The thankless droughts of teaching school can sometimes mirror our lives as believers. We find ourselves questioning the effectiveness of our witness. We offer a gentle "God bless you" to someone in the supermarket only to be summarily rebuffed, or we volunteer for years in community service with few or no confirmable souls saved.

Lord, I sometimes think, *I feel myself drying up inside. Am I producing any fruit at all?*

Like the psalmist, I covet a visit to this vine. I long for a watering, to feel the message of eternal life flowing, not just inside me but through me into others. It is then that I recall what the Lord said: "Whoever drinks the water I give them will never thirst. Indeed, the water I give them will become in them a spring of water welling up to eternal life" (John 4:14, NIV).

Only after I remind myself that it's not my assignment to monitor my contribution toward God's kingdom do I stop worrying about where the dewdrops fall, how many there are, or if they are absorbed. Instead, I realize it is mine to keep my eyes on the source of the eternal fountain, that continual well that flows through my soul, and let God do the rest.

> *Jesus, help me to remember that I am forever watered by the*
> *Eternal Fountain and connected to the True Vine.*
> —Jacqueline F. Wheelock

Digging Deeper: Acts 3:19–20; John 15:4–5

"Do not worry, saying, 'What shall we eat?" or 'What shall we drink?'
or 'What shall we wear?'" —Matthew 6:31 (NIV)

Each year, my family (thirty-one and counting!) heads to the beach to run relay races on the shore, have mini-Bible lessons with Nana, play for hours in the pool, and eat family style for twenty-one meals straight.

When our five-year-old daughter, Olivia, looked at the calendar and saw that the beach was still *pages* away, she sighed, "It'll never get here!" with the dramatic despair that only a five-year-old can conjure. I offered her the chance to skip ahead.

"We could go to the beach right now," I told her. Her eyes lit up! "But your cousins can't come this week, so they won't be there. And you'll miss Vacation Bible School. And your dance recital, Charlotte's birthday, and your school field trip." Her eyes narrowed.

"Do you want to skip all those things?" I asked her, in a neutral tone.

"No!" she said, aghast I'd even make such an offer.

With that, we chose a family motto: "Be present." The Bible tells us not to be anxious, but in my child's case, she was anxious to get this party going! So this year, we're being present.

We work on this daily. Rushing through dinner won't get you a treat any faster. Wishing away a school week won't make the weekend come sooner. Trying to fast-forward rest time only means you'll be tired when we ride bikes this evening. Instead, be present, which is really the only place you can be anyway, and find joy where you are.

Lord, thank You for the reminder to slow way down and
drink in the beauty of each day.
—Ashley Kappel

Digging Deeper: Philippians 4:6–8; Hebrews 13:5; 1 Peter 5:7

Tuesday, August 11

Train children in the right way, and when old, they will not stray.
—Proverbs 22:6 (NRSV)

Wwwhat are your goals for your daughters?" my former student, Gabe, asked at lunch the other day. Now that we're peers, she divulges personal details I rarely hear from the perfect-seeming Christian young people I teach: her struggles as a family member and believer. She sounds remarkably like me growing up, like my daughters.

Gabe's question surprised me, though. While I routinely second-guess my parenting, I've never really thought about having "goals"—something I worked to accomplish—for Charlotte and Lulu.

"You mean my hopes?" I asked.

Gabe nodded, and I blathered on about how I'd modeled this and that over the years—church attendance, cooking, gardening, reading, a healthy marriage, a clean house—hoping they'd copy what they saw. But Gabe's question pitched me into self-doubt. *What, if anything, had I tried to achieve in my daughters?* Had I stopped trying, now that they were adults? I hadn't deliberately set out to shape them. Should I have?

I grew up in an unhappy household, so my main parenting goals were to avoid my own parents' errors—constant yelling, scary punishments—and in these I'd been largely successful. Except for an episode Charlotte and Lulu still refer to as "Mommy's closet fit"— which occurred when, as toddlers, they piled up all their clean clothes to construct a trampoline—I never once screamed at them. I'd rarely punished them, certainly never physically. And we talk about everything.

And though I'll likely always worry that I'm a parenting failure, I know this: my daughters, like Gabe, are lovely women I'm proud to have influenced, even imperfectly. Surely God translates our parenting groans into just the right way to accomplish His goals.

Father, bless my parenting and teaching of Your children.
—Patty Kirk

Digging Deeper: Proverbs 13:24; Luke 11:11–13; Ephesians 6:4

Listening to gossip is like eating cheap candy; do you really want junk like that in your belly? —Proverbs 18:8 (MSG)

A cool breeze drifted across the lake as the rays of the sun poked over the mountains. Soft waves rocked my kayak. I paddled toward the snowcapped peaks that rimmed Lake Como. Only the sounds of birds, welcoming the dawn, could be heard. That is, except for the voices that floated through my mind from a conversation that I'd had a couple of days earlier.

Sandy [name changed] and I had many friends in common. Like women do, when we got together, we'd share news about them. But invariably it would turn to gossip. When we parted, I knew the words we'd spoken did not edify our friends. Inside, I felt dirty. And this morning, our last gossip-session swirled through my thoughts. *Lord, still my mind.*

Suddenly the sunlight illuminated the peak in front of me. *Wow!* Resting my paddle across the bow, I pulled out my phone to take a picture. Unfortunately, by the time the peak was in the viewfinder, the kayak had drifted sideways from the momentum of my paddling.

Setting down the phone, I picked up the paddle and lightly dipped it to correct the kayak, but the kayak moved sideways in the other direction. For several minutes, the momentum kept taking me off course. Frustrated, I ordered the boat, "Stop it!" And when I did, it was as if a still small voice echoed those same words. Instantly I knew that eliminating gossip wasn't about God changing me or stilling my mind. It was about my choosing to stop the momentum before it started.

The next few weeks were tough. I limited my time with Sandy and chose to close conversations early. I don't love Sandy any less; however, I made the choice not to dip my tongue into gossip anymore.

> *Lord, thank You for showing me that the choice—to edify*
> *and uplift, or to gossip—is mine.*
> —Rebecca Ondov

Digging Deeper: Exodus 23:1–3; Leviticus 19:16; Proverbs 17:4

Thursday, August 13

We desire that each one of you show the same diligence to the full assurance of hope until the end, that you do not become sluggish, but imitate those who through faith and patience inherit the promises. —Hebrews 6:11–12 (NKJV)

I bet you don't get visitors often. At least not a second time," the delivery guy said as he unloaded the last of ten boxes from his dolly onto my front porch. He stopped for a moment to wipe the sweat from his brow and then trudged down to his truck.

Funny how my husband and I hadn't given much thought to buying a house on a hill. We were more concerned about whether the interior layout met the needs of our family, whether the yard provided enough space for the children to play, and if the school system was to our liking. But the hill is always the first thing people notice, especially since they have to park along the street and walk (or should I say climb) up.

As for my family—from the youngest to the oldest—we take the hill with an easy stride, and it certainly doesn't seem as intimidating as most people claim it to be. We're accustomed to checking the mailbox, rolling down the trash and recycling bins, or chasing down the occasional runaway ball. With every ascent and descent, the tasks have become easier and definitely not as taxing on our bodies. Our home has given us more than a safe place to live. In its own way, our little house on a hill has shown us that things get easier with practice and perseverance. So keep climbing!

> *Father, even when my legs grow weary, I'll still run to You.*
> *Pull me up to a higher calling in Christ Jesus.*
> —Tia McCollors

Digging Deeper: Galatians 6:9; James 1:4

*My God will meet all your needs according to the riches of his glory in
Christ Jesus.* —Philippians 4:19 (NIV)

I sat on my parents' porch swing and shucked off my boots. I placed
one in my lap, dipped a rag into a bucket of soapy water, and then
ran the rag across the leather.

"What are you doing?" My ten-year-old brother Isaiah asked.

"Cleaning and polishing my boots." I dipped the rag back into the
bucket. The water turned dark.

"Can I help?" Isaiah asked.

I patted the seat next to me and handed him a boot and a rag.

"Will these scuffs come out?" Isaiah asked. He ran his thumb along
the scratches in the dark leather.

"Most of them," I said. "But first we have to get this grime off."

I remembered when my boots were smooth and new, a gift from my
mom after I got accepted to law school. I always wanted to live out
East, but I ended up deferring that dream and attended law school in
Iowa. Instead of hiking Appalachian trails, these boots had tromped
through Iowa mud.

The washcloth made a splash as Isaiah dropped it into the bucket.

"Polishing time," he said.

"Wait a minute, Bud," I said. "They need to dry first." We set the
boots in the sunlight. Isaiah twisted open the can of polish and touched
its surface. He smiled when his finger came back brown.

"I miss you when you're gone," he said. "I'm glad you came home
this weekend."

If I lived in Virginia, I would be thousands of miles away this morning instead of sitting on a porch with a ten-year-old shoeshine boy.
"Me too," I said. "I wouldn't trade this for anything."

> *Lord, thank You for blessing me in unexpected ways.*
> —Logan Eliasen

Digging Deeper: John 1:16; James 1:17

Encourage one another and build each other up, just as in fact you are doing. —1 Thessalonians 5:11 (NIV)

I'd just finished playing my guitar and singing songs to a group of tiny birthday guests. I took on more of these birthday gigs to make money since my writing career had hit a lull.

"Who's ready for face painting?" I asked, and the children lit up with requests for animals, superheroes, and princess crowns. I tucked my guitar in its flimsy case and placed it behind me on the grass. Children crowded around me as I transformed their faces. I didn't even see the child who stepped on my case and broke the neck of my guitar in half.

When their faces were done, I reached into my case to play more songs. I held back tears as I saw my guitar held together only by its strings. The adults gasped, but the party wasn't over. I had to sing songs a cappella with lots of animation and a big smile, even though I wanted to cry. The money I would make from this party would not go toward bills as I'd hoped. It would have to go toward another guitar.

I walked home feeling defeated. It seemed as if no matter how hard I tried in life, I would always have to struggle. It wasn't just my guitar that was broken that day.

A few days later, the worship leader led me to the stage of our church. There were four guitars lined up like soldiers on their stands. "Pick the one you want," he said. He went on to tell me how much he believed in me and my talent as a musician. With each encouraging word, I felt new again, just like the beautiful new guitar I chose—its sound so much richer than the one that was broken.

Thank You for those who lift me up when I'm discouraged.
Help me to learn from their example and encourage others as well.
—Karen Valentin

Digging Deeper: Romans 8:28; Philippians 4:19

THE FRIENDSHIP OF WOMEN: Better Together

Now you are the body of Christ, and each one of you is a part of it.
—1 Corinthians 12:27 (NIV)

While in my early twenties, I was in college to earn my Bachelor of Science degree in nursing. For my senior project, I designed a community hospice program for my little town of Huntington, West Virginia. Local physicians referred terminally ill patients to me, and I modeled my program after the esteemed work Cicely Saunders did with the terminally ill in England.

Patients, their families, and their caregivers loved the economic, emotional, and spiritual dimensions of patients' being able to live until they died in their own homes. But I lacked administrative and fiscal skills to sustain it. In the end, it was just a lofty idea. I was crushed.

Then the next semester, an older, more experienced student named Laura needed a project she could plan from her ill father's bedside. The two of us met, and I told her about my discarded dream. I gave her all of my research materials, and we prayed about the future of Huntington's hospice. Laura, who excelled in the skills I lacked, took the hospice concept to a fully realized level.

As the years passed, Laura and I became terrific friends and two of the program's initial volunteer nurses. One day, I lamented to her that all my work had been a failure. "Look at all *you* did compared to *me*," I said. "*You're* like the right hand in the body of Christ, Laura. *I'm* just a fingernail."

She laughed. "Really? Have you ever tried to live without a fingernail? Hospice of Huntington would've never come to be without *you!*"

Thank You for friends, Lord, who remind us of our unique
role in Your body.
—Roberta Messner

Digging Deeper: Romans 12:4–5; 1 Corinthians 12:12

Monday, August 17

"Peace I leave with you; My peace I give to you...." —John 14:27 (NASB)

A spectacular story is told of Jesus in Matthew 8:23–27. He had been teaching large crowds and healing many who were ill. Then He and His disciples took their boat to the other side of the Sea of Galilee, a large freshwater lake.

Before they reached the opposite shore, a "great storm" swamped the boat with waves. This was an open wooden fishing boat, similar to the one exposed in 1986 when drought caused the Sea of Galilee waters to recede. One can presume Jesus was drenched and tossed about. His disciples—many of them seasoned fishermen—were terrified.

And Jesus? He was asleep. A deep, satisfying rest. The others had to wake Him, crying to Him to save them.

In the NASB, the passage says Jesus "rebuked the winds and the sea, and it became perfectly calm." He shut down the storm, imparting His peace to the forces of nature. His amazed disciples questioned, "What kind of a man is this, that even the winds and the sea obey Him?"

When I need to claim the peace of Jesus in a crisis, I climb in the "Jesus Boat"—what the ancient fishing vessel is frequently called. I found this deep unexplainable rest in the storm most recently when I traveled the end-of-life journey with my beloved mother-in-law.

Mom's sudden illness broadsided us. Our family felt deluged by what was happening. I cried out to Jesus to speak His Word into Mom's life and for me to accept His authority. He invited me to trust Him, even as He welcomed Mom home with Him. His peace carried us across troubled waters.

Jesus can rebuke the storm, but to experience His calm in the storm is no less a miracle.

> *Son of God, in turbulent times, show me what it means to*
> *rest in—and with—You.*
> —Carol Knapp

Digging Deeper: Exodus 33:14; Psalm 62:1–2;
Matthew 8:23–27; John 16:33

Praise be to the God and Father of our Lord Jesus Christ, the Father of compassion and the God of all comfort, who comforts us in all our troubles, so that we can comfort those in any trouble with the comfort we ourselves receive from God. —2 Corinthians 1:3–4 (NIV)

T oday's the day," my daughter Kendall texted me. "I'm taking Baby in at 9:30."

Her words caused an instant wave of grief. Baby is her eighteen-year-old cat that she and her husband got shortly after they married. Their first "child." I knew how long Kendall had been dreading this day as she watched her cat's health and body deteriorate. I also knew how she felt. I'd made that final painful journey to the vet's office many times, most recently with Kemo, my faithful ten-year-old golden retriever who had cancer. I had vivid emotional recall.

"I'm so sorry," I wrote in my text message back to her. "You are brave and this is the most loving thing you can do for her."

"Ugh," she wrote back, adding a crying emoji.

"Makes me feel like crying with you," I answered. "Before taking Kemo in, I asked myself whether I could allow him to become a happy memory instead of a painful daily reality. The thought helped me make that hard choice."

"Thanks," she replied. "Helps me too."

"You've been dreading this day, but I know God will comfort you afterward. You've been a great cat-mom, Kendall."

"I gave her lots of treats this morning. It's just so hard."

"I'm praying with you," I wrote. "It is a very hard, right thing."

Lord, You love us in many personal and powerful ways through our pets. Thank You for comforting me when I've had to let them go, which helps me understand others when they face that same painful experience.
—Carol Kuykendall

Digging Deeper: Isaiah 50:4; 2 Corinthians 1:3–7

Wednesday, August 19

I have the desire to do what is good, but I cannot carry it out.
—Romans 7:18 (NIV)

I'm not good at being friends," I warned a new friend recently, hoping to sidestep—or at least account for—her inevitable disappointment at my unwillingness to "do something" together. I don't know what's wrong with me—introversion, social anxiety, or sheer self-centeredness—but making plans to get together, even for the delightful bird-watching walk in the woods she proposed, makes me feel trapped.

I love encountering a friend in town somewhere and sitting down to a serendipitous coffee. I often stop by a friend's house unannounced just to say hi or drop off a loaf of bread. And I like it when friends show up uninvited. I like spending time together; I just hate scheduling it.

"Didn't you schedule visits with your mother-in-law?" my brother asked on the phone as I was going on about my latest friendship failure. "Can't you just commit to it like that?"

"I had to visit Mamaw," I said. "But with friends, I don't. Somehow I just can't make myself do it."

Some of my friends live far away, so our friendships consist of long catch-up phone calls and visiting every decade or so. Others—those with small children, for instance—are busier than I am, so getting together is typically spur of the moment. But increasingly, as my friends age and their free time expands, I know I neglect them.

I neglect Jesus, too, I know. I wonder if someday He'll tell me, "I was lonely, but you didn't want to hang out."

What I want to confess here is that though I'm aware of my tendency to isolate and I am determined to do better (I'm eager to enjoy good things like birds, trees, and friendship), I routinely fail as a friend. I have to rely on God's promises that I'm forgiven and that He will ultimately make me perfect.

Lord, mold me to Your will.
—Patty Kirk

Digging Deeper: Luke 6:31, 22:39–46

He was buried with the kings in the City of David, because of the good he had done in Israel for God and his temple. —2 Chronicles 24:16 (NIV)

As my family and I were flying from an overseas assignment back to the United States recently, I noticed something out of place about a fellow passenger wearing his military dress uniform. Having lived overseas for a number of years, I knew that soldiers, for security reasons, are not supposed to wear uniforms while traveling.

My curiosity was finally satisfied when we landed and heard that our flight carried the remains of a World War II casualty being returned home to family for burial. The pilot asked for respect as the person in uniform escorted the body. I am proud to live in a country where such care and effort is taken to bring fallen service members home. Decades after this service member lost his life, he was returned home with great dignity and respect. Service to others is service to the Lord.

I believe that every American on board sat solemnly while the service member left the plane and retrieved the remains. I prayed. Unfortunately, some of the passengers from other countries carried on as if nothing was happening. While this was disappointing, I took comfort in the reverence with which many Americans do honor our fallen service members.

Displaying your beliefs, whether because of national pride or religious convictions, can often meet with misunderstanding, lack of regard, or even outright opposition. Standing true sometimes means standing alone. Even when I am surrounded by people who do not understand my convictions, I hope I will always have the courage to stand up for my beliefs and to honor those who deserve my appreciation and respect.

Dear Lord, we thank You for those who have loved others above themselves, for those who have sacrificed their lives so that freedom can reign in our great nation. May we continue to revere their sacrifice.
—Jolynda Strandberg

Digging Deeper: Luke 20:36; 2 Corinthians 5:8

Friday, August 21

I thank my God every time I remember you. In all my prayers for all of you, I always pray with joy. —Philippians 1:3–4 (NIV)

Most days I tune in a classical-music radio station that features old standards rather than modern dissonance. The music melds into the background "landscape" of my day. I hardly distinguish one piece from another. But last week, Tchaikovsky's *Fifth Symphony* riveted my attention. Not because of its superior artistry. Because a college friend in the 1970s had given me an album of the symphony, performed by the Cleveland Orchestra. Yesterday's broadcast took me back in time. Not to the loneliness of my twenties, when I frequently played the record, but to the friendship of the gift-giver, Bob. His distinctive take on life, his sense of humor, his talents. I found his contact info and sent him a thank-you. He was happy to hear from me, though he doesn't remember the vinyl. I remembered it so well that when I listened to it last week, I noticed the symphony's telltale clarinet squeak was missing.

Over a lifetime, I've been graced with pleasing gifts that nurture my spirit and suit my tastes. The most memorable ones connect me to the giver. Like Bob. Like Camilla, who gave me a silk-screen cloth. Like Leon, who framed it. Like Angi, who brought me a rooted fig shoot. Like my Creator God, who provided the growth and the fruit I plucked this morning from the maturing tree.

Naming several gifts and givers prompted me to take a break to package up a book I enjoyed and mail it to an out-of-town friend I haven't seen in years. The memoir's theme reminded me of my friend's life's work. I've just returned from the post office. I pray she'll value the gift and the renewed connection, and maybe remember me with thanksgiving.

> *Lord, I thank You for the gift-givers who have enriched my life.*
> *May I, in turn, bless others.*
> —Evelyn Bence

Digging Deeper: 1 Corinthians 1:1–9; 1 Thessalonians 1:2–3

"Not one of them is forgotten before God." —Luke 12:6 (NKJV)

It was a blistering hot day, a Saturday, and my hard-working daddy must have been ready for a bit of leisure. But my seven-year-old self was having a meltdown unrelated to the temperature.

A sparrow had somehow made its way into our low-ceilinged attic and become frightened.

"Daddy," I wailed, "you've got to save the poor bird!"

The attic was sweltering, and it offered only room enough for my six-foot-four father to crawl on his hands and knees. No matter how many tricks he tried, he couldn't coax the bird to fly out of the attic opening.

Daddy realized that catching the sparrow was its only hope for survival. He improvised a net, but there wasn't enough room to swing it in a way to capture the bird. The temperature was getting hotter, and my mother was beginning to worry about heat strokes and exhaustion, not so much for the bird but for Daddy. All we could do was to stand below and encourage him as he crawled back and forth across the rough wood floor.

And then, "Gotcha!"

We were cheering now, as Daddy backed down the wooden steps. He was wet with sweat, but there in his big, gentle hands, the bird lay, equally exhausted. Outside, Daddy opened his hands. The sparrow hesitated for only a second, and then flew free.

The Bible offers many promises of God's loving care for us. It tells us that He will never give up until He delivers us from harm. Thanks to my earthly father and the bird in the attic, I have an idea of the lengths to which our heavenly Father is willing to go to save His children. It's really nice to know that even when we try our hardest to avoid being rescued, He is there, hatching yet another plan to save us.

Father, I know that You will never give up on Your children. I cheer You on.
—Pam Kidd

Digging Deeper: Matthew 6:26, 10:31

Sunday, August 23

Beloved, let us love one another, for love is of God.... —1 John 4:7 (NKJV)

The two-mile trek up Monument Mountain in Great Barrington, Massachusetts, is a ritual adventure for me and all the dogs I've loved. Especially Gracie, our three-year-old golden retriever. It is her favorite place in the world. She's not a huge fan of the car, but when we head toward Monument Mountain, she nudges me from the back seat, tail a-wag, as if to speed us along.

The other day, a hot sunny morning, we stopped halfway up the mountain at a cherished trail juncture so we could both have a drink. I rested my sunglasses on a rock and busied myself getting her portable water bowl out and filled after stealing a peek at my work e-mail on my phone (I know better, but I did it anyway). Meanwhile Gracie scurried off into some undergrowth, her hindquarters to me. *Wonder what she found?*

"Gracie, come get a drink."

She didn't come right away. She bolted up the trail instead and then darted back to lap sloppily at her bowl, glancing up at me. A group of hikers passed by, greeted cheerily by my golden. Then we were on our way. Except I couldn't find my sunglasses. My new, pricey prescription sunglasses. I knew at once: Gracie.

I searched for five minutes before I found the mangled remains a few yards up the trail, gnawed nearly beyond recognition and then crushed underfoot by the recent hiking party.

There had been intent. There had been deceit and concealment. "How could you?" I wailed, shielding my eyes to better glare at her.

She had moved on up the trail by now, tail aloft, while I clutched the remnants of my glasses. I wanted to scream—or to weep. Instead I laughed. *No*, I thought, *love is never easy*. If it were easy, it wouldn't be love. Maybe that was the lesson on this hot sunny day.

> *Dear God, keep teaching me to love when love is the hardest.*
> —Edward Grinnan

Digging Deeper: Proverbs 17:17; 1 Corinthians 13

"Prepare yourself and be ready, you and all your companies that are gathered about you...."—Ezekiel 38:7 (NKJV)

Grandma had a readiness factor I admire. She always kept homemade cookies in her freezer. It seemed every time I visited her, someone would drop by unannounced. This never appeared to fluster her. She would welcome the person with a cup of hot coffee and a plate of very cold cookies from the freezer. Her guests got their coffee up front, but she placed the cookies a little beyond their reach. Grandma would masterfully steer the conversation, asking questions and drawing out her guests. Through silent observation (and a snatched cookie or two), I learned quickly that the longer they chatted, the softer the cookies became. After about twenty minutes, Grandma would make a point of "remembering" to offer the plate to her guests. By this time, the cookies seemed as fresh as if they were baked that day. Her thoughtful conversations made lifelong friends. Her always-fresh cookies kept people coming back.

Being ready for the unexpected is a talent I'm still mastering, especially when there is a Scripture I could share to help someone. The verses I easily memorized as a child are harder for me to recall now. But one practice I've started has really improved my retention of Scripture. Each day of the month, I read a chapter of Proverbs. The thirty-one chapters makes it easy to follow through. I love having a pithy Proverb on the tip of my tongue for nearly any situation that arises. And I'm working at having a stock of cookies on hand in the freezer too. The trouble is, I have developed a taste for frozen cookies. They remind me of Grandma.

Lord, make me ever ready to speak Your Word.
—Erika Bentsen

Digging Deeper: Deuteronomy 11:18; Proverbs 3:3;
Matthew 24:44; 2 Timothy 4:2

Tuesday, August 25

You are all one in Christ Jesus. —Galatians 3:28 (NIV)

As the registration deadline for a popular writers' conference approached, I asked a friend, a successful author, if she was going. "No. They're very cliquish."

Shocked by her answer, the word *clique* summoned dreadful memories from my teenage years. Back then, *clique* meant the "in crowd," that special group of people I never seemed to fit into: the popular, the athletic, the pretty, the smart, the confident. I always felt on the fringe of that group—friends, but not one of "them."

It started in the ninth grade when all the girls began training for the high school booster club. Every day after school, we marched in unison, practicing the required drills. Then I got sick, and I missed school for the next six weeks. I couldn't practice, so I missed the tryouts and subsequently, being in the boosters.

The boosters were the first step toward my goal to get into the "Highsteppers," an elite corps with the cutest uniforms. By missing out on boosters, I felt doomed to never being in the "in crowd." A friend told me that I could try out the next year, but by then, I thought it was too late.

The experience wasn't totally bad, because I learned a couple of things from it: One, don't quit too soon, and two, start your own group when you feel left out of another. I became a leader of whatever club I joined, rallying other girls who felt left out and giving them something to belong to.

Long after my high school years, I continued to start groups when I wasn't invited to one. It's been a long time since cliques have threatened me. As an adult, those barriers don't matter. As a Christian, we all belong to the same "club."

> *Thank You, Lord, that we don't have to be in a clique for*
> *You to accept us. Help us to be inclusive of all others.*
> —Marilyn Turk

Digging Deeper: 1 Corinthians 12:12; Ephesians 1:5–6

The young lions suffer want and hunger; but those who seek the Lord lack no good thing. —Psalm 34:10 (ESV)

As I hauled yet another gallon of milk into my cart, I glanced at the cart and did some mental calculations. At $6.49 for one gallon, times four gallons per week, the milk adds up to—well, a whole lot of money. It's hard to maintain a grocery budget when you have growing children in the house.

Can I get an Amen?

I considered putting the fourth gallon back and trying to get by with three gallons for the week, but my children need calcium for their growing bones. And I certainly couldn't give up milk for my coffee, could I?

I stood in the dairy section and assessed my cart. I still needed to cut twenty dollars in order to keep to our budget. What else could I eliminate? Certainly not the ground beef and chicken that would provide protein, or the fruits and vegetables that helped us stay strong and healthy.

"Lord," I silently prayed. "I'm trying to be wise with my money, but it's hard to stick to a budget when my family needs so much."

I stood there for a few minutes, contemplating my grocery budget and imagining bread and fish multiplying in my cupboards as they did on that hillside in Galilee long ago. Wouldn't that be nice?

Just then, my phone buzzed in my pocket. A text message from my friend Megan: "Erin, our garden is going gangbusters. I put together a basket with tomatoes, green beans, blackberries, and watermelon for you. Drop by and pick it up."

I smiled. A grocery-store miracle. I walked back to the produce section and put back the fruit and veggies. Then I walked to checkout and my total came in just three dollars under budget.

Thank You, Jesus, for answering even the tiniest of prayers when I need You most. Thank You for meeting every one of my needs in abundance. Amen.
—Erin MacPherson

Digging Deeper: 1 Chronicles 29:11; Philippians 4:19

Thursday, August 27

Each of you should give what you have decided in your heart to give, not reluctantly or under compulsion, for God loves a cheerful giver.
—2 Corinthians 9:7 (NIV)

As part of the hospitality ministry at our church, I provide food for funerals, shut-ins, and special events. Now I had begun to cook for an interfaith program, Family Promise, where local churches take weekly turns hosting a family in need of housing. Some parishioners stay overnight with the guests; others, like me, provide an evening meal. I hadn't cooked an entire dinner for a large group in years. Nowadays, "dinner" at my home served only one or two people. What could I prepare this week for three adults and five children who might not be adventurous eaters?

I zeroed in on a hearty casserole full of ground beef, cheese, onions, corn, beans, tomato, chilies, corn chips, and Mexican seasonings. At the grocery, I found what I needed, added brownies and watermelon mostly for the youngsters, and proceeded to the checkout. Wow! Nearly twenty dollars for just one meal! I had quite forgotten the cost of feeding a family of eight. Granted, I had volunteered to serve only one meal this week, but I hadn't expected it to cost quite so much.

Back home while the beef browned in a skillet, I lunched on a veggie omelet leftover from a leisurely breakfast downtown the day before. That's when it hit me: I had blithely spent almost as much on *one* meal for myself as I had grudgingly spent for a family of eight. I flushed in hot shame. May God be generous in forgiving my self-absorption.

Giver of all good things, teach me to be more like You.
—Gail Schilling

Digging Deeper: Matthew 10:8; Romans 12:13

You have rescued my soul from death, my eyes from tears, my feet from stumbling. —Psalm 116:8 (NASB)

Today my husband, Dwight; my stepson; and I were getting ready to wash the dog. "I forgot the shampoo," I said. "I'll be right back." But I wasn't right back. When I did return, Dwight asked, "What took you so long?"

I told him what had distracted me: a chipmunk had gotten onto our screened back porch through the propped-open door. Problem was, poor little fellow couldn't find his way back out. I watched him struggle, trying to get through the screen, not seeing the open door through which he could easily escape. "I put a trail of popcorn to the door to help him find his way out," I said. Dwight laughed, shook his head, and gave me a hug.

Maybe it was silly to worry so much about a chipmunk, yet I couldn't help but feel that I understood him somehow. Here he was, trapped in an impossible situation of his own making, trying all the wrong ways to get out of it. *Boy, can I relate!* It seems that every time I've found myself in a tough spot, it was my own doing that got me into it. If only I'd trusted God and not gone off on my own path, I could have spared myself such trouble. So many times I've said, "I wish I'd done what Jesus would have done," but not once in my entire life have I said, "If only I hadn't done things God's way!"

I checked back on my furry friend later, and he was gone. No word on whether he enjoyed the popcorn, but I like to think he appreciated the gesture.

Father, You have rescued me from my own self-sabotage more times than I can count. Thank You for Your mercy and Your abounding grace.
—Ginger Rue

Digging Deeper: Isaiah 43:1–7; Romans 7:24

Saturday, August 29

Let each of you look not only to his own interests, but also to the interests of others. —Philippians 2:4 (ESV)

Sarah and I stood in the movie ticket line, talking. Titles and showtimes crawled across an overhead screen. The words moved much faster than the line, but I didn't mind. I liked Sarah. We had been out several times, and she was always easy to talk to. She made me feel comfortable.

We reached the front of the line, and I told the cashier our movie and time. When he totaled up the cost, I reached for my back pocket. But Sarah reached into her purse first.

"You paid last time," she said. "This one's on me."

"No, I've got it," I said. But even as the words came out of my mouth, Sarah passed her cash across the counter. I no longer felt at ease. I didn't like being a burden. I pulled my hand from my back pocket, wallet-less. My hands felt out of place.

The cashier gave us our tickets, and we headed across the atrium.

"You didn't have to do that," I said.

"I wanted to," she said.

As we walked into the theater, I still felt uncomfortable. I was used to being self-reliant. I took care of people, not the other way around. I lowered my voice. "I mean, I didn't expect you to pay," I said.

She touched my arm. "It makes me happy to treat you," she said. I looked into her eyes; they were full and happy. She didn't feel that paying for me was a burden; it was a blessing for her.

It was wrong for me to want to take that blessing away from her—an ironic form of selfishness to try to fight her desire to pay. Today, the best way that I could take care of Sarah was to let her take care of me.

"Thank you," I said.

In the glow of the movie screen, I saw her smile.

> *Father God, give me a heart that can both give and receive.*
> —Logan Eliasen

Digging Deeper: Proverbs 18:1; 1 Corinthians 10:24

Since we live by the Spirit, let us keep in step with the Spirit.
—Galatians 5:25 (NIV)

I'm fuming as my husband, Michael, and I wait in the car for our daughter Micah, as we do most Sunday mornings. She's late. Again.

We amble into the darkened sanctuary. Everyone's standing. We've attended this church for more than a decade, so I figure our usual place down front, left center, is available.

Micah pushes past me to lead. Instead of going to the section where we normally sit, she turns toward the rear rows. I shake my head, but Michael furrows his brow as if to say, "Let it go."

They know I don't like sitting in the back where people are disengaged. Heck, half of them clear out right after the sermon is over. Back here is not where we belong. Not where we should be.

The choir's on their final song. I'm too cross to sing. Micah playfully peers around Michael who's next to me. When we sit, Micah moves down a chair. Michael follows, which leaves an empty seat between us. They motion me over. I'm not moving. Neither do they.

We greet people around us and have announcements. As the sermon begins, a woman with a preschooler rushes to the seats beside me.

At the end of his message, the pastor asks us to write a prayer on provided note cards and exchange them with someone behind us. I scribble a prayer, and turn. A family of five behind me stares right through me. *This wouldn't happen if we sat up front.*

"I'll trade," says the woman with the preschooler next to me.

I read her card. "Pray for my children during our divorce: Emma, Charli, Asher." Our eyes meet. I'm a prayer warrior. I've got her covered.

Perhaps Micah didn't choose my seat, after all.

> *Lord, thank You for reminding me that when circumstances don't*
> *go my way, You could be leading me Your way.*
> —Stephanie Thompson

Digging Deeper: Psalm 25:4; 2 Thessalonians 3:5

Righteousness guards him whose way is blameless, but sin overthrows the wicked. —Proverbs 13:6 (ESV)

A few months ago, my puppy Zeke chewed a hole in the couch cushion and tore out all of the stuffing. I came home to a blizzard of cotton puffs in my living room and spent an hour cleaning up the mess and stitching up the hole. Problem solved.

Or not.

The next night, we came home once again to find the living room a blizzard, my careful stitches torn into an even bigger hole than before.

This has now been going on for three months. I stitch up the cushion, Zeke tears it open. I stitch it. Zeke rips it.

Last night, after another cotton-stuffing disaster zone, my son Joey said, "Mom, I think it might be time to throw away the couch cushion."

I started to retort that the puppy had to learn right from wrong and that soon he would figure out that it is a bad idea to tear apart the couch day after day. But then I realized that Joey was right.

The puppy had found a weak spot and he was exploiting it. He knew exactly where to find the hole, and exactly how to cause yet another blizzard. While my efforts to keep sewing it up were well-meaning, they put the temptation right back in front of my dog's face. So this morning, the couch cushion went into the trash and a new, hole-free cushion was ordered.

It cost seventy-eight dollars. That is, seventy-eight dollars to stop the cycle, to pull away the temptation, to assure that my dog and I can co-exist without my losing my mind. Seventy-eight dollars to remind me that sometimes to get rid of a sin, drastic steps and a fresh start are necessary.

Otherwise, a tiny hole can quickly be torn into a gaping hole.

Lord, give me a willingness to throw out sin, into the garbage,
and to walk forward blamelessly, following You. Amen.
—Erin MacPherson

Digging Deeper: 2 Timothy 1:7; 1 Peter 3:11

HE PERFORMS WONDERS

1 _____

2 _____

3 _____

4 _____

5 _____

6 _____

7 _____

8 _____

9 _____

10 _____

11 _____

12 _____

13 _____

14 _____

15 _____

August

16 _____

17 _____

18 _____

19 _____

20 _____

21 _____

22 _____

23 _____

24 _____

25 _____

26 _____

27 _____

28 _____

29 _____

30 _____

31 _____

SEPTEMBER

Bear with each other and forgive one another if any of you has a grievance against someone. Forgive as the Lord forgave you.

—Colossians 3:13 (NIV)

Tuesday, September 1

FIRSTS: Childlike Faith

"I am with you always...."—Matthew 28:20 (KJV)

Ritchie was four the first time he darted away from his mother in a crowd. On a sunny Saturday, she'd taken him to the Bronx Zoo. "We were standing in the ticket line for the camel ride," Jean told me. "I let go of his hand just long enough to reach in my purse."

Looking frantically around, Jean thought, *He loves polar bears!* She ran to the North Pole habitat. No Ritchie. She raced back past the camels, crying now. "Have you seen a little boy in a red shirt?"

A guard pointed her to the headquarters building. "That's where they take lost kids. He's probably there now." He wasn't. Just another couple reporting a lost child. "We broadcast a description to all personnel," the attendant said. "We usually find the child in twenty minutes." Giving Ritchie's particulars—blonde hair, blue eyes, red-and-white-check suspender pants, red sneakers—he seemed to Jean a perfect kidnapper's target.

In twenty minutes, as predicted, the other couple's seven-year-old son arrived in a zookeeper's truck. Another twenty minutes passed. Half an hour. Forty-five minutes. Each minute an eternity. Jean had waited at the headquarters an hour-and-a-half before the truck arrived with Ritchie.

What had taken so long, the driver told her, was that lost children are invariably crying. Ritchie had been spotted several times, but he was so composed that they assumed he belonged to some nearby family.

Discovering him outside the penguin house with no one else in sight, the driver had asked, "Are you lost, little boy?" Ritchie nodded.

"Let's go in my truck to find Mommy."

The child seemed to hesitate. "Can Jesus come in the truck too?"

It wasn't the last time Jean's escape artist slipped away. Just the first time she realized that her four-year-old's faith was stronger than her own.

Lord, Who makes all things new, give me the awareness
of Your presence, wherever I am.
—Elizabeth Sherrill

Digging Deeper: Joshua 1:9; Isaiah 41:10–13

"There will no longer be any mourning, or crying, or pain...."
—Revelation 21:4 (NASB)

My first days of classes each fall semester at Mercer University are often tinged with nostalgia. I am both a professor and an alumnus of Mercer, class of 1973. As I now meet new students and thrill to their fresh vitality and eagerness, I also recall my old classmates, most of whom I haven't seen in forty-five years. I wonder where they are and if we would recognize each other at homecoming weekend.

In the midst of my excitement as I greet returning students, I also miss last year's seniors whom I have grown to love. Life seems to always be "a tear and a smile," a time of saying hello and goodbye.

Tonight as I reflected on these thoughts, I recall the words of the writer of Revelation: "I saw a new heaven and a new earth...and He will wipe away every tear from their eyes; and there will no longer be any death; there will no longer be any mourning, or crying, or pain.... Behold, I am making all things new" (Revelation 21:1, 4–5, NASB).

This is the promise of our life in a new dimension beyond death. Some call it heaven. Some call it eternity. No name is adequate to express what the future will be, but there will be laughter and joy and sweet reunion. My deepest intuition tells me this is true.

> *Lord, may my longing be a poignant prelude to a*
> *symphony of eternal reunion. Amen.*
> —Scott Walker

Digging Deeper: John 14:1–3; 1 Corinthians 15:51–58

Thursday, September 3

My soul will glory in the Lord; let the poor hear and be glad.
—Psalm 34:3 (NABRE)

Mom looked small standing next to Dad's hospital bed in the intensive care unit. She held his hand in both of hers, her thumbs tracing his knuckles and veins.

"How did I get so lucky to have found you?" she asked as he lay there listening (or so we hoped). She glanced up at us, gathered nearby. "And how did we get such incredible children? Oh, we had such fun, didn't we? You've given me a rich and wonderful life."

I was surprised to hear her say this. She was telling a different story than the one I told myself about their marriage. Oh, I knew they loved each other. But I saw that I had dwelled on the times I saw them lose patience with each other. I had prioritized their complaints, not their compliments.

Clearly, I need to be more charitable. But what about those compliments? To be honest, I felt a shiver of embarrassment trickle through me as my mom openly spoke of her love for her husband, my father. I felt like I was eavesdropping. Yet her words were a gift. They enriched my understanding of my parents and their imperfectly perfect union. They gladdened my grieving heart.

Public praise is an act of love. It's how we're encouraged to express our love for God. The psalms exhort us, again and again, to make music for God, to sing to Him, to shout to the Lord with joy. It is in the shouting that others hear and are made glad.

If so with God, then so with one another. Saying to all who will listen "I love him" and "I love her" is just as important as saying "I love you."

God, I give my self-consciousness to You so that I may let the world know how much I love the special people in my life.
—Amy Eddings

Digging Deeper: Psalms 96:1, 149:3, 150:4

We may make our plans, but God has the last word. —Proverbs 16:1 (GNT)

I thought *for sure* I knew what would happen next. I'd become a grand-mother—a grandmother who knits! I'd crocheted years ago but never learned to knit. Knitting seemed a step above crocheting. Posher. Fancier.

After our daughter Katie married in 2005, she and her husband began trying to start a family. I enrolled in class to knit a baby blanket.

But Katie couldn't get pregnant, and I couldn't knit.

She divorced after eight years of marriage, and I donated my knit-ting needles and instruction books to Goodwill. I almost tossed the thin strip of green and yellow yarn—my failure of a blanket. Instead, I shoved it into the back of my closet. I never wanted to see it again.

Then something unexpected happened.

Katie met a good man—a Purple Heart recipient who'd served in Afghanistan and who had a brown-eyed, three-year-old daughter named Rilynn. Katie and Chris married, and I became an instant grandmother. A few months after the wedding, Katie resumed her infertility treatment.

Two and a half years later, she called me after another pregnancy test. Her last chance. No more treatment options available.

Listening to her sobs, I held the phone and prayed.

What do I say, Lord? She's completely broken. And I'm empty. I have no words of consolation left.

I dropped to my knees. "I'm so sorry. Want me to pray for you?"

"No, Mom," Katie's hysterical crying turned to choppy laughter. "It's positive. One hundred percent positive. I'm pregnant!"

My laughter and tears blended with hers. We were a mother-daughter mess.

Several months later, I ripped out my knitting and returned to my first love. Crocheting. I finished the yellow and green blanket and then made another one. Baby blue for my grandson, Caleb James.

> *Lord, Your plans are always the best. Hallelujah!*
> —Julie Garmon

Digging Deeper: Proverbs 19:2; Ecclesiastes 8:7

Saturday, September 5

"I am your God and will take care of you until you are old and your hair is gray. I made you and will care for you; I will give you help and rescue you."—Isaiah 46:4 (GNT)

Everything okay?" my dad said from behind me.

I was digging through a small closet upstairs in the hallway, next to my parents' bedroom.

"I scraped my finger," I said. "I wasn't sure where you kept the Band-Aids but just found them," I said, holding up the small box.

My dad shook his head. "Those are cheap," he said. "I have better ones in the bathroom."

I followed him, where he opened a drawer stuffed with a variety of sizes of them. He started to unwrap one.

"Dad, I can put it on myself," I said. "It's not that bad."

"Hold out your hand," he said. He hovered the bandage over my wound, carefully aligning it. His concentration was strong.

I felt like his little girl again. Just like a daydream, these minutes became fragile, as if the scene could fall away at any second.

I sensed that Jesus wanted me to pay attention to the way my father's fingers felt as they wrapped the Band-Aid around my finger. Gently. Lovingly. Securely. He wanted me to think about how much joy this moment was bringing my father—being able to take care of his thirty-two-year-old daughter as though she were six years old again.

Then, Jesus planted these words in my heart: "Now, imagine how your Father in Heaven feels when you let Him care for you. It's His nature to help you, but you must learn to let Him, just as you let your father today."

Father, the older I get, the more I try to fix things by myself. But it's Your desire for me to experience all of Your character and to receive Your sweet fatherly qualities, even in seemingly minor situations.
—Desiree Cole

Digging Deeper: 2 Corinthians 6:18; 1 John 3:1

The Lord gives strength to his people; the Lord blesses his people with peace. —Psalm 29:11 (NIV)

When my mother, Maria, was a senior in high school, she came down with rheumatic fever, an inflammatory disease that can develop as a complication of inadequately treated strep throat or scarlet fever. The disease can cause permanent damage to the heart, joints, skin, and brain. When my mom was in her early sixties, she had open-heart surgery to repair her damaged heart valves as a result of this disease. It's now about fifteen years later and she is in need of another heart surgery.

Recently, my mother had been experiencing shortness of breath and was unable to walk for long periods; yet she refused to see a doctor. The painful heart surgery and long recovery process were a lot to handle the first time, and she didn't want to go through that again. However, her condition continued to worsen, leaving her no choice but to seek medical attention. After several exams, she was informed that she would need heart valve replacement surgery. Thankfully, this procedure, unlike the last, could be done through small incisions in the groin. Though this was a relief to the family, Mom was still anxious about the process.

Soon after my mother received this news, I decided to drop by to see how she was feeling. When I arrived, I found her sitting outside on the deck reading a book. When she spotted me, the first words out of her mouth were, "God spoke to me." I was taken aback; this is not her typical greeting. Then she showed me what she was reading: *What Prayer Can Do*, a Guideposts book. "I just finished reading a story of a woman diagnosed with an abnormal tricuspid heart valve and God healed her. I needed this message." Her faith and spirit were uplifted by the story. God calmed my mother's fears and gave her the peace she needed to move forward with the procedure.

God, calm our fears and give us peace.
—Pablo Diaz

Digging Deeper: Job 3:25–26; 1 John 5:14

Labor Day, Monday, September 7

Oh, yes. Affirm the work that we do! —Psalm 90:17 (MSG)

With mild irritation I read the e-mail subject line: "Please tell us what you think." The message seemed to come from corporate headquarters of a hotel where I stayed recently in Leavenworth, Kansas. My initial response? *Not more inbox clutter.*

Then I thought back to the lodging experience. Sparkling clean rooms. Pleasant staff. Breakfast buffet of Canadian bacon; fresh cheesy scrambled eggs; guava, cranberry, and orange juice drink options. With memories of the delightful stay, I quickly filled out the online survey. Gratitude was the theme.

Being a retired chaplain, I'm often shown appreciation for work rightly done. When a West Point Washington Gate security officer sees my US Army retired ID card, he'll often say, "Thanks, Sir, for your service." Frequently, after a TSA agent inspects my ID card and boarding pass at an airport check-in line, she'll say, "Thank you for what you've done."

My usual response to these words of affirmation is something like: "Yes, and thank you for your work. We're all in this together. Each one of us, working side by side, is helping to keep our nation strong. Thank you."

Labor Day celebrates the dignity and healthy pride we can take in the callings we've been given. Our collective work contributes to the betterment of us all. Showing mutual thanks for shared vocations uplifts and encourages. Our world is positively affected for much good. We are all blessed.

Three days after completing my hotel survey, I opened an unexpected e-mail. "Dear Kenneth Sampson: Thank you for choosing to stay with us! We appreciate your kind words and hope to see you again." A real person, the assistant general manager of a Kansas hotel, sent the response. It was a moment of grace. In expressing gratitude for a pleasant stay, I was blessed as well.

> *Gracious God, show me opportunities where I may say a word*
> *of thanks today, and empower me to do so.*
> —Ken Sampson

Digging Deeper: Ephesians 4:1; Colossians 3:15–17

PRAYING IN PUBLIC: A Change of Heart

"Leave your gift there before the altar and go; first be reconciled to your brother or sister, and then come and offer your gift."—Matthew 5:24 (NRSV)

I've never gotten along with the young woman who owns the apartment below ours. Our building's walls, floors, and ceilings might as well be made of cardboard when it comes to noise. So I get to hear her arguments, parties, loud laughter, and television, while she gets to hear my walking, sometimes at night because I'm a night owl. The difference between us is that I accept the noise as part of apartment living, while she thinks nothing of screaming at her ceiling and pounding on it with, I assume, a broom or some tall tool whenever she hears me. If my husband, Charlie, and I come in after an evening out, I can't even walk in my good shoes for the ten steps necessary to reach my closet before she lets me know the noise is bothering her.

So when she starts to sneeze, sniffle, and cough with seasonal allergies every year, I am not as sympathetic as I should be. I'm embarrassed to admit that after hours of listening to her, I'm ready to scream myself. But I don't.

Most days, I pray for an hour in our bedroom, which is above her bedroom. One afternoon I was praying upstairs as she was coughing downstairs. I started praying louder, and I can't say I was doing it out of love. But then her coughing slowed down, and I realized that she could hear me. I kept praying, but changed my heart and my tone. I willed my words to go through the floor and into her room. I asked the Lord to help this child who had annoyed me so often over the years. I felt hope. It grew quiet down there.

When I finished praying, I stood up and took off my shoes.

Father, help me to pray with empathy. Help my prayers to change me!
—Marci Alborghetti

Digging Deeper: Proverbs 3:5–8, 27–30

Wednesday, September 9

"When I consider Thy heavens, the work of Thy fingers, the moon and the stars, which Thou has ordained; what is man that Thou dost take thought of him? And the son of man, that Thou dost care for him?"
—Psalm 8:3–4 (KJV)

Every fall semester, I teach a freshman class at Mercer University titled "Understanding Self and Others." As we survey ancient events and realms, we more fully realize how old our planet is. Thoughts swirl as rational questions bounce against the unfathomable expanse of time and eternity. The depth of creative mystery and the immeasurable wisdom of God becomes so apparent. A sacred and intuitive sense of mystery is experienced by all.

My father, a theology professor, once told me when I was an inquisitive teenager, "Son, the more I know, the less I know. But the more I know, the more I believe in a creative and loving God." Over the ensuing decades I have discovered my father's words to be true. Sacred mystery is at the center of the greatest truths.

Centuries ago, the prophet Isaiah wrote, "For as the heavens are higher than the earth, so are my ways higher than your ways, and my thoughts than your thoughts" (Isaiah 55:9, KJV). Yet this holy God, shrouded in mystery, has made a way for us to know him.

Father, may I embrace Your mystery as I seek truth
and understanding. Amen.
—Scott Walker

Digging Deeper: Genesis 1:1–31; Job 38:1–33; 1 Corinthians 3:18–19

The wrath of man does not produce the righteousness of God.
—James 1:20 (NKJV)

D ad, I have a flat tire. What should I do?" The text message came from my daughter, Josie.

I replied, "I'll be right there."

Josie discovered her dilemma at the end of her school day. I was only minutes away and arrived quickly.

It was a hot day, but my tenacious teenager wanted to change the tire herself. I talked her through it. She got out the jack and the spare tire. Removed the lug wrench. Positioned the jack and snugged it up. Time to loosen the lug nuts a little. No problem on the first three nuts. The fourth one was tricky, though she got it. But she just couldn't get the wrench onto the last lug nut.

She resisted asking for help but finally gave in. That's when I discovered she would never get that nut off, because the tire shop had put on the wrong-sized lug nut. They'd done that not only on the fifth, but on the fourth nut too. My daughter's tire had three different sizes of lug nuts on it.

I was angry. Had she been stranded alone, she would have never been able to change her tire. Josie's shop teacher lent her tools to finish the job. We traded cars. Josie drove my car home while I drove hers to the shop.

The angry-dad speech in my mind never came out of my mouth. I'm not sure why, but I'm glad. The tire had a hole in the sidewall, so the warranty didn't cover it. The job would cost about eighty dollars. I sat in the waiting room, breathing the aroma of new car tires, thanking God that this flat had happened close to home.

Finally, the mechanic called me over. He apologized for the lug nuts. Everything was finished.

And no charge. Someone else had covered the cost.

> *Lord, I confess that You never need my help—especially*
> *my anger—to accomplish Your grace.*
> —Bill Giovannetti

Digging Deeper: Psalm 34:8; 2 Timothy 2:24–25

Friday, September 11

As iron sharpens iron, so a person sharpens his friend. —Proverbs 27:17 (NET)

Throughout my childhood and teen years, I lived in the same house in Maryland. When friends and classmates moved, I had mixed feelings—excitement about the new, nicer homes they were moving into, and sadness for their transitions as they joined new neighborhoods, communities, and schools. As an adult, I have relocated several times, each time with that same joy and sadness for my own children and the challenges they face as they adjust to new people and surroundings.

Our last move returned us to our previous Tennessee hometown of nine years. We loved this quaint, growing city, and had stayed in touch with several friends while living in other cities. Still, those familiar feelings that I have felt with each move unexpectedly creep up from time to time. I have been surprised by loneliness and a struggle to find my fit here.

And yet, God has amazed me with some sweet sister-friend moments. Recently, I sat among a small, intimate gathering of women at an eclectic urban restaurant celebrating a friend's fiftieth birthday. That same week I shared some laughs with a college friend who had flown into town for a mutual friend's daughter's graduation. A day later, I sat across from a friend who had moved from Tennessee to a small town in Virginia. My heart broke with hers as she talked through finding her fit within her new community and career. Lord knows I have been there.

As I continue to find my own fit, the Lord reminds me of the precious friendships I've made over the years. A few friends live nearby. Several live in other towns. Most would be strangers to me if I'd remained in my childhood hometown. My life is richer for having uprooted several times over the years. And each stop has added new and sweet friends to my life.

Lord, thank You for continually moving me out of my comfort zone and planting precious friends along the way.
—Carla Hendricks

Digging Deeper: Genesis 2:18; Ecclesiastes 4:9–10; 1 Corinthians 12:18–19

Jesus said to them, "I am the bread of life; he who comes to me shall not hunger, and he who believes in me shall never thirst." —John 6:35 (RSV)

We had a lot of bread to give out at our church's soup kitchen, more than ever before. On Friday nights, the "midnight marauders," as we call them, pick up extra inventory from the nearest Whole Foods for us to hand out to our usual guests. But this Friday it seemed that Trader Joe's had jumped the gun and dropped off bags and bags of bread. Now it was Saturday morning and we were trying to figure out how to give it away. This was more than our food pantry could begin to accommodate.

After tossing around a couple of ideas, we finally settled on setting up a table at the church's front door around the corner from the soup kitchen's entrance. "Free bread!" we called to passersby. There was pumpernickel, rye, raisin, sour dough, whole wheat, sprouted wheat. There were English muffins, bran muffins, hot-dog buns, soft rolls, low-sodium bread, all of it quite fresh. A few people came up to investigate, more followed. Soon a line formed up the steps. "Thank you, thank you," came the responses. "God bless you," we said.

By morning's end, we had given away hundreds of loaves. We folded up the table, gathered up the trash bags and crushed the extra boxes, and I took one loaf home. On my way back through the church, I looked up at the writing above the altar: "I am the Bread of Life," it said, "all who come to me shall not hunger." I was used to seeing those words on a Sunday morning. How nice to give them this nourishing spin on a Saturday morning.

Give us this day our daily bread.
—Rick Hamlin

Digging Deeper: Ezekiel 4:9; Matthew 6:26

Sunday, September 13

He leads me beside quiet waters, he refreshes my soul....
—Psalm 23:2–3 (NIV)

I've wondered why an adolescent neighbor friend has been eager to come to church with me for several months now. The service is traditional and liturgical. Think page-turning in hymnbooks and prayer books. Think stained-glass windows, a robed choir, and a somber doxology. It's not the jazzed-up hour that young teens stereotypically enjoy. It's not the exuberant Spanish church she attends when visiting her grandmother.

Last week, wondering if the novelty was wearing off, I asked, "Do you want to come again next week?"

"Definitely"—a word I'd never heard her use.

But a different phrase in her repertoire identifies her need that helps me understand the church's draw. Lately she's been asking for what she calls "peace and quiet" in her grandmother's kitchen or extended hours in my dining room. It's something she misses at home, where she shares a room with a rambunctious sister.

"Where did you hear about 'peace and quiet'?" I asked.

"It's what the teacher wants. Sometimes."

In chaotic seasons, I've sought out a serene setting, if not at church (some congregational worship services don't engender a beside-quiet-waters experience) then on a nature walk, at a courtyard fountain, or with soothing bedtime music.

In lonely times, when I've complained about having too much peace and quiet, I've allowed the Good Shepherd to fill and still my thirsty heart, soul, and mind—if not at church, then in a friend's kitchen, or with an open book of psalms or songs.

Do I find refreshment?

Definitely. Eventually. God restores my soul.

> *Lord, lead me to a rippling brook or some other peaceful place*
> *where You can—and will—refresh my soul.*
> —Evelyn Bence

Digging Deeper: Isaiah 44:1–8

All kinds of animals, birds, reptiles and sea creatures are being tamed and have been tamed by mankind. —James 3:7 (NIV)

I'm usually upstairs working when I hear the shriek of our dog, followed by a howl and the growl of a very angry cat. Sounds that can mean only one thing: Kirby attacked Soda again.

Our cat Kirby is an alpha male. All white and strong but for a low belly that is getting increasingly plump, he is an odd sort of bully. He hides under the skirt of the living room chair and waits for his victim, and then when the moment is right he pounces. A few times, he jumped right on Soda's back and rode him like a pony until Soda shook him off.

We've tried all the pet suggestions of how to make Kirby accept our dog. Most of the time, they get along fine. It's just that every once in a while something happens and a cat-and-dog fight ensues.

Kirby's saving grace is that he loves to sleep with our son Henry. Every night, just as Henry gets into bed, Kirby follows. He jumps up and settles right at Henry's feet.

Last night, Henry spent the night at a friend's house. I went to bed early and when I woke in the morning and came downstairs, I noticed Kirby was curled up on the hardwood floor right at the foot of the front door.

"He slept there all night," my husband, Tony, said, "He misses Henry."

And so it is—a beautiful gesture of love from an unlikely source.

Dear Lord, thank You for cats and dogs that keep life interesting.
Bless our family and help make us complete.
—Sabra Ciancanelli

Digging Deeper: Genesis 1:26; Proverbs 12:10

"Consider what great things he has done for you." —1 Samuel 12:24 (NIV)

Pastor Bryan asked my wife, Pat, and me to serve as two of four co-chairs for the church's upcoming capital campaign. I told Bryan we would help, and that Pat wanted a behind-the-scenes role. "That's fine," he said, "I know Pat likes to stay in the background."

We were soon asked to share our stewardship journey at an upcoming gathering. Pat said, "Let's think through our journey together and you give the talk." We remembered our first year of marriage and our struggle between paychecks. Inspired by a sermon on tithing, we started giving. It took a while before our giving reached a tithe, but we never struggled financially once we decided to give. The real story in our journey is not about our giving; it's about God's generosity. We began exchanging memorable blessings. Each blessing we recalled sparked another. And we realized our greatest treasures are truly God's nonfinancial blessings like His presence, Jesus taking our place on the Cross...a list without end.

A couple of days before the talk, Pat said, "I will tell about these parts...you talk about the rest." She told about being a child growing up in low-income projects, seeing her dad, no matter how little they had, help others with less. She shared the time we felt guided to donate the money from a property we sold. With concerns about needing the money to fund our son's college education, we stepped out in faith and gave it away. A few years later, when his college acceptance letter came, included was a generous four-year scholarship we never expected. Again, God's blessing was exponential to our giving!

Pat couldn't stay in the background. We told parts of our journey neither of us had been comfortable sharing before.

God, keep us so immersed in the great things You have done
in our lives that we boldly tell others about Your generous
response to steps in faith we take for You!
—John Dilworth

Digging Deeper: Psalms 64:9, 66:16; Luke 6:38

Remember this, my dear friends! Everyone must be quick to listen, but slow to speak and slow to become angry. —James 1:19 (GNT)

Iregularly record the birds I observe using the app *eBird*, the crowd-sourced database of the Cornell Lab of Ornithology. I like contributing to our collective knowledge of birds and take my identifications seriously, sometimes worrying that they might not be correct. After all, I'm no expert. Even so, it irks me when an *eBird* volunteer e-mails me asking for photos, sound clips, or descriptive information to confirm my identification and to distinguish it from other similar-looking birds.

Whenever I get one of these e-mails, I feel combative and insecure and defensive all at once. I have to humble myself past those emotions and remind myself of our shared goal—collecting accurate information about global bird populations—before responding. Even then, I have to ruthlessly edit the resentment out of my reply e-mail. Recently *eBird* invited me to become a volunteer checker myself, so I've been considering whether I want to be on the other side of these tricky conversations with arrogant fellow birders like me.

The whole process reminds me of my interactions with believers as I reapproached faith after years of atheism. My many questions inevitably made people uncomfortable. "Because the Bible says so" was their usual response, but when I probed further or compared contradictory-seeming passages from Scripture, they got defensive—sometimes outright mad. They seemed to think I was fighting with them, not trying to get answers.

As a professor at a Christian college, I'm often in similar scenarios with students. Despite my own past struggles as a believer, I sometimes have to remind myself that questions are not attacks but opportunities for both the questioner and the answerer to participate in our collective understanding of God.

Father, help me to listen better and to answer slowly and with love.
—Patty Kirk

Digging Deeper: John 3:1–15; Ephesians 4:2

Thursday, September 17

The prayer offered in faith will make the sick person well; the Lord will raise them up. If they have sinned, they will be forgiven. —James 5:15 (NIV)

One of the strongest women I knew was my grandmother, Maw Maw Bea. She was always steadfast in her faith despite her circumstances and managed to smile through them all. From when I was a girl, she encouraged and inspired me. She died many years ago, but I still think of her often. On a recent trip to my hometown, I stayed at my grandparents' home. Everything in the house reminds me of my grandmother. I was looking through old photographs during my stay and found my grandmother's prayer journals and calendars.

As I read through the years of writings, I found the prayers of her heart. She struggled for years with cancer, ultimately succumbing to it. When she received reprieve from the cancer in remission, she cared for her daughter who died of cancer within nine months of her diagnosis. I knew her heartbreak, because it was my entire family's heartbreak. She prayed for strength, but most of all she prayed for Jesus to be with us all. More often than not, she was thankful for anything and everything. I found, at particular times of my life when I was struggling, she would note the phone call and pray for me. I lived her answered prayers. Maw Maw Bea's prayers showed that she was not strong in and of herself. Her closeness to Jesus and her rich prayer life sustained her body and spirit throughout her lifetime.

Like my grandmother, I pray for others every single day. Do they know I have prayed for them? Knowing my grandmother's prayers for me humbled me; it allowed me to realize that her strength, and mine, comes from our relationship with Jesus. He is the One Who sustains us and is faithful to us.

Father, help me to share Your love for others through prayer.
May I continue to grow in my prayer life.
—Jolynda Strandberg

Digging Deeper: Deuteronomy 12:11; James 5:13–18

*We do not have a high priest who is unable to empathize with our weaknesses, but we have one who has been tempted in every way, just as we are—yet he did not sin. —*Hebrews 4:15 (NIV)

Nobody loves me! Nobody cares about me!"

Years ago, my little girl—shoulders slumped and lips drawn into a severe bow—made her objections clear about the praise showered on her older brother. That moment during the 1970s is memorable and a tad humorous. But several months ago, when that same daughter's three-year-old lobbed a similar complaint, I laughed out loud. "Is *anybody* gonna say hooray?" she inquired after her ear-assaulting, unsolicited song performance met with a mute response.

While it's obvious both mother and daughter took vernacular liberties, it's equally clear that, at an early age, they had grasped the human concept of pity-partying and self-absorption.

That need for affirmation wears on us at times, especially when it pushes against the boundaries of control and is levied in a demanding way that shames us. Still, when we find ourselves feeling foolish about such needs, we can be solaced by the boundless love of our God Who, through His Son, understands, because He allowed Himself to be tested by the same undignified needs.

Since I'm aware of no other religion whose very definition of God is love, it's necessary that we remind ourselves of His sacrifice to feel what we feel, "yet without sin" (Hebrews 4:15, KJV). The Lord lowered Himself to understand each one of us perfectly, giving us the right to proclaim, "Yes, Jesus Loves Me" (Anna Bartlett Warner). Even when our grumblings and other failures prove childish and embarrassing, all it takes to face another day is to know that He understands and forgives.

*Lord, though I need others' encouragement, help me to value
Your empathy more than any other, for Your love for me cost
You the most, and it never disappoints.*
—Jacqueline F. Wheelock

Digging Deeper: Psalm 139:3; 1 Peter 5:7

Saturday, September 19

You will keep in perfect peace those whose minds are steadfast, because they trust in you. —Isaiah 26:3 (NIV)

I have been avoiding cleaning out my son's bedroom. Although Henry is way past picture books and playing with little toys and action figures, he still has a lot in his room and closet. Why I thought to take on this chore this morning, in the midst of my current workload, looming deadlines, and other commitments, I have no idea.

The chaos of my schedule is mirrored by the heavy boxes of books that crowd the hallway and a huge crate of mismatched figures that needs to be sorted into keep, donate, and toss piles. I drag the box downstairs for Henry, just off the school bus, to go through and sort.

He loves this type of job. Among the hundreds of old toys are treasures he had forgotten all about. Things that make him laugh. He sits on the couch, up to his elbows in little toys from his early childhood. My mind races across work, shopping, and a phone call I have to make in an hour. Then I hear Henry's giggle, so I go in to investigate.

"Remember this guy?" Henry says holding up a little plastic man the size of my thumb, a figure with oversize and weighted feet. "Remember? You can throw him any way and he always lands on his feet."

Henry tosses him up. Sure enough, the little plastic man whirls through the air and lands standing. Henry tosses him right into the giveaway pile.

"You're not keeping him?"

"No, I don't need him."

"I think I want him."

"You do? Why?"

"So I will remember that no matter what life throws at me, I can always land just like this guy."

> *Heavenly Father, thank You for encouraging me,*
> *always at the right time and in the best ways.*
> —Sabra Ciancanelli

Digging Deeper: Psalm 27:1; Romans 5:3–5

Her children rise up and call her blessed.... —Proverbs 31:28 (NKJV)

Today, September 20, is my mother's birthday. For the first time, I forgot.

Even though she's been gone twenty years, I always remember her birthday. I think most people are like that about their moms. Had it not been for a friend reminding me on social media, I might not have remembered at all. That bothers me.

So I thought back to a piece I wrote years ago that got a lot of response. It was about how as a little boy I played a shaky "Happy Birthday" to my mom on the trombone I was learning to play at school. It was just the two of us that year. My father was on a business trip, my two older siblings were at college, and Bobby, my brother with Down syndrome, had died the year before. It was Mom's first birthday without him.

I had never felt sorry for my mother until that day and my mother never would have wanted pity. She was tough like that. But watching her sit at the table after dinner, all by herself, broke my nine-year-old heart. I didn't know what to do. I felt a little panicky.

That's when I ran to my bedroom, grabbed the used trombone my dad had reluctantly agreed to rent, and marched down the stairs blaring the birthday song, perhaps every third note actually in tune. Not that it mattered to Mom. She looked like the whole world was singing her a happy birthday.

That trombone is long gone—as is my embouchure—but the Internet is an amazing place. It didn't take me long to find "Happy Birthday" played on the trombone. I even found a child playing it almost as badly as I did. And that's what I listened to while saying a birthday prayer for my mom.

Dear Lord, thank You for mothers. And if You see mine today,
tell her happy birthday for me.
—Edward Grinnan

Digging Deeper: Proverbs 6:20–21; Ephesians 6:2–3

Monday, September 21

Being confident of this very thing, that He who has begun a good work in you will complete it until the day of Jesus Christ. —Philippians 1:6 (NKJV)

I have photographs of all three of my children when they were toddlers, their stick-size legs stuffed into boat-size shoes. It's laughable to watch children shuffle along in oversize shoes. My sons used to trudge along in my husband's brown loafers. Even my daughter, Reagan, went through a period when she was obsessed with teetering along in any pair of my high-heel shoes she could find.

It hit me one evening when Reagan, about four years old at the time, clopped into the kitchen in a pair of my black pumps. One day she will have bigger shoes to fill. She'll possibly carry the weight and responsibilities of balancing a career with raising a family and living a purpose-filled life. She'll have her own expectations, hopes, and prayers—even disappointments and trials. The thought has stayed with me, and I pray I've shown her how to walk with the Lord. She's a preteen now, wearing small heels of her own. Growing up in front of my eyes. Filling her shoes. And now I'm the one wondering if I can fill mine.

Some tearful nights I cry out to God because I'm not sure if the shoes He's given me fit. Perhaps they were oversize in comparison to what I thought I could handle. *Am I worthy? Do I have what it takes? Why does He trust me with this calling?* Then God speaks to me, assuring me that I will grow into it. Growth takes time. So I'll continue to walk in the shoes He's given me for now, knowing that I'm not alone. When the journey seems too much to handle, I know He will carry me. And He'll carry you too.

Lord, everything I'm able to do is because of You.
—Tia McCollors

Digging Deeper: Luke 12:48; Ephesians 3:20

A gift… whithersoever it turneth, it prospereth. —Proverbs 17:8 (KJV)

E lla Grace was waiting when I got home from work.
"Daddy, Bebe sent me a rainbow today," she said.

Ella Grace was a baby when my grandmother, Bebe, made her way to heaven. Yet once again she was talking about Bebe.

I thought of my nephew who insists that his mother surrounds him with a safe "Bebe-Bubble" when she tucks him in at night. Our oldest daughter, Mary Katherine, draws pictures of Bebe. Both my niece Abby and my son Harrison speak of her often.

There was something about Bebe that's not easy to explain. Brilliant, but lacking college opportunities, her only paying job was behind a Woolworth's counter. After she married my grandfather her real life's work began.

My grandmother was an investor—in people.

She invested herself in her children, her grandchildren, and her great-grandchildren, but it didn't stop there. There was always a neighbor or a lonely homebound person to care for. She invested in hungry families, children who needed clothes and shoes, and adults with special needs. Her investments defined her life, and she prospered.

She spent years as a volunteer, answering a hotline for people in trouble. She wasn't supposed to "get involved" with callers, but she constantly broke the rules, delivering meals, paying an overdue bill, or rounding us up to help someone move to a better apartment.

She always had an inspiring book or poem or cartoon to share with her clan and there was no doubt in our minds that she loved us completely.

I make my living in the investment business, and I have to confess, I've never seen returns to match the ones that still multiply and divide from the investments that Bebe made in each one of us.

> *Father, Bebe never passed up a good investment.*
> *Give me wisdom to follow her example.*
> —Brock Kidd

Digging Deeper: Isaiah 58:10; Hebrews 13:16

Teach us to number our days, that we may gain a heart of wisdom.
—Psalm 90:12 (NIV)

With a heavy heart, I sat at the kitchen table in Dad's apartment. Dad had died a couple of weeks earlier. We'd flown his body back to Minnesota to bury him next to Mom. My brother Chuck and I were cleaning out Dad's apartment. A thought drifted through my mind. *There's just over thirty years between Dad's age and mine; Dad lived to be old. What if I only have thirty years left? That's not very many.* I felt like I'd barely started on this mission from God called "life."

The finality of both Dad and Mom being gone seemed to smother me. *Lord, I've wasted a lot of years. I need You to show me how to live—intentionally—with the time I have left.* As I glanced through the greeting cards Dad had kept from friends, I noticed a common theme. People frequently expressed what an encouragement he and Mom had been to them. A couple of minutes later, I heard a shout from Chuck. "Hey, Sis, come here." I hurried into the other room. Chuck held a letter in his hand. "It's for you."

My hands quivered as I read Dad's handwriting. "Dear Rebecca, God must have had a great time when He was creating you. Love, Dad." Tears welled up as Chuck and I searched and found more notes to us kids. Although Dad had been healthy until he died, he knew death was inevitable. He focused on his end, living "forward" by leaving behind words of wisdom and love for family and friends.

Armed with some heirlooms and Dad's notes, I left his apartment determined to stop drifting through life and to set a course to live forward, leaving a legacy of love behind.

Lord, please be my compass as I launch out on new adventures.
—Rebecca Ondov

Digging Deeper: Psalm 103:15; Isaiah 40:7

P.S. Recently I found a book *Living Forward: A Proven Plan to Stop Drifting and Get the Life You Want* by Michael Hyatt and Daniel Harkavy. It's a step-by-step guide to writing a life plan!

THE FRIENDSHIP OF WOMEN: A Clean Slate

Bear with each other and forgive one another if any of you has a grievance against someone. Forgive as the Lord forgave you. —Colossians 3:13 (NIV)

I blasted my horn, but not in time to stop a woman from backing into my silver Nissan in the convenience store parking lot. She leaned her curly white head out of her car window. "I'm so sorry, honey," she said, followed by, "My husband is going to kill me!"

I surveyed the damage quickly and determined she had struck my door in almost the same spot as another parking lot driver had recently. I had postponed having it repaired because of some expensive medical tests I'd undergone.

"My car doesn't have a scratch on it," the lady said. "But yours—oh my! And I have a five hundred dollar deductible."

My eyes fell to the charm dangling from the bracelet on my wrist. A gift from my now deceased friend Kay who taught me about the path of forgiveness. We had been hospital nurses together. Once when I was headed to a board meeting to determine the fate of another employee accused of a minor infraction, Kay whispered: "To err is human, Roberta; to forgive, divine."

Mindful of Kay's words that day, I listened carefully as the situation was described at the board meeting. The damage was minuscule, the employee repentant. "I vote for a second chance," I said to the board. The others concurred.

Now, I smiled at the lady in the parking lot. "I wouldn't want your husband to kill you, dear. How about if I just give you a clean slate?"

Thank You for friends, Lord, who model forgiveness and point me to You.
—Roberta Messner

Digging Deeper: Matthew 6:14–15; Luke 17:3–4;
Ephesians 4:31–32

Friday, September 25

If our heart condemns us, God is greater than our heart, and knows all things. —1 John 3:20 (NKJV)

The fall morning is veiled in mist. The path down our hill is paved with a mosaic of leaves—red, brown, yellow, orange. At the bridge leading to our neighborhood, I pause and look across the road and into the park. To my left, I see a newly acknowledged cemetery where countless ex-slaves are buried, marked only by indentations in the soil and a few mossy rocks. These people whose names are lost to history worked harder than I can imagine. To my right, a long stone wall outlines the park's boundaries. Such walls were built by young men during the Great Depression, through the Civilian Conservation Corps, a government program that gave many of them their first chance in life. Below the bridge are railroad tracks, and who knows who laid the first backbreaking ties there?

I am humbled by those who came before us—the ones whose hands built the world we enjoy today. How is it that I am here, now, living in privilege that those before me never knew?

I cross the road and walk on. I wrestle with the thought that I am somehow entitled, simply because of my family background and country of birth. I honestly don't know what to do with these feelings. I know what God expects of me. I am to use my blessings to bless others, but guilt lingers. I cannot shake the feeling that people like me are walking on a path paved by the downtrodden.

For now, I can reach out and help those who need what I have to give. I can stand for those who are treated unjustly. I can extend a hand to those who have fallen. I can pray that God, the Father of all, calms my struggling heart.

Father, help me to be mindful of those people who have worked hard to provide many of the blessings I enjoy.
—Pam Kidd

Digging Deeper: Psalm 82:3; Micah 6:8

But you, Lord, do not be far from me. You are my strength; come quickly to help me. —Psalm 22:19 (NIV)

My husband, Chuck, and I stood on the sidelines watching our grandson Logan play soccer. At eight years old, soccer was the only sport he'd tried that he liked well enough to continue.

But Logan likes attention, even if it's not for the right things. In the running scramble that characterizes youth soccer, kids often fall down. And Logan was usually the one who fell down the most. While the game continued, he lay there, waiting for someone to notice.

We're not unsympathetic, but we knew he wanted special attention even if it meant interfering with the game. When we and the coaches called to him to get up, he did, often limping to the bench for sympathy. After the game, he'd show us where he got hurt, invisible to the naked eye.

This was the same child who ran with abandon when playing chase with his friends, bouncing back up if he fell down lest he miss the fun. How could we get him to do the same in soccer?

Trying to emphasize the importance of getting back up again, we offered motivational advice.

"Everyone falls down, but you have to get back up to play the game."

"You're tough. You can take it."

"Your team needs you to play."

Eventually, Logan caught on and started getting up quickly when he fell down. As a result, he contributed to the success of his team.

Sometimes, I get knocked down too. Not physically, like Logan, but by emotional blows and frustrations. It's tempting to lie there and feel sorry for myself. But like Logan, I have to get up again, and the quicker I do, the more productive I am. I may not feel strong enough at times, but thank God, He has enough strength for us both.

Thank you, God, for the strength to get back up when I'm down.
—Marilyn Turk

Digging Deeper: Psalms 28:7, 46:1

Sunday, September 27

Then you will call on me and come and pray to me, and I will listen to you. —Jeremiah 29:12 (NIV)

W e are focusing on family prayer this month at church," I texted our grown children. "Do you have any prayer requests?"

The pastor's sermon on the importance of praying for children and grandchildren was fresh in my mind. My mom had been a praying giant. Since her death, I had felt the responsibility to step into the very large prayer shoes she had left behind. I knew the monthly focus at church would be the perfect opportunity to grow in this spiritual habit.

I glanced at the incoming phone messages. Nothing. I waited ten minutes. Nothing. Thirty. Nothing.

"Nobody wants prayer," I complained to my husband, Kevin.

"Give it time."

"How can I pray if they don't tell me?"

He laughed, knowing my propensity to make a list for everything. "Don't overcomplicate it."

Harrumph! Easy for him to say, I thought as I got ready for the day. *He doesn't carry the weight of a praying matriarch.*

Later, at lunch, our daughter Aleah shared about a doctor's visit, one in a long line of appointments to find relief from daily, chronic pain. That afternoon, our daughter-in-law Rachel texted me to say she was taking baby Madelyn to the doctor with an eye infection. Over dinner, our daughter Katelyn chatted about a struggle she was having with a college professor. Each conversation led me to pray.

"Your simple text wasn't for them, but for you," Kevin said when I shared my observations from the day.

I agreed. "It wasn't about a list at all, but about relationships."

Open my eyes and ears today, Lord Jesus. May I see the keys
You are giving me to open the door of prayer for those I love.
—Lynne Hartke

Digging Deeper: Psalm 17:6; 1 John 5:14–15

"Do not forsake wisdom, and she will protect you; love her, and she will watch over you."—Proverbs 4:6 (NIV)

For the past few years, my aging father-in-law's health challenges have made driving more difficult for him. But this retired bus driver wasn't ready to hang up his keys.

The fact is, he was still *able* to drive. His home state renewed his driver's license, even though the family realized that it wasn't a good idea for him to be behind the wheel. In our phone conversations, he would ask me what kind of car he should buy next. Most times, I said, "Didn't we all decide that Mom would just drive you where you wanted to go?" And then I'd change the subject.

One day, with Mom's blessing, he decided to take the car to go on a short errand in the neighborhood. Shortly after leaving his driveway, he drove too close to a neighbor's mailbox, and the driver's side mirror was sheared off the car door. Realizing the gravity of the situation, he drove right back home, confessed to his wife what happened, and proclaimed that his driving days were over. Then they contacted the neighbor to make amends.

When Mom called to tell us what had happened, I was nervous. I thanked God that he struck only a mailbox, and not a child, an adult, or a pet, as their neighborhood is filled with people and animals. And then I began to fret for them, as Mom told us about the high cost of replacing the car's mirror and repairing other damage caused by the crash. But my ever-wise mother-in-law praised God for another reason. "Thank God that the accident happened right in our neighborhood," she said, before he reached a nearby commercial roadway with more traffic and potential for greater harm.

Heavenly Father, thank You for protecting us always,
even when we are not aware of the dangers that surround us.
—Gayle T. Williams

Digging Deeper: Psalm 25:21; Proverbs 2:20–21

Tuesday, September 29

"I was hungry and you gave me food, I was thirsty and you gave me drink, I was a stranger and you welcomed me." —Matthew 25:35 (ESV)

The homeless man walks onto the train with his cup of loose change and a speech that begins like many others. "Ladies and gentlemen, I apologize for the interruption."

I know what's coming next. My oldest son Brandon nudges me with his elbow. That's his signal for me to look through my bag for a dollar. I make sure to keep a few singles handy to avoid the heartbroken look on his face. Sure enough, I find one. Brandon smiles as he hands the bill to the man. Another woman extends a plastic bag and tells him there's a sandwich inside.

Suddenly Brandon remembers the tangerines I've packed for him. "Mami," he says, in a frantic tone, "hurry up and open your bag!" But it's too late. The homeless man has left the subway car.

"It's fine, Brandon," I say, as I see his disappointment. "He has a sandwich. He's going to eat today."

He shrugs his shoulders. "I know, but it would have gone nicely with the tangerine."

This comment grabs at my heart in a new way. I already know my son's burden for the homeless. I've seen him cry over the suffering he's seen. I've heard his dreams of buying mansions where the homeless can live and be cared for. But the tangerine goes beyond wanting to help a hungry man eat. I can see that Brandon wants this man to enjoy his meal. In a city where the staggering presence of homelessness can desensitize, he teaches me that compassion goes beyond handing a dollar to someone I can barely look in the eye. With a simple piece of fruit, my son reminds me to look deeper and see their humanity.

Lord, give me a heart for Your people, that I may see them as You do.
—Karen Valentin

Digging Deeper: Proverbs 21:13, 22:9

I sent them messengers.... —Nehemiah 6:3 (JPS)

I live in a really beautiful place. The small city lies in a bowl, three sides of which are evergreen-covered slopes leading to the peaks of the Cascades on the east, the Canadian Coastal Range on the north, and the foothills on the south. To the west is the coastline—islands set in the waters of the bay, with the Pacific beyond.

The changing seasons provide new beauty all year, and having lived in Los Angeles, California, where there was barely any weather at all, I welcome the simple phenomena of rain, snow, and wind. Indeed, for the first few years after we moved here, my husband, Keith, and I would look at one another almost every day and say wonderingly, "We live here now!" After Keith died, the very beauty of this place was one of the things that helped me to learn to appreciate life, even without him.

The more I thought about it over the years, the more I recognized how much our home here meant to me. One day I was talking with my rabbi about the blessings of life here—she had moved here at about the same time we had—and she was agreeing with me, though with perhaps more restraint. Suddenly, a thought crystallized. I said to the rabbi, "If heaven isn't like this, I think I'm going to be very disappointed."

She thought about that for a few moments, and then said quietly, "Maybe heaven won't be anything like this in any way." She paused, and then added, "And maybe you won't be disappointed at all."

Please, Lord, don't stop sending me the messengers I need
at exactly the times that I need them. You always know.
—Rhoda Blecker

Digging Deeper: Proverbs 25:3

September

HE PERFORMS WONDERS

1 _____

2 _____

3 _____

4 _____

5 _____

6 _____

7 _____

8 _____

9 _____

10 _____

11 _____

12 _____

13 _____

14 _____

15 _____

16 _____

17 _____

18 _____

19 _____

20 _____

21 _____

22 _____

23 _____

24 _____

25 _____

26 _____

27 _____

28 _____

29 _____

30 _____

OCTOBER

*And God said, "Let the land
produce living creatures
according to their kinds…"*

—Genesis 1:24 (NIV)

"Do not worry, saying, 'What shall we eat?' or 'What shall we drink?' or 'What shall we wear?' For the pagans run after all these things, and your heavenly Father knows that you need them. But seek first his kingdom and his righteousness, and all these things will be given to you as well."
—Matthew 6:31–33 (NIV)

Pippy, our nine-pound Yorkie mix, sat in my lap shivering. Her white hair trembled as pitch black eyes scanned the room. She tucked her muzzle into my arm. Her annual checkup with the vet turned her into a quivering mess, and we hadn't even gotten past the waiting room.

I held her close. I stroked her mop-like hair. I spoke in soothing tones. Nothing worked. She simply couldn't stop shaking. "It's the same every year," I said. She should've known the vet was her friend by now.

Things kicked into high gear when Pippy's name was called, and I carried her to the exam room. She crammed her muzzle into the crook of my arm and turned the vibration to maximum. The dog couldn't fathom the simple fact that we had only her good in mind.

The vet was kind and quick. She looked into Pippy's ears and nose. She felt her belly. Gave a quick shot. Asked a few questions. All the while, she petted and stroked the frightened animal.

Then it was over. Two minutes later, I stood outside, as Pippy ran in circles, wagging her tail and celebrating like she'd just received a pardon. The trauma was forgotten.

I laughed as the words *needless drama* came to mind. I thought of my life. How many times had I fretted over my children, finances, or health concerns. Had I prayed instead of worrying, I would have remembered that God only has my good in mind.

And I would have avoided a whole lot of needless drama.

Lord, help me to always relax in Your presence and
to remember Your presence is everywhere.
—Bill Giovannetti

Digging Deeper: Psalm 139:7; Romans 8:28; Philippians 4:6

Friday, October 2

PRAYING IN PUBLIC: Faith on Display

The message about the cross is foolishness to those who are perishing, but to us who are being saved it is the power of God. —1 Corinthians 1:18 (NRSV)

"Why do you wear those crosses?" My friend's question did not sound friendly. She was referring to the three crosses I wear, one around my neck, and one in each ear. Taken aback, I gave her my own less-than-friendly look. She continued, "I mean, why do you and your church focus so much on the crucifixion of Christ? Why so morbid?"

Now I was really taken aback, though no longer annoyed. I wear my crosses because I want to pray by displaying my faith, and I've been asked the question before but not so negatively. I've often commented on the crosses I've seen others wear, whether in line at some store or once while checking out books at the library. In fact, some great, faith-filled conversations have come about because of these crosses we wear. I worried that this wasn't going to be one of them. My friend was from an orthodox church, and it surprised me that she would find it morbid to feel close to the Cross of Jesus.

Maybe it's because I've never thought of focusing on Christ's crucifixion as morbid. I think of Jesus Christ on the Cross as the greatest act of love ever shown to humankind. I think of it as the ultimate kindness, the deepest gift, the reason to live and keep trying to do better and be better. I think of it as sanctification and forgiveness. I think of it as the one chance we are given to be redeemed from ourselves and our worldly world. And I wear crosses to remind me of Whom I follow and who I should be, not always who I am.

I wear crosses to show my passion for His Passion. I think of the Cross as a prayer. Suddenly, I was ready for this conversation.

Lord, thank You for the cross.
—Marci Alborghetti

Digging Deeper: Psalm 61:1–7; 1 Corinthians 2:14–16

The Lord stood with me and strengthened me, so that the message might be preached fully through me.... —2 Timothy 4:17 (NKJV)

Listening to the radio on my way to town, the topic is that ninety percent of Christians are uncomfortable talking openly about their faith. I'm in that camp. I'm shy around people, so I've never considered myself a good evangelist for God.

At the store, I bump into a dear soul I haven't seen in years. In catching up, I hear of her pain and fear as she faces the end of an abusive relationship. She worries about her abuser, if he will be okay after she leaves. Guilt makes her stay.

As my heart breaks for her, I see striking similarities in our lives. I tell her about my ranching career being cut short by injuries. I, too, thought I needed to stay, even though the job's demands were harming me. I felt overpowering guilt at leaving my work for others to do. It took years to find the strength to give my life over completely to God, to honestly say I choose to follow His path instead of trying to go back to where I was before. Then I tell her how once I surrendered to His will, He restored me to a much better place. Those I left behind survived. He made me whole again and free to follow Him. I urge her to be strong. She matters. God will help her through this. He will lead her to a new and better life. He did it for me; He'll do it for her.

Her chin lifts. I see a trace of hope behind her tears. Back in my pickup, the radio announcers conclude that witnessing doesn't mean standing on a street corner holding a sign and shouting to passersby. It's simply sharing how God has touched our lives.

Wow. I'm a witness after all.

Lord, I thank You each time Your light shines through me.
Make me brave enough to speak for You.
—Erika Bentsen

Digging Deeper: Deuteronomy 31:8;
John 1:7–9, 15:27; 1 Peter 2:9

Sunday, October 4

Whoever is kind to the poor lends to the Lord, and he will reward them for what they have done. —Proverbs 19:17 (NIV)

Do you remember the first time someone taught you the joy of giving? For me, it was sitting in church, when my dad let me pick the shiniest coins for the collection plate. I didn't understand what our church was doing with the money, but I did know that it felt good to give my very best.

This year, Olivia's Sunday school teacher has challenged the children to raise money for a local women's and children's shelter. Our five-year-old daughter understands that the moms and their children need help and that we have money we can give to help them. She also understands that she's supposed to earn the money, so each day she goes down a chore checklist she can't even read yet: make bed, tidy room, and so on. And each night, she and I sit on her bed and count her check marks, and then I pull out my old tin full of loose change.

I dump out the change in my hand and allow Olivia to pick a coin for each check mark. Each night we go over how much the coins are worth. I've showed it to her visually, counted it out, and talked about it every night, and yet each evening she carefully selects the shiniest coins to send to the shelter.

What Olivia doesn't know (that is, doesn't know yet, because her challenge isn't over) is that her dad and I will double whatever she earns. While earning the money allows her to understand the work and effort, we hope that providing over and above will show her God's grace for us, how He can bless our works and turn even our shiniest coins into something wildly more than we could have imagined.

Lord, let me praise You with my first and best. Help me remember that loving my neighbors means caring for those who need You most.
—Ashley Kappel

Digging Deeper: Luke 6:38; Acts 20:35; 2 Corinthians 9:7

Rejoice in the Lord always. Again I will say, rejoice! —Philippians 4:4 (NKJV)

My name is Grace, known as Gracie the golden retriever. I'm three years old. I think you've heard about me from my person, Edward Grinnan. Today I want to talk about my tail. Dogs have them. Humans don't. There are reasons for that.

You wouldn't believe how many ways I use my tail. When I am happy, it wags like crazy. I have no control over it! Sometimes when I am really happy, my whole back end wags. I think there is no greater expression of joy in the world than a wagging tail. Dogs wear our hearts on our tails, that's for sure. If I'm having a good dream, my tail wags even though I am asleep!

If I am sad or disappointed, my tail droops. It's like I'm just too down to even raise it. Not all wagging is happy or sad. Trust me on this. I wag slowly when I am uncertain about something, like if other dogs will allow me to sniff them. Occasionally I misinterpret other dogs' wags. I've run into trouble because of that. I must be more sensitive to others!

As noted, it's a good thing people don't have tails. I think people would put too much importance on them. They'd spend lots of money on tail-grooming products and tail ornaments. Their tails would be status symbols. I also worry that people with certain sorts of tails would not like people with different tails. There would be tail prejudice! Maybe this is why God did not give people tails. Dogs don't do this. We respect all tails, even those short and stubby ones. All tails are important!

A tail is good for many things. But most of all, it's how we dogs smile at the world.

Hardly a day goes by, Lord, when the dog You gave me doesn't teach me something. Help me to be more like she is, seeing the world with an open, accepting heart.
—Edward Grinnan

Digging Deeper: Psalms 16:11, 118:24

Tuesday, October 6

My soul is depressed; lift me up according to your word. Lead me from the way of deceit; favor me with your law. —Psalm 119:28–29 (NABRE)

My e-mail wasn't intended for James. I had sent it to the members of the committee I was leading, tasked with creating a special community event. A good crowd attended and it generated a lot of excitement. Flush with energy after its successful conclusion, I had typed up my thoughts for next year, listing what I thought were the event's strengths and areas that were lacking.

James's involvement fell into the "lacking" category.

Under the guise of candor and transparency, I made this clear. When I pressed the "send" button I did not stop to think of James, his feelings, his actions, or his reputation.

When he called me, I could hear the anger and hurt in his voice. He read my words back to me. I winced. They sounded harsher and sharper upon hearing them than they did in my head while I was writing them. I tried to explain myself but could not. He hung up on me, leaving me red-faced and stammering.

My first thought was how I had been wronged, not James. He should not have received my confidential e-mail. Now it was my turn to be hurt. I was indignant. Then, moments later, I felt fresh shame at my thoughtlessness and error. For days, my conscience somersaulted from remorse to anger, and regret to self-pity. I knew I should apologize to James and to my committee members, but I was stuck.

I reached out to a friend who simply asked, "How did you start this ball rolling?" I looked back at my unreasonable expectations, my pride, and my self-centered need to run the show.

Finally I called James to admit how I had him all wrong and how sorry I was to have been so public about it. Only then did my heart stop aching.

God, help me to see more quickly where I am wrong and to ask forgiveness.
—Amy Eddings

Digging Deeper: Job 42:4–6; Proverbs 15:1

"If I were you, I would appeal to God; I would lay my cause before him. He performs wonders that cannot be fathomed, miracles that cannot be counted." —Job 5:8–9 (NIV)

Behind the wheel of a car, I sometimes forget all the Christian virtue I try to cultivate in other aspects of my life. I'm usually relatively patient, caring, and thoughtful—but not in traffic. I don't actually gesticulate or scream, but I grumble and simmer. I sin in my heart, for sure.

But I'm working on it. People can change, even slowly.

One afternoon, while stuck in traffic at rush hour, I kept looking at the clock on the dashboard of my rental car to see how late I was getting to the airport to catch a flight home. Each time I glanced, another minute had passed. I knew this was ridiculous—to keep looking—but I kept glancing.

Once, while I was checking the clock, a Volvo cut me off, zooming through a yellow light and leaving me sitting at a red one. My simmer began to boil. But just then I looked to my right and saw an anxious-looking young man in the car next to me. You know what he was doing? He was looking at his watch, loosening his tie, and sweating. I suddenly saw myself in him, and I didn't like at all what I saw.

I prayed, eyes open, "Your will be done, Lord."

Did I make my plane? I did, but the story would be better, perhaps, if I hadn't.

God, please perform the miracle of faith in me, every day. Thank You.
—Jon M. Sweeney

Digging Deeper: Psalms 9:1, 136:4–6

The words of a wise man's mouth are gracious....—Ecclesiastes 10:12 (KJV)

I had never met him, yet I considered this man my mentor. That's why, even though a night at home would have been nice, I insisted to my wife, Corinne, that we attend the gala where he would receive a big award.

"He's a brilliant investor and a real mover and shaker in the business world. I expect I can learn a lot from him," I explained, "Who knows, maybe I can get some good investment tips to share with my clients."

We arrived to find a large audience, a mix of local and national people, some prominent and others who seemed to be just plain folks.

The room went quiet as the honoree took to the podium.

"This is quite an honor," he began, "one I never expected to receive. But as I stand here before you, I feel compelled to be completely honest. Totally honest. This award is not mine. It belongs to those who made whatever success I enjoy possible. Some of them are here," he smiled, sweeping his hands across the audience.

"This award belongs to that lady at the reception desk in our building, the one who makes everyone feel at home. It belongs to the man who polishes the floor and cleans the windows to make every visitor feel welcome. It's for the woman who prepares the briefs and the man who fixes the copy machine. It's for the person who fills the water cooler and keeps the coffee hot. It's for the new ideas that our youngest employees pitch, and the devotion of those employees who do the hard work to keep our company going."

He continued on, never acknowledging an ounce of personal praise. Speaking from his heart, he spoke the truth that surrounds every person's success.

"So, did you learn anything?" Corinne asked later, as we headed to our car.

"Everything I really need to know," I answered back.

Father God, let me lose my ego as I strive for success as You see it.
—Brock Kidd

Digging Deeper: Proverbs 3:13, 13:7

"I am still as strong today as the day Moses sent me out; I'm just as vigorous to go out to battle now as I was then."—Joshua 14:11 (NIV)

My colleague Bill and I were excited once again to meet with Dr. Chan and his lovely wife, Stella, to discuss ministry partnership opportunities for *Guideposts*. Dr. Chan and Stella have read Guideposts and been in ministry for more than fifty years. When Bill and I first met with them, I realized just how passionate and enthusiastic they were about their ministry, which focuses on the Chinese community within the United States and abroad. We couldn't wait to hear about the projects they were working on lately.

Charged with emotion and compassion, Dr. Chan shared about his new organization, which focuses on compassion work in China. He expressed concern about the challenges that families face and the increase in the divorce rate. Because of these concerns, he has made it his mission to help families in China remain together and strong.

After telling Bill and me about the new organization, Dr. Chan shared that he is turning eighty years old and is excited to start this new ministry. He said, "God still has me here for a purpose. All I want to do is God's work." Stella then commented, "He should have been dead at fifty-nine."

Stella's comment caught me off guard; I asked her what she meant. She told us that when Dr. Chan was forty-seven-years old, he became suddenly ill and was rushed to the hospital. The doctors determined it was a heart attack and that he needed open-heart surgery. They told him that if all went well with the procedure, he could live to be fifty-nine. Though the doctors predicted he would live only another twelve years at most, here he was in his golden years, starting a new work for God's kingdom. I left the meeting with the Chans feeling inspired to keep doing God's work.

Lord, may we continue to fulfill our life mission with passion and joy.
—Pablo Diaz

Digging Deeper: Numbers 14:24; Ephesians 3:20

Saturday, October 10

"Can you discover the depths of God? Can you discover the limits of the Almighty?" —Job 11:7 (NASB)

My youngest son has been preparing for an oral report on Voyager 1 and 2 to give his sixth grade science class. This weekend was crunch time. We sat at the dining room table with a big stack of handwritten notes to organize onto lined index cards.

I am embarrassed to say I do not retain a lot of science information, and if I ever learned about Voyager 1 or 2, that knowledge left me long ago. Henry rattled off interesting facts. "You know, Mom, they are the farthest manmade objects away from earth. And then there's the Golden Record."

"The Golden Record?" I asked. "What's that?"

Henry told me that during the 1970s, a committee of scientists put together a time capsule of sorts to include on the spacecraft for someone to find in the distant future. It was an actual disk with information about earth, a short welcome snippet in many languages, a ton of images, a baby's cry, a collection of animal sounds, the sound of footsteps, a human heartbeat.

As Henry went on, I pictured a spacecraft billions of miles away containing carefully curated fragments, pictures, and sounds of life on earth. I thought about the baby's cry, the elephant's roar, the sound of a mother kissing her child. The heartbeat. Over ten billion miles away, a heartbeat is captured on a spacecraft that travels outside of our solar system. I was pondering that cosmic and eternal question and what it means to be alive, to be human, to be on earth—and trying to grasp the universe and that heartbeat.

"Mom? Are you listening?"

"Henry, you just blew my mind."

Dear God, there is so much to learn, so much to know. And yet, even a billion miles away, it always seems to come back to the majesty, the mystery, and the grace of life and a beating heart.
—Sabra Ciancanelli

Digging Deeper: Job 9:4; Proverbs 3:5

We were all baptized by one Spirit so as to form one body—whether Jews or Gentiles, slave or free—and we were all given the one Spirit to drink. —1 Corinthians 12:13 (NIV)

The military can sometimes keep me from visiting extended family as often as I'd like, and my relationship with them is not as close as we would choose. So, on an unseasonably chilly Louisiana fall day, I found myself walking alone into a small church for the sad business of honoring and laying to rest Granny. I was surrounded by extended family but felt isolated. With the exception of my sister and me, all of my family had remained geographically tied to the Louisiana bayous. They were much closer to one another than I was to them because of the physical distance between us.

My aunts and cousins had each other, my sister had her family, but I had traveled by myself because my husband could not get away. Even though no one in my family intended for me to feel alone, I still felt disconnected and sad. I had already lost my father and grandmother.

As the pastor honored Granny, I began to remember that the members of my biological family are not only the people with whom I share blood. My family also includes those who believe—all of the children of God who came before, and all of the children of God that will come. What a comforting thought!

My work and military life will take me many places, exciting and new. Despite all the transitions and the challenges of it, I will always belong to a family. I am part of the universal Body of Christ, unchanged by this temporal life. It is reassuring to know that faith extends my family.

Heavenly Father, help me to remember that You are in me and with me, always abiding, always present. Though my body travels many places, my spirit remains in You.
—Jolynda Strandberg

Digging Deeper: Romans 8:15, 9:26; Galatians 3:26

Monday, October 12

May the words of my mouth and the meditation of my heart be pleasing to you, O Lord, my rock and my redeemer. —Psalm 19:14 (NLT)

The woman at the DMV counter leaned toward the microphone. I shifted in my plastic chair. *C-57,* I thought. *Please call C-57.*

"C-57," she said.

I closed the book I was reading and headed for the counter. But before I got there, a man cut in front of me. I craned my head around him so I could see the woman at the desk. "You called my number," I said.

"No, she called C-57," the man said.

"Which is my number," I said. I unfolded the slip of paper I had been given an eternity ago and planted it on the counter. It read C-57 in boldface—physical, indisputable evidence that it was my turn. That's why I was shocked when the woman turned to me and said, "I'll help you after I'm done with this gentleman."

I clenched my jaw and returned to my seat, anger boiling beneath my surface. My frustration didn't subside when I was called back up to the counter. The woman ran through the obligatory questions: eye color, weight, height. She directed me to stand in front of a camera. There was a click and a flash. An ancient printer stuttered as it dispensed my temporary license.

The cardstock was still warm when the woman handed it to me. I looked down at my picture. I didn't like the man who stared back at me. His brow was furrowed, and his mouth was a tight line. He was standoffish; anger was etched across his face in grainy black and white.

Instead of exhibiting patience and kindness, I had been hard and curt. I didn't want to be the man in the picture anymore. I opened my wallet and slipped in my new license. It would be a daily reminder to change my heart to reflect Christ's.

Lord, help me to show Your love in everything I do.
—Logan Eliasen

Digging Deeper: Psalm 51:10–12; John 13:34

For now we see through a glass, darkly.... —1 Corinthians 13:12 (KJV)

I was in the drama teacher's classroom, waiting for my daughter to finish rehearsal for the school play. I found myself studying the whiteboard, where the students had drawn hearts and smiley faces and doodled their names. I was surprised to see the name Amos, but there it was, in all caps: AMOS. I wondered who had named their son after the Old Testament prophet who foretold the day of the Lord.

A teenage boy came into the room. Maybe he was the one. "By any chance are you Amos?" I asked.

"Ma'am?" he replied, confused.

"I wondered if you might be Amos," I explained. "I just wondered which of you boys had been named for Amos, the prophet from the Bible." I pointed to the name on the whiteboard.

That's when the boy nearly fell over laughing. "That means 'Add Me on Snapchat,'" he explained.

All I could do was laugh with him. Oh my, what fun he had telling the other kids as they trickled in!

People say you learn something new every day. I learned what Snapchat is (it's a social networking app, by the way), and my daughter's classmates got a mini-crash course in the minor prophets. I'd say it was a good learning experience for all of us.

Father, thanks for the laugh.
—Ginger Rue

Digging Deeper: Proverbs 17:22; Ecclesiastes 3:2–4

Wednesday, October 14

Isaac: "I am an old man now, and expect every day to be my last."
—Genesis 27:2 (TLB)

A few weeks after his ninety-eighth birthday and just after his pacemaker surgery, Dad asked me to write down words he wanted my brother, sister, stepmother, and me to hear.

He wrote, "God is all merciful, nobody can deny that. I don't think He would want me to suffer anymore. You are totally correct in that I still feel loved, more than ever. But it seems so futile when I have had a full life. I just feel tired and no longer able to live with the suffering. If there was an easy way out, I'd take it."

I held Dad's hand and asked softly, "Dad, can you tell me the things that make you so miserable that you want to die? You say you're not in pain."

"Lying here, it's a labor to just keep breathing. All my physical abilities are going. I have to rely on everybody to take care of me. The food doesn't taste right. I think the end of the road is near... I would feel blessed, and it would be a big relief to just go to sleep and never wake up. As much as you try to make me feel comfortable, there is always something that stands in the way... Every night when you and Catherine take turns sleeping in my room and you can't sleep, I'm miserable. I want to go to sleep and call it a day. I've lived through my years and past my contemporaries. It seems unbearable to have to go on and on. I'm just plain worn out."

Five-and-a-half weeks later Dad passed peacefully in his sleep. Thanks to the letter he dictated, we were all able to accept his death as he did, by remembering the joy of his life.

Lord, thank You for Dad's example of knowing and accepting
that the end was near. When my turn comes, please give me
the same gentle peace and anticipation.
—Patricia Lorenz

Digging Deeper: Ecclesiastes 9:5–10; Philippians 1:21–28;
Revelation 2:10

Be kind to one another, tenderhearted, forgiving one another, as God in Christ forgave you. —Ephesians 4:32 (RSV)

I had just finished breakfast and was putting stuff away. I opened the freezer to put the banana peels in the compost bin (we keep it in the freezer so it doesn't smell). To my surprise, there was a half-gallon of milk sitting there. It hadn't been there long—it wasn't frozen. But obviously, it was in the wrong place. I laughed to myself.

"Did you just put the milk in the freezer?" I said to Carol, carrying exhibit A into the bedroom where she was working on her computer. My wife who *never* forgets anything. My wife who already that morning, when I was scrambling to come up with the name of a friend of a friend, rattled it off perfectly. My wife who a couple of days earlier had discovered that *I* had left the stove on, burning gas, long after I had taken my pot of oatmeal off the flame.

"I can't believe I did that," Carol said.

"I can't believe you did it either," I said. Did I say, *Okay, we're even now?* No. Because I am still more forgetful than she will ever be. But it made me think that as forgetfulness creeps up—as surely it will—I must be certain of not forgetting a few essential things: kindness, faithfulness, forgiveness. May I always keep those in their rightful place.

I put the milk back in the fridge. At least I remembered that.

Let me never forget to love You, Lord, and those You love.
—Rick Hamlin

Digging Deeper: Daniel 9:9; 2 Corinthians 5:17

Friday, October 16

You are no longer strangers and aliens, but you are fellow citizens with the saints, and are of God's household. —Ephesians 2:19 (NASB)

A few weeks, a few thousand miles, and a whole lot of stages. One night, after a concert in California, my son, Ransom, and I stood talking to people and making new friends.

"It must be great to be able to play music with your son," someone said to me.

I looked over at my boy—a man now. A lifetime of memories flooded. "More than great," I replied. "It just doesn't get any better."

Having the opportunity to spend a few weeks alone with Ransom, family had been on my mind a lot that trip. I saw the way people responded to us when we were onstage together. Their joy made me happy. I contemplated this later that night as we drove south on the I-5 corridor, stars swirling above the land of Steinbeck and Buck Owens. It struck me: from the beginning, we humans were created for family. It's molded into our DNA. We need it like we need air. We love togetherness. We love *love*.

The older I get, the more I realize that family is a gift like no other. Husband and wife, parent and child, grand, great-grand (fill in the blank)—we all want to belong. We want someone who will have our back. Who is in our corner no matter what. That's what a real family is. That's what a real family does.

It's true, sometimes earthly families fail. But what a miracle in the lives of believers: we have been rescued from the tempest of sin and self and welcomed with open arms into the great family of God! A Love that *never* fails. Just imagine—sons and daughters of the King of kings!

Oh how I love my earthly family. And to think, it only gets better from here!

> *To the God Who imagines stars and they burst into being—*
> *thank You for calling us Your sons and daughters!*
> —Buck Storm

Digging Deeper: Psalm 27:1; Ephesians 1:5

Jesus immediately said to them: "Take courage! It is I. Don't be afraid."
—Matthew 14:27 (NIV)

I watched my eight-year-old grandson, Logan, race around the ice as if his life depended on it. He'd only attempted ice-skating once before, two years ago, when he hung onto the side of the rink the whole time.

Here in Florida, we don't have many places to ice-skate. After all, nothing freezes over except for an occasional puddle if we have an unusual cold snap. However, an hour west of our home is an ice arena where a hockey team plays.

For a special Scout Appreciation Day, my husband, Chuck, and I had taken Logan, a Cub Scout, to watch the hockey game. One of the event's perks was the opportunity to skate on the ice after the game was over.

Logan stepped onto the ice, testing his balance as he briefly held onto the side. Soon he was ready to fly. Never having been trained in technique didn't stop him. He ran, literally, in circles around the ice for the next hour, skating with abandon. Of course, he had his share of falls, but they only served as temporary pauses in his pursuit before he quickly got back up and sped on.

Today's word of the day at a Website I frequent is *intrepid*, meaning "resolute fearlessness, fortitude, and endurance." The example was right before me as I watched our intrepid skater.

As an adult, I am more careful and more aware of hazards and what-ifs that make me tentative about pursuing something new. Too often, I let fears hold me back. Was I ever an intrepid anything?

Jesus was an intrepid follower of God's will. Why should I fear then when He tells me not to?

*Lord, when fear threatens to stop me, help me to be fearless
and as intrepid as my eight-year-old grandson.*
—Marilyn Turk

Digging Deeper: Joshua 1:9; 1 Corinthians 16:13

Sunday, October 18

WAYNE: Part One

"The Lord will fight for you; you need only to be still."—Exodus 14:14 (NIV)

After years of struggling with debilitating back pain, Wayne had finally agreed to have the necessary surgery. Although the surgeon would be fusing discs and putting hardware in his spine, he would only need to be in the hospital for one night. On the day of the surgery, we drove to the hospital in high spirits, our hearts filled with hope. As I waited to talk to the doctor following the surgery, I thanked God for my husband and for the new lease on life this surgery would give him.

Wayne did come home the following day, but only a few hours after he arrived, he was in excruciating pain. Nothing helped to ease it. Unable to bear seeing him in agony, I brought him back to the hospital where he was readmitted and given high doses of painkiller. Later, they sent him home, only to have the pain return in unrelenting degrees.

I prayed hard and couldn't understand what the problem could be. According to the surgeon, Wayne should have been getting better, only he wasn't. In the weeks that followed, Wayne was in and out of rehab, doing the physical therapy, but nothing helped. I felt I had no option but to take him back to the hospital on three different occasions. Each time they gave him a shot for pain and sent him home. It seemed as if God wasn't listening as I fervently prayed for answers.

> *Lord, You ask us to pray and to leave the results to You.*
> *Being still is an act of faith, and my faith is in You.*
> —Debbie Macomber

Digging Deeper: Psalm 46:10; Proverbs 3:5–6

WAYNE: Part Two

"I will ask the Father, and he will give you another advocate to help you and be with you forever." —John 14:16 (NIV)

I had taken Wayne into the hospital emergency room three times. Nearly four months had passed since his back surgery, and I knew something was terribly wrong. I wasn't about to let the staff give him another pain shot and send him home. With my lower lip quivering, I squared my shoulders, stood as tall as my 5′1″ frame allowed, and told the attending ER physician, "I am *not* leaving this hospital until you find out what's wrong with my husband." I'm not sure how I had the courage to stand up for my husband, but the doctor took me seriously.

Pictures were taken, and something showed up that convinced the doctor to admit Wayne. Not long after, we learned that Wayne had a massive infection that had eaten through two entire discs in his spine, and an infectious-disease doctor explained that Wayne had developed meningitis. Another surgery was scheduled to remove the hardware from the previous surgery and to replace it with new hardware. After several more weeks in the hospital, he returned to the rehab facility, and it was months before he could return home. The road to recovery was arduous and lengthy.

I can't imagine what would have happened to my husband if I hadn't held my ground that day. Wayne was far too sick to be his own advocate. He needed me to speak for him, to refuse to be pushed aside.

After this ordeal I thought about how Jesus comforted His followers with the news that He wasn't leaving them alone. He sent them an advocate in the Holy Spirit. Our advocate steps in on our behalf and speaks to the Father when we are beaten down to the point that we don't know how to pray. What a comfort to have Him always with us.

Thank You, heavenly Father, for not leaving us alone.
You gave us the Holy Spirit as our Advocate.
—Debbie Macomber

Digging Deeper: Joshua 1:9; Psalm 94:19

Tuesday, October 20

*"Some pour out gold from their bags and weigh out silver on the scales; they hire a goldsmith to make it into a god, and they bow down and worship it." —*Isaiah 46:6 (NIV)

Dr. Edwards waits beside me as I check out after my chiropractic appointment. He lifts the handbag strap slung over my shoulder. "No wonder your neck aches. This thing weighs a ton. Do you really need this much stuff?"

It's a valid question since my purse doubles as a tote bag. My oversize habit began after Micah was born. Babies need lots of stuff: snacks, diapers, bottles, a change of clothes, wipes, toys, etc. I need stuff too: makeup bag, tissues, phone, billfold, brush, sunglasses, bifocals, a small notepad (to record infrequent yet potentially brilliant thoughts), checkbook, pens, hand sanitizer, and a bottle of water, just in case.

But now Micah is fifteen and carries her own purse.

Back home, I drop my satchel on the scales. Eight pounds. I do need to lighten my load!

I dump it on the bed. When did I last take an aspirin? Yep, these are expired. I never remember to reapply makeup. I could trade my full-size hairbrush for a collapsible one. Sunglasses can stay in the console, as well as the nonfiction book I keep hoping to start. Dr. Edwards is right. I don't need all this stuff.

Carrying around unnecessary items weighs me down. It's time for a makeover. My stylish, new cross-body bag weighs less than two pounds. Because of the design, it doesn't put pressure on my shoulder or neck.

Switching purses made me think: *What else needs to be updated in my life?* Am I hanging on to other baggage that doesn't serve me anymore? Maybe I need to metaphorically dump some things and start fresh. Lugging around too much stuff really is a pain in the neck!

Lord, help me take inventory of what I need to hold on to
and what I need to let go of in all areas of my life.
—Stephanie Thompson

Digging Deeper: Haggai 1:5; Luke 12:33

God created great sea creatures and every living thing that moves....
—Genesis 1:21 (NKJV)

If you ever doubted that animals are capable of deep, rich emotions, you need only to have observed the friendship between my dog, Millie, and a friend's dog, Winky. I had a skeptical friend who used to crow at me, "Find me a dog that understands differential equations!" To which I'd reply, "Find me a human who can sense when a loved one is one hundred miles away and heading to them."

For those who believe, as I do, that many animals possess a kind of soul and a complex consciousness able to form deep relationships, then nothing proves it better than the way Winky and Millie loved each other.

Millie was a puppy when she met six-year-old Winky. Millie was starstruck. Winky was a bit standoffish. But slowly, amazingly, Winky took responsibility for Millie. She taught my puppy how to walk confidently on the streets of Manhattan. She introduced her at the dog park and made sure she wasn't bullied. All you had to do to get Millie's attention was to whisper Winky's name and she would head for her leash hung by the door. Later in life, when Winky's eyesight was failing, Millie repaid her devotion by protecting her from a young black bear that the three of us encountered on the Appalachian Trail.

It's no wonder we form such deep relationships with the animals who share our lives. It is surely a God-given miracle that we can reach across the boundaries of species to form bonds that last a lifetime. Anyone who has experienced grief at the passing of a pet knows how deep that bond is.

The day Winky died, Millie was at our apartment across town. At that very hour, she let out a soft cry and a deep sigh. Somehow she knew. Not differential equations, just love.

> *Lord, thank You for the blessing to love and be loved*
> *by the animals we share our lives with.*
> —Edward Grinnan

Digging Deeper: Proverbs 12:10; James 3:7

Thursday, October 22

"The Lord will fight for you; you need only to be still."
—Exodus 14:14 (NIV)

"L ook out!" my son James cried, imaginary sword in hand. It didn't matter that I was trying to cook dinner; there was obviously a shark trying to devour me, and James was my shining knight.

I played along, crying out for help, tippy-tapping my feet while I chopped veggies, until James appeared to lose interest. While he had been backstroking on my kitchen hardwoods to reach the beast, he suddenly stood up and walked away.

"Where are you going?" I asked. "I thought you were going to save me from this shark!"

He shrugged. "Only God can save you now, Mommy."

I used to doubt people when they told me things their children had said. Then I had James. James learned to talk in full sentences at eighteen months because it was about time someone understood him. He changed his name when he was barely two, telling me Jake, the nickname we'd always intended to call him, "is a baby name. I'm James now." At three, he can repeat movies verbatim, which is great, until he's in line at a birthday party and yells, "Olivia! I'm tired of looking at your [you-know-what]!" (Thanks, Ferdinand.)

But I have always believed that James has a wise, old soul. He feels things deeply and responds passionately. The day he gave up saving me from the shark must've been hard on his hero heart, but it showed me that even a three-year-old can know when it's time to fully lean on God to help finish off those pesky sharks.

If you're facing a shark in your life, rest easy. God is here fighting for you, and He has way more than an imaginary sword.

Lord, save me from the sharks nipping at my heels today. Help me remember that I can give up the fight and fully lean on You in times of trial.
—Ashley Kappel

Digging Deeper: Deuteronomy 3:22; 2 Chronicles 20:17; Ephesians 2:8–9

You have tasted the kindness of the Lord. —1 Peter 2:3 (RSV)

I was in my get-on-the-road, make-the-best-of-the-time travel mode. My nearly fifty-pound suitcase and travel bag stuffed with books were in hand. I entered Terminal 5 of New York City's JFK International Airport for a Hawaii-bound Guideposts military outreach flight, content to be in a focused, traveling frame of mind.

A gracious airline representative greeted me at a self-service kiosk. After fumbling to find my confirmation number, I began the computerized boarding pass process. When I had difficulty getting my credit card to register, the friendly agent went out of her way to assist me.

I walked directly to the bag-drop aisle. The counter agent was kind and seemed genuinely appreciative of my military service. As I made it through TSA screening, the lift in spirit I received from check-in officials remained. I was being drawn into a restorative and calming state of mind.

Upon entering the wide-bodied Hawaiian Air Airbus A330, considerate flight attendants gave friendly and warm greetings. Then, while viewing the preflight instructions video, I heard the words, "When you're here with us, you're in Hawaii."

Ah, I thought. *I'm still physically in New York City, but I'm being treated as if I were already in the Aloha State.*

The tone set by the airline personnel made for a delightful visit. Whether staying at the Kaneohe Bay Marine Air Base guesthouse or working out at the "Semper Fit" Marine Fitness Center, I experienced the same charm that started my trip.

Upon returning to JFK, the same check-in kiosk representative smiled as I exited the jetway. I prayed, "Thank You, Lord, not only for safe travel, but for gracious airline personnel who make it all possible."

Creator God, give us expansive hearts today to experience You through encounters and interactions with Your people.
—Ken Sampson

Digging Deeper: Matthew 7:12; Ephesians 4:32

Saturday, October 24

You also were included in Christ when you heard the message of truth, the gospel of your salvation. When you believed, you were marked in him with a seal, the promised Holy Spirit. —Ephesians 1:13 (NIV)

I've loved this life of little boys. Today my sons made vintage maps and messages for a treasure hunt. They tore paper into ragged edges and stained their maps old—their contribution to preparing our home for sale. The new owners will have clues to secret spaces. My boys have old souls, so they had a seal stamp.

"Mom, is it ready for the seal?" twelve-year-old Gabriel asked.

I looked at the tiny drawing of our Victorian's lower level, complete with closet cubbies and the hideout under the stairs. I nodded.

"Get it ready," Gabriel instructed ten-year-old Isaiah.

Isaiah folded the map. Small fingers creased and pressed. "Ready," he said. He handed the map to his brother. This was serious business.

Gabriel took a tiny, wax-filled spoon and warmed it over a candle. Soon the wax was liquid smooth and Gabe let it pool where the map's edges overlapped. Isaiah took their seal, an ornate *E*, and pressed it into the wax puddle. "Sealed," Isaiah said. The boys set the map aside and reached for paper and pencils to begin the process again.

I thought about what I had seen. The sealing.

It's what happens when we come to the Lord through faith in Jesus Christ. He marks us as His own with His holy seal. We're set apart for future glory with the One Who saw us, heart and soul, beauty and barbs, and loved us anyway. No matter what this life holds, no matter the struggle or strife, it's a promise of life to come.

It's grace flowing forward.

My boys continued the enterprise of making messages and maps. Later they'd hide them in the hushed places of this old house.

But for those sealed by the Spirit, the bounty has already been found.

Lord, Your seal is security.
—Shawnelle Eliasen

Digging Deeper: 2 Corinthians 1:21–22, 5:5

THE FRIENDSHIP OF WOMEN: Lasting Bond

There is a friend who sticks closer than a brother. —Proverbs 18:24 (NKJV)

When I was a little girl, Sue, the pianist at my church in Huntington, West Virginia, was the prettiest lady I had ever seen. I adored watching her fingers fly across the keys, so Mother allowed me to sit in the second row, piano side, for a closer look. One Wednesday night at prayer meeting, I asked God for Sue to be my friend someday.

Eventually Sue started sitting beside me when she left the piano. I felt so honored. Then when I was a teen and my mother sustained a severe brain injury, Sue reached out to me. As I progressed into young womanhood, Sue, nineteen years my senior, began to mother me. She never tried to *become* my mother; she was simply by my side, which has continued throughout many periods of my life.

Sue taught me about creating a beautiful home with affordable antiques, and when I couldn't drive because of seizures, she would take me to places where I could find them. She taught me strange but fascinating terms like "coal hod," "sugar shell," and "paper punch samplers." She was with me when I bought my first antique at an old farmhouse in Ohio. "This oak washstand is only thirty-five dollars and doesn't take up a lot of space," she told me. "It would be wonderful in your bedroom now at home and in a little apartment later on. It's a great investment too." When I got that first apartment, Sue ironed my criss-cross curtains and helped me arrange all my treasures.

When I have recurrent surgeries to remove nerve tumors that bleed, Sue washes and styles my hair afterward. When I'm away at the Cleveland Clinic, she leaves comfort foods in my refrigerator. I turn to her first when things go wrong—and when things go right. She's the one I always call.

> *Thank You, precious Lord, for the joy of friends*
> *who help me endure hardships in my life.*
> —Roberta Messner

Digging Deeper: Proverbs 17:17; John 15:13

Monday, October 26

"Love your neighbor as yourself." —Matthew 19:19 (NIV)

I heard the ambulance siren roaring through the neighborhood and then it abruptly stopped. At our neighbor's house. *Oh no! What could that mean?* Later in the day, I learned: Jake, the husband and father in that house, had suddenly collapsed. He was taken to the hospital, where he died. Cars gathered in the driveway as adult children showed up. With a note on their front door, they closed their family circle, telling neighbors they needed privacy in their grief.

I understood and respected their wishes, of course.

Yet I kept looking at the house, thinking there must be something I could do. I fell asleep that night praying for Jake's family and asking God to give me some way to reach out to them. The next morning, I woke up thinking about pumpkin bread. That's not surprising. I love pumpkin bread but hadn't made it in many months. And it wasn't even close to Thanksgiving, when many people think about pumpkin bread.

As I made coffee, I decided to bake Jake's family some pumpkin bread, which I did that afternoon. Two loaves. While they were still warm, I wrapped the loaves in foil, tied bows around them and attached a note about sharing their sadness. In the gathering darkness, I left the two loaves just outside their front door, confident that with all the cars in their driveway, they would find the pumpkin bread.

Later that evening, Jake's wife—now widow—texted this message: "I absolutely love pumpkin bread. In fact, your pumpkin bread was my dinner. It was just what I needed! Thank you."

Who knew that pumpkin bread would be just what she needed?

Lord, when I fall asleep with a prayer in my heart, You sometimes put an answer into my waking thoughts. I praise You for that, and ask that You continue to nudge me toward ways to meet my neighbor's needs.
—Carol Kuykendall

Digging Deeper: 1 John 3:18–20, 5:14–15

*Even when I am old and gray, O God, do not forsake me, until I declare
Your strength to this generation, Your power to all who are to come.*
—Psalm 71:18 (NASB)

Gray hair. Wrinkles. Stiffness. These can make a person feel "old." But
the list lengthened when our fourteen-year-old granddaughter visited.
Sarah was excited to take digital photos of family pictures stretching
back decades. She got right to work with her phone camera. I remembered one taken in the age of film that I didn't want preserved. Sarah
asked, "If you didn't like it, why didn't you just delete it?"

Next came the moment she waved a photo under my nose. Our oldest
daughter on her sixteenth birthday talking on her new telephone—
receiver to her ear, twisty cord in full view. Sarah said, "I just find this
such an odd way of communication!"

The final blow was how she referenced our pictorial collection. She
would question, "Is this something from the 1900s?" She was throwing
the 1900s around, as I would talk about the 1800s!

Sarah's comments during her visit made me reposition myself. I have
more years behind than ahead. As I contemplated this one morning,
I noticed the sun lighting a big puffball in the woods. The bright
blossom had disappeared. Now the cottony head, filled with seeds, was
ready to release its bounty in the first good breeze.

It's like me, I thought. Youth's bloom might be past. But the seeds
are there, poised to disperse new growth. Decades of experience—of
learning—of faith reside in me. Ready to spread wisdom to a fourteen-
year-old granddaughter and all the other grands in our family.

I don't regret being a "relic from the 1900s." I feel on the threshold
of an exciting season of life—the future!

*Lord, it seems I'm becoming an old puffball. Use Your precious
seeds in me to secure Your truth in the generations to come.*
—Carol Knapp

Digging Deeper: Job 12:12; Proverbs 17:6; Isaiah 46:4;
1 Thessalonians 2:8

Commit to the Lord whatever you do, and he will establish your plans.
—Proverbs 16:3 (NIV)

I'd been struggling all week with a writing project. Nothing I'd put down on paper seemed right—until this morning. Finally, I hit my stride, and words seemed to flow. It was a good thing, too, because it was due the next morning. What a relief it was to finally place the period at the end of the last sentence. I knew it still needed a little tweaking, but overall, I was happy with what I'd written. Until I checked the word count: 2,293.

My limit was 1,400.

I glanced at the clock on the wall. Company was coming soon. I hadn't started dinner, and the house needed to be vacuumed before guests arrived. A stack of bills glared at me from my desk, and it was my daughter's turn to take snacks to her preschool in the morning. Time for personal reflection and prayer hadn't even made the bottom of that day's list. I sighed. My calendar was as overstuffed as my article. Something had to give, but what? It all felt important.

Scrolling back through the pages I'd written, I started hacking—a sentence here, a paragraph there. Each strike-through made me cringe. As I'd typed them, every word had felt necessary.

Finally, I checked my count again and was rewarded: 1,396 words. With trepidation, I read through what was left. I was surprised to find the article's message hadn't suffered at all. In fact, this shortened version was less cluttered, more straightforward. In a word: *better.*

I looked at my to-do list on the counter, and I picked up a pencil. Time to start hacking here too.

God, help guide my decisions about what belongs on my to-do list,
so I always have time for the things that are important to You.
—Erin Janoso

Digging Deeper: Proverbs 19:21; Isaiah 26:3

"When a foreigner resides among you in your land, do not mistreat them."—Leviticus 19:33 (NIV)

The Statue of Liberty is green.

Yes, I realize this is not news, but in some ways, it is news. The outer skin of the statue is made of copper, so it looked like a shiny new penny when it was shipped from France and assembled in the United States in 1886.

But standing alone and exposed to the elements changed the composition of Lady Liberty. After a few decades, she started to look a bit different. A subtle but inevitable natural process forever altered her outer appearance.

Some were disturbed by this change. In fact, some historians suggest money was set aside in the early twentieth century to paint the structure its original hue, but the plan was scuttled.

I was reminded of this when I came across a religious statue that I had never noticed before, despite walking past it many times. I know it's a saint but I don't know which one because the saint, too, had turned green and I couldn't really see the face.

I'm glad the Statue of Liberty is green. I'm sure the original color was beautiful, but things change. As the composition of the statue changed, we too would change with her. But it's just the outside that is different; Lady Liberty may have taken on a new patina, yet she remains the same. She is undergoing an understated but relentless natural process that we don't really see—just like we have to look closely to notice the nameless saints who live among us, the ones we walk past every day.

Lord, let me see beyond the surface and understand
the hearts of Your people.
—Mark Collins

Digging Deeper: 1 Samuel 16:7; Ephesians 2:11–13; Hebrews 13:1–2

Friday, October 30

"You are most kind...to comfort me."—Ruth 2:13 (JPS)

For almost five years after my husband, Keith, died, my cat, L.E., represented my ongoing grief at losing him. She slept most of the day pressed against his slippers, which I still kept on the rug in front of his sink in our master bathroom. She deigned to notice that I'd filled her food dish, and she'd endure—for a short time—my brushing her or clipping her claws occasionally. I could see her missing him.

Then one day I became aware that she had started ordering me around—complaining when I got ready to leave the house, yowling at me when she thought I should already have fed her, coming into the living room at 10:00 every night to tell me it was bedtime. I began to believe that she had recognized I was the only person in the house and had decided to put up with me, but Keith was still first in her heart the way he was in mine.

On the nights when I would dream about Keith—and I had several dreams of him every week—I didn't want to get out of bed in the mornings. It felt as if my staying under the covers would keep the dream alive in my mind, and I just didn't want to let it go, like the way L.E. stayed cuddling against Keith's slippers. As if L.E. noticed my reluctance to move, she began to climb onto my chest, butt her head into my nose until I opened my eyes, and then meow at my face until I finally gave in and got up.

The morning I realized she had really, finally, moved on was one day in the fifth year when I found her stretched out on the bathroom rug in front of my sink. She didn't move back to Keith's rug.

Thank you for the creatures that share my house, God, especially when they show me that we share more than just geography.
—Rhoda Blecker

Digging Deeper: Nehemiah 2:2

Hatred stirs up conflict, but love covers over all wrongs.
—Proverbs 10:12 (NIV)

I had to turn it off. I'd been listening to the radio on my way home from work, and the news of another volcano, another shooting, and more international policy changes was more than unsettling.

Frustrated at my own inaction, I gripped the steering wheel tighter. When our local food bank requests donations, we show up with macaroni and cheese. When a local mom needs diapers, we donate a value box so she's covered for a month. But when these great, hugely important things happen all around the world, I'm at a loss.

"What is it you want me to do?" I asked, partially of the news anchor but mostly in an irreverent prayer.

Love.

The word came to me almost instantly. God didn't need me to go and do something this time. He needed me to stop feeling overwhelmed and grumpy; that wasn't helping anyone. What He needed from me was to love.

Now when I'm faced with a situation I can't directly affect, I turn to how I can put out more love to those around me. In the face of oppression, we love. In the face of anger, we love. In the face of violence, we love.

In God's New Testament commandments, He called us to love Him with all that we have. In the same breath, He called us to love our neighbors (see Matthew 22:36–40).

The next time you're faced with an overwhelming newscast, a difficult situation, or an event that causes you to wonder what God would think of it, approach it with love, because God loves each one of us, and calls us to do the same.

> *Lord, help me to serve those around me. Open my heart to truly*
> *love with great abandon, even in the face of trial or difficulty,*
> *or when I don't fully understand Your ways.*
> —Ashley Kappel

Digging Deeper: Matthew 5:43–48; Philippians 2:4; 1 John 4:11

October

HE PERFORMS WONDERS

1 _____

2 _____

3 _____

4 _____

5 _____

6 _____

7 _____

8 _____

9 _____

10 _____

11 _____

12 _____

13 _____

14 _____

15 _____

16 _____

17 _____

18 _____

19 _____

20 _____

21 _____

22 _____

23 _____

24 _____

25 _____

26 _____

27 _____

28 _____

29 _____

30 _____

31 _____

NOVEMBER

"I have loved you with an

everlasting love..."

—Jeremiah 31:3 (NIV)

FIRSTS: To Dance

I will sing of mercy and judgment.... —Psalm 101:1 (KJV)

I'll never forget the first time I put on nail polish. I was twelve years old, staying with my father's father in California. Grandfather's house in Pasadena was near a five-and-dime store where for fifteen cents I'd bought a bottle of Razzle-Dazzle-Red. I remember laboring over my hands for what seemed hours. Draw the little brush carefully over each nail, scrub away the splotches on my fingers, put on another layer to cover the smears. At last, I was ready to display my new sophistication.

Grandfather lowered his newspaper, glanced at my hands spread proudly before him, and went back to reading. "Bleeding stumps of fingers," he pronounced from behind the paper.

I looked at my "glamorous" hands—and now all I could see was blood spouting from chopped-off fingers. It was twenty years before I colored my nails again.

Going polish-less is not much of a loss, but it's made me sensitive to how a put-down can hurt when you're trying something for the first time. For my husband, John, it was his first (and last) dance class at age eleven. "All the boys had to wear white gloves," he told me, shuddering at the memory, "and stand exactly eight inches from our partners." It was one-two-three to the right, one-two-three to the left. The fourth time John collided with another couple, the teacher made him sit down: "You're off beat! You'll never be a dancer."

When we were first married, John would dutifully lead me onto a dance floor, but he was so stiff and awkward and miserable that I stopped urging him to try. No encouragement of mine could stand against that harsh judgment on his first attempt.

Lord, Who makes all things new, as You know first-times can be fragile times. Help me to treat them gently, in myself and for others.
—Elizabeth Sherrill

Digging Deeper: Ephesians 4:2; Colossians 4:6; 1 Thessalonians 5:11

Monday, November 2

Write them on the tablet of your heart. —Proverbs 7:3 (NIV)

When I was a child, my mother insisted I attend a Sword Drill at church. Sword Drills mean memorizing the books of the Bible, locating Scripture verses on command, and reading them aloud. I dreaded the pressure of competition, and the words I recited were about as interesting as reading a phone book.

We kids stood in a circle, with me, repeatedly clearing my throat, terrified the teacher would choose an obscure book like Obadiah.

"Swords ready?" she would ask.

We stood tall, our swords (Bibles) clutched under our arms.

"Draw swords!" she proclaimed.

Then we placed the spine of the book in our palms. With arms stick-straight, we thrust our swords midair, keeping them high. No cheating.

"Ready? Deuteronomy, chapter four, verse twelve!"

We repeated the charge in unison.

Finally, she said, "Go!"

Such pressure! The first one to locate the verse read it to the group.

I memorized a lot of Scripture in Sword Drill, but I didn't grasp the power of the words until I grew up and got desperate.

1981. I became a mother.

1983. Daddy died from a brain tumor.

1991. Our infant son was born without a brain.

2002. I visited my brother in drug rehab.

2007. I was diagnosed with two autoimmune diseases.

2018. After ten years of infertility problems, our daughter had a baby.

Mother was right. Sword Drill mattered. With every triumph and trial, precious verses planted in my heart years ago now sprang to life.

> *Lord, I'll never outgrow my need for the Bible.*
> *As Hebrews 4:12 says, Your Word is "alive and active"*
> *and "sharper than any double-edged sword."*
> —Julie Garmon

Digging Deeper: Deuteronomy 11:18; Jeremiah 15:16

Elisha prayed, "Open his eyes, LORD, so that he may see."...
—2 Kings 6:17 (NIV)

For the first time in months, I awoke before my alarm. The temperature had dropped. *Good morning, Lord. I love You,* I said silently. Then I went to make coffee.

I smiled as I walked into the kitchen of our new apartment. It is a separate room, not the mere three-foot stretch of counter adjacent to the living/dining area in our old place. I luxuriated in it, thankful, as I poured hot water into the French press and stirred the ground coffee with a chopstick. Then I padded across the new blue carpet to my chair in the living room. Early-morning sun glinted off the bricks of the apartment building across the street. Sparrows twittered somewhere. Life felt good.

I sipped my coffee and chuckled. Absolutely nothing was different that morning except the temperature and a good night's sleep. Every problem I'd had the day before still existed. One of my kids was in the hospital after a suicide attempt. Another was struggling mightily with the stress of the situation. Our prior landlord refused to return my calls to negotiate an end to our lease. Many things in my life were *not* good, yet I was feeling reasonably content.

I prayed (wryly): "You were right, Lord. Feeling helpless doesn't mean everything is hopeless." Fortunately, when I stress because I can't imagine a way out of a bad situation, God gently corrects my thoughts: *Right now,* I can't see the way. Perhaps tomorrow I will. I may wake up, smell the coffee, and see the light, and what felt impossible will feel more doable.

I can't always imagine that possibility. What I can do, is pray:

Lord, teach me to trust in You more than I trust my feelings.
—Julia Attaway

Digging Deeper: Proverbs 3:5–6

Wednesday, November 4

God demonstrates His own love toward us, in that while we were still sinners, Christ died for us. —Romans 5:8 (NKJV)

I was in a twelve-step meeting the other day when I heard the speaker mention imposter syndrome. Before she even explained it, I knew what the condition was: the fear that deep inside, you are not who you want people to think you are. That God knows it and doesn't love you because of it. I asked a friend after the meeting if he ever experienced it.

"I think we all do," he said. "For instance, people say I am bright and hard-working, but sometimes a little voice inside says, 'No, you're not! You fake being bright and you don't work all *that* hard. You've got everyone fooled. But someday people will find out.'"

"Do you really believe that?" I asked.

"Not like I used to when I was drinking and drugging. So I talk back to that voice. I say, 'No, I'm not a phony and how would you know anyway?' A sponsor once told me that the voice was my disease talking, trying to bully me into a slip. He was right. When I was drinking, that voice talked to me all the time, telling me that I was a bad person and people were going to find out. Now that I'm sober I just shout down that little voice."

I have to admit that there are times when that voice speaks to me. It tries to whittle away at my self-esteem and undermine my sobriety. It's more than an attack of low self-esteem, though. It's an assault on my very identity. It tries to tell me that I am unworthy of God's love. Yet how could that ever be? Who knows me better than God? Whomever God knows, God loves—even the worst of us at our worst.

Lord, today, help me to shout down that little voice that says I am undeserving of You. Keep me in Your love, even when I do not love myself.
—Edward Grinnan

Digging Deeper: Psalm 86:5; Ephesians 2:4–5

Your eyes will see the King in his beauty; you will see a vast land.
—Isaiah 33:17 (CSB)

I was driving home on a street that brought with it a flood of memories. After eight years of living out of state, I had moved back to my hometown in Kansas. What was most striking to me about being back was how open the view was on any given street. I could see for miles in any distance, without a skyscraper breaking up the horizon. And the sunset tonight—a recipe of gray, white, and yellow clouds against a pure blue sky—was doing something to my heart.

I started to think about when I was a little girl on this same street. How a lot of things had changed since then. But at thirty-two years old, I had never lost the desire to want to look into Jesus's eyes.

He often bends low and hums words to me in moments like this, especially when I'm captivated by the beauty ahead of me, above me, in the sky. After all these years of wanting to see into His eyes, He did one better tonight on this drive. Perhaps He felt I was finally ready for a deep look. Tonight His eyes were the sea of colors holding still in the sky.

He was revealing Himself, and my spirit began to soak in His Spirit on that quiet road. His gaze was more magnified than I ever thought it could be. I was enveloped in his attention.

Father, I want to see You in everything that You've created on earth,
and every new thing You create each day. I know that beauty and
nature are pure reflections of You.
—Desiree Cole

Digging Deeper: Psalm 19:1; Romans 1:20

Friday, November 6

Whoever loves God is known by God. —1 Corinthians 8:3 (NIV)

I lace up my running shoes and start jogging around the indoor track. I'm at the gym to clear my head. Last night, Diana told me that she has a new boyfriend. I expected this to happen soon. I knew that she and I couldn't be together. We'd talked about this. It wouldn't work because we didn't share the same faith. But that didn't change my feelings for her.

I glance up at the clock above the track. The seconds tick by in blocky LED.

Lord, I am so tired of relationships that don't work out. Why do You keep letting this happen to me?

I wrestle with God as I tread rubber track. Soon, I loop back under the clock and pick up my pace.

God, why did You put Diana in my life? I was already lonely. Why rub salt in my wound?

My breathing is heavier now. My heartbeat is faster. I crank up my speed as I pass the clock again.

How long am I supposed to be single? I don't deserve this.

The digital clock is a blur of red. I'm sprinting. My T-shirt is drenched.

Do You care? Are you listening? I can't keep living alone like this!

Invisible claws are squeezing my lungs. I skid to a stop and lurch for air. My pulse thunders in my ears. My calves are on fire.

And my face burns as well, because I realize I bottled up my frustration for too long. Instead of being open with God, I tamped down my anger. But I can't hide my feelings from Him.

I breathe in and out, hands on my knees, head lowered in fatigue. I know that I need to be transparent with God. I need to trust the One Who knows my heart better than even I do.

I was right: I can't keep living alone. And, because of God, I don't have to.

Father, help me to be open and vulnerable with You.
—Logan Eliasen

Digging Deeper: Jeremiah 1:5; John 10:14

I prayed to the Lord my God.... —Daniel 9:4 (JPS)

I asked the veterinarian, "What can I do for her?"

My dog, Anjin, was ill, and I felt I had to be able to do something. She had been diagnosed with a mass that resisted identification in her abdomen. It didn't appear to be attached to any of her organs. Two ultrasounds and two biopsies showed no malignancy. The radiologist and the vet could not pinpoint what the mass was, and both said that all the cells were normal. When the vet told me that exploratory surgery might not tell us what we were dealing with or show us how it could be fixed, it wasn't the $9,000 price tag that made me rule it out. Anjin is an elderly greyhound, whose quality of life is most important to me. If there were complications from the surgery, even in the unlikely event of a real diagnosis, she was too big for me to lift to get her to further treatment.

And, her symptoms were not severe. She was drinking a great deal of water, panting more often than she used to, and doing lots of stretching, but she was clearly not in any pain. She was very good at the stretch that consisted of bowing and pulling back on extended front legs. She did it for us just as I was asking the vet what I could do to help my dog.

"That's what my friend who does yoga calls 'the downward dog pose,'" I said to the vet. "Anjin does it about ten times a day."

"We say the dog is praying," the vet said. "Now what did you ask me?"

The light went on. "Never mind," I told her. "I think Anjin just pointed out to me what I can do for her."

Lord, if I forget to pray, please forgive me. I was thinking of her,
when I could have been thinking of You.
—Rhoda Blecker

Digging Deeper: 2 Kings 4:33; Psalm 4:2

Sunday, November 8

The people who walked in darkness have seen a great light....
—Isaiah 9:2 (NKJV)

Daylight Saving Time had ended, and the sun had sunk below sky-scrapers well before 4:00 PM. After a delightful day babysitting my little grandson in Boston, I felt my mood darken as early twilight seeped into my soul. Ambiguous shadows on the bus platform had rendered my favorite city vaguely sinister. Alone and edgy, I boarded the bus to New Hampshire and squeezed into a window seat.

Soon the coach swung into bumper-to-bumper traffic for the ninety-minute ride home. Electronic devices flickered in the dim light as commuters caught up on work or mail or played games. I rarely did this, as I preferred to look out the window to enjoy the cityscape. This night, however, as traffic crawled north, I reasoned that I would continue reading for a Bible study if I could access it online. I fiddled with my phone, and sure enough, the Gospel of Luke appeared right in my hand.

Perhaps it was the novelty of the luminous screen in the darkness or the Gospel plucked from cyberspace just for me. Perhaps it was the relief and reassurance I now felt as I moved through the dusk. Suddenly, an ordinary act had flowered into an epiphany. The metaphor was clear: Electronics provide the means, but the Holy Spirit provides my certainty. God's Word truly lights our darkness.

*Father, You created light and called it good. We invite You to
draw us from our darkness into Your light.*
—Gail Schilling

Digging Deeper: Genesis 1:3–5; Isaiah 58:8, 10;
John 12:36; 2 Peter 1:19

"For this child I prayed; and the LORD has granted me my petition which I made to him." —1 Samuel 1:27 (RSV)

It was a busy day at the office and in the middle of a million things, I told my colleague, Diana, that a story from our contributing editor, Peggy, could be used in an upcoming workshop with some of our writers. Diana e-mailed Peggy and within minutes, Peggy e-mailed me.

"You wouldn't have known this," she wrote, "but this morning I asked my mom to pray with me for some guidance, because I wanted to write a story for the workshop but just didn't have time and didn't know what to do. Then I got Diana's e-mail. What an answer to prayer."

I sent back a string of smiley faces, but it got me thinking. How many times do I unwittingly turn out to be someone's answer to prayer? How often do you? You send an e-mail, you have lunch with a friend, you are a listening ear or a port in a storm, you recommend a favorite book, you buy a card, you share a devotional, you have a long rambling conversation that you're not sure made a scrap of difference. Turns out you said just the right thing. You didn't know it at the time. Sometimes you never find out, sometimes you do.

Time and again, you are someone's answer to prayer. I don't doubt it. I was.

Thank You, Lord, for the part I can play in the unfolding of Your plan.
—Rick Hamlin

Digging Deeper: Psalm 66:19; 1 John 5:14–15

Tuesday, November 10

I keep going on, grasping ever more firmly that purpose for which Christ grasped me. —Philippians 3:12 (PHILLIPS)

The Hudson Valley Honor Flight #19 gave recognition to World War II, Korea, and Vietnam era armed forces members. I joined nearly eighty-five veterans as one of the guardians accompanying each veteran, one to one. We gathered at 0545 for a spectacular dawn sendoff.

We flew to Washington, DC, and toured the World War II and Korean war memorials. But near the end of the day, the careful, one-foot-in-front-of-the-other steps of my 85-year-old veteran, Richard, became labored and uncertain.

Our final destination was the 5:00 PM changing of the guard at Arlington's Tomb of the Unknown Soldier. After some hesitation, Richard agreed to wheelchair transport to guarantee a front-row view. Following this awe-inspiring ceremony, I wheeled my veteran to witness "Retreat," the taking-down of the national colors. Along the way he remarked, "Let me push you." After a few more appeals, I thought, *Why not?* Giving in to Richard's urgings, I sat in the wheelchair, and with great satisfaction, he pushed me.

My eye-to-eye view with other veterans in wheelchairs altered my perspective, and I was thrilled to identify with fellow Honor Flight veterans.

At day's end, I asked my risk-taking "wheelchair guardian" how he was doing. Richard said, "Very fine, but the trouble with folks my age— they don't step out and pretty soon are doin' nothin'."

While the Honor Flight prompts many good memories, none matches being pushed in the wheelchair by my veteran friend Richard. His wonderful humor, wise perspectives on faith and life remain. Because of him, I can say to myself *Step out, Sampson. Take prudent risks. Embody courage steadily, step-by-step, and like Richard, be blessed.*

> *Living God, propel me forward to take risks for You,*
> *knowing Your firm hand is on my shoulder.*
> —Ken Sampson

Digging Deeper: Psalm 27:14; Hebrews 10:23–24

Whoever protects their master will be honored. —Proverbs 27:18 (NIV)

When I was fourteen years old, I won a Veterans Day essay contest. I expounded the virtues of courage and of sacrifice. It was a good essay based on an ideal; however, very little of it was based on experience. I had no real understanding or witness of what it means to serve our country or the sacrifices it entails.

Much has changed since I wrote the essay. Living and working with soldiers for the past twenty-two years, I have been blessed with a first-person witness to the meaning of courage, honor, duty, loyalty, and sacrifice that our service members impart. I have watched them truly sacrificing not only their personal safety but also the personal blessing of being with their loved ones, a sacrifice often unseen. There are countless missed births, birthdays, anniversaries, and holidays. Many service members will miss many "firsts": a child's first steps, first words, or first days of school.

Growing up, I used to think of Veterans Day as a celebration, a holiday, and a day off from school. Because I have since been blessed to witness the personal sacrifice of those defending our nation on a daily basis, I now know that Veterans Day is a day to honor, not simply to celebrate. Honor their service; honor their sacrifice; honor their lives. Service members pour out their lives in fidelity to our nation; we are called to respect that fidelity.

Lord God, may we honor those who selflessly serve or have served our great nation. May we never take for granted their sacrifices and their duty. Bless all who have answered the honorable call to service.
—Jolynda Strandberg

Digging Deeper: Judges 7:8–22; John 15:13; 2 Timothy 2:4

Thursday, November 12

I prayed to the LORD, and he answered me. He freed me from all my fears. —Psalm 34:4 (NLT)

I gripped my armrest as our plane lurched suddenly up and then down. The seatbelt light dinged overhead. I glanced over to check my five-year-old daughter's belt.

"Ooh Mom!" she said. "That was fun!"

I smiled at her, remembering how, not that long ago, even the slightest turbulence would send me into panic-mode.

I hadn't always been afraid of flying. As a child, I remembered enjoying it, as Aurora was now. But somewhere along the way, fear crept in. When flying, and honestly, in most other things, too, worrying felt like something I could *do* to help keep us safe—like I was showing God I knew how fragile my life, and the lives of those I loved, was.

My husband opened my eyes to the folly of this idea. "You focus on outcomes opposite of the ones you're praying for," he pointed out. He was right. I prayed fervently to God to keep us safe, and then spent the rest of every flight sure we would crash. Where was the faith in that? So I changed my airplane prayers. I still asked for safety. But I started asking for help with my fear as well. When things got bumpy, I stopped indulging in thoughts of catastrophe, and I worked hard to at least pretend my stomach wasn't in my throat.

Eventually, I realized I wasn't pretending as often. Those menacing bumps and shudders weren't as terrifying as they'd once been. I still didn't like turbulence, but I no longer believed it meant a crash was imminent.

Our plane shook again, and Aurora patted her tummy, a big grin on her face. "These bumps tickle!" she said.

"They kinda do, don't they?" I answered, and we laughed together.

Thank you, Lord, for showing me that You are the
conqueror of all my fears.
—Erin Janoso

Digging Deeper: Matthew 6:27; 2 Corinthians 12:9

"Give us each day our daily bread." —Luke 11:3 (NABRE)

We were keeping vigil by my dad's bedside at the hospital's intensive care unit. My siblings and I stood around the bed's railings, watching him sleep.

"Shall we pray over him?" I asked my brothers and sister. We looked at each other and nodded but then fell into embarrassed silence. None of us was comfortable extemporizing, and the Lord's Prayer felt too rote in that intimate moment.

"Let's say the prayer Dad would say before meals," my oldest brother suggested. We held hands and started: "Thank Thee, our precious heavenly Father, for Thy many blessings...."

We faltered with the words and giggled self-consciously as we did so. Even after more than fifty years of hearing Dad recite it, we never had the prayer down. Mom had taught us as children the traditional Catholic blessing, "Bless us, O Lord, and these Thy gifts...." But Dad was Methodist, and the prayer was uniquely his, heard on Sundays and holidays when it was his turn to say the blessing before meals.

Dad also distinguished himself by always pausing before every meal to pray silently. He did this whether he was at home having a peanut butter and honey sandwich for lunch or out to dinner with friends.

After Dad died, we talked a lot about his special qualities and habits: how he loved to make things, weaving baskets and carving soapstone; the way he always drove the speed limit; his precise penmanship; his big hugs. How special, indeed, that we also remember him for the way he prayed.

God, I know how to pray but I don't always do it. Help me
get into the habit by talking with You at my meals,
as I would with any guest at my table.
—Amy Eddings

Digging Deeper: Acts 2:46; Romans 8:26

Saturday, November 14

Who is the man who delights in life, who loves to see the good days? Keep your tongue from evil, your lips from speaking lies. Turn from evil and do good; seek peace and pursue it. —Psalm 34:13–15 (NABRE)

At the funeral home, I heard the same thing again and again about my dad. "He was such a kind man," said those who came to pay their respects. "Always smiling, cheering, and encouraging," said the now-adult friends of my brothers, who remembered Dad's enthusiastic shouts from the stands during their football games in high school. "He was a friend to everyone."

My siblings and I were hard-pressed to recall times when our feelings were hurt by a sarcastic remark or put-down from Dad about our hair, our clothes, our choice of friends, our divorces, or our bad decisions. I don't ever remember his being rude or impolite. I've fallen, too easily and often, into the temptation to criticize loudly a colleague for a mistake or to dress down a server for a cold, botched meal, but Dad never behaved that way. He never resorted to profanity or other forms of verbal aggression. He found a way, when displeased, to get his point across without the withering glance, the harsh word, or wagging finger.

At the funeral home, I saw the prosperity he enjoyed. He was rich in friends. He had a long and loving marriage with my mom. He did not suffer estrangement from any of his six children. His memory brought smiles to us and leavened the sadness of his death with joy.

God, be the Minder of my words today.
Make them an instrument of Your peace.
—Amy Eddings

Digging Deeper: Psalms 126:2–3, 141:3; 1 Peter 2:23

*He said to me, "My grace is all you need. My power is strongest when
you are weak." So I am very happy to brag about how weak I am.
Then Christ's power can rest on me.* —2 Corinthians 12:9 (NIRV)

One by one, the yellow balls of cookie dough rolled out of the
overturned bowl, off the counter, and onto the floor. My granddaughter, Lula, who'd accidentally tipped the bowl, looked horrified.
Her eyes met mine. I could tell she was searching, unsure of what she'd
find. Anger? Impatience? Criticism? Adopted less than a year ago from
foster care, five-year-old Lula was still testing the waters of acceptance
within our family.

"Accidents happen," I reassured her. "Do you know that one
Thanksgiving I made a pumpkin cheesecake, and as I was taking it out
of the oven, it slipped off of my oven mitt? It twirled up in the air and
then fell—*splat*—right on the kitchen floor!"

"What did you do?" she asked, wide-eyed.

"Well, your grandpa and I had a good laugh. Then, we got forks and ate
a few bites off the part that didn't touch the floor! After that, we cleaned
up the mess. How about you help me throw away this cookie dough?"

Together, we gathered up the errant dough balls and pitched them into
the trash. Then, we continued rolling the remaining red, green, and blue
balls together to make our tie-dyed sugar cookies. When we served the
cookies that night, Lula immediately recounted the story of my cheesecake debacle. Then, buoyed by the reassurance that she wasn't the only
one who makes mistakes, Lula shared why there was no yellow in our
rainbow-colored cookies. I found myself feeling grateful that my cheesecake had done a half-gainer onto the kitchen floor all those years ago.

*Dear Lord, thank You for Your mercy and forgiveness. Help me to be
honest about my faults. Perfection is found in You alone.*
—Vicki Kuyper

Digging Deeper: Proverbs 28:13; 2 Corinthians 12:9–10;
Ephesians 4:31–32

Buy the truth, and sell it not; also wisdom, and instruction, and understanding. —Proverbs 23:23 (KJV)

The man sitting in my office was, simply put, obnoxious. He knew he had it all. He was certain that it would always be so.

I was digging for an extra measure of patience when Matt Wiggington popped into my mind. For a moment, I was fifteen and back in his living room. He was about eighty and the most successful businessperson I knew. I'd chosen him as my mentor. He'd kindly obliged. Had I been Catholic rather than Presbyterian, spending time with him would've been like having an audience with the Pope.

With all the surety of a teen, I asked, "What's the secret to your success?"

Mr. Wiggington said: "Love people, and try to understand them."

His words reverberated through the years.

I looked at the man seated opposite me and tried to channel Mr. Wiggington's spirit. My client was bragging about his wealth and describing his jet-setting lifestyle. I knew his days on top were numbered. Money dwindles. A life void of meaning grows lonely and empty.

Caught in Mr. Wiggington's motto, compassion was washing over my irritation. I found myself moving toward concern.

What caused this man to focus on things that lead to unhappiness? *Love people, and try to understand them.*

I looked into his eyes and asked. "What's your hidden talent?"

"Uh, well, I—I used to paint. I thought I might be a painter."

"Now, that is interesting," I answered. "Tell me about it—all about it." And he did.

The invitation to his first show, two years later, had "Thank you" scrawled across the bottom. Mr. Wiggington was surely smiling.

> *Father, let me be wise and kind and live in Your truth as*
> *I try to love and understand Your children.*
> —Brock Kidd

Digging Deeper: 1 Peter 1:22; 1 John 4:20

"Inasmuch as you did it to one of the least of these...you did it to Me."
—Matthew 25:40 (NKJV)

If you live in Nashville and you are looking for a hero, might I recommend Darlene Stephen.

You can find her every Tuesday morning working with her volunteers in the little kitchen at Spruce Street Baptist Church (the oldest African-American church in the area). By noon, far more than one hundred homeless people will be welcomed to a lovely lunch. Every day in November, in addition to the usual luncheon, Darlene oversees the preparation and delivery of 220 meals to homebound people.

Sure, this is admirable and many communities offer similar programs, but Darlene serves her meals with a twist: Each meal "must be beautiful." That's right. The food is not only nutritious, it's "color-coded" and placed on the plate with care. It all goes back to Mama Mac, Darlene's grandmother who started the program many years ago.

Each person who comes to dinner is considered a guest. It's that simple. You serve your best to company. Even in her final earth-days, Mama Mac insisted that Darlene send over a few photos of the food once it was plated. And under Mama Mac's eye, it better be pretty!

There are numerous lessons in Darlene's story. You can pick your own. For me, whether I'm just fixing lunch for my husband, David, creating a birthday feast, or setting a buffet table for a celebration, Darlene is always hovering in the back of my mind, going far beyond "I was hungry and you gave me something to eat" (Matthew 25:35 NIV).

If you're going to serve, her big smile tells me, you might as well go all the way. I can't help but smile, too, imagining the pleasure Jesus must feel when he looks through the eyes of a homeless person at Darlene's plate of beautiful food.

Father, thank You for the joy that comes with serving "big"!
—Pam Kidd

Digging Deeper: Proverbs 14:21; 1 John 3:18

Wednesday, November 18

Nevertheless the solid foundation of God stands, having this seal:
"The Lord knows those who are His...."—2 Timothy 2:19 (NKJV)

Spice?"

I've just placed a call to Tom, a friend from my youth. We haven't seen each other or talked in probably twenty years, but when he answers, he calls me by my old moniker, a play on my name, Ginger. Only a small handful of people ever called me by this nickname, coined in the 1980s in Tom's basement, where our group passed the weekends on an old couch and plastic chairs—watching TV, goofing off, talking about nothing. I can't recall why hanging out at Tom's was so much fun, but it was. No one has called me Spice in decades, and now, it occurs to me that I have never once heard Tom call me by my real name. I'm suddenly taken aback by the comforting familiarity of this gift: the gift of being known.

I was Spice long before life changed me, throwing in my path so many things that helped me gain hard-won wisdom or altered the way I look at the world. It feels peculiar to hear my long-lost friend call me by the name of the girl I used to be. But this peculiarity comes with a side of wistfulness. I realize that my old friend knew a "me" that my husband, my children, and many of my closest friends do not. I haven't been Spice for a long time, but I feel lighter somehow, knowing that someone else remembers her.

At the end of the conversation, Tom tells me I haven't changed a bit, that I'm the same girl he always knew. I'm sure that's not entirely true, but it makes me smile to think that somewhere inside, Spice is still there.

Lord, only You know me fully and completely. How precious it will be
someday to hear You call my name!
—Ginger Rue

Digging Deeper: Psalm 139:1–4; John 10:14; 1 Corinthians 8:3

As the deer pants for the water brooks, so pants my soul for You, O God.
—Psalm 42:1 (NKJV)

Thanksgiving was a week away. While many were probably fretting over holiday traditions, I was grateful for a reprieve from the everyday stresses of my life. With three young children and the caregiver responsibilities of helping a mother who was battling cancer, I was physically and emotionally depleted.

Because an out-of-town speaking engagement would pull me from home, my sister drove in from North Carolina to help my husband juggle the household. I hopped in the car with my best friend for the trip from Atlanta, Georgia, to Kiawah Island, South Carolina. Our conversations, car karaoke, fits of laughter, and moments of thoughtful silence were refreshing.

Upon our arrival, we didn't have much time before the opening session. By the end of the night, I nearly collapsed into bed. A beachside prayer session was scheduled for five o'clock the next morning, and I couldn't fathom where I'd get the energy.

However, before sunrise, I bundled up and walked by flashlight along the beach pathway. We were welcomed by mist and the calm roar of the ocean. When my feet touched the sand, my soul awakened. Looking across the vast ocean, I marveled at God's workmanship and the impending sunrise painting the sky in hues of orange and gold.

God renewed me there. With each breeze that rolled across the water, I inhaled a greater sense of hope. Suddenly, a reverential hush fell over our group. A deer appeared from the brush and walked to the edge of the water. It dipped its head in the water several times and then bounded away.

Tears welled in my eyes. I thirsted for more of God's presence. In Him is where I've always been refreshed. In Him is where I can cast my cares and trust that no matter the day, His grace is sufficient.

God, I seek You in times of joy and sorrow. Let me thirst for Your presence.
—Tia McCollors

Digging Deeper: Jeremiah 31:25; 1 Peter 5:7

Friday, November 20

The Lord replied, "My Presence will go with you, and I will give you rest."
—Exodus 33:14 (NIV)

My grandfather sat in the parlor of this old Victorian when it held only one cane chair and hope. He sat in the corner, a gentle, humble, quiet man, and spoke a blessing. Six days later, he was in heaven.

"God will be with you here, Lonny, Shawnie, and boys. He'll be with you in your new home."

Fourteen years blew by. Beautiful grains of life. We loved and laughed. Found struggle and strife. These walls held us through our happiest and hardest times. But our family is changing. Now it's time to move across the Mississippi to the community where our boys will attend high school after years of home learning.

I've prayed for the family who will live here next as I've painted doors and washed panes of glass. I've asked the Lord to help us find another home while I've polished the banister and emptied the secret space behind the stairs. And I've decided that what I ache for is more than just missing the scrawls on the wall that measured the boys' heights. Or the kindness of the maple that stood tall as my sons scaled her branches.

I long for my grandfather's blessing.

We're closing one life stage and opening another. I'm afraid.

But today, as I pack the attic and fill cardboard boxes with treasure from this trove, I consider that the blessing doesn't need to be left behind. Maybe it can move with us. It's rooted in God's Word. It's righteous and true. God's presence isn't tied to a time or a dwelling that's been dear.

God goes with His people. He goes with them through moves. Through changes. Through journeys of life and journeys of the soul.

"God will be with us as we go," I speak it aloud. I imagine the words rising to the rafters.

I claim the blessing anew and already there is rest.

Lord, Your presence is powerful.
—Shawnelle Eliasen

Digging Deeper: Joshua 1:9; Matthew 28:20

"The LORD, the LORD, the compassionate and gracious God...."
—Exodus 34:6 (NIV)

Our Australian shepherd, Sage, nearly thirteen years old, was declining rapidly. We had tried what we could to revive her failing kidneys, but now she was refusing food and water. For the last few days, she had simply laid on the floor, her breathing labored. It broke our hearts to see her struggle.

It had been snowing and cold, but on November 21, Colorado sunshine broke through, melted the snow, and warmed the earth. Sage teetered to the door. We let her outside. Somehow, she found the strength to walk to the field below our home, the field where for nearly her entire life she'd run freely with her inseparable friend, Montana, our other Aussie. I watched from the door as she sat, paws outstretched in front of her, head held high with dignity, looking out over her familiar domain. Then she lay down on her side.

For the next four hours, Montana, my husband, David, and I sat with Sage. She rested her head in our laps, and Montana never left her side. The sun shone brightly, and a warm breeze stirred the air. As we stroked Sage and Montana, David and I reminisced about our years with them. Then he gently lifted Sage, now too weak to walk, and placed her in our car for her final journey.

The next day, snow fell again.

Thank you, gracious God, for the gift of that sunny day of togetherness—and for remembrance.
—Kim Taylor Henry

Digging Deeper: 2 Corinthians 1:3–4; James 4:6

Sunday, November 22

Ye are no more strangers and foreigners, but fellow citizens with the saints, and of the household of God. —Ephesians 2:19 (KJV)

Before I head to a turkey dinner with my family, I take time to enjoy one of my most favorite celebrations here in Concord, New Hampshire—the Thanksgiving service sponsored by the local Interfaith Council. The location varies from year to year as churches take turns hosting the gathering. Participants vary, as well, but the diversity of the group remains constant in this city that is home to so many refugee people and new Americans.

Last Thanksgiving, we gathered in the Unitarian Church. Some participants wore yarmulkes, others headscarves or embroidered stoles. Clergy of several Protestant denominations read from the Bible. The cantor from the Jewish temple sang songs in Hebrew, and then led the congregation in songs from the hymnals. A woman professing Baha'i faith read a poem, and about half a dozen teenage girls wearing colorful silks—and giggling with nerves—recited verses from the Koran.

After the service, there was much hugging and happy conversation. We know each other from work, from school, or perhaps the community garden. We are friends. Today we share our faith traditions knowing our various ways of communicating with God will be respected by those around us, even when we do not agree on particulars.

I am thankful to live in a community that does not simply tolerate diversity but celebrates it. In our multicultural microcosm, we see a glimpse of a harmonious world. Peace on Earth is possible. In fact, this blessed Thanksgiving—it is already here.

Creator God, You make us all in Your image.
—Gail Schilling

Digging Deeper: Leviticus 19:18; Deuteronomy 10:19; Luke 10:21

We have this as a sure and steadfast anchor of the soul, a hope that enters into the inner place behind the curtain. —Hebrews 6:19 (ESV)

Those who have read *Daily Guideposts* for many years may have noticed that my bio has changed. Yes, I still have a trusty golden retriever as my writing partner. I still spend my days with a dog at my feet, his warm breath keeping cadence with the tapping at the keys. Same breed, same tender heart, but now it is Zeke, not Jack, who keeps me company as I write.

We had to put Jack down. He was sixteen years old, loyally holding steady in his spot underneath my desk, but I knew he was in pain. His dark eyes seemed to beg me to let him go, to let him leave me with dignity. Oh, how I cried. It hurt. Jack had slept under each of my baby's cribs after they came home from the hospital. He had walked down country roads at my side as I contemplated my next book. He had watched my children's first steps. He had helped me say goodbye to lost loved ones. He had been my anchor in many storms.

I miss him. Still.

Zeke is different. He has a different spot under my desk, still close enough to warm my toes but a little farther back, a little off to the side. Where Jack calmly looked at me with big brown eyes, Zeke jumps and licks my face. Where Jack walked, Zeke runs.

But Zeke is still here, still my writing partner, my soft, warm touch when things start to feel overwhelming. Writing just doesn't feel the same without my guy under my desk.

I am thankful. For my beloved dogs, but even more for my God Who is sure and steadfast, unchanging, unmoving, steady. Anchoring me in the midst of countless storms. Being that warm touch, that soft landing place, that resting place for my soul.

> *Father God, thank You for Your steady, sure,*
> *and unmovable love for me. Amen.*
> —Erin MacPherson

Digging Deeper: Psalm 91:1–2; James 1:17

PACKING LIGHT

Do not neglect your gift, which was given you through prophecy when the body of elders laid their hands on you. —1 Timothy 4:14 (NIV)

I've met some amazing, fun people on planes. On a recent trip, flying from Houston back to Seattle, I sat next to a friendly young woman. We struck up a conversation and she asked me, "What do you do?" It's a common question we ask when we first meet someone. I explained that I was a novelist and the conversation went from there. It wasn't until later that I thought about that introductory question. It's certainly a popular one. Our identity is tied up in our occupations, in what we do.

The truth is, I've always felt a bit uncomfortable talking about my career. I am a lot more than a writer and storyteller. God has given all of us gifts. While it's gratifying when people tell me they enjoy my stories, I feel somehow undeserving. God is the One Who should get the praise, not me. As a result, I've come up with a response that redirects the praise where it belongs, "God and I thank you."

From our brief encounter on the plane, I could see that this friendly young woman had a huge heart. She spoke about her love for her family and her enjoyment in entertaining. It was clear she had the gift of hospitality. I thought about her as we parted ways, and in the future, how I should best handle the question, "What do you do?" I no longer ask that question when I meet others. Instead, I ask, "What gifts has God given you?" This puts the emphasis where it should be and sets the right tone for the conversation.

Thank You, Lord, for the gifts and talents You have given each of us.
May I always reflect the glory back to You.
—Debbie Macomber

Digging Deeper: Ephesians 2:10; 1 Peter 4:10–11

"Behold, I am with you and will keep [careful watch over you and guard] you wherever you may go...."—Genesis 28:15 (AMP)

Picking myself up from a fall, I was thankful that nothing hurt too much. Walking on to the building where I was going to attend a meeting, I noticed blood was marking my path in the fresh snow. Distracted by an ambulance with screaming sirens approaching the same building, I had missed the step from the parking lot up to the sidewalk. Walking fast, I had fallen hard and there was nothing to grab hold of on the way down.

Once inside, I examined my wounds with a mirror. The blood was from a couple of scratches to my lips that had brushed across the sidewalk along with my chin and nose. Thankful to have fallen in a way that minimized the injuries to surface scrapes and a slightly chipped tooth, I moved from frustration to praise. Silently giving thanks that the damage was not what it could have been if I had fallen at a slightly steeper angle, I was filled with gratefulness.

Earlier that morning, I had prayed for God to guide me through the day. I ran through my planned events, asking for His insight to deal with a couple of challenges I faced and His grace and wisdom for the meetings and conversations scheduled at various hours. But falling—that was an unplanned event, one for which I had not prayed. As my gratitude grew, I realized that there was something between me and the cold and unforgiving concrete that I had missed before—the hand of God and an unspoken prayer. It is in moments like these when God goes immediately to work for our good and the Holy Spirit prays for us!

Thank You, God, for softening the blows that come when things spin quickly out of control—things that happen before we can pray—even things caused by my ineptness.
—John Dilworth

Digging Deeper: Psalm 73:23; Romans 8:26–28

Thanksgiving, Thursday, November 26

For everything God made is good, and we may eat it gladly if we are thankful for it, and if we ask God to bless it, for it is made good by the Word of God and prayer. —1 Timothy 4:4–5 (TLB)

Over the years I've celebrated Thanksgiving at my parents' home, my grandparents' home, aunts' and uncles' homes, and my own homes in four states and now in Florida. I've celebrated the feast at my siblings' homes, and in recent years at five of my husband Jack's adult children's homes, and at my cousin Judy's. I've spent the holiday in restaurants with close friends when there was no family around. It's always an experience with different foods, people, atmosphere, and customs. Some of the food is better than others. Jack's daughter-in-law, with her Egyptian heritage, makes the best turkey stuffing I've ever eaten—even better than my own fabulous recipe!

Wherever I am on Thanksgiving Day, nearly every dinner begins with a prayer and an opportunity to share what we're most thankful for. Since I rarely get to spend Thanksgiving with my own children and grandchildren who are scattered across the country, this year I sent individual letters detailing exactly what I'm thankful for. The letters begin:

Jeanne, I am thankful for your sense of humor, your amazing artistic talent and your devotion to your daughter.

Julia, I am thankful for your persistence in finishing your education and in following your dreams that include your three children.

Michael, I am thankful that you are such an amazing single-parent dad to your three young adults.

Andrew, I am thankful that you are enamored with our family's heritage and ancestry and that you are such a good dad to your two boys.

Heavenly Father, guide my hand when I write notes of thanksgiving to friends and family members. Help me to be filled with gratitude every day of the year.
—Patricia Lorenz

Digging Deeper: Psalm 100:1–5; Isaiah 25:6–9

The Spirit also helps in our weaknesses. For we do not know what we should pray for as we ought, but the Spirit Himself makes intercession for us with groanings which cannot be uttered. —Romans 8:26 (NKJV)

This autumn I offer a prayer for folks affected by Seasonal Affective Disorder (SAD). Sometimes we sufferers are too emotionally paralyzed to pray for ourselves.

About fifteen autumns ago, I felt increasingly mopey. First, I blamed grim New England weather for the melancholy. Endless rain exacerbated the end of Daylight Saving Time; black nights followed gray days. Next, I blamed my mood on an empty nest, as my younger daughter had graduated from high school and moved away from home. Teaching satisfied me, but the dark, hour-long commute drained me. Even a move closer to work, friends, and family didn't help. I sank deeper and deeper into depression. I'd rather sleep than appeal to God. My prayers felt dry and useless.

When my daughter and excited little granddaughter set up their Christmas tree the first Sunday in Advent, I watched numbly. At home, I slung a string of twinkle lights on my tall houseplant; it was all I could muster. That awful year, I did no baking, sent no cards, and bought no presents—not even for my children.

Mercifully, my daughters sensed something was wrong and helped me seek professional care. SAD symptoms described me exactly: lethargy in winter due to lack of sunlight, oversleeping, and overeating. Simple fixes such as medication, a light box, and exercise would restore energy to my body and, eventually, hope to my soul. God restored my health, even when I could not ask for it.

Omniscient God, You supply our needs even when we cannot speak them.
—Gail Schilling

Digging Deeper: Psalms 42:11, 61:1, 70:4–5

*The whole assembly bowed in worship, while the musicians played.... —*2 Chronicles 29:28 (NIV)

The fireplace in our living room sits between two tall (seven foot) wooden organ pipes, which I purchased at a rural salvage yard. I don't know which musical notes were assigned to each pipe, but I'm guessing one was "very low" and the other was "really very low."

I retrofit them with LED bulbs; they now serve as overhead lights. It's an interesting decoration, albeit a bit Phantom-of-the-Opera-ish. Guests either ask, "Are those organ pipes?" or say something distinctly ambiguous like "Oh. Huh. They're—something."

I repurpose a lot of things, but these lights are something special. I asked the seller where he got them. "Dunno," he said. "Some little church around here."

"Around here" could mean anywhere, but chances are they came from one of the countless small coal towns that dot the western Pennsylvania countryside. It's hard to imagine that a hardscrabble hamlet could afford an organ of this magnitude. Weren't there other priorities?

There surely were. (The economic history of Appalachian coal country is distinctly ambiguous.) Yet, somehow, a faith community decided on making magnificent music. For how many decades did the congregation rise up to sing "Amazing Grace," accompanied by the beautiful bass notes that poured forth from the tall wooden throats that now stand like sentries in my living room?

Maybe I didn't "repurpose" anything. Maybe I merely extended their continuing mission: illuminating our path from above in whatever form they can.

Lord, let me repurpose my own life toward Your will and not mine.
—Mark Collins

Digging Deeper: Psalm 96:1–2; Ephesians 5:19

Each of you should give what you have decided in your heart to give,
not reluctantly or under compulsion, for God loves a cheerful giver.
—2 Corinthians 9:7 (NIV)

We sat in the auditorium as elementary schoolchildren flooded the stage with instruments under their arms. They scanned the audience, smiling nervously. The music started. A little girl in the back row with a trumpet in her hands swayed back and forth and a flute player fidgeted, but it was the boy in the front row that captured our attention.

Adorably, he balanced himself on the edge of a tall stool. His black oversize glasses hung low on his nose as he edged toward the huge instrument: a bass clarinet that was literally as big as he was.

As the students played "Away in a Manger," my eyes darted between the beaming little girl with the trumpet who waved her free hand back and forth as if she were in the audience at a rock concert and the boy in the front with the seemingly enormous clarinet. The music teacher cued a solo and the band went silent except for the boy on the stool. He leaned toward his instrument with eyes wide, cheeks full, face red, and blew and blew and blew his heart out.

The notes weren't important. I have no memory of what the instrument sounded like. It was the intention, his effort, his giving it all that came like a beam of light right out of him and into us.

He finished and took a bow. When I got to my feet to join the crowd bursting with applause I thought, *This is it. This is Christmas.*

Heavenly Father, thank You for the moments when we realize
what Christmas is all about.
—Sabra Ciancanelli

Digging Deeper: 1 Chronicles 29:14; Proverbs 11:25

Monday, November 30

Shout for joy, you heavens; rejoice, you earth; burst into song, you mountains! For the LORD comforts his people and will have compassion on his afflicted ones. —Isaiah 49:13 (NIV)

B e careful while applying the hot wax," the craft instructor cautions. My length of white silk is stretched taut over a cardboard frame on a table in front of me. I brush the wax wherever I don't want any additional color on the finished scarf.

"Close the wax lines so you have a contained area for the paint."

I outline several flowers. Three butterflies. Beside me, my twenty-eight-year-old daughter, Aleah, traces the sunflowers on her pattern.

"The doctor can't find anything wrong," she told me yesterday after a long-anticipated appointment with a specialist, one more doctor in an endless line of doctors. "He wants me to try an experimental pain program." *More tests. More medications.*

I replay the conversation as I watch Aleah paint her design with bold colors. Sunset orange. Brilliant yellow. The paint blends into the fabric, following the thread lines, until it hits a wax boundary. Aleah's cane is propped on the table in case she needs it.

I choose a bottle of magenta paint for my butterflies, filling in the small spaces carefully. A tiny opening in the wax allows the paint to escape. The color flows freely into the unrestricted space.

"Don't worry," the instructor says. "The scarf will be beautiful."

"My therapist will be so proud of me," Aleah says, as she paints her remaining scarf with deep blue and purple. She strokes red paint into the center of the sunflowers for added depth. "I got out of the house today."

My daughter's smile cannot be contained.

Give me understanding of those who live with daily pain,
Lord Jesus. On days they escape the boundaries of their restrictions,
help me to notice and to celebrate their victory.
—Lynne Hartke

Digging Deeper: Psalm 103:13; Isaiah 49:15–16

HE PERFORMS WONDERS

1 _____

2 _____

3 _____

4 _____

5 _____

6 _____

7 _____

8 _____

9 _____

10 _____

11 _____

12 _____

13 _____

14 _____

15 _____

November

16 _____

17 _____

18 _____

19 _____

20 _____

21 _____

22 _____

23 _____

24 _____

25 _____

26 _____

27 _____

28 _____

29 _____

30 _____

DECEMBER

*I want to know Christ
and the power of his
resurrection....*

—Philippians 3:10 (NRSV)

Tuesday, December 1

FIRSTS: Pass It On

Anyone who loves God must also love their brother and sister.
—1 John 4:21 (NIV)

The parking meter needed quarters but all I had were dimes, nickels, and pennies. I was fumbling through my purse in a final search when a man who'd parked a few cars away handed me a quarter as he walked by. "Wait!" I shouted after him, holding out two dimes and a nickel. "Pass it on," he called back as he crossed the street.

Pass it on. As I fed the meter, I thought back some fifteen years to the first time someone said those words to me. I'd done my grocery shopping and wheeled my loaded cart to the checkout line. My purchases were on the counter when I searched my wallet for my credit card—library card, AAA, Medicare, driver's license—and a sinking sensation grew as I recalled running a quick errand the day before and stuffing my credit card in a jacket pocket.

I got out all the cash I carried, some twenty-four dollars in bills and coins. The empathetic clerk helped me set aside some costlier items. Coffee. Cheeses. Blueberries. Olive oil—there wasn't much left in the keep-it pile and still I didn't have enough to pay for it.

By now, everyone in the line behind me was watching the little drama. "How much does she need?" came a voice from the rear.

"Forty, with what she has, would cover it all," the clerk said.

The next moment two twenty-dollar bills were handed down the line. As the clerk bagged my groceries, I asked the thoughtful woman for an address where I could mail a check. She shook her head. "Pass it on."

And of course I did. And do each day. Not always money, more often a smile, a note, a helping hand. *Pass it on.* What a lifestyle for children of a God Who never stops giving.

Lord Who makes all things new, to whom will I pass on Your love today?
—Elizabeth Sherrill

Digging Deeper: Proverbs 19:17; Luke 6:38; 2 Corinthians 9:6

"Obey the Lord your God and follow his commands and decrees that I give you today."—Deuteronomy 27:10 (NIV)

I had a voice message from someone named Janet. The message said, "Mom is not doing so well. Please call me."

I didn't know Janet or recognize her number. Immediately I called her back, envisioning that this woman was intending to tell someone that her mother was close to death, but misdialed. Her voice-mail picked up, and I left her a message saying that she called me by mistake. I then said a prayer for her and her mom.

Later, Janet returned my call. "I got your number from Mom's book," she said. "Maybe she has the wrong number in here."

I asked her for the name of the person she was trying to reach.

"Gayle Williams," she said.

"I'm Gayle Williams," I said hesitantly. "Who is your mom?"

She spoke her mother's name—first, middle, and last. I had to sit down.

Janet's mother, Olga, had been my grandmother's caretaker in her final years. A lovely lady and a retired nurse, she came to our home to do crossword puzzles and watch soap operas with my grandmother. Olga was a godsend. I had been in touch with her until about ten years ago, exchanging Christmas cards and infrequent phone calls. I had assumed Olga had passed away, and so I was stunned that Janet was showering me with this flood of treasured memories in her one call.

Olga passed away that night at the age of one hundred.

Just hours before this happened, I had been on the train reading my Bible on the way to work. I felt that God told me, "Pray for each other, with the same fervor that you pray for yourselves." I'm so grateful to have obeyed. Because I listened to God, called Janet back, and prayed for her mom—without knowing who her mom was—*I* was blessed.

Lord, thank You for Your ways, which are always completely right and just. Help me to follow Your perfect example.
—Gayle T. Williams

Digging Deeper: Psalm 25:4–5; James 5:13

Thursday, December 3

You hide them in the secret place of Your presence.... —Psalm 31:20 (NASB)

When I visit three-year-old Alice, she says, "Grandma, let's read in our secret spot." Our hideaway is a living room corner behind the rocking chair where we enter a world of imagination in stories.

Since childhood I've liked finding secluded nooks: A maple tree in a backyard down the street where I'd climb and read my book. Pretend camping with my little red wagon, a blanket, and water and soda crackers. The neighbors didn't mind my pulling alongside an opening in their hedge.

As I grew up, I still liked to search out a hidden corner—indoors or out. In the woods behind our home there's a towering cedar tree ringed by young firs. Recently when I was upset I sought refuge in my cedar chapel. Anger subsided and soon I whispered praises to God interspersed with the gentle snowflakes that had begun to fall.

Perhaps my history with "secret spots" is why I'm drawn to accounts of Jesus going away to pray and renew. Luke 5:16 relates, "Jesus Himself would often slip away to the wilderness and pray." He "proceeded as was His custom to the Mount of Olives" (Luke 22:39). Following John the Baptist's execution and after a demanding time of ministry, Jesus and His disciples "went away in the boat to a secluded place by themselves" (Mark 6:32).

There is something about getting away to be alone with God—entering His world of authenticity in prayer—that is immensely bolstering. But I am not always able to physically leave or search out a quiet place. That's when I find my true secret spot in the invitation of Jesus: "Come to Me, all who are weary and heavy-laden, and I will give you rest" (Matthew 11:28).

Jesus offers Himself as my sanctuary—anytime, anywhere.

Quiet Savior, gather me in all my need to the "secret place of Your presence."
                                                        —Carol Knapp

Digging Deeper: Psalms 46:10, 91:1–2; Matthew 6:6; Luke 6:12

Satisfy us in the morning with your unfailing love, that we may sing for joy and be glad all our days. —Psalm 90:14 (NIV)

This morning I was drawn to a picture forming outside the window in the room where I exercise. The sun, punching its bright light through a dark sky, filtered through the trees to a captivating soft glow below, as though our neighborhood were under a photographer's lamp. It was so distinct from anything I have ever seen that I called my wife, Pat, to come see it. "Wow! I'm really glad I didn't miss this," she said.

We lingered a few moments longer, mesmerized by the unfolding panorama. I began working out on our cross-country ski machine, watching the scene transform into a stunning canvas of light and color. When I finished exercising, the extraordinary spectacle was gone, blotted out by the return of dark clouds.

Seeing the scene move full circle so quickly was like watching a series of time-lapse photos that reflect life's ups and downs. Mountaintop experiences often spring out of a dark struggle when a prayer is answered, a distressing issue solved, or a worry erased. And the mountaintops seem to pass much more quickly than times of struggle as our exhilaration gives way to a new storm—a health concern, a job loss, a broken relationship, or other challenging circumstance.

This brief experience changed my outlook for the entire day. The cloudy weather remained, but my mind held to the light of the beautiful early morning scene. We may not be able to stop a life struggle or change an outcome, but we can decide how to weather each storm. We can stay focused on God's faithfulness, or we can become absorbed by dark clouds of fear that shriek *What will I do?*

What will you do?

God, etch upon our minds the wondrous things You have done for us so we will rejoice in Your unfailing providence and confidently trust You to light our way through the storms.
—John Dilworth

Digging Deeper: Psalms 30:5, 63:5–6; Lamentations 3:22–23

Saturday, December 5

You are the God who performs miracles; you display your power among the peoples. —Psalm 77:14 (NIV)

I have a hard time believing the story about Mary's pregnancy," a mom said, as she sat snuggling her baby at our MOPS (Mothers of Preschoolers) meeting. "I just don't understand."

I'm a mentor at MOPS, a ministry that welcomes moms of young children, no matter where they are in their life stories or faith journeys. We'd just watched a video about the Virgin Mary who's told by an angel that she's pregnant and will give birth to the Son of God.

"Mary's pregnancy is a barrier for me too," another mom added. "How do you explain it?"

All eyes turned toward me. As a mentor, I'm supposed to offer perspective because I've lived through more of life's seasons.

My heart was pounding. How would I answer such an important question?

"I don't have a logical answer," I admitted, "because a miracle is impossible to understand." I hesitated. "But I have my story.

"Today is the fifteenth anniversary of my diagnosis of stage 4 ovarian cancer. I was given a two-year life expectancy and a doctor told me that stage 4 ovarian cancer is not curable. Many people expected me to die. I think I did too. Obviously I didn't die. I'm now declared cancer free and some people call me a miracle.

"I can't make sense of it. Why have I survived when so many others have not? I don't have an answer, and I feel both grief and gratitude. But this is what I've learned about accepting the wonder of a miracle: I don't have to understand in order to believe."

Lord, each December, when I celebrate the wonder of a miracle that I don't understand, I thank You for my health. I pray that You continue to meet each one of us, right where we have a hard time believing in You.
—Carol Kuykendall

Digging Deeper: John 20:30–31; Romans 10:9–10

The light shines in the darkness, and the darkness has not overcome it.
—John 1:5 (NIV)

The new lights have to be here somewhere," I said to my husband, Tony. I'd already searched the attic twice and was on the stairs to go down to the basement. I had a vision of them in my mind: a huge wheel of white and bright Christmas-tree lights we had purchased the year before, right after Christmas at an incredible discount.

Now with our tree in the stand and ready to be decorated, it was either use the old multi-colored big-bulb lights or keep hunting for the brand-new smaller white ones.

As I dug around the basement, I found a box of ornaments I'd completely forgotten about and a pair of snow pants, hand-me-downs from our son Solomon that would just fit his younger brother, but no new lights.

"We'll just have to use the old ones," I said, giving up. Trimming the tree, I tried to let go of the nagging feeling that I'd lost something. We were down to the dregs of our ornaments—the ones missing hooks or with broken pieces. "I like the big lights," Solomon said. "I like that it looks like it always looks."

He was right. The tree was gorgeous and there was something to having the tree look the same—with big red, blue, green, and gold bulbs.

As I sat down on the couch, my eyes went up toward the ceiling. I laughed. There were the lights! The long string I'd spent hours looking for, we had strung across the ceiling beams back in the early fall to bring more light to the dark afternoons. The elusive lights were there the whole time.

Heavenly Father, in the days ahead, help me to look up when
I need answers and to always see the bright side when I feel
something is missing.
—Sabra Ciancanelli

Digging Deeper: Psalm 119:130; Ecclesiastes 2:13

Monday, December 7

"For to the snow he says, 'Fall on the earth'; and to the shower and the rain, 'Be strong.'"—Job 37:6 (RSV)

I didn't grow up with snow. In my Southern California childhood, the only way we ever saw it was to bundle up in old parkas and mothball-smelling woolens and drive up to the mountains to build a snowman or to go sledding. I came east to college and it seemed such a novelty to see snow falling outside my dorm-room window. I loved the way it transformed the world, the brown grass turning white, highlights sketched out on the bare limbs of a dark tree, the roof of a building changing color.

I remember studying for finals that freshman year and feeling completely inadequate. I had too many papers to write and too much learning to cram into too little time. Then I looked out my window. Snow was swirling around the branches of the bare maple tree, collecting on the ground, covering the paths we students rushed back and forth on, heading to classes. It was as though God were saying: *I'm right here. Don't worry. Look what I can do with just a few inches of powder.* After staring at books for too long, my roommate and I dashed outside to laugh and throw snowballs. I was happy, free, glad to be alive.

I still feel that way about snow days. They remind me that God is bigger than anything I could possibly accomplish on my own. I want to raise my head and catch snowflakes on my tongue, tasting the Creator's goodness. He's always there, ready to transform my world. Heck, I might even get the day off.

Lord, I give thanks for the unexpected goodness of the Creation.
—Rick Hamlin

Digging Deeper: Psalm 148:8; Jeremiah 18:14

I lay my requests before you and wait expectantly. —Psalm 5:3 (NIV)

Mountains of black plastic trash bags and boxes filled with donations were stacked by the doors of the gymnasium. Volunteers scurried around, getting ready for the "Giveaway," a huge community event that took place a couple of weeks before Christmas. Our community had gathered donated furniture, clothing, housewares, and more. We were setting up tables with neatly folded and displayed goods—offered for free. Many underprivileged families would come here to do their Christmas shopping.

I stood at a table, sorting the contents of the bags, while in my mind I wrestled with a conflict I was trying to resolve. *Maybe I should...* For hours as I folded clothing, I considered options of things I could do, but I couldn't figure it out.

Reaching into a cardboard box, I pulled out a child's jewelry box. *Some little girl is going to love this.* Gently I arranged the individual necklaces and bracelets for display. In the bottom of the box was what appeared to be a round black container. It was heavy. *I wonder what kind of jewelry is in here.* I tried unscrewing it. Then looked for a way to open the lid, but there wasn't a visible seam where I could slip in a fingernail to pry it off. For minutes, I wrestled with it and couldn't figure it out.

A friend, who had been walking by, stopped. "What are you doing?"

"I need some help. I can't get this open."

My friend frowned, "It doesn't open. It's a hockey puck." We both burst out laughing.

After she walked away, a still small voice whispered in my spirit. *Like the hockey puck, your conflict is not for you to open. I've been waiting for you to ask me for help.*

I swallowed, hard. *Lord, I'm sorry.* Over the next couple of weeks, God coached me on how to work things out.

Thank You, Lord, for reminding me that I need to ask for Your wisdom.
—Rebecca Ondov

Digging Deeper: 1 Corinthians 1:19–25; James 1:5

Be not forgetful to entertain strangers: for thereby some have entertained angels unawares. —Hebrews 13:2 (KJV)

Perhaps because strangers have been so kind to me during my travels, I try to return the favor wherever I am. Sometimes I receive far more than I give.

Last December, while I was waiting for the subway on Boston's Red Line, a young woman pulling a suitcase approached me. "¿Downtown? ¿Orange-a line?" Her creamy accent hinted a Spanish background.

She must mean Downtown Crossing. "Okay. Follow me, and I'll show you where to get off." She studied my face, translating. When the train screeched into the station, we boarded together. She sat very close.

At first, we did not speak as we lurched toward Harvard Square. Then she beamed at me as though admiring fine statuary. "You are beautiful!" she gushed. *She must be* really *glad to have help,* I thought.

I regarded my companion's fine black wool coat, matching pillbox hat, leather boots, and quality suitcase. I had to know more. Garbling each other's languages, we established that she was from Colombia. She flashed a phone photo of herself and about twenty youngsters.

"Ah! *¡Enseña!* You are a teacher!"

"*¡Sí! ¡Sí!*"

"Me, *Abuela.* Grandmother." Then I shared my grandbaby photos. She nodded in delight.

All too soon, I told her that her stop was next. "I thank God we met."

"*¡Sí! Gracias a Dios.* ¡Thank you!" As the train slowed, she rose, bent low, and lightly as a snowflake, kissed my cheek. Then she was gone.

My friends say I met an angel that day, or perhaps we were angels to each other. Either way, unexpected joy on a dreary subway train tells me God is very near.

> *Father, how I love when You surprise me with joy!*
> —Gail Schilling

Digging Deeper: Exodus 2:22, 22:21; Galatians 5:22–23

Think of what is above, not of what is on earth. For you have died, and your life is hidden with Christ in God. —Colossians 3:2–3 (NABRE)

Friends and acquaintances ask me how I'm doing, weeks now after my father has died. "I'm doing really well," I tell them. "His death was amazing."

My dad got very sick, very suddenly. He died of multiple organ failure two days after going to the hospital complaining of severe abdominal pain.

We were all with him when he died—Mom and my five siblings. We took turns witnessing the joy he gave us and the meaning his life held for us.

"Dad," I said, holding his face between my hands, "are you ready? Are you good to go?"

His words were barely a whisper: "I'm fine."

I needed to know if he was scared. He let me know that he wasn't. I could let him go.

I had no unresolved issues with my father. I have no feelings of "if only," no doubts about his love for me or whether I had made him proud. He told me so, told my siblings, all the time, bucking the parenting tendencies of the men of his generation. He was affectionate and generous with praise and encouragement. He was never rude or impolite, mocking or mean, and so we had no need to seek resolution or reconciliation. He was, indeed, good to go.

We put our hands on him. His breaths came in short sips and then they stopped coming altogether. I had the curious feeling of being a spectator at the finish line of a long and spirited race. I thought of Dad like a runner, leaning in to break the tape, the bonds of earth, the veil between here and the "what's next." A deep peace and quiet joy settled over us. It is with me still.

God, show me how to lead a good life so that I may experience a good death. Help me to be good to go when it's my time.
—Amy Eddings

Digging Deeper: Revelation 21:4, 22:4–5

Friday, December 11

Mary kept all these things, and pondered them in her heart.
—Luke 2:19 (KJV)

An older friend seems to be losing ground mentally. "What day is it?" "What time was I expected?" "What's her name?" "Where did I vacation? Oh, really? I didn't know that,..." On its own, each question is innocuous. But their frequency concerns me and concerns her also.

If a downward slide continues... Well, I've traveled this road before, standing by a friend, John, who remained physically present but mindfully distant; eventually he was completely absent mentally. I treasure a photo of us in his waning days. We're assembling a Christmas table centerpiece. I'm handing him dried red florets that he's carefully placing among evergreen twigs overflowing from a small ceramic basket. His intense gaze betrays his deliberative effort. My assisting gesture marks a moment of peace on earth, prevailing goodwill.

John passed away several years ago. When I mentioned a few details of his funeral, a social media friend commented, "What you've done is important." Puzzled, I asked for clarification. Did she mean traveling to a funeral? Posting a picture?

No, she replied. "Sticking by him" in his decline. Calling. Connecting. Tethering.

I thanked her for her affirmation and remember it today, as I set out some holiday table decorations. They're different this year. The little basket vase didn't survive an ill-advised season outdoors. But the activity itself opens my heart to positive memories, which in turn stretch my vision for walking alongside another friend down a potentially perilous road. It feels important. Help me, God.

> *Spirit of God, remind me of positive memories that can*
> *draw me toward faithful friendship and service.*
> —Evelyn Bence

Digging Deeper: Psalm 77

Rejoice in the Lord always... Let your gentleness be evident to all,... Do not be anxious about anything, but in every situation, by prayer and petition, with thanksgiving, present your requests to God. And the peace of God, which transcends all understanding, will guard your hearts and your minds in Christ Jesus. Finally... whatever is true... noble... right... pure... lovely... admirable—if anything is excellent or praiseworthy—think about such things. —Philippians 4:4–8 (NIV)

We lost a role model of faith this year in our Bible study group. Even during the hard days of cancer treatment, Katie exuded a kind and gentle spirit, a treasured sweetness. And she was always glad for what God did to meet her daily needs.

Why was Katie so peaceful? How did she stay joyful despite difficult circumstances? The answer was within her faith, but where?

I read a New Testament passage at Katie's funeral. They were verses she chose—guideposts from her journey, anchors for her soul. As I read Philippians 4:4–8, I realized that through these verses Katie was sharing the secret to the peace and joy she discovered by:

Finding gladness in the Lord each day, even in difficult days;
Being gentle with others, including irritating ones;
Praying about everything, while thanking God for His goodness!

A friend said, "When we discussed things, Katie always had good thoughts." I last talked with Katie when my wife, Pat, and I visited her and her husband, Don, after she began hospice care. True to her character, Katie told us about good things—a butterfly park to visit, the birds and animals enjoying the natural beauty that surrounded their lakeside home. Throughout the years I knew her, Katie focused her mind on true, pure, and lovely things—thoughts worthy of praise—even in hospice.

Lord, thank You for the Katies in our lives who live the Scriptures and reflect Your indescribable peace. Let their memory inspire us to seek the same!
—John Dilworth

Digging Deeper: Isaiah 26:3; John 14:27, 16:33

Third Sunday of Advent, December 13

When they saw the star, they were filled with joy!
—Matthew 2:10 (NLT)

Every December, my sister, my mom, and I gather evergreen boughs and weave them into a beautiful grave blanket to decorate my sister Maria's final resting place. Only this year our schedules have been crazy—and a huge storm hit last week, thwarting our plans.

This morning when I looked out the window at the gray day I thought, *If we don't do something soon, it just isn't going to happen.* A grave blanket takes time and a lot of pine boughs.

As though he could read my mind, my husband, Tony, said, "What if we put a Christmas tree at the cemetery? We can decorate it and take it today. I can go pick one up right now. I saw them. They're almost giving them away."

A tree? I thought. Decorating a full-sized tree would be fun, but was it allowed? It had been ten years, ten Christmases, without my sister. A full-sized tree might be just the way to honor more than a decade in heaven.

That afternoon our family came over. We played Christmas music and wired the brightly colored decorations we usually use for the grave blankets to the tree's branches. Carefully we placed the tree in our truck. It looked like a greeting card—a tree decked to the hilt with decorations in the back of a pickup.

We drove to the cemetery laughing as we saw people's reactions. We reached the very top of the hill. Together, we carried the Christmas tree to Maria's headstone. Tony pulled the star from his coat pocket and placed it on top. For a moment, I thought I heard my sister in heaven laugh, but it was my mom. Clapping her hands, her face lit up as she said, "Isn't that just perfect!"

Heavenly Father, thank You for helping me fill this holiday season with love.
—Sabra Ciancanelli

Digging Deeper: Psalm 34:18; Matthew 5:4

Heal me, O Lord, and I shall be healed; save me, and I shall be saved, for You are my praise. —Jeremiah 17:14 (NKJV)

G racie, here again, Edward's golden retriever (with Edward's help): Recently I got sick. I felt horrible. I just wanted to sleep and be reassured by my people. I didn't even want to eat, which is unbelievable.

I want to share some things about being sick, in case you ever experience it.

REST: I am usually quite adept at napping, but when I was sick, I felt bad that I wasn't doing my usual duties—guarding the front door, scaring deer from my backyard, helping clean up food my people dropped on the floor. I had to give myself permission to rest.

TAKE YOUR MEDS: I am suspicious of pills. Unless they taste like liver, I try to conceal them in my cheek pouch. When I was sick, eventually I allowed pills to be administered in a bit of turkey. I believe they actually helped and I enjoyed the turkey. So take your pills.

LISTEN: I think of myself as a dog who listens, but sometimes I don't. I chew on items I shouldn't. I eat stuff before I know what it is and get sick as, well, a dog. I should listen!

STAY HOPEFUL: I am optimistic. We dogs always have hope of something good happening. Yet at times during my illness, I feared I would never feel better. I had to make a deliberate effort to believe I would get better.

PRAY: My people did this for me. I know it helped. Like the pills, prayer is a bit of a puzzle to me. Yet when my people held me at night and asked God to make me better, it somehow had an amazing effect.

These are some things that helped me get better. I hope they work the next time you get sick. Be careful what you chew on.

Father, thank You for looking out for all Your creatures,
especially the ones we love most.
—Edward Grinnan

Digging Deeper: Proverbs 17:22; Matthew 4:23

Tuesday, December 15

"So that your giving may be in secret...."—Matthew 6:4 (NIV)

St. Nicholas of Myra tops my hit parade of saints. This generous man from what is now Turkey anonymously left gifts where they were most needed, sparking legends of miracles and the Santa tradition still observed today. I'm a believer.

My first Christmas as a single mother, I despaired of scraping together decent gifts for my children, ages two, four, five, and eight. A couple of days before Christmas, while I was shampooing my boys in the tub, the doorbell rang. Eight-year-old Tess ran to answer it and then raced to me.

"Mom! It's Santa!"

"Okay. But who *is* it?"

"SANTA!"

I hastily rinsed and toweled the boys, urged them into their jammies, and rose to investigate. Sure enough, a bewhiskered man I did not know waited on my porch. He wore a furry burgundy suit with white trim and a leather strap of sleigh bells across his chest. Beside him rested a canvas sack. I hesitated, but when Santa greeted me by name, I invited him in.

By now, all four little ones in various states of undress circled our unlikely guest. Saint Nicholas greeted all four by name before presenting each with a lavishly wrapped gift. "Well, open them!" They shrieked to find toys that had topped their wish lists. I could never have afforded them. With a tinkle of sleigh bells, he left as mysteriously as he had come.

Eventually I sleuthed out our Saint Nicholas's identity. What really matters, though, is that all of us have the potential to be saints: just learn each other's needs and give in secret.

Gracious God, may we find imaginative ways to give to
one another—just as You do.
—Gail Schilling

Digging Deeper: Psalms 16:3, 30:4, 31:23, 145:10

We are His workmanship, created in Christ Jesus for good works,
which God prepared beforehand.... —Ephesians 2:10 (NKJV)

I was going through cards you'd sent us over the years, which makes
me thank you again for that coffeemaker you bought us last year,"
Mom said over the phone. "It works great."

I laughed. "It was hard to find one that only made coffee. Most of
them came with too many features. You didn't need an alarm clock,
an AM/FM radio, a milk steamer, or a data port. All you needed was
a coffeemaker."

"Do you remember what you wrote when you sent it?"

I didn't, so Mom read it to me. "This gift is not fancy or expensive.
No bells, no whistles, no distracting features. It does only one job, but
does it very well. It is efficient. There is no mistaking its purpose. May
we all live up to its example."

I chuckled. "I write goofy cards."

"It's not goofy at all," Mom insisted. "Whenever I read this, I think
about people unhappy with the way they look or with their natural talents. They exhaust themselves trying to be something they're not. We
would be so much more at peace if we simply accepted how God made
us and tried to be the best 'us' we could be."

I thought about the times I fought my Maker's plan before I accepted
me for me. The wasted trips to the salon for the "right" hair, which was
never right for me; wishing I were shorter; wishing I'd been born in
England so I could have a cool accent.

Actually, I'd like most of all to be more like my mom—staid, solid,
comfortable in being the wonderful person she is.

"You know, Mom, you're about the best coffeepot I've ever met."

"You, too, honey. You too." *Not yet, but maybe someday...*

> *Lord, please give me satisfaction in Your purpose for me so*
> *I will fit into the artwork of life You designed.*
> —Erika Bentsen

Digging Deeper: Deuteronomy 14:2; John 1:3; 1 Peter 2:9

Thursday, December 17

He covers the sky with clouds; he supplies the earth with rain....
—Psalm 147:8 (NIV)

Mollie, my rust-colored mutt, pranced while I searched for her leash. "Where are you going?" my husband, Kevin, asked, tying the belt tighter on his bathrobe. "It's still dark outside."

"To walk in the rain."

"Did the storm wake you last night?"

I nodded, grabbing a light jacket. "I heard the rain hitting the roof."

Kevin smiled and held the door as I stepped outside into the clouded morning. He didn't ask why I was leaving a dry house to walk in a downpour because he knew. It had been 116 days without rain.

The night before, with a storm in the forecast, I had done a computer search to discover the date of the last desert rain. I had to go back to August 23—back when we were in the full-blown heat of summer and the thermometer on the patio stretched red above the century mark. Back when iced tea brewed in my refrigerator and flip-flops adorned my feet.

But since then—not a drop of moisture. No rain in September. October. November. One hundred and sixteen days.

The annual desert cycle was familiar, but this year my memory had grown thirsty, wondering if the winter rains would pass us by.

Water dripped from the neighbor's palm tree as Mollie and I splashed through puddles. The asphalt was a mosaic of reflected colors from the holiday lights hanging on nearby trees. Gold. Red. Green. Mollie sniffed the shimmering jewels, puzzled by the unfamiliar scent of rain.

A blown-over Frosty the Snowman took a long winter's nap next to a cactus. We dodged fallen branches and storm debris. We walked until we were soaked to the skin.

Heavenly Father, in seasons of dryness, help me to remember that You are faithful. You never forget to send necessary rain.
—Lynne Hartke

Digging Deeper: Isaiah 55:10; Acts 14:17

"I will make you...a company of peoples...."—Genesis 48:4 (JPS)

My congregation sold our old synagogue building months before we had an occupancy permit for the new one. That left us in need of wider community support for places to meet until we could move into our new space.

Our Torah study group was able to use a community gathering room at one of the local grocery stores, but the room was too small for Friday night services, so several of the local churches stepped up and offered us use of their buildings. Their meeting rooms were steeped in the kind of atmosphere that ongoing prayer creates, and we were grateful to be worshiping in that mood of serenity and reverence.

In our service, as in almost all Jewish services that take place outside Jerusalem, there's a point when the congregation is asked to stand up and turn to face toward that city (in the Pacific Northwest, it's east) when we say specific prayers of praise—the Amidah (also known as the Tefilah, which is the Hebrew word for "prayer") and the Aleynu (which translates, approximately, to "we must praise God"). The week before Christmas, this custom gave our rabbi an opportunity to say something that had never been said at one of our services—and likely not at any other Friday night service in any synagogue anywhere.

The rabbi said, "Please rise for the Amidah, turn, and face the Christmas tree in the corner."

The congregation laughed, and I felt that this particular recitation of the prayer must have delighted God not only because of the praise, but because it acknowledged the generosity of our neighbors in sharing their sacred space with us. Friday night services are supposed to be joyous. This one also included some real fun.

Please be generous to those who show generosity, O God, and kind to those who show kindness. And thank You for a good laugh.
—Rhoda Blecker

Digging Deeper: Genesis 12:3; Deuteronomy 15:8; Isaiah 6:3

Saturday, December 19

Let us be grateful for receiving a kingdom that cannot be shaken, and thus let us offer to God acceptable worship, with reverence and awe.
—Hebrews 12:28 (RSV)

The train is stuck in a tunnel, not going anywhere. *I can't believe this is happening again,* I think. It happens all too often. The conductor makes an announcement that "due to signal problems" or "an earlier incident" (which could cover a multitude of sins) or "a sick passenger" (okay, I feel bad), we are "delayed." Then she says, "Thank you for your patience." And I'm thinking, *But I'm not feeling patient at all!*

It's like when someone says in a letter, "Thanking you in advance." How can you thank someone in advance of something? Then I think of a note a friend once wrote. She was invited to a Christmas party and would be immediately rushing out of town afterward. She wanted to be sure her friends knew how appreciative she was. So she wrote a thank-you note *before* the event, saying what a wonderful party it was. And her husband, thinking he was being helpful, *mailed* it before the event.

When she arrived, the hostess, having just received the note, thanked her for "thanking me in advance." My friend was hugely embarrassed and apologized, but what harm was done? The party was as good as she had anticipated—if not better. Gratitude is welcome at all times. In fact, it's worth seeking out. At all times.

> *Lord, help me see that there is something to be grateful*
> *for in every situation and circumstance.*
> —Rick Hamlin

Digging Deeper: Psalm 107:1; 1 Thessalonians 5:18

Monday, December 21

He knows the secrets of the heart. —Psalm 44:21 (NKJV)

It was a small nativity scene. A little box holding a few plastic pieces my mother had brought home from her travels. I had hesitated before I shoved it onto a shelf. *Shouldn't I just put it in the garage-sale box?* I had wondered. Since the baby Jesus had gone missing a few years earlier, the nativity set had no real point, but I hated to toss it out.

In reality, the nativity made me sad. I looked back on the years my husband, David, was the minister of a vital, enthusiastic church, and I missed the fanfare of Christmas. It was easy to find Jesus there, in the march of toys for underprivileged children, presenting gifts to our disabled members, welcoming the lonely and elderly to our home on Christmas morning.

Now our Christmas was family centered. We had a quiet Christmas Eve candlelight service in our living room, and then lots of activity opening presents. Christmas breakfast rang with the laughter of friends, and our Christmas dinner was festive with English poppers, overfilled stockings, and too much food. It was good, in a different way. But Jesus seemed missing in the action.

I soon forgot about the incomplete nativity and began my decorating marathon. There were two trees and an entire snow village to set up. Looking for some extra balls to hang from the chandelier, I came across a forgotten container marked "miscellaneous." I opened the box and suddenly, to my complete surprise, there he was! A tiny plastic baby with outstretched arms. He had come unexpectedly to remind me of something eternal.

Our church Christmases were over, and for a while, Jesus had seemed out of sight. But he was there, tucked away haphazardly, waiting—all new and waiting to be found, embraced, and experienced in new and joyful ways.

Father, you remind me that Your Son is always tucked somewhere
in my heart, patiently waiting. With joy, I find him again.
—Pam Kidd

Digging Deeper: Luke 1:14; 1 John 5:1

I will instruct you and teach you in the way you should go; I will counsel you with my loving eye on you. —Psalm 32:8 (NIV)

The most beautiful 1920s lithograph of the Sacred Heart of Jesus hangs in my office, right above my computer. I bought it more than twenty years ago at a huge flea market. I almost didn't see it leaning against a bunch of broken frames when I passed the open truck. I asked the vendor if I could take a closer look, and he dragged it out from the back saying, "Wow, I didn't even know I had this."

I brushed grime from the glass and uncovered Jesus's beautiful eyes. They drew me in and I felt I had to have it for my little apartment. The seller looked at me curiously, surprised that a young woman would want a religious antique. "What are you going to do with it?" he asked.

"Pray," I answered.

I paid ten dollars for it, priceless now, decades later, and hundreds, thousands of prayers later. My eyes have spent countless hours locked on His—sometimes, most times, simply "being." I pray with words. I pray without words. I pray with intention, with frustration, with confusion, with understanding, with peace. I pray with sorrow. I pray with gratitude. I pray.

> *Lord Jesus, as we get ready to celebrate Your arrival, thank You, thank You, thank You for always being there to guide and shape our lives.*
> —Sabra Ciancanelli

Digging Deeper: Psalm 119:10; Matthew 11:25

"Give, and it will be given to you . . . pressed down, shaken together, and running over . . ."—Luke 6:38 (NASB)

Three years of foot and back surgeries had altered my husband Terry's mobility. He used a crutch now. Walking was slow and uncomfortable.

One day in early December, we were reminiscing about past adventures. Suddenly, tears trickled down my cheeks. "We've lost so much," I sighed. Then I thought of our nearly two dozen grandchildren and the tears came faster. "There are so many things you might have done with them. The older kids will remember how you were, but the little ones only know you like this."

A few days later, three of the youngest grands, six and under, spent the day. We started stringing lights on the Christmas tree. The children helped Terry—sitting in a chair—untangle the lights, trotting back and forth plugging the strands into the socket to see if they worked.

Terry lowered himself carefully to the floor and rotated the tall tree while I wrapped lights around the top from the loft. He joked with the grands, "I'm the first present under the tree!"

The next week he set out amid swirling snow to mail packages. The same three children accompanied him to carry boxes into the drop center. When they returned he bragged about the big help they'd been.

That's when I got my Christmas gift. Far from losing "what might have been," our family was being added to in heaps. Terry required extra assistance for things he'd previously done himself, but our grandchildren were experiencing the opportunity to develop a giving spirit, learn the value of serving, gain that good feeling of meeting others' needs.

Witnessing a grandpa whose faith injected bravery and humor into a tough situation was definitely the best present under the tree.

Praise You, Servant God!
—Carol Knapp

Digging Deeper: Mark 9:35; Philippians 2:5–7;
Hebrews 6:10; 1 Peter 5:5

Wednesday, December 23

Let all that you do be done in love. —1 Corinthians 16:14 (ESV)

M y friend from law school, Diana, pulled into the snow-covered drive. I put on boots and went out to greet her.

"Merry Christmas," I said, embracing her.

"Thanks for inviting me to your family Christmas," she said. "I thought I'd have to spend Christmas alone after my flight home was canceled."

"I wouldn't let that happen," I said, leading her down the walkway to the house. "Here's a heads-up before we get inside. My parents are getting the house ready to sell, so there are a lot of projects going on."

"I won't mind," she said.

Yet, despite her reassurance, I was self-conscious. The entryway's trim was half removed and power tools were pushed against the walls. My uneasiness didn't settle as I introduced Diana to my family. Conversation was smooth, but I wondered if Diana was comparing my family's home to hers. I imagined that her family lived in a trendy home full of sleek appliances—a far cry from this messy Victorian.

On the way to the dinner table, Diana pulled me aside.

"It's unlike anything I've ever seen," she said.

I surveyed paint buckets and drop cloths, trying to determine what she was talking about.

"Your family loves each other so much," she said. "I can see it in the way they look and talk to each other. And I feel so loved being here."

She was right. Regardless of the mess, we loved each other. And that was more important than the painting and patching that still needed to be done.

"So does that mean you're coming back to help us retile the kitchen next week?" I asked.

She laughed, and we joined the rest of my family in the dining room.

Lord, help me to focus on the things that matter and the people I love.
—Logan Eliasen

Digging Deeper: John 13:34–35; 1 John 4:7

May the God of hope fill you with all joy and peace as you trust in him,
so that you may overflow with hope by the power of the Holy Spirit.
—Romans 15:13 (NIV)

My oldest Christmas tree ornament is from when I was four years old. I can still remember seeing him in the department store—a cute little mouse with big eyes and a felted Santa suit. I had to have him.

My mom carefully took him down from the display. "You really want him?" she asked.

I nodded. "I guess we can get him," she said.

For the rest of the afternoon, my mom held my hand and I held the paper bag with the ornament. On the way home, I took off my mittens. The bag seemed light. Opening it up, my heart sank. The mouse was gone.

The next day Mom and I went back to town and searched the slushy pavement. We returned to the store hoping to buy another one, but the owner had no memory of a mouse dressed like Santa. Christmas Eve I prayed for my Santa-mouse ornament to be under the tree or in my stocking, but it wasn't.

A whole year passed and Christmas music filled the streets. As Mom and I walked on the sidewalk, something caught my eye on the curb by the drainage grill. I looked closer, bending down.

The little mouse was a wreck. His Santa suit had worn off completely. His head was flat. Gritty filth covered his face. I held him in my hands, hardly believing my eyes.

"How on earth?" Mom said, "After all this time."

Mom soaked him in a bowl of detergent and dried him by the coal stove. She fashioned a new coat and hat of red felt and all these years later he is still with me, making a special appearance each year. Time sweetens God's gifts.

Heavenly Father, on this beautiful Christmas Eve night, thank You
for life's little miracles that remind us of the power of Your love.
—Sabra Ciancanelli

Digging Deeper: Deuteronomy 10:21; Jeremiah 32:27

Thanks be to God for his indescribable gift! —2 Corinthians 9:15 (NIV)

The sun isn't up, but I am. I slip out of bed and sneak down the stairs. The tags on our dog Soda's collar jingle, ringing in the special day. I pour myself a cup of coffee in my favorite mug and open the curtain. The dim light of the streetlamp shows a new blanket of snow.

I hit the switch for the Christmas tree lights. Brightly wrapped presents wait for the boys to wake up. For now, I sit quietly and take in the moment.

My mind travels to my nephew, in heaven for two years now. How I miss him. Then I go to our first year in this house where Santa brought for our son Solomon a motorized train that circled the entire perimeter of the house. I can still see the expression on his face of sheer magic and delight.

The bittersweet feeling of missing family in heaven layers between comfort and love, a symphony of reassurance—of family and memories, of little boys becoming men, and all of us growing older. In the silence of Christmas morning, circles and swirls of love embrace me.

Today is a day to feel with our whole hearts. To give generously and receive graciously. To take in every amazing moment. I could go on and on, but the dog sits up. I hear footsteps on the stairs. First the light, fast pace of our younger son Henry, followed by the solid footing of my husband, Tony, and last, the slow tread of half-asleep Solomon.

And so our day of magnified love begins.

Heavenly Father, thank You. Thank You. Thank You! You have
my whole heart, for my whole life and beyond!
—Sabra Ciancanelli

Digging Deeper: Isaiah 9:6–7; Luke 2:1–20

"He will yet fill your mouth with laughter and your lips with shouts of joy."
—Job 8:21 (TLB)

A study said ninety percent of people who were asked to describe their past week in one word replied either "stressful" or "hectic." I was astounded. Imagine defining your life that way.

I did some research and learned that laughter and a good sense of humor can reduce mental and physical stress considerably. So I resolved to work at putting more fun in my life and in the lives of those around me.

Since I live in Florida, I get a fair number of houseguests, especially during the winter months. Every child, friend, or relative who comes to sleep in my condo will, more than likely, find a rubber chicken tucked in between the pillows of my guest bed. Sometimes I put plastic roaches, frogs, or spiders in unexpected places in the bathroom or kitchen. I have one of those old mink shoulder wraps from the fifties, and often I put that furry piece at the bottom of the bed between the sheets for the excitement and laughter of my guests.

One time I had the man at the meat counter wrap my rubber chicken in Styrofoam and cellophane as if it were a real piece of meat. He even put a price tag on it. I put it in the meat drawer of my refrigerator just before my friends Shirley and Wally came for a visit. They were houseguests for a couple of weeks, so Shirley did her share of the cooking. When she opened the meat drawer and took out the rubber chicken, she ended up rolling around on the floor laughing hysterically. We laughed about that for days, and I'm pretty sure there was no illness caused by stress in my home for months.

Being funny takes planning and a few trips to the dollar store for plastic bugs. Definitely worth it.

Jesus, help me to help others be healthier mentally and physically by putting more laughter into their lives.
—Patricia Lorenz

Digging Deeper: Psalm 126:2–3; Luke 6:21

Sunday, December 27

Don't be fools; be wise: make the most of every opportunity you have for doing good. —Ephesians 5:16 (TLB)

After a visit to a retina specialist, I had to put in eye drops three times a day.

It was easy to remember to do it every morning and night, but that middle-of-the-day dose had me remembering the drops hours late or sometimes not at all. It dawned on me that I could set my new cell phone alarm clock to ring every day at 3:00 PM so I would remember to put in the eye drops. It worked so well that I began to think about other ways I could use the alarm as a reminder.

I can set the alarm to remind me to say my prayers, I thought. The older I get, it seems that more people are on my prayer list. At my age, all my friends, relatives, neighbors, and fellow church members seem to always be asking for prayers. The week I set my phone alarm clock to ring to remind me to put in my eye drops, I was praying for many others: my daughter Julia who was about to undergo open heart surgery, my dad in hospice care, my stepmother who at age ninety-three was dealing with health issues of her own and her sister who was near death, and my son Andrew who was on a trip to New York for his job and ended up sick, two thousand miles from home. Even I needed prayers because that month a horrid cold had turned into pneumonia.

So I did it. I set my phone to ring every day at 3:00 PM. Eye drops in first, then I began praying. Long after the swelling in my retina went down, my three o'clock prayers continued. And as always, my list of people to pray for continues to grow.

Father, thank You for listening to my prayers, for granting favors, and for working things out in Your own way and time.
—Patricia Lorenz

Digging Deeper: 2 Kings 20:8–11; Psalm 89:52

If anyone says, "I love God," and hates his brother, he is a liar....
—1 John 4:20 (ESV)

My daughters—who chose grad schools near each other and have always been close—had a falling out this summer. The ensuing months of their ill will were agonizing. No cheery shared texts planning our usual fall-break visit. No Ethiopian dinner with them and the boyfriends while we were there. No family meals at all. They came home separately for the holidays, Charlotte for Thanksgiving, Lulu for Christmas. Neither holiday felt normal or convivial.

The girls were toddlers when I regained my belief in the divine Father I'd worshipped as a child, and I've always associated their sisterly relationship with my realization back then that God feels loved when we love our human siblings. Whenever Charlotte and Lulu were kind to each other, I thought, *This is how God must feel!* With them incommunicado, I so shared God's parental pain! I became obsessed with Jacob and Esau, their rivalries and heartening reconciliation—but after twenty years! I was in despair.

I longed to request prayer amid the medical problems and traveling mercies at church. But no one ever mentioned such needs—or indeed any of the relationship-related struggles that occupy my prayers—so I couldn't do it. Too embarrassing.

I did tell some friends, who consoled me by confessing similar feuds of their own. Siblings cutting off from one another is fairly common, I learned, and talking about my pain allowed me to intervene meaningfully in rifts among my own siblings. Still, I winced through the months, hoping for a miracle.

I've never felt such an overflow of gratitude as when Charlotte and Lulu reconciled. Oh how delightful is the love between siblings. No wonder Jesus mentions it so often!

Father, help me love Your children, my many siblings!
—Patty Kirk

Digging Deeper: Matthew 5:21–24; 1 John 4:7

Tuesday, December 29

I can do all things through Christ who strengthens me.
—Philippians 4:13 (NKJV)

"Missy, get in the house," hollers my husband, Michael, from the living room. Like a slow motion video, our schweenie (shih tzu/dachshund mix) moves toward the backyard doggy door. Just before her head hits the flap, Missy stops. Repeating the motion again and again, her front legs start to jump and then halt when she's within an inch of the opening. From the back porch, she whines and yips.

"Missy, get inside!" Michael repeats, his pitch louder.

The twenty-five-pound dog squeals as she musters all her might and bolts inside as if she's entered another dimension at warp speed. Michael shakes his head. We don't know why she has trouble. We taught our Pug to leap through the opening after several attempts. She exits and enters at will. The cat figured it out. But with Missy, it's drama every time.

We try teaching her. We lift the flap and coax her through. We reward her with praise and doggy treats. Nothing, short of yelling, works.

I'm not sure what traumatized her. Maybe she bumped her head once on the door. Maybe she was startled by the cat. Maybe her short legs force her weenie-dog belly to sometimes touch the frame.

Why can't she simply leap through that door?

The same reason I can't.

I've had a project I've wanted to start for years but something irrational is holding me back. Maybe it's fear, but that seems as ridiculous as a dog that wants inside and won't come through a doggy door. Maybe, like Missy, I need to take a leap of faith.

Lord, only You can teach an old dog new tricks. Motivate Missy, and me, to conquer the things that seem impossible.
—Stephanie Thompson

Digging Deeper: Proverbs 18:10; Romans 8:15

*Jesus called the Twelve and said, "Anyone who wants to be first must be the very last, and the servant of all." —*Mark 9:35 (NIV)

Have you ever stopped to think about how you receive love? Years ago, I read a book called *The Five Love Languages*. It broke down the five ways we can receive love, which are, according to the author: receiving gifts, words of affirmation, acts of service, quality time, and physical touch.

I realized, if I had a preferred way of receiving love (words of affirmation!), then others did too. My older son loves physical touch, so I scratch his back. My daughter loves gifts, but really craves quality time.

This year, my mom gave me the gift of service. My youngest, Beau, refused to take a bottle, which was quite the problem when I went back to work. Mom drove the "milk runs," shuttling him to my office twice a day, every day, for six weeks until he gave in and took the bottle.

The extra time I had with Beau was wonderful, and the relief that I didn't need to worry about his crying at day care all day was real. But the reminder of how much we are loved by our earthly parents, that my mom would schedule her life around *my* child's needs, was breathtakingly beautiful. "He's only little once and I'm happy to be useful," she would say as she lugged him into my office each morning and afternoon, kissing him behind his ear to make him laugh.

But I saw more. Mom beamed God's love, soaking Beau and me with it daily. As a handyman we share once said, "I love Jesus, but your mom, wow. She can out-Jesus me any day!"

Before, I had been quick to think that I knew how others received love. Now I know to pay closer attention, and to ask how they give and receive love, so that I may better show my love to them.

Lord, help me to model Your love for my children.
—Ashley Kappel

Digging Deeper: Galatians 5:13–14; Philippians 2:1–11;
1 Peter 4:10–11

Fear not, for I am with you; be not dismayed, for I am your God; I will strengthen you, I will help you, I will uphold you with my righteous right hand. —Isaiah 41:10 (ESV)

My mom offered to take my children on an outing so I could have some quiet time to work. The plan was to head to the library to get new books, and then have lunch, ice cream, and some time at the park. She borrowed my car so she would have room for all of them.

What started as a sweet day with Grandma quickly turned sour. Just as my mom spotted an open space in the parking garage, a car whipped around the corner and cut her off, causing her to crash my car into the support pole.

It was a minor collision—just some large scratches on the passenger side—but my mom was devastated. She pulled over to the side and started crying.

My mom said that as she sat there feeling like the day was ruined, a tiny voice in the back seat began to sing the words to a familiar worship song based on Scripture. "Bless the Lord, O my soul..." she heard.

Two other voices joined the first voice and within minutes of the accident, the car was full of worship.

Tears were dried, laughter commenced. They parked that scratched-up car and headed into the library. Then to lunch and ice cream and finally a long sunny afternoon at the park.

When they got home, all were in high spirits.

"How was it?" I asked.

"We had a great day," my mom answered. "I do need to talk to you about a small issue with the car, but first, let me tell you about the blessed time we shared."

Lord, whenever my heart begins to despair, draw me close to You and buoy me with Your strength. Amen.
—Erin MacPherson

Digging Deeper: John 14:27; 2 Corinthians 1:3–4

HE PERFORMS WONDERS

1 _____

2 _____

3 _____

4 _____

5 _____

6 _____

7 _____

8 _____

9 _____

10 _____

11 _____

12 _____

13 _____

14 _____

15 _____

December

16 _____

17 _____

18 _____

19 _____

20 _____

21 _____

22 _____

23 _____

24 _____

25 _____

26 _____

27 _____

28 _____

29 _____

30 _____

31 _____

"In a rather blessed way, the more our life together presents challenges, the more I am aware of God's power to perform wonders," says **Marci Alborghetti**, adding, "Even as we learn to live with loss and illness as we, and other family members age, the Lord shows us His wonder in various ways: in watching our godsons grow up into great kids; in the joy of laughing with friends new and old; and in the simple pleasure of savoring a bowl of popcorn while watching a favorite movie or television show. We are so grateful for all that God does for us, in the moment, every moment."

"This was a year of change," writes **Julia Attaway** of New York City. Aside from moving to a new apartment in a new neighborhood, Julia began writing about mental health issues for the nonprofit organization Child Mind. "Helping other parents who grapple with their children's struggles is a tremendously gratifying—and positive—use of the difficulties I've encountered," Julia says. Some of her own children continue to stagger emotionally, yet honing her ability to see light in the darkness has kept her faith alive. "Much as I wish it were otherwise, loving the Lord doesn't mean I always get the outcome I desire," Julia admits. "We are called to praise Him in all circumstances, even those that cause us pain."

Evelyn Bence of Arlington, Virginia, notes, "I write this in the season of redbud, lilac, and dogwood blossoms. Every spring the world is full of such promise. As an exercise in gratitude, I recently filled a poster board with a flowchart diagram of my editorial career. What a study in networking over several decades, starting with my first job in publishing—one contact leading to another and another—including Van Varner, legendary Guideposts editor (RIP), and this *Daily Guideposts* opportunity. My church congregation, extended family, and array of culturally diverse neighbors broaden my world. God is good."

Topping **Erika Bentsen's** list of God's truly unfathomable wonders this year is the out-of-the-blue opportunity to illustrate a series of children's books for an author in New Zealand. "Ever since I was little I made cards for my family." As God would have it, the author's granddaughter was friends with Erika's niece, Haley. "I made a card for Haley's twelfth birthday, and word about my silly drawings made it back to New Zealand. The author came to the states and hired me on the spot!" It was a lot more work than she anticipated. "The learning curve was about ninety degrees straight up since this was the first children's book for both of us. It's taken a lot of prayer and late nights, but I persevered. I never would have had the chance without God's amazing help."

"This has been a 'the Lord giveth and the Lord taketh away' year," **Rhoda Blecker** says. "In March I was asked to become part of a family in my synagogue. They needed a Jewish grandmother for their five kids, and for whatever reason, they chose me. So that was the first 'giveth' part. The 'taketh' part was hard. On July 25, my wonderful greyhound, Anjin, reached the end of her struggle, and we gave her the kind of gentle death that we can only hope we get ourselves. I didn't have a lot of time to grieve, however, because on July 26, I re-homed a seven-year-old Silken Windhound who'd had a traumatic life and needed a safe forever home. Halle is now a firm part of the household, much to the dismay of the cat, who thought—for twenty-four hours—that the place was all hers at last."

Sabra Ciancanelli of Tivoli, New York, says: "I have a clear memory of being in the second grade and thinking *One day it will be 2020!* We probably had just learned about perfect eyesight or something, but the number, the year itself, seemed magical and impossible. I imagined spaceships and teleporters being part of everyday life. Now that it's here, my focus is not on grand inventions, but rather simple blessings—the joy of apple blossoms in spring, the warmth of a wood fire, the beauty of a single bird soaring across a blue sky, the gratitude I feel when I hear my sons' laughter, and, of course, the infinite love I feel when I pray. Ah, the wonders of 2020!"

"I've learned how amazing it can be to trust Papa God with all your heart," writes **Desiree Cole** of Olathe, Kansas. After many successful years as an editor in New York City, Desiree was bewildered when God invited her to enter another story somewhere else—her hometown. "I couldn't see why He wanted my husband and me to drop what we'd built in New York, but we leaned into His voice that was leading us back home to Kansas." Since then, Zach and Desiree were able to buy their first house together—a big dream—and things kept getting better. Just days after moving in, they welcomed their first child—an even bigger dream come true. "I don't always know what He has in mind, but I've always believed He's good."

"Pittsburgh's topography makes it easy for newbies to get lost," says **Mark Collins** of his hometown. "A few weeks ago, a couple asked me how to get from Calvary Church to Duquesne University. I knew the straightest route was under construction, so the best route wasn't the one on the map. 'Listen, take Shady Avenue, follow signs for I-376 toward town, take the Boulevard of the Allies, go past Pride Street, then look for Mercy.' Recent events with my daughters—Faith's upcoming wedding, Hope's new job, Grace's graduation from college, plus my own circuitous journey through the metaphorical wilderness—have given new meaning to those directions: the straightest route isn't the best route. The best route starts at Calvary, usually includes allies, never includes pride, and is always, always, always in search of mercy."

Pablo Diaz writes: "Over the course of this year, I'll celebrate several milestones. In March, I turn sixty years old and while some people have told me that with age comes wisdom, others warn that it just comes with lots of aches. I'm not quite there yet, but I already feel some aches and pains, especially after a round of tennis, but I anticipate gaining wisdom. While I don't know what the future holds, I do know that God holds my future. I'm looking forward to celebrating my sixtieth birthday with friends, but especially with my wife, Elba, and our kids.

Fellowship Corner

"This year also marks my forty-fifth anniversary of preaching and thirty years since I was ordained. I'm blessed to have been called to ministry and thank God each and every day for aligning my steps to serve Him and others. Several years ago, I came across a quote that made a big impact on me and has remained in my mind, 'Most people overestimate what they can do in a day and underestimate what they can do in a lifetime.' I've come a long way, but I can't wait to see how the next chapter of my life unfolds. God's blessings are limitless."

Starting with good news, **John Dilworth** writes, "Our son relocated to the Washington, DC, area. We're happy he's only a half-day drive away, enabling us to be together more often. This past year we enjoyed a wonderful trip to New Zealand and Australia filled with splendid excursions. Sad news came when our sweet dog, Tish, passed away and crossed the rainbow bridge. It was a tough loss for Pat and me. The void Tish left was filled with lots of *no mores*: no more hauling bags of dog food, no more cold rainy walks, and no more getting up to let the dog in and out. We quickly missed the *no mores*—all the joy and activity a dog brings. Soon Skipper, a young rescue dog—part beagle, part Labrador with a bit of "rascal" thrown in—made his way into our lives. He's smart, has a gentle nature, delights in exploring, and has selective hearing! Now Skipper, Pat, and I enjoy fun, adventurous days together; and at day's end, the dog is more tired than we are—and that's really good news!"

Amy Eddings is a writer, broadcast journalist, and podcaster. She is the host of NPR's "Morning Edition" on 90.3 WCPN-Cleveland. For three years, she and her husband, Mark, ran a bed-and-breakfast, Easter House, in Ada, Ohio. Both had previously lived in New York City where they worked in radio. "When I was writing these devotions, I was going through a lot of change, loss, and hardship," writes Amy. "My introduction to Guideposts readers was a story in 2015 about leaving my radio job in New York City and moving to rural Ohio to be closer to family and to open a B&B. That entrepreneurial adventure has run its course, despite many delightful guests. I returned to public radio, to WCPN in Cleveland, my hometown. I relish being on the air again and being with public radio news geeks. Being in Cleveland also put me within twenty minutes of my parents' home. That meant more time hanging out with them at what turned out to be a critical time. My dad, Lloyd Eddings, died about a year later. I was blessed to be there, with all of my family, when he died. But being in Cleveland has meant living apart from Mark during the work week and making the long drive to and from Ada on weekends. The grind convinced us to sell our beloved Easter House and relocate to Cleveland. We recently signed a lease on an exciting new apartment in downtown Cleveland."

 "This past year has been the end of an era for me," says Logan Eliasen. "I graduated from law school, so my days as a student are over. And while that's a relief in one sense, it's unnerving in another. It means leaving a small world that's comfortable and launching into the unknown. But God has shown me His faithfulness again and again during my time as a student. So I know that the hands opening new doors for me are hands I trust beyond compare."

 "I'm hearing God's voice in personal ways again," says **Shawnelle Eliasen** of Port Byron, Illinois. "And it brings me the sweetest joy. We've been working through some hard circumstances, and He's been kind and compassionate." A phone call from a long-distance friend was significant to Shawnelle this year. "She didn't know my struggle, but she shared Scripture and reminded me that the battle is the Lord's. What a beautiful, intimate thing for God to do! My friend's phone call took me from a place of powerlessness to a place of peace." Shawnelle and her family are currently preparing to move from a home where they've lived a long time. "It's another opportunity to lean into the Lord," she says. "Change can be tough, but I want to trust Him. I think that sometimes God's greatest works of wonder take place inside the human heart."

Julie Garmon writes: "I attend a women's prayer group. At the Christmas meeting in 2016, our leader asked us to voice a prayer request we'd like God to answer in 2017. I knew what I wanted to say, but I hated to bother my friends with the same request, year after year. My daughter, Katie, had been struggling with infertility for ten years. With only a speck of faith, I said, 'My prayer for 2017 is that Katie will get pregnant.' The following spring, our leader prayed for Katie according to Ezekiel 37: 'Thus says the Lord God to these (dry) bones, 'Behold, I will cause breath to enter you that you may come to life.' On November 3, 2017, Katie called me, laughing and crying. 'Mom, [the test] is positive. I'm pregnant!' I dropped to my knees and cried with her. Our grandson Caleb was born on July 11, 2018—six pounds, three ounces. His name means faithful and brave. *Lord, I'll never stop thanking You. You speak life into hopeless situations.*"

Bill Giovannetti serves as the senior pastor of Neighborhood Church in scenic northern California. His wife, Margi, an attorney, serves alongside him in ministry. They have two kids, one in college and one about to head to college, and two adorable little dogs. Bill continues bass fishing and playing tennis, along with a busy schedule of writing and speaking. You can visit Bill at www.maxgrace.com.

"I'll let you in on a little secret," says **Edward Grinnan** of New York, New York. "Because of book publishing deadlines, we write these bios way in advance of publication. Who knows where my life will be in 2020?" But what an opportunity to visualize his hopes and dreams for the future! He continues, "I pray that by the time you read this everyone in my family has stayed strong and healthy, especially my wife, Julee, whose lupus has been making an unwelcome comeback, and my brother, Joe, who recently had a kidney transplant. I hope Grace, our golden retriever, still has a young, playful spirit, though she will be turning five in 2020. I hope to be finishing another book for Guideposts, this one on Alzheimer's disease and the effect it's had on generations of my family. Most of all, I trust that each day between now and then brings me closer to God."

Edward is Editor-in-Chief of Guideposts and Vice President of Guideposts Publications. He has published two books, available from Guideposts: *Always by My Side: Life Lessons from Millie and All the Dogs I've Loved*; and *The Promise of Hope: How True Stories of Hope and Inspiration Saved My Life and How They Can Change Yours.*

Rick Hamlin and his wife, Carol, celebrated the marriage of their son William to Karen a year ago. Two weeks after the wedding the young couple bought a dog. Rick writes, "We were hoping for grandbabies. We got a grandpuppy instead." Their younger son, Tim, is going to seminary with hopes of entering the ministry. They continue to sing in their church choir, Carol in the soprano section, Rick with the tenors. Rick will be leading a group of Guideposts readers to see the Passion Play at Oberammergau, Germany, later this year. "Can't wait," he says. His newest book *Prayer Works* can be found at shopGuideposts.com. "When I think about this world of wonders, I treasure the words of the legendary John Wooden: 'Make each day your masterpiece.' Each day has that possibility."

Lynne Hartke says she often hears the Sonoran Desert, where she lives, described as "a desolate place, even godforsaken." At one time, Lynne would have agreed with that statement. But after three decades of exploring desert trails with her husband, Kevin, and rust-colored mutt, named Mollie, Lynne has encountered the beauty found in barren places, a beauty enjoyed by the couple's four grown children and four grandchildren. An author and breast cancer survivor, Lynne receives inspiration from other survivors at the cancer organizations where she volunteers. Connect with her on Facebook and Instagram, and at www.lynnehartke.com.

"I have a heart that can discern hurting people," says **Carla Hendricks** of Franklin, Tennessee. "When I enter a room, it's not long before I laser-focus on the person in an emotionally painful season of life. My own painful seasons— my parents' deaths, two miscarriages, and challenging family dynamics—help me serve others with compassion.

Serving begins at home with my husband, Anthony, and our four children, two of whom were adopted, and extends to the support ministry for adoptive and foster families that I lead at church. Through it all, I've witnessed over and over again that God is truly 'close to the brokenhearted.'"

Kim Taylor Henry writes: "Amazingly, our three children and five grandchildren, who had been living on both coasts and in between, all ended up in the Portland, Oregon, area. Now my husband and I can see them all together in one place instead of traveling the country to visit them. We've taken advantage of this gift from God, splitting our time between Colorado and Oregon. We've also continued traveling internationally, spending almost two months experiencing other countries. One favorite memory is seeing the Matterhorn up close, another reminder that I will never stop being awed by God's creation. I'd love to hear from you. E-mail me at kim@kimtaylorhenry.com or visit my Web site at kimtaylorhenry.com!"

Erin Janoso writes, "For years, my husband, Jim, daughter, Aurora, and I spent our summers in Fairbanks, Alaska, for our microscope company. But in 2018, we discovered it was better for business if we spent winters there instead. We have learned to love our annual snow-filled adventure. The Fairbanks community has provided us with countless opportunities to enjoy the cold winter days. Jim has gotten involved with search and rescue as well as the group that keeps the steam engine running at a local park. I love participating in the Fairbanks Community Band, and Aurora is exceling in homeschool kindergarten. What a season of blessings!"

In the age-old quest of finding work-life balance as a working mom, **Ashley Kappel** tells us that she fails daily! She's grateful that His mercies are new every morning and that God has filled her life with hilarious tiny people of her own creation to make the quest truly a joyful journey. Ashley lives in Alabama with her husband, Brian, her three children (Olivia, James, and Beau), and her golden retriever, Colby.

"Never a dull moment!" reports **Brock Kidd** from Nashville, Tennessee. "Even though my oldest son, Harrison, has successfully launched into college at George Washington University, located in our nation's capital, his two sisters, Mary Katherine and Ella Grace, and baby brother David keep Corinne and me hopping!" In addition to his bustling family, Brock celebrates passing the quarter-century mark in his career in wealth management. "While Corinne and I continue enjoying family time, it makes our occasional date night that much sweeter!"

Pam Kidd writes: "'Why, who makes much of a miracle?' Walt Whitman asks in 'Leaves of Grass.' And, when he goes on to say, 'I know of nothing else but miracles,' I'm on his page. Miracles abound! abound! Think of it! I type on a computer, unimagined fifty years ago, with hands inexplicable in their abilities. In a world full of people, somehow we have found the right friends and the ideal people to love. Walk outside and study a tree…always a miracle in progress, along with birdsong and the smell of flowers. Children, grandchildren, coming and going, opening up new worlds to us. Opportunities cropping up that invite us to say 'yes' to God's work on earth.

"Saying that 'yes' to Zimbabwe is a constant joy to our family. My husband, David, and I thrive in our love for each other, for our family, and in our attempts to make the world better for others. Miracles—I, personally know of nothing else!"

Patty Kirk spent her year, as always, teaching, writing, gardening, running, and birding. While her daughters were home visiting, they wanted to watch the OKC Thunder, Oklahoma's NBA basketball team. Living in the country without a satellite dish, they were forced to watch blurry, illegally streamed videos on the computer. Figuring out who was who was like identifying birds in a rainstorm, more by their behavior than what they looked like. Soon Patty and husband, Kris, were able to differentiate Russell Westbrook from PG, Adams, Schröder, and the rest. Now they're hooked and hold private watch parties for every game, legally, using the fast Internet at Kris's office in town. Go Thunder!

One wonder God has performed in my life is becoming a *Daily Guideposts* contributor, **Carol Knapp** writes. "Over thirty years ago I heard inside myself, 'You can do this!' as I was considering entering the Guideposts Writer's Work-shop contest. Since then God has encouraged me and others as I journeyed from young mother to grandmother. Writing truthfully has been a tremendously freeing, flinging act of faith. My life has taken joyous leaps and bounds! My husband, Terry, has serious health challenges…we have grandchildren who are now out on their own…we lost our last parent recently…I still dream of writing my book. This magnificent Savior we serve continues with us in every heart's desire—and every deep sorrow. He is the Wonder of wonders! Terry and I couldn't live life apart from Him."

Carol Kuykendall writes: "Our family marked a once-in-a-lifetime event: my husband, Lynn, and I celebrated our fiftieth wedding anniversary. Ten grandchildren, their parents, and Lynn and I spent a week in a house on the beach in Mexico! I love the three phases of a celebration: looking forward to it, living it, and remembering it. After eight years leading a Stories ministry in our church, I stepped aside to let a new ministry grow in its place. I'm still a MOPs (Mothers of Preschoolers) mentor with renewed empathy for the responsibility of caring for young children. Lynn and I recently became parents of a golden retriever puppy who wakes up in the middle of the night, chews shoes, and jumps on the couch. I dare not let him out of my sight but he makes our house happy."

When she isn't hanging out with her three grandkids, **Vicki Kuyper** spends her time writing, and has authored more than fifty books over the past thirty years. Although Vicki calls Colorado Springs, Colorado, home, she's just as likely to be found in some remote corner of the world, hiking, taking photos, and exploring God's great gallery of creation. In between speaking, writing, travel, and playing peek-a-boo, she'd love to connect with you at vickikuyper.net or on Facebook at vickikuyper@1wittybiddy.

 **Patricia Lorenz** of Largo, Florida, writes: "Jack and I met one sunny day in the deep end of our beautiful community pool. We were a couple for eight years and married in 2012. During those years we swam in the outdoor heated pool and did water aerobics nearly every day, twelve months a year. In the spring, summer, and fall we also swam in the Gulf of Mexico, just minutes from our home. Jack loved cruises when we would sit for hours watching the ocean waves from the deck of a ship or swim in the small pool on the open deck. Water, one of the basic and most blessed ingredients of life, became the thing that bonded us. Jack died on March 10, 2019, after a year-long battle with stage-four melanoma. The day after my 'Hunka Hunka Burnin' Love' died, I went to the pool in the early morning so I could swim by myself, pray, and think about my beloved husband. It's a habit I've continued nearly every day since and hope to continue for the rest of my life."

 "The things that God has been teaching me this year! Even in times of suffering, when God seems so far away, I learned to persevere in my walk with Him. He's a good, merciful, divinely wise, and loving God. I can safely leave my life in His hands." **Debbie Macomber**, a New York Times #1 best-selling author, hopes to share this message with you through her devotions. With over thirty-five years as a published author, Debbie has written a multitude of novels, three cookbooks, several inspirational nonfiction titles, as well as two acclaimed children's books. Debbie serves on the Guideposts National Advisory Cabinet, is the international spokesperson for World Vision's Knit for Kids, and is a Youth for Christ National Ambassador. When not writing, Debbie loves to spend time with her husband, Wayne, her children's families, and her writing companion, Bogie. A good cup of coffee and a current knitting project are never far from her side.

Fellowship Corner

In what feels both wonderful and a bit frightening, **Erin MacPherson** went from chasing around a gaggle of toddlers to ferrying around teenagers. As she traded in car seats for soccer cleats, one thing has remained: Even in the midst of the most hectic, busy, and frustrating days, His miraculous acts of love are what hold Erin's family together. Erin lives in Austin, Texas, with her husband, Cameron; their three kids, Joey, Kate, and Will; and the Golden Retriever, Zeke. Visit her at www.christianmamasguide.com to share your own stories of wonder, awe, and God's unfailing love.

Tia McCollors is a born and bred North Carolinian who now raises her family in Atlanta, Georgia, along with her husband, Wayne. She grew up seeing *Daily Guideposts* books on her grandmother's nightstand and credits most of her deeply rooted faith to her upbringing. In addition to balancing her family's needs and their growing businesses, Tia has been writing Christian fiction since her first bestselling novel in 2005. Recently she's expanded to writing devotions. When Tia doesn't have a pen in hand, she enjoys speaking into the hearts of women by bringing uplifting messages of faith. You can find her on Facebook or follow her on Instagram @ TMcCollors.

God indeed performed a wonder in **Roberta Messner's** life this past year. For a long time, *Daily Guideposts* readers have prayed for her to be free of the pain of a lifelong neurological condition, neurofibromatosis. Roberta is thrilled to report that a new medication, which is also used for severe diabetic peripheral neuropathy, has completely relieved her pain. It specifically targets the nerve cells where her tumors reside.

"I am so incredibly thankful to my heavenly Father and to the many readers and fellow writers who have never given up on me," Roberta says. "Though I am in my early senior years, I feel as if I am finally really living for the very first time. Thank you, thank you, thank you to everyone. Your love and caring have sustained me. It is truly a miracle. If we don't meet up here on earth, I will comb heaven searching for each one of you."

Dwelling in God's ever-present love was **Rebecca Ondov's** focus this year. Her favorite time with God is the stillness of the morning from the back of her horse, while riding through the mountains with her dog, Sunrise, trotting beside them or while bobbing on the lake in her kayak. She says, "After decades of being a Christian, I'm still overwhelmed when I ponder the miracle that the God Who created the universe, Who hung each star in place, is madly in love with each one of us—especially when I review who I am when I'm not 'in Christ.' That is truly a marvelous—life-changing—wonder." She invites you to connect with her via her Web site at www.RebeccaOndov.com and on Facebook.

Ginger Rue jokes that for the past decade and a half, she's been preparing to win big on *Jeopardy!* "We have three children who are all in high school and college now, and I always used to quiz them before their tests and sometimes still do. At this point, I feel as though I've taken every science, math, English, and social studies class four times: once myself and three times vicariously!" she says. "I was a little relieved when they made it to subjects where I was no longer useful to them. It happened earliest with math, since I can't do much past basic algebra, and not even that very well. But I believe that even our limitations bless us because they remind us to rely on God."

"It's like living in a 'cathedral in the air,'" says **Ken Sampson** on being settled in Cornwall-on-Hudson, New York. Upon retiring from the US army Chaplaincy five-and-a-half years ago, Ken and his wife, Kate, moved to the Hudson Highlands. They marvel at the natural beauty, expanse of trees, and deer that regularly stroll through their yard. A sense of wonder comes also knowing that the adoption of their granddaughter Chanel is complete. "To see this two-year-old child," says Ken, "is to see the exuberance and delight of our Creator." God's ongoing miracles occur week after week at Cornwall Presbyterian Church, where the Sampsons sing in the choir. Ken's job as Guideposts outreach military liaison is a marvelous gift from God as well. "To travel to military camps, posts, and stations and know how Guideposts publications directly touch our armed forces and veterans affairs members with faith, hope, and prayer is a real blessing."

Daniel Schantz's daughters, Natalie and Teresa, are both doing paralegal work, now that their children are grown. Granddaughters Hannah and Rossetti are both engaged to marry soon. Grandson Abram is studying languages at Truman State, in Kirksville, Missouri, and grandson Silas is doing marketing for a large gift shop in Kansas City.

Dan and Sharon went on a fifty-fifth anniversary trip to Kentucky and visited some small towns from their childhood—Germantown, Brooksville, Augusta, and Maysville—and also went on a few tours, including the Noah's Ark replica in Williamstown.

Gail Thorell Schilling of Concord, New Hampshire, writes: "God performs wonders and miracles daily. I just need to discern them. For example, after several cat-less years, the fluffy Mitzi turned up as my perfect companion. Both toddler grandchildren began talking and calling 'Nana!' so I better appreciated the wonders of language acquisition when I spent six months learning Greek before a visit to Athens, Delphi, Nafplio, and the holy island of Tinos. This year I led even more memoir groups, and several writers have already finished their books for family. I especially rejoiced in the publication of *God Threw Me Back: A Child Survives War in Sudan*, the memoir I helped to ghostwrite with Gatuk Digiew whose survival is, indeed, a miracle. Now I am eager to launch my own memoir, *Do Not Go Gentle. Go to Paris: Travels of an Uncertain Woman of a Certain Age*. I often wonder how God led me to writing...."

Penney Schwab writes: "My husband, Don, and I are spending more time with family. We travel to school, sports, and 4-H events for our two youngest grandchildren, Caden and Naomee. We've enjoyed short excursions to natural wonders in Kansas and Oklahoma with my sister and brother-in-law; visits with my brother and his wife; and attended graduations and special events. It was a surprise and delight when our oldest son, Patrick, and his wife moved to Garden City, just fifty miles from our house. Our church has the blessing of an experienced and godly pastor, and the congregation is growing both numerically and spiritually! In good times and in difficult ones, God continues to perform wonders of healing, growth, and love."

An unwelcome "first" for **Elizabeth (Tib) Sherrill**, who writes about special first-times in her life this year, was getting along without a car. "I couldn't write a devotion about giving up driving because so far I haven't found anything good about it, other than encountering a lot of helpful and generous people." One wonderful first-time was meeting Desmond James Sherrill, son of grandson Andrew, a professor at Emory University in Atlanta, Georgia, and his wife, Erin, a career counselor at Oglethorpe. "They've decorated Desmond's room with maps because they hope to do a lot of traveling." He's Andrew and Erin's first child and Tib's fourth great-grandchild.

Buck Storm is a critically acclaimed singer/songwriter and the author of two novels, *Truck Stop Jesus* and the Selah-Award finalist, *The Miracle Man,* as well as the nonfiction book, *Finding Jesus in Israel—Through the Holy Land on the Road Less Traveled.* His short story, "A Waffle Stop Story of Love and Pistols," is featured in *21 Days of Grace: Stories That Celebrate God's Love.* Buck and his wife, Michelle, have a happy love story, a home in Hayden, Idaho, and two wonderful grown children.

Jolynda Strandberg, who serves as a Director of Religious Education, has spent twenty years with the military as a civilian. She and her family have recently returned from an assignment in Europe to Clarksville, Tennessee. She is also a proud wife and a mom of three children.

Jon M. Sweeney and his wife adopted a teenage daughter last year. They also moved back to the Midwest, leaving Vermont for Milwaukee. "It's been a year of changes and blessings," Jon says, with gratitude. He's the author of thirty books, including *The St. Francis Holy Fool Prayer Book*, published last year, and his first book for children, *The Pope's Cat.* He's a busy father and husband and also the editor-in-chief at Paraclete Press.

Stephanie Thompson started waking up half an hour earlier each morning to pray. "I want to talk to God first thing—before I brush my teeth or brew the coffee. I set an alarm on my phone for 5:30 AM, kneel by my bedside, and pour out my heart until the second alarm sounds. God may not be performing more wonders since I started this practice, but I'm noticing His works with much more clarity." Stephanie, husband, Michael, and daughter, Micah, live in an Oklahoma City suburb with a pug named Princess; Missy, a schweenie (shih tzu/dachshund mix); and a tuxedo cat named Mr. Whiskers.

Marilyn Turk writes: "The past year has been one of stepping out on faith and watching God do wonders. Because of the popularity of the first Blue Lake Christian Writers Retreat, I directed the small writers' conference again and was as astonished the second year as the first to see the way God provided everything needed to make it a blessed event. In addition to the retreat, I've been busy writing historical Christian novels and seeing the publication of all four books in my Coastal Lights Legacy series. Instead of long vacations, Chuck, Logan, and I have enjoyed seeing God's wonders on short camping trips as we travel in our RV to the many beautiful campgrounds in our home state of Florida."

Karen Valentin writes: "I put the finishing touches on a new oil painting I've been working on and then get ready to join my band for a gig uptown. The boys are now old enough to stay home without supervision for a few hours, so I kiss their cheeks and head out the door. My life with children has always been about their happiness. This is the first year I've given equal attention to my own. I've revived the artist in me, made an effort to meet up with friends, and have participated in activities that speak life into who I am outside of motherhood. These parts of myself were never lost, they were simply on hiatus while my children were small and needed so much of me. As they grow older, they need less and less. And while it's heartbreaking to watch my babies slowly bid farewell to their childhood, it's an exciting new season for us all. Together, we are growing apart in the most beautiful way, giving each other permission to walk a path of his own and seeing what God has for each of us along the way."

Scott Walker writes: "This year has been a merging of generations for our family. Our third grandchild, Jayne Jenkins Walker, was born and she is delightful. My mother turned ninety-seven-years old and promptly broke her hip. Her ninety-five-year old brother, a World War II veteran, died last week. Suddenly Beth and I are learning what being part of the 'sandwich generation' is all about—sandwiched between the young and the old and trying to hold everyone together.

"Yet, this 'merging together' is also a privilege. I'm learning a great deal from my elders as they face inevitable decline. And from the smiles and laughter of our children and grandchildren, I'm reminded that life is wonderful. Through all stages of life, God remains loving and good. The best is always yet to be!

"I continue to teach at Mercer University and direct The Institute of Life Purpose. My students are a gift to me. I'm learning as much from them as they're gleaning from me. Education is a collaborative venture between the idealism of youth and the wisdom of age. I gain hope from my students' idealism and vigor."

Recalling her sister's fear of her own shadow that was cast on the wall of their tiny childhood bedroom, **Jacqueline F. Wheelock** finds Psalm 91's "shadow of His wings" a fitting foil to her sister Gloria's version of a "boogeyman" produced by lamplight. Unlike the shadows imposed by the kerosene lamps of her Mississippi upbringing, Jacqueline now savors the shadow of the Lord's wings that shield her from the sometimes scorching sunrays of life. Jacqueline's aim is to remain under His protection while also reaching out to the lost and despondent. "How marvelous that God's shadow always moves into the fray right along with us!" she comments. The mother of two adult children, Jacqueline treasures her retirement years spent writing and enjoying the company of her husband.

Gayle T. Williams has been a journalist for more than thirty years and has been a committed Christian for much of that time. She is so very grateful for a chance to meld her professional skills with her faith by writing devotions. As the parents of two adult sons, she and her husband, Terry, are beginning to experience what life is like when the kids have graduated college and start to make a life of their own. Gayle loves her church home, New York Covenant Church in New Rochelle, New York, where she is active in a ministry that welcomes new members, and waves flags as part of the church's praise dance team. She never passes up a chance to play a good game of Boggle, Scrabble, or to tackle most any kind of word puzzle. A confirmed news junkie, NPR [National Public Radio] is her friend, and she would easily give up her television for a radio. Besides her family and friends, Gayle's loves include jazz and seventies, eighties, and nineties pop music; cats; baking; and chocolate—perhaps in that order. An only child from a fairly small family, she is blessed with so many friends that she considers them *framily*.

SCRIPTURE REFERENCE INDEX

Scripture Reference Index

AUTHORS, TITLES AND SUBJECTS INDEX

Authors, Titles, and Subjects Index

Authors, Titles, and Subjects Index

Authors, Titles, and Subjects Index

Authors, Titles, and Subjects Index